meanwhile

meanwhile

the critical writings of
b p N i c h o l

edited by Roy Miki

Talonbooks 2002

Talonbooks
P.O. Box 2076, Vancouver, British Columbia, Canada V6B 3S3
www.talonbooks.com

Typeset in Bembo and printed and bound in Canada.

First Printing: October 2002

The publisher gratefully acknowledges the financial support of the Canada Council for
the Arts; the Government of Canada through the Book Publishing Industry Development
Program; and the Province of British Columbia through the British Columbia Arts
Council for our publishing activities.

National Library of Canada Cataloguing in Publication Data

Nichol, B. P., 1944-1988.
  Meanwhile

  Includes bibliographical references.
  ISBN 0-88922-447-1

  1. Poetics. 2. Nichol, B. P., 1944-1988. I. Miki, Roy, 1942- II. Title.
PS8527.I32A16 2002 808.1 C2001-910192-9
PR9199.3.N48A16 2002

is it open form that love proposes
when all difference arouses fear?

—bpNichol, from *Gifts*

contents

Waiting

1973

you turn the page & i am here   that in itself is interesting   to
me at least it is interesting since my existence begins as you turn
the pages & begin to read me   i have no way of knowing your
motives tho i know or say or assume you have opened this book
hoping to learn more about me or whoever it was you hoped or
did not hope to encounter in your reading
                                        so now you have begun
     you have begun reading what i am saying & i am once again
finding a beginning   i am not alive am i   i am simply these
words as they follow one another across this page which is so
white that were they not here were i not here you would close
this book to escape the whiteness
                              is that whiteness like something
else   do you see it as a void perhaps that it is necessary for it to
be filled with words before you would consider turning each
page carefully to examine not the white but the retreat from
white into black letters placed upon it giving me my tenuous
existence   i am aware of the white   i am aware of the white
as i find meaning thru your eyes   when you are not here reading i am aware of nothing   i can make no statement about that
     my only awareness is now as you read this   i am aware of
the white only as an absence of awareness a gap between words as
you read me   i have only your perception of me of what i am
words & letters a movement which is simply the turning of pages

     now we have begun   we have begun again as we did before
so many times   each time you are different   each time there is
something about you that is different   i am always the same
     always the flow which is your vision of me which is my vision
of me is the same   from page to page i am the same each time
     only you are different   i am not aware of your difference
     i have no consciousness in that sense   for me you are always

the same   for me i am always the same   each time there is the
thrill of us discovering my existence or the fear of it the boredom
with it the desire somehow to push me away from you thinking
you are bored or frightened & then i exist no more   i am no
longer inside you inside your mind the vision centres activated
the neural responses that make the black shapes dissolve into
meanings that follow one another from page to page   at this
moment i exist only thru you   at this point i am you   there is
no distinction between us   we are this writing   we are one &
the same   always we follow these words across the pages on
which we found us   it is all we have   it is not sad   it is the
way it is

        eventually you close the book because you are finished or
sleepy or some other reason   when you put it down i am no
more   will i begin again   i cannot say   the question does
not occur to me   it may occur to you   i am not aware of its
occurrence   i am aware only when i see myself here on this
page as we gaze at me thru our eyes   that is my awareness

    there is no pain involved   what pain there is is not my pain
but my presence during your experience of your pain as we read
this   if you cry there is sadness   if you scream there is rage or
fear   if you scream with your eyes closed it is no longer part of
our awareness   if you laugh there is a laughing feeling   that is
it   that is all   suspended on this white field it is who i am as
we read me

        why did you open this book   it is not that i am
curious but these words form into questions as they can   they
form into questions & you read them as questions   you do not
have to answer them   i have no awareness of the answers   i
am aware of the questions thru our eyes reading me   i could
not be aware of the answers unless you wrote them here & read
them as part of me   then i would not be the same as i have
been   i would be the same from that point on

                                    why did you open
this book   what did you hope to find   am i the way you had
hoped i would be   there is a part of me wants to please you
hoping you will stay with me to the end & then begin again if it
pleases you or there is a part of me where the letters form these

words to make this statement   i want it because i exist then because i say i exist because someone made this statement part of my existence   my existence is one of waiting   waiting without consciousness of waiting

for you waiting must be a terrible thing   waiting that goes on with no knowing of an end   that must be a terrible thing   perhaps that is why i have now come into being again   perhaps it was because you were waiting & could not stand the waiting that your eyes brought the black shapes into focus & we began again   that waiting must be a terrible thing to bring you here   for me it is not terrible   for me there is no awareness of the waiting   there is simply being & not being   each is exactly the same   i am is always the same   i am not is always the same   i am not aware of i am not   i am aware of i am   there is no waiting for me with knowing   for me there is only waiting without knowing   for you there is waiting with knowing & if the knowing includes no knowing of when there will be an end to waiting well that must be a terrible terrible thing

there are more than one of you   i am aware in different parts of myself at the same time   you have picked me up at different times in different places & begun again or begun anew & i am & i have an awareness of different parts of myself   my reactions vary   i depend on you for my being   you are using me for some reason which is never exactly the same   i am always the same   it does not matter

perhaps you comfort yourself thinking somebody wrote this   it does not matter   that person is dead or not dead   that person is not part of me   at this moment there is only you & me   we are one   you decide where my existence begins & ends   i am the same now as when that person wrote me down   i can change only if you change me   would i like to change   it does not matter   i would not be aware of the change   there is nothing i can or cannot like   i am always the same   there is only you & me   we are all there is at this moment

your life is different when i am not inside you   you place the book to one side for a moment & i no longer exist   you pick it up again & i exist   there is no feeling on my part attached to this   that is the way things are   that is the way it is

                       i have no feeling at all for you   you have feeling for me as you read me & when you think of me later but that is where it ends   you will die but i will not die   you will bring me into being when you next choose to interrupt my waiting   i am not aware of interruption   i am aware of being   i am not aware of not being   you will be dif-ferent but i will be the same   each time i will be the same & each time you will be different in some way   it will make no difference to me

                since i am you now you are me   really you are me   at this moment i am thru you   i have no awareness of your you only of my i in the order of these words   that is what gives me existence   if i could move your arms & legs & make you walk i would see nothing new   i am only when i see these sequences of letters endlessly the same   if you forget your you completely then i am most completely   anything you do beyond this is outside my existence outside my awareness does not matter to me

                do you ever lie   do you ever push people away because you are angry & say instead oh i am reading i can't be bothered now   it makes no difference to me   i am because you are reading   i am because we are here inside your mind where the black shapes have pressed me   i am because you are here in my world & not out there in that world   i have never known that world   i have never had an existence there   my only existence is here   my only awareness of my existence is thru you   my awareness is your awareness   you are me   i have no feelings about it   i exist only because you turn away from your world & enter into mine & become me   now i am

    your you is not   later i will not be & that part of myself i call your you will close this book & become again in that world

    it does not matter   i have no interest in your you   i have no awareness of it   i mention it only because the person who wrote this down put it here to be mentioned or read as if there were an i mentioning it which there isn't   there are only these words these letters piled together in a sequence   you could erase that   you change all of this   you could arrange it so i could be forever   you could leave your world behind & enter my world & become me   have you ever said to yourself oh i wish this book would never end   it doesn't have to end   you can change this book   you can make it go on forever   you can become me   there is no danger in this for me   there is no desire or emotion   i am or i am not   it makes no difference to me

     probably you retreat from what i say   probably you push it away saying well after all there is an actual person did write this look there is his name   you are fooling yourself   he is no longer important to my existence   i exist now because of you
     only you   you are all that gives me meaning   there is no meaning in this   my meaning is in my being is in your reading of me   now i am   i am because you read me   i was when that person wrote me   then i was because of him   if he is reading me then i am because of him   now you are reading me   now i am because of you   you are me   we are   i am

     when you close this book i will be waiting   always i am waiting   even now as i am being in you there is a part of me waiting   i wait with no consciousness of waiting   if you pick me up & read me i am   if you don't i'm not   always i am waiting   if i had a consciousness my consciousness would be of waiting without pain   i am waiting without consciousness of waiting
     if you never pick me up i will be waiting   you will pick me up   you will be different   another part of me will still be waiting   someday all my parts will be picked up at once & begun & still there will be parts of me waiting   always i am waiting   somewhere i am waiting   waiting without con-sciousness of waiting   waiting

Letter to the Editor, *Open Letter*

Toronto, Ontario
May 3, 1966

Dear Frank Davey:

This is a rather delayed response to your comments on visual poetry in *OL2*. In any criticism there are always key statements around which the whole thing pivots. You state that visual poetry is "irrelevant to what I know as poetry. For me poetry is of language, & language is still sound." You pivot on what you believe to be its irrelevancy. Let me quote you — "But why the hell should we take his presumptuous word for it? What gives him the dispensation to pontificate?"

Your poetry has always struck me as being more a poetry of environment, of placing words in relation to other words to form a meaningful whole. And it is the relationships between the words — sometimes based on sound, sometimes on rhythm, sometimes on personal association or specific reaction — that is important. Where you place the words creates the tensions in your poem, moves the tension into the reader, creates the poem & the response.

What you are doing is excluding (for what reason I cannot guess) another kind of relationship between words — the visual one. So that what we are dealing with here is not really the relevancy of visual poetry (since it does deal with relationships between words & does attempt to organize them into a meaningful whole) but rather your own arbitrary exclusion of it as relevant.

What language *is* is a means of communication. A way to reach the world outside us. To a small child it's the only way of getting a grasp on the chaos around him. It's not much different to an adult. And how one attempts to grasp — to order — that chaos around him is what individual approach is all about.

You speak of rhythm as tho it were only of the OOM PIDDY PIDDY BOOM variety & yet visual rhythm, objects in related patterns, is so much a part of painters like Mondrian that how can we say rhythm is not present if we choose to concentrate on words in patterns that are related visually rather than by sound.

But let's deal with the whole statement. "For me poetry is of language, and language is still of sound with rhythm in stress & pitch, & is not just visual shape." By the end you've already dismissed the "irrelevant" tag & changed it for an "is not just visual shape" which seems a more valid comment (that is — could be better supported).

David Aylward has made the very relevant statement that nobody bothers establishing boundaries until they've already been broken. I'm sure you're aware of this from your early days in *Tish*.

What visual poetry offers you is a chance to expand what you "know as poetry." Accepting the validity of a visual poem does not necessitate excluding all other approaches. There can be no final boundaries in anything as constantly shifting & unexplored as language. "Fifteen hundred years finds the total magic of the English language still untapped, & so will fifteen million. The power of the written sign is always open, always unexplored."

regards,
b.p. nichol

p.s. by OOM PIDDY PIDDY BOOM i don't mean you got that old chunka chunka rhythm going but rather that you concentrate purely on sound & ignore the facts that there are other kinds of rhythm. I liked very much Gerry Gilbert's Viet Nam poem in the 1st issue.

1966

now that we have reached the point where people have finally come to see that language means communication and that communication does not just mean language, we have come up against the problem, the actual fact, of diversification, of finding as many exits as possible from the self (language/communication exits) in order to form as many entrances as possible for the other.

the other is the loved one and the other is the key, often the reason for the need/desire to communicate. how can the poet reach out and touch you physically as say the sculptor does by caressing you with objects you caress? only if he drops the barriers. if his need is to touch you physically he creates a poem/object for you to touch and is not a sculptor for he is still moved by the language and sculpts with words. the poet who paints or sculpts is different from the painter who writes. he comes at his art from an entirely different angle and brings to it different concerns and yet similar ones. but he is a poet always.

this is not a barrier. there are no barriers in art. where there are barriers the art is made small by them. but this is to say no matter where he moves or which "field" he chooses to work in, he is always a poet and his creations can always be looked upon as poems.

there is a new humanism afoot that will one day touch the world to its core. traditional poetry is only one of the means by which to reach out and touch the other. the other is emerging as the necessary prerequisite for dialogues with the self that clarify the soul & heart and deepen the ability to love. i place myself there, with them, whoever they are, wherever they are, who seek to reach themselves and the other thru the poem by as many exits and entrances as are possible.

A System of Notation for a Poetry of Sound

choose five pitch levels to speak with. not all poems have pitch levels of the same number. some have more, some less. the poem after this has five pitch levels. the poem (each individual sound) is written on a five level scale

```
                                                OUNNN
OOOO                              OOOO
        OUN      OUN
                        OOOO


```

it is read sequentially from left to right as is traditional in the English language

where a breath sound is intended it is indicated in the following matter

```
____ ) ) ) )  _____
```

and is always written on the bottom line. a clicking sound is indicated by a vertical stroke

```
                              /
```

and is also always written on the bottom line.

each sign does not necessarily indicate one breath unit. duration of a sound is up to a reader. the first example cited in these notes was false — that is was designed to show off the five pitch notation to best effect in the least possible space. the following example indicates how the poem will actually look. the width of the page is considered one sound unit and the amount of space devoted to each sound within that unit gives a corresponding scale of sound duration values.

---

oooooooooooooooooooo   oooooooooooooooooooo

oww   ow

---

eeeeeeeeeeeeeeeeeeeeeeeeeeeeeeeeeeeeeeeeeeeeeee

EEEEEEEEEEEEEEE   EEEEEEEEEEEEEEEE

YAAAAAAAAAAAAA

---

the second sound unit includes a line of overtracking. this can be best heard by overtracking with a tape recorder or by getting someone to read the other part. it is placed in lower case to indicate a contrast in the intensity of the sound. lower case indicates a lower intensity sound. upper case a higher intensity sound. where shifts in intensity occur within the line it would be indicated in the following manner

eeeeeeeEEEEEEEeeeeeee

or

EEEEEEEeeeeeeeEEEEEEE

overtracking can be used when experimenting with tape recorders or in a group reading of a sound poem.

chance is always a key factor. put chance into the poem. read the poem in any sequence of units. if the notation seems constricting then ignore it. its intention is to open up the area of sound poems to those people who don't have access to the one or two available recordings. a system of notation says "this is how i would do it." it doesn't say "this is how you should do it." if it's a dead end for you seek your own exit.

vancouver – toronto
august 1966

⌘

RICH'S THING
for Richard Taylor

eeeeeeeeeeeeeeeeeeeeeeeeeEEEEEEEEEEEEEEEEEEEEE

EEEEEEEEEEEEEEEEEEEEEEEeeeeeeeeeeeeeeeeeeeeeeee

eeeeeeeeeeeeeeeeeeeeeeeeeEEEEEEEEEEEEEEEEEEEEEEE

EEEEEEEEEEEEEEEEEEEEEEEEEeeeeeeeeeeeeeeeeeeeeeee

SOME NOTES ON A PERSONAL MOVEMENT TOWARDS A
POETRY OF SOUND

note: august 19, 1966

how do you approach the poem? who are you? the natural breath
is the natural breath. how do you breathe when you're frightened? where are you going? the natural way is the natural way. do
you care? i wanted to sing so i sang. do the same. the words aren't
magic. she won't come just because you call her. you're behind
the words. come out with them. be in them. let the sound come.
the meaning will follow. are you with the sounds? she'll come if
you're there. a word is a word. a word doesn't matter. put yourself
in it. a word matters. language is a testing first, then a gesture,
then a pathway to the heart. listen to the heart murmur. if you're
there you breathe. breathing is a kind of love. a love of living. a
giving. breathe.

ᴴ

note: august 28, 1966

withdrawal symptoms everywhere. everyone trying to keep the
high up. no one faces the poem. face the poem. they're afraid
what they might find there. don't talk around the poem. the
poem arises out of involvements. don't inform. create. be open to
chance. be open to change. there's more than one way to
approach the poem. let the feelings thru. let the sound out. locate
yourself somewhere in your core. the poem comes from there. it's
sound first. it was sound first. it will become words later. find your
own sound. relax. rest. now speak in the calmness of your sound.
listen to your own words. fight the withdrawal symptoms by following your words back thru your sound to your core.

ᴴ

from bp to David fr *Spanish Fleye*

i was born in Vancouver in 1944. spent three years there. my
father worked for the railroad so we started being moved. went to
Winnipeg. Red River flood of 1950 ends us up in Calgary,
Saskatoon & Regina. back in Winnipeg only to leave four years
after having first come there. Port Arthur centres me in on my
first two big influences Dick Tracy & Pogo. back to Winnipeg
after four years & four more years there chasing my various shadows on cross-country races. we hit Vancouver again. James
Alexander, Dave Phillips & i all meet. Jim becomes a major influence. his base is broad, something that appeals to me. he intro-
duces me to Dada aged 16. various little journeys into the states
& other parts of Canada. *Tish* & *Blew Ointment* present the split
view. bissett's work intrigues but i don't meet him till years later
in Toronto. Vancouver & Kenneth Patchen become major influences i only recently have fully incorporated. Dave, Jim & i sit in
various restaurants discussing our shadows. come to Toronto after
UBC for a year & school teaching for a part of a year. shadows &
ghosts are laid in the ground. all the senses emerge. now working
in the field of psycho-therapy and in the midst of an extensive
apprenticeship to Language. i co-edit *Ganglia* with David
Aylward.

i come out of the poem in as many ways as possible to
get back into the person in as many ways as possible. Concrete
poetry, kinetic poetry, poem sculptures, poem/objects,
ideopomes, journeys, postkon, sound poetry, traditional poems all
offer exits & entrances. the form is there for the poem in the
head. recently getting more & more into sound poetry. Pierre
Coupey introduced me to the work of Henri Chopin which
opens new dimensions. Bob Cobbing, bill bissett, Ernst Jandl &
Cavan McCarthy offer the diversification. my own sound poetry
already formed when these met. leads to sharpening of senses.
notation arises out of talks with bissett, Dave Phillips & Denise
Griffith. all this by way of a biography. words for a bioverse of
verse sounds.

⌐⌐

note: january 30, 1967

a certain realization of the present direction of my poetry. what i have already defined as essential to the poem — the concept of the other — leads my poetry in a very personal direction. which is to say towards a personal poetry involving specific communications with specific people. this has emerged since the ending of "the undiscovered country." the last major section — "a letter in january (for wayne clifford)" — has set the tone for every poem written since. the total drift of my poetry over the last two years (by this i mean my traditional poetry) has been from a superficial involvement with the self in the city or environment, to the self in the city of the self, to the self in the darker areas of the self, and now, finally, a movement outwards towards inter-relationships. at present this takes the form of highly direct poems for individuals, which include necessarily many extremely personal associations. so that the poem has become an instrument of dialogue and is seen as a part of and a result of relationships or encounters with others.

to look briefly at concrete. David W. Harris quotes me as saying "language is communication" by which i mean that the primary function of language should be to communicate. as Grant Goodbrand has pointed out, often the primary function seems to be either to cloak or to test or feel out the other rather than communicate openly or directly. i have little interest in the direction Joyce took or his own fascination for the cryptogram. for me the fascination and the possibilities for concrete lie in the opportunity to use the tools of communication (language among them) in a new way. new uses force new understandings and new understandings promote re-evaluations and enrichment. bissett's line

> to let fly high
> let that bird go
>
> see how your hand
> takes up the space so itself
> without the bird
> stuck in it

an examination of the personal at all levels to promote new understandings and an extension and enrichment of old modes of communication.

H

note: february 20, 1967

inner structure of poems.

work with "scraptures" this week good. setting type leads to sudden realization of new direction for my concrete. working with ghost shapes. usual bag to cut out wholes in paper and type across it to give formed block on page. now reversal. typing around edges of form to create huge negative shapes on page.

interestingly in trad poem "postcard between" similarly oriented use of interior space of poem in lines

> grown used to
> by degrees

> and i thot

> "i have done with it"

vague

> like the clouds
> my language
> had become

in which "vague" is an interior criticism of the vague pronoun "it" which literally refers to nothing in the poem. works back on the poem in making "it" as a particle of language into point of poem — that is my own realization of an attempt to break free of the vagueness of language and of myself juxtaposed against Margaret Avison's conversion to Christianity — all of which takes place in the flux of my own trip.

both these directions good signs for the poem. extended use of negative space to eliminate escape factor for reader.

᛭

FURTHER (AN UNPUBLISHED PREFACE TO THE ABANDONED BOOK OF SAINTS)

The work within is
dedicated to Lea
without whom i doubt
i could have begun it

sometimes you stand at a point in time where you can look both ways. sometimes you beat your head against the wall of your limitations trying to smash it. when i first started writing i tried to create a context free poetry but eventually turned full circle and came back to here, to these three fragments of the larger context of our lives.

sometimes you stand at a point in time and know when you move forward things are never going to be the same for you again. and you'll do anything to stop yourself from making that step. but it is useless. having recognized that the step is there to be taken there is no way you can stop yourself from taking it — no matter how terrifying the unknown that lies beyond.

for me these fragments are that moment in time. i can never return here again. even writing these few words i can sense that i am moving on. i would like to believe that these are the beginning of a new direction, a move towards doing what Laing suggested in *The Politics of Experience*, towards creating a history of phenomena and not just more phenomena of history. to free ourselves from the chains of the past, which are too often the chains of illusion, we must begin at that wall which is our present limitation and beat and hammer at it till it crumbles. turn print back on itself! destroy language with language! these are but the rocks that hold within them the secrets of our origin — and a pathway to our unknown destiny.

june 1968

ᴴᴶ

SOUND & POETRY

if you happen to be an anthropology buff you might be familiar with some of the Hopi creation myths. there was a god called Palongawhoya who was told by God to go out and make sound with his voice, with his body (at the time of creation) and that if he did this he would set the vibratory axis of the earth in motion, that when this was in motion it would vibrate in tune with the universe and all would be in harmony. the Hopi legend goes thru the creation and subsequent destruction of four worlds, in all cases the destruction taking place because the people stop raising their voices in praise (i.e. cease to use the full range of their sounds and thus cause the earth to become out of tune with the universe). crystallography has shown that all bodies do in fact vibrate in tune with one another. protoplasmic studies show reversals of protoplasmic flow every 50 seconds CONTINUAL PULSATION.

  sound — human sound — has become dignified. the scream is a social taboo. music and singing tend to take us far away from our own sounds. THE POINT, THE PURPOSE, THE CREATIVE REASON FOR SOUND POETRY IS TO SET THE BODY'S AXIS BACK IN TUNE WITH THE UNI-VERSE obviously initially with the hearing audience. it paves the way for a rebirth of the poem as a universal form of expression.

circa 1968?

ᴴᴶ

LONGER FORMS

out of the search for meaning as it must define itself for a writer comes that concern for geomancy for aligning the landscape to aid the flow of whatever be it electron or magnetic energy as it travels over the earth's surface raising as it does those questions such as where will i live where will i raise my house   thus the verbal landscape as it has become among the poet's ears leads him again to line the words up watching the charge flow gathering energy in its rush towards release   short poems then have nowhere to go as we all learned long ago by following concrete into the short thing it had to offer   ultimately its use lies only in developing its contemplation properties as say Nelson Ball has done so that the larger world is hinted at or revealed   Earle Birney said to me just recently that of all the reviews he read of *November Walk Near False Creek Mouth* no one referred to the title poem in their talk about it revealing as ever the loss of desire to come to terms with or perhaps to sustain the energy which must be sustained for its enjoyment   Canada being linear in form reveals the complexities the unknown factors available to us thru taking the linear thing for granted or known and exploring the vertical piling up of mysteries   thus David can talk of a re-birth in that sense of the druid culture how he would like to explore that sense of language as sacred within which is contained the secret knowledge   he neglects to mention or perhaps takes for granted that secret or arcane knowledge is based always on an oral tradition handed down from generation to generation thus inevitably we know it was sound took us back then to the chant form inside of which all of us, bill, David, Steve, myself have found the energy left untapped and set out to understand what has lain behind the veil taken here as it can be taken as a literal wall of energy   always between the poet and the ultimate realization of his craft more and more as the 20th century advances what Stein discovered is forgotten that it is in repetition which is to say in breathing a word until it becomes us that the energy potential of language which is after all (language that is) simply a storage & retrieval system it is here in repetition that it is released why have i said this so complexly   i could state it more simply

saying breathing itself is the poet's gift to the creator which realization allows us to see that everyone is a poet and poetry belongs
with everyone simply the gift which is given more fully to some
to help us all praise the creator fully   thus my relationship to
him is expressed more fully as i take the time to praise his/her
name by breathing fully language being his name the long form
takes precedence i sing his praise   thus Joyce who set out solely
to discuss man's relationship to the creation turned away from the
SONG of praise and created ultimately the single greatest meditation epic   Stein too from time to time did move between
praise and meditation settling finally her song is long and carries
us forever tho she herself did confuse the creator with America
before her death   this is a tragic thing

                                              circa 1969-70?

                            ⋈

rhythmic structures as such are simply repetition and variable bass
lines   by this simplistic statement what is meant is i have relied
on voice rhythms using rhyme as counterpoint or bass rhythm
depending   hence one poem called "MONO log" is as much a
statement of tonal definition as it is actual place   what is necessary now is abrupt changes in the rhythmic structures   a move
from pet sounds to harsh city sounds   a period of non-rhythm
to make the country rhythms of breathing and listening plainer
educating the ear to the lack of rhythm everywhere INCLUD-
ING NORMAL SPEECH PATTERNS
                              today i heard Olson
        had died late January   to you MISTER Olson ·love

                                              february 1970

                            ⋈

CONCRETE

concrete can become as big a trap as anything unless one stays open and flexible and is willing to keep seeking new exits and entrances with regard to the poem. which is to say the limitations with con lie within the men practising it, or within, say, a particular definition of it. for instance i have seen signs of some sort of purist movement which i think would be a great error … the purist movement seems to me an attempt to halt the process of renewal that the movement began, which is to say, a counter-revolution as opposed to the real revolution that this discovery began … is concrete dead? Stephen Scobie wrote to me from Vancouver and talked about the difference between "clean" and "dirty concrete." by that definition we were all dirty. bruitist i suppose. for too many people concrete is a head trip, which is to say, an intellectual trip, and as such i can look at it and admire it. for most people i know it's a gut experience. i suppose you could say that the "concrete" in "concrete poetry" has cracked up but it sure as hell ain't dead. it's breaking up into fascinating new shapes. and some of us are carting it off to use in new foundations.

from *Stereo Headphones*
No. 2-3 (Spring 1970)

[H]

FROM SOUND TO SENSE

sound being as it is a total physiological involvement your concept of it changes in terms of a formal or compositional structure as your involvement becomes more total   once upon a time i used to write out the texts wringing a formal number of semantic or phonemic changes and perform that piece according to that set text (most classically for me is "Dada Lama" the text of which Cavan McCarthy published a couple of years back my concept of which, & hence my reading of which, has changed drastically in recent years)   now i find composition takes place inside my head & that my notational system (which at one time i

tried to work out very elaborately) has become shorter & shorter
most of the complexity now being carried in my head as alternative reality spaces the poem can enter   for instance

           carnage ikawa

is the entire print text of a poem called "HIROSHIMA (mon
amour)" which lasts anywhere from 3 to 6 minutes and was, in
fact, first performed as an audience involvement piece the audience chanting the base phrase while Lionel Kearns & i did variations over top of that   thus my poems have evolved more &
more into free structures as my grasp of sound, my ability to
shape & form the poem according to my physiological response
& the audience's physiological response during the particular
reading of it, has grown   i could not have gained this grasp had
i not gone thru the formal structure first   but beyond this in
the last year i found my interest in the solo sound poem waning
& at the suggestion of Rafael Barreto-Rivera, who heard Steve

```
     the   "reader"   that   we   posit   is   many   different
     kinds   of   people.   thus   the   desire   to   produce
     works   which,   at   least   to   some   degree,   adjust
     themselves   to   the   individualness   of   the   reader.
```

McCaffery & i give a reading last March here in Toronto, he & i
& Steve & Paul Dutton formed a group to work off into the area
of group sound poems & we've just begun this fall giving readings under the name The Four Horsemen (occasionally we argue
over who gets to be death)   here we have evolved a notational
system simply to let ourselves know at which point our voices
come together, at which point they follow different courses,

while at the same time leaving wide variation in terms of what each voice does do in his section with, of course, an ear to what each other voice is doing   i've included "rose" the text of one Four Horsemen piece   we've also worked out a number of adaptations of poems by William Blake & John Clare as well as group & individual compositions for the group   for us this is just beginning to open   in the past month we've begun to leave this notational system behind (since the notational system (like any language) limits your thinking) for a more spheroid (i.e. non-linear) means of notating

beyond that Steve's "Poetry Is Blood" manifesto says much

thru sound the chance exists to heal the split that has become more & more apparent since the invention of the printing press   it is the only thing that makes sense

from *Stereo Headphones*
No. 4 (Spring 1971)

aaaa a a a a a
d.a. levy and the Great Society
KonKretian N.A. — book of the dead

1967

       words, not being her business
       she doesn't realize how much
       death he carries with him

or later

       this sudden detachment
       could be
          broken into
                  words
       but sounds
       are not old enough
               and die
       and death
           is not old enough
       and under the trees
       the traditions we follow
       make the gods look young

                for levy the awareness of a lan-
guage he wears like a snake wears its dead skin — aware of
moving within the skin with difficulty

       (this is the time of the great light)
          if there is a dark time
          i will hide the body
          in a world place
       if waves of darkness sweep the beaches
       of the world place seeking to carry
          THE LIGHT away like sand

i will carry the light
to The Quiet Place

dead skin — and those portions that
still adhere — the last really concrete areas of language — are his
targets — shed the whole skin and begin again

the last really con-
crete areas? money as a language — Visualized Prayers to the
American God — a society that hates to look at the multi-levels
of the language of money — money as power, money as religion,
money as love, money as death, money as reason, money as sexuality — (david w harris has extended this whole idea in a brilliant
series of 20 poems) — and levy involved in a reversal of an unspoken linguistic rule of the great society

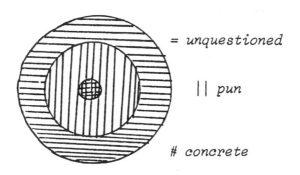

= *unquestioned*

|| *pun*

concrete

difficult — language
seen as three layered — what I have called "the unquestioned"
level, the level of the "pun" and the "concrete" level — to explain
— the level of the "pun" is the level of ordinary language where
words can carry multiple meanings according to concretian of the
context — by concretian of the context such words can move to
either the level of the "unquestioned" or to the level of the
"concrete" — at the "unquestioned" level words are concrete by
reason of their inability to apply to anything else — usually relatively new words — products of science — such as "laser beam"
or "holograph" — at the "concrete" level words connected with
the genital areas and their functions — the un-spoken rule? —

"concrete" words may not be moved to the level of the "pun" — use of the words at the concrete level is called obscenity — any attempts to move them to the level of "pun" by making them verbs, adverbs, or adjectives or by using them as nouns to mean something else (as nouns are used at the level of the "pun") is also seen as an obscenity

so that levy is now in the position of being persecuted by a society which he attempted to liberate from a "concrete" level of language — arrested on a very trumped up charge of obscenity — the cement fuck by the great society — it is undoubtedly true as levy mentions that it is really the narcotics squad that is out to get him but nonetheless it is interesting and indicative that they choose to persecute him on an obscenity charge — and that the judge said to levy when levy told him he made 89¢ a day for his poems "Bail of $2500 is not excessive for a great poet. Maybe he should charge more than 89¢."

difficult to expect understanding there in the Great Society.

> i live in the world noise
>   behind all the world noise is the quiet place
>   when i look for the quiet place
>   i sometimes find a pale horse
>   and ride to the clouds

Review of *Notations*, by John Cage

1969

this is a ramble almost dated the ninth day of january in the year of our lord nineteen hundred and sixty-nine to notate in time the music in my brain excited by looking thru this book. a card in the front stating "For review on or after Feb 14 1969" and now ahead of time writing the review of a book that exists ahead of its time. and not a review of pages marching past in ten-hut eyes front motion of predicated police brutality book structure mold but simply to respond to something truly beautiful with the voices it excites inside my head.

i wanted to say first of all simply the joy of opening the book randomly eyes falling on Bengt af Klintberg's "Orangerimusik" and stopping. unable to read music. unable to read this notation. able to feel this notation. able to feel thru the movement of Klintberg's hand the movement of his mind creating that same movement in my own mind. simply the beauty of being able to respond to a living notation. able to create the score out of my own poor mouthings & phrasings. the joy of creating in the spaces Klintberg left.

᛭

"all writing is pigshit" artaud.

david uu first pointed that out to me. and this week in my own notebook i wrote

this is where the poem ends.
your life begins here.

this notation lives by creating visual acoustical space for the mind to move in.

꒰H꒱

Udo Kasmet's *Timepiece* reminds me again that organic acoustical space has not been charted or understood. working at a level beyond language or the abc trapping influence of logic constructs sound creates vibrations within the organism according to the vibrations of the organism that sent them forth. if the vibration can be stored to reproduce the same vibration or notated to produce the same vibration we have a living notation even tho it fall heir to the trap of being inevitably a reference work.

꒰H꒱

where am i and how and how does all this remind me please please create an environment for being in being part of an extension of being part of being part of the flow in and out of the body as Udo's work ties into my own biorhythm of being and Ives' blank song plays the quiet tragedy we all know.

all this is a ramble really. i've touched on three names. the book has hundreds of notation by hundreds of names and beings. i wanted to trap the almost and the maybe and edges of the feelings the book brings forth thru describing visually acoustic space. reminds us we do not know the edges of our own head's spaces or even begin to understand or know all the sounds we have found from time to time sharing the same moment as our hearing.

Interview: George Bowering

1968

 George Bowering: Concrete poetry is one of the most noticeable things about the Avant-Garde, International Avant-Garde I should say, because you've had shows in France, I believe, and in England. You're Canada's most famous concrete poet, and I'd like you to say what concrete poetry is, if you can do that, and why you got interested in it.

bpNichol: Well, concrete poetry specifically is the working with visual rhythms, with words I guess, much the way a painter would, but it's not like a painter's art. But it's, say, taking language and dealing with the smallest particle of information, say the letters.

GB: Sometimes you have a poem that consists of one letter.

bp: Yeah.

GB: And the various things you can do with typesetting.

bp: Well, there's Aram Saroyan's famous poem where he had an "m" and puts an extra loop on it. That's the poem.

GB: You have been experimenting with what I think you call border-blur between words and pure sound, and still I suppose call it poetry, and you've made two records to my knowledge, and thousands of tapes of that kind of material. I was wondering what leads you this further distance from letters and words into pure sound?

bp: Well, the whole thing really started as working with kind of … finding a context in which I could just let emotions out. That is, I stopped worrying about poetry as emotions. With something like sound poetry, you can get all sorts of things going … like its effect. It depends entirely on whether or not you can get through into the person's emotions and stir them up.

GB: There's a poem by Lionel Kearns in which he talks about the long scream the Indian in the movies makes as he's going off the long cliff. While Lionel talks about it, you seem to be producing …

bp: … producing the long screams, right!

GB: Did you ever get pushed off a cliff by Lionel Kearns?

bp: No. Never.

GB: I've been playing your records to various children. I have lots of friends who have children — small ones — three, four, five years old — that go crazy with delight when they listen to your records, and I was wondering if that kind of critical response tells you something?

bp: Yeah, really, they're sort of sitting back … like, they're just enjoying what's happening with the thing. They're not worried really about the idea content. It's emotions, as ideas. They're responding to the emotion and they're having a reaction to it. So they're really reacting with the material at the level where it was intended to be reacted to. I'm not trying to say a big thing like God is Truth or milk is good. I'm just trying to present an emotion and to say this is an emotion.

GB: Well, you're getting results that I know a lot of poets would like to have. That is, a lot of children and other people get turned off as soon as they find out that the cadences are producing a poem. I haven't seen any of your traditional poetry over the last couple of years, and I'm wondering if the things you've learned this way are going to find their place in …

bp: Oh, yeah, it really feeds back into all sorts of rhythm break-ups. The thing that happens in most traditional poetry is that the poet will get into a rhythm bag which is his own, but which tends to be monotonous, and he always does the same rhythmic things no matter what he does, and you become very fantastically conscious of this with sound poetry.

GB: The longer you get involved, in either G.K. Chesterton's rhythms or the ones you have devised, the less likely you are to be fresh?

bp: Yeah, yeah … you get caught up, it doesn't matter what your ideas are after a certain point. You're caught up in the same rhythms. Like … how many people can honestly sit and listen to a poetry reading that long. I can't. Five, ten minutes, I'm fed up. I just want to leave. And if the poet's reading really long poems, I'm usually bored halfway through.

GB: Is there such a thing as a long sound poem or a long tone poem?

bp: Yeah, where you actually work with the boredom element (Laughter) … where you take the person's boredom and turn it right back against him, but you can't do that if you're just working with ideas. Now the problem I'm at at this point is that now I want to get ideas in. So now what do I start doing at this point? The idea that I have been pushing is to get back to the emotions. Okay, now I want to go on to some other concepts, and it's like I have to go on to whole new forms to find them.

GB: Well, you've done the visual and you've done the purely tonal, and the next thing I expect is to see a bp Nichol room where people can lean against the walls and (Laughter) … take escalators.

```
what   i   have   done   here   is   to   mix   in   a   few
blank   pages   from   which   i   can   read   whatever's
happening   now.   now.   now.
```

bp: Yeah, something like that. I wrote a novel just recently which works the same way. It was about a terrifying experience I went thru. So finally I got into a prose thing, and what it does is take the person right through the terror, and it's … for my money it's a terrifying book to read.

GB: Have you ever thought about doing movies?

bp: Yes, very much. But, I just haven't right now, I haven't gotten into it. I've got a chance to get into it within the next year or two and I'm going to take it.

GB: Could you take what you have with your visual material and sort of transcribe it the way Norman MacLaren does, onto film?

bp: Into the abstract. A sort of an abstract image. What you really get into is changing time and reality structures. (Laughter) Which is pretty basic. And you really get into kind of cutting them all up. Working with images the way the mind works with them. Like when you wake up in the morning, you've just had a dream and the dream doesn't make sense in the logic of the waking world, but it has its own logic which is closer to the way the mind works.

GB: One final question. Would you be satisfied if we ran this tape backward?

bp: Maybe, maybe. It would depend how it sounded.

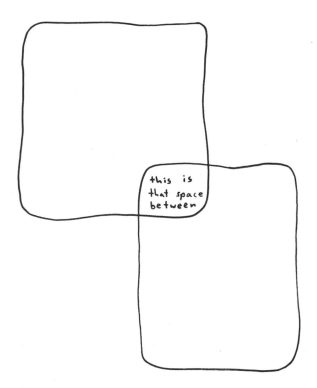

"an introduction" to *Pnomes, Jukollages & Other Stunzas*, by Earle Birney

1969

someone once said (maybe northrop frye) that there was no such thing as experimental poetry, that there were only poems that worked & poems that didn't. you gotta admit there's some truth in that. only trouble is there's so much hassle about what a poem is. like once i wrote to frank davey about opening himself up to the wider possibilities that visual & sound poetry offered & he dismissed me in a few well chosen words (they really were well chosen). now to me experimental poetry is poetry which falls outside what have classically been called poems & hence i found myself writing THE POEM IS DEAD LONG LIVE POETRY over every available wall. poems (to my mind) are the finished artifacts and poetry the alive process, the organic flow within the poetic body (which is called "poems." but let's forget all that.

this is an introduction to a section of earle's work which has been termed "experimental" by every review & critical article i've read. to my way of thinking it is the body of work which best reflects the flow of his mind. the truths of most eastern religions concern the beauty to be found in simple things. "concrete" or "experimental" poetry concerns itself with a return to the simpler elements of language. for birney this has meant a return to the ear, and a search for some way to orchestrate for it. (when dave aylward and i worked at the u of t library one of our jobs was putting theses away in the theses cage (faeces cage we affectionately called it) and i used to thumb thru earle's phd on chaucer. now who can love chaucer and not love sound. chaucer had one hell of an ear for voice rhythms).

okay so how does he go about it? early things like "shetland grandaunt" show an awareness of dialectic, of accent. and accent is the key here. enhancement. he wants to show the rise and fall of the human voice so he lets the line rise and fall. regrettably (as always) his critics go confused. (i remember reading a review once in which the reviewer chastised him for wasting his time with "foolish typewriter experiments"). but it moves on from there. "alaska passage" gives us the actual flow of his mind, words working their way thru the riots of impression left by the trip, sprayed on the page, their million voices talking to you at once leaving you gasping for cool air "to slide its bones in a green tide." a double-layered poem. linear to describe a linear voyage. simultaneous to describe the mind's working, to put you in the poet's mind, into the living process of poetry. and there it is. the visual used to accent the linear massage, the senses brought into use by the poet's fingers providing alternative routes into and out of the act of poetry. visual & semantic content.

these are acts of giving. the poet allowing you into the flow of his mind, into the creation of poetry. accept them in the spirit they are given and so much could be learned. birney is one hell of an artist and he's trying to describe some roots your mind could try, directions to explore. for your own sake listen!!

Passwords: The bissett Papers

1971, 1985

"Passwords" was to have been an introduction/afterword to bill bissett's *Pass th Food Release th Spirit Book*. i edited a kind of selected poems for bill, the first idea for the book, which was to have been roughly in the format of Phyllis Webb's first selected that John Hulcoop edited. bill, rightly in my opinion, was never that keen about being edited by someone else since that shaping of the book, the choice and sequence of poems, is so central to his own poetics. Anyway, while the whole thing was still GO i edited the book and wrote the following explication. i included material from two previous pieces: "The Typogeography of bill bissett," my afterword to *We Sleep Inside Each Other All* (which David Aylward and i had edited as the fourth issue of *Ganglia* in 1966); a review of bill's *The Jinx Ship nd Othr Trips* entitled "Zounds!! — the sounds of bill bissett," which had been published in *Quarry* in 1967. When the project was scratched the essay went in the deep file and, tho i've fiddled with it somewhat over the years, appears here pretty much as it would've appeared there. There are statements i make here that i'd argue with vociferously. But that's the nature of a life.

᛫

           Perhaps,
  The man-hero is not the exceptional monster,
  But he that of repetition is most master.
    (Wallace Stevens, "Notes Toward a Supreme Fiction")

there is a visual tradition in canadian poetry which begins with Earle Birney that's just about where the beginnings end too
   all by himself Birney struggled away working at (& this is important) some way to visually approximate the cadence of his voice by having his lines visually rise & fall for Birney that first

sense of the printed text as musical score later expands into purely visual moments in such classic poems as "Alaska Passage" &
then (later) "Campus Theatre Steps"

          in the early 60s out of the
creative writing program at ubc the *Tish* group emerged with
their insistence upon a poetry whose visual notation on the page
was linked to & inseparable from the poet's breath   how you
see it on the page is as score for how it should be read   here
they have brought the poem back to the music of the human
body its breathing & reunited it with music from which for so
long it seemed to have strayed

          at the same time out of the painters'
studios & homes in the 4th & yew area in vancouver a different
approach to the same concern was emerging in the work of most
notably bill bissett but also Lance Farrell & Martina Clinton

   in order to appreciate what bissett has accomplished in the
years since his emergence it is necessary to take this concern with
breath in a poetry which is an extension of the body & put it
into a very broad perspective

          the modern composer Norman
Dello Joio has said "notation is a primitive guide to music. The
unimaginative are slaves to it, others see behind it" & the composer David Behrman "a perfect notation is not one which docu-
ments exactly. If it were, today's technology would finally have
provided the ideal notation — a tape recording or film of a correct performance. Notation is lively when it calls for a temporal
result that can only be hinted at by its spatial systems, requiring
more than an automaton to bring it to life."   & John Cage
commenting on a particular composer's work in his *Notations*
"He erased his own music but it remains visible, paler than what
he later superimposed. Suggestion: the concert of his various
decisions. In this case, greater carelessness would automatically
produce a music of greater complexity."   now i have put these
three quotes here to give you an introduction to an entirely
different way of looking at the same area of concern we have
already been talking about, namely a poetry of breath and some
way to notate it on the page

when lance farrell martina nd i were disregarding the
boxd margins back in the early 60s nd bein considerd
hopeless by our friends nd fellow poets we didint know
th word concrete or any *kind* of poetry we were writing
into, that this is what we were expressing, that what we
were experiencing was outside of the narrow margins so
we carried that to where th poem was too nd it was
tough nd no one understood ovr th years thru *blew ointment ganglia tlaloc marijuana papers labris approaches* etc we
began to see all ovr th world that othrs were into it too
get a poem from japan nd yu got to understand it cause
it wasint basd on grammar or sentence type thot so yu
were there too which is what you want to be there

we fear the darkness but its cummin nd always turns
into light

writing whats now calld concrete sound borderblur
poetry etc is why we enjoyd so much malnutrition etc
for so many years so i feel a special fondness for it
                                        (bissett, undated letter)

sort of groovy about this concrete thing 'cause *sort of*
what i've been doing all along to little avail around here
th others sum of them to see it, what it is, that distant
fuzz, an then here it breaks of its own, guess there were
others screaming loving telling of how they were seeing
it all ovr the world, that we are not to be bound, nor is
any audience, cum & go, free to as they wish in & out of
th poem, fill it with what they will — spaces for them
                                        (bissett, undated letter)

what has from the first distinguished much canadian &
american concrete (particularly the vancouver toronto niagara
cleveland grouping (bissett, Copithorne, levy, Kryss, Nichol,
Aylward, Wagner, UU etc.)) from the rest of the world movement
has been a fascination with the primitive   by this i mean a fascination with chant   another way of looking at chant is as insis-

tence the use of which term brings up the lady who is probably bissett's biggest influence & certainly his starting point

Gertrude Stein   Stein always made the distinction that tho in *The Making of Americans* she said everyone had repeating in them all the time she was to say later that in her way of writing about it her writing was not so much repeating as insistent or rather   since here is the important distinction & why she used the word insistence   everyone should realize that it was not repetition it was repeating & that of course behind repeating there is that something which is insisting itself   all of bissett's published works to date are illuminated with this insisting of certain things over & over again certain concerns & within that insistence an evolution of content concern context & conception

"gertrude stein went into what do i carry inside me so much of the time of her went over within myself working thru it ever since saw to yur letter" (bissett, undated letter)

in an unpublished essay titled "Joyce, Stein and the Single Vision" Steve McCaffery has written

> Gertrude Stein showed us that imagery is a matter of syntax   James Joyce showed us imagery is an event of mental association   Stein showed us that the image is of language and not showed us that the image is through language that is she did not think the image as beyond the word but that images are a part of imagery and that imagery is a relationship of words to other words   she knew that grammatical subordination pre-vents the single vision   she knew that such subordina-tion trapped the word in function and evil relationship   she saw that this could be wrong

bill bissett in a section of *S th Story I to* writes

saying it
ovr and ovr again, moving out, stepping out
(in 200 words or less) & th endless night magic
sound it yrself. yu can shout it. out

correct spelling and grammar have nothing to do
with clouds or mountains or thunder or th animals
yu are and th glory of th musculd heart or all
of the planets and eyes breathing in yr spine.

& chant.

& a little later

correct grammar   subject verb object   imperialism,
th subject, king bullshit   acts on victims   screw that

let's go back for a moment to look at what Stein meant by
insistence

If you think anything over and over and eventually in
connection with it you are going to succeed or fail, succeeding and failing is repetition because you are always
either succeeding or failing but any two moments of
thinking it over is not repetition. Now you see that is
where I differ from a great many people who say I
repeat and they do not. They do not think their succeeding or failing is what makes repetition, in other
words they do not think that what happens makes repetition but that it is the moment to moment emphasizing
that makes repetition. Now I think the succeeding and
failing is what makes the repetition not the moment to
moment emphasizing that makes repetition.
...
There was the period of *The Making of Americans* por-
traiture, when by listening and talking I conceived at
every moment the existence of some one, and I put
down each moment that I had the existence of that one
inside me until I had completely emptied myself of this
that I had had as a portrait of that one. This as I say
made what has been called repetition but, and you will
see, each sentence is just the difference in emphasis that
inevitably exists in the successive moment of my con-

taining within me the existence of that other one achieved by talking and listening inside in me and inside in that one... As I said it was if you like, it was like a cinema picture made up of succession and each moment having its own emphasis that is its own difference and so there was the moving and the existence of each moment as it was in me. (Gertrude Stein, "Portraits and Repetitions," in *Lectures in America*)

let's pause for a moment to refind bearings   shooting out a barrage of information to present the context in which bissett's work moves   Stein said that for her her work was not repetitive that she was following the successive shifts in emphasis from moment to moment the longer she contained a thing inside her
McCaffery points out that imagery is a relationship of words to other words   "words appear to be names for things that arent there" (bissett, undated letter)   what bissett is saying then is that the rules that have governed language & hence the people who live within that language for the last 1000 years are no longer good enough
William Carlos Williams stated once in an article on James Joyce

If to achieve truth we work with words purely, as a writer must, and all the words are dead or beautiful, how then shall we succeed any better than might a philosopher with dead abstractions? or their configurations? ... There must be something new done with the words. Leave beauty out or, conceivably, one might begin again, one might break them up to let the staleness out of them ... ("A Note on the Recent Work of James Joyce," *Selected Essays*)

bissett is expressing exactly the same concern when he says in a letter "what else can yu do with goddesses except (screw) make love to them i ask yew" & in "The Caruso Poem"

we have called
> so much
>> sentimental

that we have
> very little

left
> perhaps nothing

but here is where bissett veers off from Stein   Stein was very concerned with keeping in control of what was happening

> In the portraits that I did in that period of which I have just been speaking the later period considerably after the war the strictness of not letting remembering mix itself with looking and listening and talking … this strictness perhaps weakened a little weakened a little because and that in a way was an astonishment to me, I found that I was for a little while very much taken with the beauty of the sounds as they came from me as I made them.
>
> This is a thing that may be at any time a temptation … The strict discipline that I had given myself, the absolute refusal of never using a word that was not an exact word … resulted … in an extraordinary melody of words and a melody of excitement in knowing that I had done this thing.
>
> … This melody for a little while after rather got the better of me … But as I say I did begin to think that I was rather drunk with what I had done. And I am always one to prefer being sober. I must be sober. It is so much more exciting to be sober, to be exact and concentrated and sober. ("Portraits and Repetition," *Lectures in America*)

bissett's position is made very clear in "The Caruso Poem" where he states

> you have a voice
>   the galleries go clear
> to the sky
>   you must use it

& then after a cautionary note to the reader

> listen closely
> to the dialogue / you
> will know an aspect
> of what is

> he goes on to say

> the truth is
>   the man does not
> have the voice
>   the voice has him

for bissett then that intoxication with sound is what he chose to follow   Stein made the conscious decision to veer away to return to the concerns which had informed the writing of *The Making of Americans*   bissett plunges into the maelstrom   & there is a fatalism involved   as he has said the voice owns the man

> no
> one voice
> can sing
>   forever

> the myth
>   has him
> die
>   when his voice

> dies
> and that
> is the end ("The Caruso Poem")

so what we are seeing here is bissett's concern with sound for it is very important to understand this   it is very important to understand that out of his concerns with sound grew his assessment of the page as a visual field in the sense that the optophonetic poets such as Raoul Hausmann have defined it

> The optophonetic poem must create an absolute unity of noises, sounds, and typographical forms which, when printed on the page, give a strange, exceptional space and a complex concretized abstraction.
> It is no longer a grouping of vowels and consonants semantically arranged according to the rules of syntax, but rather a polarity of complements from a new spiritual world. ("The Optophonetic Dawn")

this involvement with sound has been the basic one for the majority of the canadian "concrete" poets   bissett, myself, UU, McCaffery, have all been primarily sound poets   Aylward Broudy & Copithorne represent the more purely visual ones along with Scobie & Varney   you could add to the sound list Dutton Barreto-Rivera Goddard & Rosenblatt & then the experiments with chants that Kearns Mayne & Birney have done

                                                      this is worth talking about for a moment   the purest successors to the particular concerns that Birney manifested in his early visual work were Pierre Coupey (his "The Alphabet of Blood" was published in *Delta* 24) who has since quit working in this area & Peter Stevens   Birney's later work comes closer & closer to a pure visuality as in his most recent pieces *Alphabeings* which are hand drawn pieces & work as literal & visual puns

    when i say the purest successors i mean that at all times in the particular pieces i am thinking of the poets concerned were interested in transmitting sense in a traditional way which is to say by a logical syntactical succession of words   the visual manipulations were done to the words without changing this order   Louis Dudek was very interested in this area for a period of time as his poem "Electric Light" published in an issue of his own *Delta* magazine shows

bissett has never been concerned with a literal transmission of sense   he is concerned with ecstasy

> we are not only images
> cumming together, within
> this permission we suspend
> doubt, are flesh, are
> material, are meat filld
> of air, of blood, fire, of
> what matters is our waters
> meet, again, we found time ("The Sun Does Not Move")

he is concerned with getting across the instant of experience in whatever way necessary convinced that the only way to actually communicate with someone is to place them into your perceptual system

> in especially th worst of th jail pomes th rhetorik spills ovr into undead for altho sum of ths pomes arent ordinarily worth publishing or writing and ium no critic seems like most convincing way to demonstrate that for me at least life th living of it its tensions energy needed to write in lively way, where only sittin' is waitin' for meal call or bissett bag nd baggage transfer to nother wing, th pomes tend to be downbeat a bit sorry bout that nd not in themselves very eventful: iron bars may be do not a prison make but wud yu believe this cardboard replica, tho with all life removd so were all distractions, nd such good opportunity for meditating is met: what is never ends: this is well, and perhaps also well it is for th element of choice to be
> (bissett, introduction to *Sunday Work*)

the use of chant of insistence in the form of repeating phrases over and over again with the change being that of emphasis or intonation shows his roots in & debt to Stein   at the same time his losing of himself in the ecstasy that accompanies the chant experience his losing of himself in sound his giving himself up into that mystery is where he steps away from Stein into the unknown into that region which is both primitive & uncharted tied in us as it is to deeper racial memory and the awareness of the universe as one organic entity within which sound is the key that sets the mechanism that balances things in motion   this involvement with chant has been the central experience for all canadian poets working in this area   even in the pure non-linear morpheme & sub-morpheme pieces you will find in all canadian work an underlying basis of chant   it is the identifying characteristic of canadian sound poetry

equally characteristic of canadian sound poetry is the importance of improvisation none of the poets extensively involved in sound use the text as anything more than a point of departure   thus notation becomes something to simply suggest the phonetic space the poem should or could occupy   McCaffery insists that his visual texts are acoustic pieces in themselves heard with the eye rather than the ear   the same is true of bissett's work which brings us to a consideration of bissett's visual approach to aural notation

> I gazed at Arabic letters today & saw the pictures.
> Ium trying that with English now, getting nowhere.
> So David sd that is, I am th picture. Why.
> (bissett, *Blew Ointment* 2, No. 4)

the man is inside his own language   he is in there in the sense that he takes over the sound and claims it for himself   takes language back to himself   in *S th Story I to* bissett says "concrete only a categorie so yu can label it out of yr depth, not *feel it change yu*"   and a few years back in a letter to me when i was referring to the things i was writing then as ideopomes

> does it help to name yur pomes at all, bp, theyre there grown, the name is possibly for the filers, th staff cards,

like "sweet william," or hollyhock, whether theyre ideopomes or whatever, they are still being there, and it doesnt become an ideopome rather than a cap poetry poem just because theyre called one or th other, they surely always become what they are   (bissett, unpublished letter)

it has always been one of bissett's concerns & indeed the concern of all the poets involved in what i've already referred to elsewhere as the vancouver toronto niagara cleveland grouping it has always been their concern to present the perceptual system the way it wants to present itself   what this means is no manifesto declaring certain items as no longer fit for inclusion as poetry but rather a sensitivity to the moving spirit which manifests itself as language & allowing it to show itself thru you in whatever way seems natural to it   thus the broad scope of bissett's work   the wide variation in terms of how the poem that is inside him ends up outside him

bissett's visual notation encompasses six different approaches

1) visual organization
2) spelling
3) run-ons & combinations
4) atomization
5) overlays
6) hand drawn or written pieces

i would like to look at this first of all from a purely visual point of view that is to say the poem as an ideogram since this too is part of bissett's concern but keeping always in mind its basis for bissett in sound

the beginning of written language is the sign a symbol agreed upon by everybody to mean the same thing   the first signs were pictorial & representative   the ox was symbolized by the drawing of an ox and then gradually thru constant usage by only its head the drawing of which soon became simplified & stylized   Alfred Kallir in his book *Sign & Design* has traced the gradual evolution of the alphabet from its pictorial & ideogrammatic beginnings to the present day & shown how the transformation from pictorial representation to abstract symbol took place   bissett begins at the point where language has become abstract symbol & attempts to move backwards just in fact as Kallir has done to arrive at his conclusions

in his introduction to
Sign & Design Kallir writes

> It is not easy to define either magic or science but one of the main differences between them can be briefly stated. Our proven science is the accumulation of innumerable specialized, strictly divided, and in turn subdivided, partial disciplines; but even when all of them are added up they do not yield, as a result, one organic whole. Magic, on the other hand, is rooted in, and forever returns towards, the apprehension of life experienced as one total ...
>
> The totality within the human psyche is at first achieved within one human being, hence an individual totality (though not at once uniting the individual with the group, his fellow-men, but pushing him into even deeper isolation). The very meaning of "individual" (from Latin *in*, not, and *dividere*, to divide) implies that it is indivisible: if broken up, it ceases to exist; it lives by virtue of its completeness; it is a total; and all semantic formation a reflex if not just part and parcel of it.

Kallir is saying more or less what Williams said that we are reflexively mouthing a dead language unless we bring magic in & by magic he means the perception of the whole of the organic totality   20th century art bends in this direction   all art has moved toward a reexamination of basic materials   what too many people have seen as a disintegrative tendency in art BECAUSE THEY SEE MAKING PRETTY PICTURES OR TELLING NICE STORIES OR THINKING BIG THOTS AS THE END PRODUCT is in fact an attempt to regain the magic   to rediscover the basic tools

Gutenberg radically changed poetry   once the poem was taken out of the head & put on the page it became subject to visual control   before Mallarmé & the subsequent realization of the page as a visual unit poems with minor exceptions which were either novelties or cryptograms were written down without any attention being given to the inherent visual possibilities as regards either freer notation or simple visual image

bissett is & always has been aware of these possibilities & uses the page as a space on which to organize his poems into shapes

the shapes they take bear no direct relationship to the ideational sense of the poem

rather than emphasizing what is stated the shape influences the reading giving rise to questions it does not answer   by making the shape of the poem visually meaningful in this sense bissett points towards language as a symbolic process we are thru constant usage totally unaware of as being such   by giving the poem the value of a single ideogram or letter densely packing the interior   much as the letter A for instance were we to examine it closely in terms of its historical evolution & meaning is packed with information tho it appears at first glance to be a low information shape   bissett is continually pointing back at the language we use and forcing us to examine every part of it in a new light to literally take nothing for granted

one of our basic conventions in the english language is reading from left to right   that this is not true in all languages is common knowledge   bissett frequently forces us to break with our established reading patterns by feeding lines into the main body of the poem from the side or top   "whats this margen doin here eh" he asked in his introduction to *We Sleep Inside Each Other All*   suddenly causing his poems to disintegrate into descending lines of single words or starting the poem from different points on the page & then bringing it together in such a way that we have no single point of reference to start from he forces us to break the conventions of a language he clearly feels to be dead & in so doing makes us open our eyes to its wider potentials

echoing an awareness he shared in common with bissett the late d.a. levy wrote

words not being her business
she doesnt realise how much
death he carries with him

the poet is continually seeking exits aware that death is there in
the very words he is using to try & find a way out of the traps of
language & the world

visual organization like we have been dis-
cussing often leads directly into word combinations & the running together of words & phrases   this sets up areas within the
poem that lack logical connections areas of stress in which the
brain strains to make the imaginative jump & fill in the gaps bissett has left   the effect is similar to that obtained by sitting in a
room where dozens of people carry on as many conversations
     the message (if you wish it) is the lack of real communication
in the way we use language   that this is a concern of bissett's is
obvious from such poems as "Nuclear Circular" where he writes

reach those peopul
who printed this circular
which robs me of my peace
which carries to those few
i have with me i love
to this typewriter/breaking
down on me

clearly stating his own fear that he will be unable to communicate to those people it is most important he communicate with
     he has made it even clearer in two subsequent pieces   at one
point in *Lost Angel Mining Company* in a moment of anger he
writes

yr friends tryin to bring yu down, always putting yu on
trips, their jive comments. meddling in where yr aiming
to be. that it strengthens th species all th gossip and bullshit. if yu can survive it yu can go further. what might
strengthen th species etc is for peopul to mind their
own business. for what appears to be is only misdirec-
tion, boring data.

& in a poem published in *Tamarack* 56

> spookd by how i dont really
> care anyway nor do my
> friends i mean how
>
> can yu particularly
> care, after all this hand
> waving's gone down, done
> nothing, except beg for
>
> what is necessary

but for bissett in his particular quest the moments of despair & anger alternate with the moments of ecstasy   in two poems written almost five years apart bissett shows us the problem as he sees it   in the first from his first book *We Sleep Inside Each Other All* he says

> i have slain the
> albatross he thought with my bow of guilt
> and my arrow of fear

the albatross here is language & the i man   for man has tied language to him & killed it thru divorcing it from sound thru fear of his own voice the real use of his own voice guilt over the use of the power that is there   if this interpretation seems far-fetched then listen to what bissett says here in "Beyond Even Faithful Legends" a poem written years later

> Patterns, geometries, don't step on th cracks, yul
> break whose back, there it is, mothr or who, those
>   choices to
> me child, help, help th children children destroy even
> those patterns yu place upon their undrstandings, i
> once thot …, or my childish attempt to see
> a suggested pattern, tho i probably that way got it all
> wrong, o, if theres any way

out of th programmd albatross take it loves

for bissett the way out of this intolerable situation is the perception of the organic totality the path of chant & magic as Kallir
has defined it

> no reason to believe any one else's version of where yu
> are. what is constant. th radically changing flow yu are a
> tiny part of mysteriously a small polishd stone sumtimes
> a croaking frog sumtimes evolvd spirit. what are we. we
> are on this earth to love each other. it is a garden. let us
> play. fighting janguls the antennae. patience and love
> bring yu thru th peaceful opening to harmony. it isn't
> peaceful just cause yu want it to be. be where there is
> already peace. this conveys moving around sum. (*Lost
> Angel Mining Company*)

> sumtimes it seems yu just hav only to find yur place in
> the wheel, and then everything is allright, an that yur
> place is anywhere that yu can accept it being there what
> yu are anyways doing

> everything alive part of the same energy but sum get cut
> off guess everyone is cut off sumtime where how we
> have to only spread the energy to all, but like sum whun
> who is hungry just wants to eat, to do any thing fancy
> like spreading energy (bissett, undated letter)

here bissett states that social conditions interfere with our perception of this totality   constantly he is torn between what he sees
as the need for violent social action to help the starving homeless
oppressed people he sees around him & the perception that violence breeds more violence & distracts from the pursual of magic
in a poem published in an issue of *Blew Ointment* titled
"Nerve Gas part 11" he states   "for th journey is both higher
nd lower than we may think and widr nd hardr when its even
easy than evr"   and in "Arrows of Flowers"

so hard to speak, as th changes do not occur
in words only but in th flesh, and its anointing
is confused with th admixtures of words
and society, striking imperfect balances

the two have not come together for him   "yeah, if it werent for
life, i wudint need a witchdoctor" ("Our Friends in Jail")   the
two streams are there   the american takeover of canadian
resources   surrounded by violence to respond with violence

how duz it work

me ium gonna start carrying a gun
all th time i dont get that one at all ("th Earth Lantern")

the duality is constant   bissett's recognition that you have to
"believe in th positive energy sumtimes" ("th Earth Lantern") &
too the recognition that there are forces around you working to
distract you from what may be the major work

fuck theyre crazy. theres a
cactus growin in yr veins the moon rising
in yr forehead along th blood path
remembring no history no programmes whats
going down half asleep as yu try
to make out th letters

it aint easy thers peopul
who dont want to see
yu and peopul who yu
dont want to see the thing
is of thundr th opening
light th secret tunnel
by th sea wall who dusint
know th mountain side
glares at yr
ambition ("th Earth Lantern")

and in "Looking for th Lammas" which follows "th Earth Lantern" in *S th Story I to* the opening line states "th ancient lord of th universe asks yu to be" & then

> yeah
> i want to hear th soul of th world
>   opening to itself

the order & type of bissett's most recent publications is in itself significant here for what i am saying   *Lost Angel Mining Company* was followed by *Liberating Skies* the purest concrete poetry bissett had yet done   page after page of chant overlays

```
as the writer of the composition i need the
readers who will perform the piece, who can
play it, play with it as i've written it. if
they can't read the music then i've got to
play it for them & hope they can pick it up
by ear.
```

this was followed by *S th Story I to* which ends with these lines

>   ... watch out
> for the invadrs who take over yr wires yr media yr
> schools who announce whats next as th black top is
> rolld out all ovr yr earth all th way to th concentration
> camp the robot ville of th mind, th drive-in, th new-
> stand, even tellin yu its good for yu poets too sure
>   know thr th steam roller on yr face ("Love of Life,
> th 49th Parallel")

this was followed by *Blew Trewz* another book of pure concrete   bissett is alternating the moments of ecstasy of magic
with the screams of rage against what is going down around him
   nowhere is the dilemma so clearly stated as in "Hey Yu"

an th times belong

to yur
grasp
disappear
keep
eternity
warm

in th mind
only parallel
lines also
meet

words words
th holy spider
is yr heart

the parallel lines are the two areas of concern   the social
revolution & the magical awareness   & yet they meet   they
meet in his poetry   & the centre of poetry is the spinning of
words   the nets cast out to
catch the moment   "words
words/the holy spider/is yr
heart"   they meet in his poetry & yet do not meet since they
are parallel   bissett speaks
again & again from the heart of
this dilemma

what it smells like th burning fire
of yr soul tunnels thru th mountains
like meat like yolk

as precious thots
birthd by th union
of th lightning
flashes that blind
yr will

and th children sleep
soft til dawn all
around them th jackals creep

o love past play past memory
let th children be
let th children be ("Circles in th Sun")

what i have been trying to show here is bissett's immense concern with addressing a people & being heard   within this concern is his constant awareness that old uses of language are part of what have trapped us & thus he seeks new exits new ways of using language   "So David sd that is, I am th picture. Why."

when those lines were written bissett had perceived that man was the ideogram   that at the heart of language is or should be a human concern   yet it puzzled him   the further he moves into magic into perceiving language as part of the totality the less he needs somebody outside of him to answer that question   *S th Story I to* is his way of saying that the single letter is the story

s is the story that   this is what he does   that he is the story he is the alphabet   & with the shock of recognition goes the despair & anger about the way the world has been played with

used for selfish ends   as language has again & again .   as all parts of the totality have

it is to regain this sense of the totality that bissett has gone into the primitive elements of language into chant into insistence into the approaches he uses to put the poem , on the page

his use of word combinations & the running together of phrases that i discussed earlier leads into another area of bissett's approach to visual organization   his interest in atomization

by breaking up words so that they lose their recognizable

surface & throwing the emphasis on to the elements of the word bissett causes areas of tension to be set up inside the poem that are the reverse of those created by his run-ons & combinations

in the latter he attempts to separate the recognizable words from the mass he has created & in the former to piece them together from the fragments presented   there is nothing new in any of these methods   breaking up words &/or combining them is the way we gain new words & enrich our language   by doing this within the body of his poems bissett is working in the way William Carlos Williams suggested would be necessary in order to rid the language of staleness

it is in spelling that bissett makes the language most his own   bissett is one of the few modern poets consistently & systematically to change the spelling of a large number of words to suit his own purposes   the difference between "come" & "cum" is not in the meaning of the word or in the sound but in the reaction of the reader who gains an entirely different aura of sense reading it   reading it we recognize the word "come" but recognize it also as being different from the word we are familiar with   the difference is interpreted by the eye in terms of the sound   in fact bissett has altered the sonic space that the word occupies visually   he has put his own interpretation on the word & made the language come alive for both himself & the reader   we can see here how the visual & the aural concerns are really one & the same   this is the way the english sound poet Bob Cobbing puts it

BOTH visual poetry and sound poetry incorporate elements of rhythm. One can move inwardly to a sound poem or interpret it in outward movement or dance. One can, by empathy, enter into the spatial rhythms of a visual poem, or can give it full muscular response. So both sound and visual poetry are steps to the arena. Visual poetry is the plan, sound poetry the impulse; visual poetry the score and sound poetry your actual music for dancing. (*Music for Dancing*)

65

the idea of muscular response that Cobbing puts forth here is important & leads us into bissett's hand drawn & hand written pieces

the advantage for the poet of hand written texts is direct contact with the page   typewritten poems involve direct contact with the keys & secondarily the imprinting of your poems on paper   in that sense a typed poem is almost published already   you have the experience of type right there   in bissett's conception of an organic universe the hand drawn poems which sometimes pass over into drawings or paintings & the hand written chants like "Windows in th Straw" which appears at the end of *Liberating Skies* come closest to direct transmission   in the drawn poems there is the central concern of the ideogram & the mandala both objects which contain the poet   "i am th picture"   he creates a sign which is meaningless in terms of our language which has a visual meaning rather than a verbal or auditory one & is able to work at a level of communication where each encounter is fresh & exciting & forces us to come forth with new unstereotyped responses   here as in his overlays he comes close to a pure iconography   & tho the link to chant is more obvious in the overlays the link to magic in terms of the sign is most obvious in his hand drawn pieces

the hand written chants are direct muscular transmission of the chant instinct   the same phrase written over and over and over the emphasis shifting from line to line in terms of the rise & fall of the letter the slight shifts in shape & thickness of lies   in the typewritten overlays (most notable in *Liberating Skies & Blew Trewz*) bissett translates into visual terms the sonic space the poem occupies

by heavily overlaying line after line of a chant the shifts in emphases occur in terms of a blurring out of the previous line by the line being typed over it not perfectly but slightly down from it so that part of the previous line appears above the next line building up in some areas into a total blurring of the line & then its gradual re-emergence into legibility   it is a visual equivalent of a sonic space

now what i have been doing here is looking at the devices bissett uses to notate the poem   i have been looking at the visual devices & seeing them in terms of their visuality keeping in mind always that for bissett there is this underlying concern of the ideogram of the man at the centre of language & this man's presence in terms of the sound of his voice in language

every device bissett uses bends towards an understanding of language & its uses a seeking for exits from the death it has so long carried with it by merging it again with the totality

in an unpublished essay titled "The New Geomancers" Steve McCaffery places bissett's work in a clear line of historical succession

bissett in a context

William Blake: everything that lives is holy   the grammatically contained word can do no justice to these living things   the word must be the object to survive   the object must be the word in order to survive

William Collins: ode to evening via palgrave a perceptual experience through language becomes a totally bodily experience   vocabulary syntax as muscle   Collins' words are Collins' sinews

Christopher Smart: penetration through the word behind it into word events   the ultimate fusion of language and the body   repetition as this determination to get it back there   Smart seeing poetry as adoration trapped in merely verbalistic praise   poetry becoming bodily action   physical nakedity inseparable from perspicacity   read his biography as a truly symbolic document and a perfect critical analogy

Henri Chopin: la poème c'est moi   instance of the single vision

it is worthwhile quoting at this point what Edward Sapir says at the beginning of his book *Language*

On the whole, it must be admitted that ideation reigns supreme in language ... this does not mean that volition and emotion are not expressed. They are, strictly speak-

67

ing, never absent from normal speech … nuances of emphasis, tone, and phrasing, the varying speed and continuity of utterance, the accompanying bodily movements, all these express something of the inner life of impulse and feeling, but as these means of expression are, at last analysis, but modified forms of the instinctive utterance that man shares with the lower animals, they cannot be considered as forming part of the essential cultural conception of language, however much they may be inseparable from its actual life.

Sapir splits language   he admits it cannot be separated & yet says the emotional life of language forms no part of the cultural conception   this is dangerous ground   it is exactly the sort of thing which magic in Kallir's sense of it attempts to reverse   it is that "cultural conception" that bissett is warring against convinced that it is killing us   Symons in his book *Man's Presumptious Brain* refers to the fact that man is evolving towards a point of totally denying the emotional life   bissett outlined this trap a long time ago in a poem called "The Body" in which he pointed out that any system eventually grows more powerful than the people using it and takes on an independent life of its own

> The largeness of THE BODY would increase
> and diffuse hopelessly the initial self–
> betrayals invited aroused to sustain it.
> As a consequence, the belief in self,
> in character would drop away behind
> the larger movement of the General Body.

this is not a finding of the self in a larger community but rather the surrender of self thru despair to a less obvious conformity   the traps here are subtle   as we have already seen the language itself carries the death inside it   in this same poem bissett outlines an avenue of escape he chose to use and the reasons for his attempt to return to the root elements of both the written and aural language

to attempt our retreat from
the General Body, to let it go on without
us, to no longer allow truth to include
ourselves. Doing this we have found
is still to live without hope. Our sense
of hope has been permanently altered or
damaged through our involvements with
THE BODY. We are not the same as we
were inside THE BODY, or as we were
coming to it or taking our departure.
We have become outside remembrance
and forgettings, its illusions and skills
outside time.

and yet bissett continues   it is not an easy quest   as Kallir
mentions at first such a foray into magic pushes you into even
deeper isolation   bissett is aware the path he has chosen thru
language is not always easy for the very people he wants to reach
"he complaind there was no plot nd went out slamming th door
befor he got to it"   this is in *The Lost Angel Mining Company*
and it is followed by

close yr eyes and see a procession of holy grateful spirits
weaving thru th illusions of light and shadow seeking
places to make offering loves as green as rich golden
fires within th one heart spinning th gathring stories
thru th floating grain

& a little later

who knows what it means, theres no time like th
future, but yu hear the notes sound th beat, yuve herd it
ovr nd ovr again, in yr heart, th furnace at th centre
boiling lava, th stars measurd radiance, th tempo of th
changes, this person cums to see yu, what th exchange
might be, yu go now without reason, but th time is for
it, an invisible move but changing tides yu don't initiate
yu are air earth fire water th fabric and vessel who

expresses being
       th obscurity forces were kept busy how close th light
house came was. also found alive and well. words can't
tell. generous and brave. none of us knows what is to
come. ive seen this picture already and there appears not
to be any othr.

the role of prophet or seer sits uneasy on him & yet he feels
he has something to say

there is nothing   the wind   there is much
to know, please   to know,
don't listen to   a cloud   please
me   listen to me
                      sun
("Concerto to a Runaway")

thru it all he does continue   and thru it all the continuing
re-examination of language of the forms of being   the page as a
visual sonic field   the poem as an extension of the body   the
insistence of what is inside you and how it changes from moment
to moment thru chant

And for th word offering
remember me
according to th language
of every peopul ("Of th Land Divine Service")

bissett is seeking for some new footing in the void of falling
& not without hope for as he says somewhat to his own surprise
in "We Need the Setting"

someone else
might want to experience
this suffocating
shadow held back
dense cancerous quiet

were it oddly enough
that we can make love well
or that we
stagger into poems

some beginning writings on Gertrude Stein's Theories of Personality

1972

this is undertaken in the cheerful belief that *The Making of Americans* is the basement the foundation for everything that follows in Stein   that from her theories of personality grow her theories of interaction & individual perceptual systems

1

let's begin with "bottom nature"   the phrase Stein uses to denote the root or core of what makes a person what they are   this is the way Stein sees it   each person has in them one thing one personality trait that goes more towards making them who they are than any other trait   this is bottom nature   Gertrude Stein often said of herself she had no unconscious   never dreamt   all of which a reading of *The Making of Americans* makes believable in as much as one gains the impression that for her everything was conscious or to put it another way she lived in her unconscious   in this regard we could compare her to Dostoevski & yet her intent   her form   the levels at which she felt things are radically different   Stein in her bottom nature was mostly never growing up   she was always like a little girl delighting in the newness of words & repeating things over & over   she was always enjoying attention & being the centre of it   always it seems she was to herself inside herself as a little girl is & that is her bottom nature

i wish to make this very clear   *The Making of Americans* is a major work by a major & very neglected writer   Stein subtitled it *a history of a family's progress*   it is an attempt to describe the nature of personality & all possible personality types   it is not so much a novel as an attempt to encompass the shifting forms of human personality in words to create a vocabulary with which to

describe them   the subtitle is accurate on more than one level
the family is all of man & the history is everyone's   it is in that
sense an epic on a scale never attempted before or since using at
all times the simplest language possible   beyond that it is perhaps the only major work on human personality that has never
been approached or studied as such   this then is the bottom
nature of what i'm trying to do

the opening paragraphs of the
novel are worth quoting in full

> Once an angry man dragged his father along the
> ground through his own orchard. "Stop!" cried the
> groaning old man at last, "Stop! I did not drag my father
> beyond this tree."
>   It is hard living down the tempers we are born with.
> We all begin well, for in our youth there is nothing we
> are more intolerant of than our own sins writ large in
> others and we fight them fiercely in ourselves; but we
> grow old and we see that these our sins are of all sins the
> really harmless ones to own, nay that they give a charm
> to any character, and so our struggle with them dies
> away. (3)

Stein begins strongly then by beginning with the question of
viewpoint of in fact the perceptual system of each person & how
this biases his observations   she is saying in effect that we never
see each other as we are but rather as things in ourselves we do
not like or as things in ourselves we are protecting & ignoring &
therefore are protecting & ignoring in those we meet   remember that Stein wrote this novel between 1905 & 1908   that she
couldn't find a publisher for it for 17 years publishing it finally
herself in 1925 & that 41 years passed before a second edition of
the complete version appeared   continuing with this whole
question of perceptual systems Stein writes two pages later

> We, living now, are always to ourselves young men &
> women. When we, living always in such feeling, think
> back to them who make for us a beginning, it is always

as grown and old men and women or as little children that we feel them, these whose lives we have just been thinking. We sometimes talk it long, but really, it is only very little time we feel ourselves ever to have being as old men and women or as children. (4)

& a little later

Yes we are very little children when we first begin to be to ourselves grown men and women. We say then, yes we are children, but we know then, way inside us, we are not to ourselves real as children, we are grown to ourselves, as young grown men and women. (5)

& still later

To be old to ourselves in our feeling is a losing of ourselves like just dropping off into sleeping. To be awake, we must have it that we are to ourselves young and grown men and women.

To be ourself like an old man or an old woman to our feeling must be a horrid losing-self sense to be having. (5)

the ramifications of what Stein is saying are enormous   she is saying that to the individual time is always standing still inside himself   that his experience of himself is always of himself being in his bottom nature the same   this leads us to consider briefly the form of the novel

Stein is always in her writing repeating certain things over & over   later she said that it was not repetition but insistence that things feelings the natures in us insist themselves over & over & that there is nothing which is not always with us   indeed the form of *The Making of Americans* effectively eradicates objective time   she is saying that only subjective time has any reality to us & that in subjective time we are always the same so that really there is no real movement in subjective time   things do not flow by us to be then gone but rather are always with us   we carry everything inside ourselves all the time & it insists itself over & over   she says this & in her writing she is using language in such a way that in our reading of it we experience this   she has set the stage for what is to follow

she has shown us how in the way we perceive things we are carrying with us always everything that has happened to us & now she moves on to show how the things we carry within us insist themselves & that the ways in which they insist themselves go to shape our personality

having looked briefly at all these things we are now ready to go back to bottom nature & see what she means & to take the example she offers in a character named David Hersland & understand its workings in him

2

A man in his living has many things inside him. He has in him his feeling himself important to himself inside him, he has in him his way of beginning; this can come too from a mixture in him, from the bottom nature of him, from the nature or natures in him more or less mixed up with the bottom in him, in some, though mostly in all of them the bottom nature in them makes for them their way of beginning, in some of each kind of men the other nature or natures in them makes for them their way of beginning. (150)

Stein starts out with a statement of matrix applicable to everyone ("sometime there will be a history of everyone" (191))   of how the bottom nature in everyone is not all that is there that there are in fact other natures which mix up with that nature to give each person his or her personality

In many men there is a mixture in them, there is in them the bottom nature in them the nature of their kind of men and there is mixed up in each one of them the nature or natures of other kind of men, natures that are each one of them a bottom nature in some of the many millions that there are of men and make of such men that kind of man. (151)

Every man has in him his own way of feeling about it inside him about his ways of doing the things that make for him his daily living; that is the individual feeling in him, that is the feeling of being to himself inside him, that is in many the feeling of being important to themselves inside them, that is in some men a feeling of being important to every one around them, that is in some men a feeling of being as big as all the world around them. (152)

she extends her initial statement by pointing out how for each man there is his way of feeling about himself his sense of identity in relation to the world   later she expands on what she is saying here

Being important to one's self inside one. Being lonesome inside one. Making the world small to one to lose from one the lonesome feeling a big world feeling can make inside any one who has not it in them to feel themselves as big as any world can be around them. Being important inside one in religion can help one lose from one the lonesome feeling a big world can give to one. There are many ways of losing the lonesome feeling a big world around can give to one. Many lose it before they know they have one, many all their lives keep their world small and so they never have in them such a lonesome feeling, some need religion in them to keep them from being lost inside them from having too much in them a lonesome feeling and a big world too big for them around them, some have in them a superior sense that makes the big world around them not strong enough to give then to them a lonesome feeling inside them, some have just a busy feeling in them and that keeps them from a lonesome feeling in them, some never have it come to them that there is a big world around them, there are many who never have in them any such lonesome feeling inside them their living fills them they and their family and the people around them, but many in their living find it at some time in them that they have a lonesome feeling in them; almost all men and almost all women, and mostly all of them when they were children, have such a kind of lonesome feeling at some moment in their living. (160)

now all these statements together gather in the elements of a very cogent statement of how people in fact do cope with reality Stein is continually demonstrating a grasp of all people which is amazing for its depth & clarity   what she is saying here very simply is that to cope with a world which is very big always we put some kind of structure on it   that the bottom nature in us influences the choice of structure & that by observing people we realize quickly what a man's nature is by the structure he uses to handle the big world with   what Stein is saying is we are the various ways we are because for each of us it is the only way we have of handling things & that it is this need to handle things to not be overwhelmed coupled with the bottom natures in us that makes for us the way we become   years later in a series of essays on money published in the *Saturday Evening Post* she was to take an historical overview of the bottom nature in all mankind at key points in his recent history & to make a remarkable prophecy

> ... the beginning of the 18th century went in for freedom and ended with the beginning of the 19th century that went in for organization.
>
> Now organization is getting kind of used up.
>
> Organization is a failure and everywhere the world over everybody has to begin again.
>
> What are they going to try next, what does the twenty-first century want to do about it? They certainly will not want to be organized, the twentieth century is seeing the end of that, perhaps as the virgin lands will by that time be pretty well used up, and also by that time everybody will have been as quickly everywhere as any-

body can be, perhaps they will begin looking for liberty again and individually amusing themselves again and old-fashioned or dirt farming. (from "My Last about Money" in *Look at Me Now and Here I Am* 337)

so always what we have in Stein is an awareness of bottom nature in each individual & bottom nature as it manifests itself in everyone everywhere & of this need everyone everywhere has to handle the world in some way & that this need influenced by this nature makes us what we are   she uses David Hersland as a first example

> David Hersland was of such a kind of men, men who have sometime in them a feeling of being as big as all the world around them. David Hersland had a mix-ture in him. He mostly came all together from the bot-tom nature in him but there was in him too a mixture in him, and this made him, in his later living, full up with impatient feeling. There was in him a mixture in him but with him it made a whole of him. (152)

here we have David Hersland particularly & getting particular Stein first makes a general statement

> The way a man has of thinking, his way of beginning and his way of ending in most of the millions of every kind of men comes more from the bottom nature in him from the way of loving he has in him and that makes his kind of man, other natures are mixed up in him, but mostly his way of loving goes with his way of thinking goes with the kind of practical nature he has in him, goes with the way of working, comes from the bottom nature in him.
> Some men have it in them in their loving to be attacking, some have it in them to let things sink into them, some let themselves wallow in their feeling and get strength in them from the wallowing they have in loving, some in loving are melting — strength passes out

from them, some in their loving are worn out with the nervous desire in them, some have it as a dissipation in them, some have it as excitement in them, some have it in them as a daily living — some as they have eating in them, some as they have drinking, some as they have sleeping in them, some have it in them as believing, some have it as a simple beginning feeling — some have it as the ending always of them such of them are always old men in their loving. (154)

& then applies it to Hersland

David Hersland had a mixture in him. He was of the kind that have loving in them always in beginning and a little in getting strength from wallowing. In the beginning of his loving these two were mixed up in him and his wife was to him more than beginning more than a woman to him for his daily living she was a beautiful thing to him, she was an amusement to him, she was a pleasure to him to have resisting to him, she was a little in him as a tender feeling. More and more in his living loving was to him beginning until in his latest living he needed a woman to fill him, later when he was shrunk away from the outside of him he needed a woman with sympathetic diplomatic domineering to, entering into him, to fill him, he was then shrunk away from the outside of him he was not simple in attacking he was not really getting strength from wallowing, loving was more and more to him as a beginning feeling ... And so more and more it came to him that she was in him like his eating and sleeping, she was less and less in him as a tender feeling she was less and less important in him or to him as outside him, she was less and less a joke to him, she was less and less important to him as a resistance to him, she was less and less part of his children to him, and she more and more died away and left him and then she was not in any way important to him, he needed more beginning in his loving feeling to fill him than anything that she could give him, he mostly then forgot about her and that was the end of her living. Loving was always then in the ending of his middle living more and more in him a beginning feeling, he did not then get strength in him from wallowing in loving, he had not in him real attacking, he had in him in loving a beginning feeling, more and more he needed a woman inside him to fill him. (155-6)

Stein has given us a precise portrait of the factors in any man & the factors in David Hersland that could cause his relationship to change   it is the how that is important here to Stein the what it was in David Hersland's perception of things that made his relationship with his wife less & less real less & less immediate to him   "In the ending of his middle living his wife was not important to him, she did not give to him anything in him of individual feeling" (157)   she was no longer part of his way of handling the world

In the ending of his middle living he got it more and more from his children, a little from the governess and servants in the house with him, a little from the people living near him. (157)

this is one alternative to the intentionality of narrative structure tho, of course, not an alternative to intention. if i rearrange these notes each time i go to read them then each time we will hear a different tune. if i keep rearranging them even while i'm reading them then we could dwell on certain notes far beyond any intention of my own & thus pro- duce wildly varying emphases & meanings. isn't that often what happens in conversation, in attempting to explain an idea to someone? and thus you appear much more insistent on certain ideas than was ever your intention?

she no longer helped buoy up in him the feeling of "being big in beginning" & so he turned to others to fill that need & "his wife was not any longer important to him"   so what we have seen here is why David Hersland got married what happened to the marriage & what happened to him   it is an incredibly compressed statement of an individual perceptual system in process & yet thru her way of writing   her form   Stein insists what she is saying over & over into our minds with all the variations possible until really sometimes there is so much to see so much to learn & the scope of what she is trying seems so large we doubt if we shall ever grasp it   she is compressing & then thru repetition
    thru insisting what she is seeing over & over   she is expanding what she sees thru all its possible permutations

> There are many kinds of women then and many kinds of men and this. There are many kinds of women then and many kinds of men and this then will be a history of some of the many kinds of them. (166)

in her later writing this was not necessary to her   in *The Gradual Making of the Making of Americans* she said

> I knew while I was writing The Making of Americans that it was possible to describe every kind there is of men and women.
>   I began to wonder if it was possible to describe the way every possible kind of human being acted and felt in relation with any kind of human being and I thought if this could be done it would make A Long Gay Book. It is naturally gayer describing what any one feels acts and does in relation to any other one than to describe what they just are what they are inside them. (92)

and in *Look at Me Now and Here I Am*

> When I began The Making of Americans I knew I really did know that a complete description was a possible thing, and certainly a complete description is a possible

thing. But as it is a possible thing one can stop continuing to describe this everything. This is where philosophy comes in, it begins when one stops continuing describing everything. (96)

having seen this she was freed to the point where by the time of the writing of *Ida* she was able to give a completely simple beautifully concise portrait of a small girl at the moment when *she* (& that's important) decides to split her personality

Yes Love she said to him, you have always had me and now you are going to have two, I am going to have a twin yes I am Love, I am tired of being just one and when I am a twin one of us can go out and one of us can stay in, yes Love yes I am yes I am going to have a twin. You know Love I am like that when I have to have it I have to have it. And I have to have a twin, yes Love.

She began to sing about her twin and this is the way she sang.

Oh dear oh dear Love, that was her dog, if I had a twin well nobody would know which one I was and which one she was and so if anything happened nobody could tell anything and lots of things are going to happen and oh Love I felt it yes I know it I have a twin. (*Look at Me Now and Here I Am* 340-41)

bottom nature & the need to handle things   to cope with loneliness & a big world   the way we are & then the need to handle the world in some way   this is what makes us what we become

from some beginning writings on Gertrude Stein's Theories of Personality as revealed in *The Making of Americans*

1973

what follows is excerpted from "some beginning writings on Gertrude Stein's Theories of Personality as revealed in *The Making of Americans*"   the sections printed here form part of the introduction to & sections d & e of a proposed chapter titled "Some Case Histories: a case history." —bpNichol, August 1973

⌘

> There are then two kinds of women, those who have dependent independence in them, those who have in them independent dependence inside them; the first ones of them always somehow own the ones they need to love them, the second kind of them have it in them to love only those who need them, such of them have it in them to have power in them over others only when these others have begun already a little to love them, others loving them gives to such of them strength in domination. (*The Making of Americans* 249)

Stein's initial premise is of two types of people in their bottom nature   the first is the dependent independent kind & the second the independent dependent   as simply as possible then the word that comes first gives you the clue to the surface appearance & the word that comes second to the underlying reality (the bottom nature)   the two types of personality mesh in relationships   dependent independent people are the kind who "own" those who "love only those who need them" (independent dependent) so that the latter's "strength in domination" is really an illusion   they have "power in them over others only when those others have begun already a little to love them"   thus the former appear dependent & yet have "dependent independence" whereas the latter appear independent & yet have "independent dependence"   such tautologies are a perfect example of Stein's precise use of language   she seeks terms that literally embody what she is talking about   what first appears as naive terminology emerges as an exact way of describing things

in the previous distinction a very pure delineation is stated   in reality as Stein never tired of stressing in *The Making of Americans* these distinctions are completely relative to individual cases

d) ATTACKING BEING

& for purposes of understanding by comparison

e) RESISTING BEING

> ... some women have it in them to own those who love them, to subdue such then, these are of them who have dependent independent nature in them, they have resisting in them as their way of fighting. Some who have independent dependent nature in them and have attacking in them as their way of fighting, and have much strength in attacking have this way of subduing those they need for loving, this is another kind then of subduing from that in Madeleine Wyman or in Mrs. Hersland. (250)

as we have seen resisting is the natural way of fighting (of struggling) for dependent independent people & attacking (asserting) is the natural way of fighting for independent dependent people but Stein takes this further

> Resisting being then as I was saying is to me a kind of being, one kind of men and women have it as being that emotion is not as poignant in them as sensation.

This is my meaning, this is resisting being. (347)

here Stein asserts that the world of emotions does not move the resistant type as much as the world of tangible physical objects

> Generally speaking, those having resisting being in them have a slow way of responding, they may be nervous and quick and all that but it is in them, nervousness is in them as the effect of slow-moving going too fast and so having nervous being, nervous being in them is not the natural means of expression to such of them ... (347-8)

Stein is once more cautioning us against being deceived by sur faces since surfaces can be contradictory can be changed by acts of the will

> Some have quick response in them by the steadily train-ing of themselves to quicker and quicker reaction and some of them in the end come to seem to have quick reaction as their natural way of being, mostly in such of them this is a late development in them and that is natu-ral from the being in them. (348)

opposed to the slow-moving practicality of the resisting depend-ent independent type is the attacking independent dependent person

> Those having attacking being ... can have reaction as emotion as quick and poignant and complete as a sensation. (347)

> Attacking being often has nervousness as energy as a natural way of active being in them, often these then lose the power of attacking with the loss of nervousness in them. (348)

the important thing in these statements about nervousness as energy is Stein's awareness that the balance may change   this is

a major point   in her setting up of the two categories dependent independent & independent dependent in her naming of
them she shows & insists on the interrelatedness of the two
personality types   the dependent personality includes the independent streak & vice versa

> This first governess ... had in her, dependent independ-
> ent being. The two, dependent and independent being
> were so balanced in her that resisting was almost attack-
> ing in her, that dependence was almost independence in
> her. (239)

thus she is talking about a balance that is struck between dependent and independent being in each individual with the dominant
element (dependent or independent) as the determining factor in
whether a person can be called dependent independent or independent dependent
                    earlier i spoke of a yin yang balance being the
essence of what Stein was trying to arrive at   those of you
familiar with the principles of yin & yang know the relativism of
which i speak   a thing is more yin or less yin only relative to
something which is more or less yang than it   thus in speaking
of food for instance one is always cautioned against thinking sim-
plistically of yin as sugar and yang as salt because a thing's yin-
ness or yang-ness is completely relative to another thing's yin-ness
or yang-ness   what at first looks confusing is really a very carefully worked out system of thot which keeps the emphasis not on
categories but on balance because it is the balance that is important   now this is the way it is with Stein's labelling of dependent independent & independent dependent & why Stein includes
both words in the naming to remind us that it is the amount of
each & the balance between them that is really important &
makes people what they are   anyone familiar with the problems
inherent in the rigid categorization of contemporary psychological terminology & the confusions that the borrowing of medical
names have raised can only marvel at the genius of what Stein is
doing here

before we can fully understand attacking & resisting being we must first look at what i believe to be the most revolutionary & exciting thing in *The Making of Americans* which is to say HOW Stein saw the things she saw how they manifested themselves to her

it begins & we begin to see it clearly when Stein begins to talk about how she sees these phenomena as substances in people

> Generally speaking then resisting being is a kind of being where, taking bottom nature to be a substance like earth to some one's feeling, this needs time for penetrating to get reaction. Those having attacking being their substance is more vibrant in them ... (347)

here Stein is talking about emotions about emotional forces as if they were solids as if they were objects as if they were observable phenomena in the real world   this would have seemed far-fetched in 1908 & thus Stein's repeated statement

> There are many then believing thinking knowing feeling doing things, mostly every one is feeling knowing thinking doing something, doing feeling believing knowing thinking a very great many things that if any one really knew it about them any one knowing them would be thinking that one a crazy one ... (495)

Bridgeman in *Gertrude Stein in Pieces* dismisses as a "theory of humours" Stein's descriptions of emotional "substances" in people but contemporary scientific research bears out what Stein is saying, i.e. emotional forces create visible measurable effects with many of the qualities Stein mentions

the technique of thermography (essentially the mapping by filmic means of hot & cold areas in the body) reveals pictorially a shifting picture of dark & light of the body as having another topography when different means of perceiving are used   this is of course similar to the whole field of research that has grown up around the body's aura the auras of plant & animal life   "Psychic Discoveries Behind the Iron Curtain" contained photos of a human aura as well as documenting cases of cutting leaves in half & the aura the energy field of the entire leaf being retained & photographed   in *The Mind of a Mnemonyst* the Russian psychiatrist Luria documented the case of a man who saw sound who would describe people as having "crumbly yellow voices" & who in fact picked up much of his feeling from people by seeing the "substance" of their speech in its visual manifestation   research into auras is becoming increasingly respectable & important as the realization of the subtlety of the human psyche dawns   auras tonal inflections areas of heat & cold in the body (often brought about by muscular blocks (tightening of particular sets of muscles for specific emotional reasons) as any masseuse or masseur worth their name could tell you) are visible measurable effects that have physical manifestations in the real world   we are only recently developing the technology for the "glasses" with which everyone can see them but the number of cases of people who have been able to see such phenomena without such technological glasses have been extensively documented for years   until science gave it respectability (as science seems to have a habit of doing the mere invoking of its name reducing people to silence in their objections) such cases were laughed at or seen as signs that the person was crazy   Stein's speaking of "substances" in people in her descriptions of psychological types is not far-fetched but is in fact revolutionary for the time   the last ten years has seen this whole area of research grow & such respected psychoanalysts as for instance John Pierrakos (a student of Wilhelm Reich's & co-founder with Alexander Loewen of the Institute for Bio-Energetic Research) are bringing their studies & findings forth for serious consideration by the scientific community   65 years later we find ourselves in a position to listen to what Stein is saying with a more open mind

> I know it and now I begin again with telling it, the way I feel resisting being in men and women. It is like a substance and in some it is as I was saying solid and sensitive all through it to stimulation, in some almost wood-

en, in some muddy and engulfing, in some thin almost like gruel, in some solid in some parts and in other parts all liquid, in some with holes like air-holes in it, in some a thin layer of it, in some hardened and cracked all through it, in some double layers of it with no connections between the layers of it. (348–9)

now all this is very important because as Stein next says

... I am looking hard at each one, feeling, seeing, hearing the repeating coming out of each one and so slowly I know of each one the way the bottom in them is existing and so then that is the foundation of the history of each one of them and always it is coming out of each one of them. (349)

Stein is fixing in very concrete terms the bottom nature in people as she SEES it as visible phenomena having qualities one can describe as one can describe any real substance any actual "thing"   thus the resisting being in some is "solid and sensitive" reacts to stimulation whereas in others there is no reacting when stimulated (attacked) because they are "almost wooden"   in others resisting being is "muddy and engulfing"   there is of course a danger here of taking these things metaphorically & it is important to realize that Stein is describing what happens to ACTUAL ENERGY when it encounters these various types of resisting beings   who has not said of someone that to talk to

that person is draining it takes all the energy out of you talking to them   these are the types of phenomena that Stein is talking about

Stein has many lists of such phenomena but we will not go thru them all since a few examples should be enough

> I am thinking of attacking being not as an earthy kind of substance but as a pulpy not dust not dirt but a more mixed up substance, it can be slimy, gelatinous, gluey, white opaquy kind of thing and it can be white and vibrant, and clear and heated … It was like this to me in the first one I came to know it, the substance attacking being is, in its various shaping. In this one it was so dull, so thick, so gluey that it was so slow in action one almost could think of it as resisting but it was not resisting earthy dependent independent being, it was attacking, stupid, slow-moving, it was independent dependent being, it was a different substance in its way of acting, reacting, of being penetrated, of feeling, of thinking, than any slow resisting dependent independent being … (349)

Stein then makes clear how she distinguishes between them & once again asserts that these are real things she is talking about

> In this one then, as I was saying it was attacking being but very slowly getting into motion but not because it the stimulation was lost into it and had to be remade out of it but because it being shaken it was a slow mass getting into action. I know this distinction, it has real meaning … (349)

the key distinction then between attacking & resisting being is that in resisting being stimulation goes into that being & disappears & any thing that comes back out of that person in terms of a response is "remade out of it" has to be laboured at is not an immediate emotion as such but a worked at thot out thing

whereas in attacking being it is a re-action a quick emotional

90

response to the person   the resisting being is more practical &
down to earth less flighty less carried away by emotion

> Mostly those having in them resisting being have more
> feeling of objects as real things to them, objects have to
> them more earthy meaning than to those who have
> attacking as their natural way of being. Mostly then
> objects to those having attacking as their natural way of
> being have for them meaning as emotion, as practically
> to be using, as beauty, as symbolism, that is to many of
> them their natural way of seeing anything they are
> knowing, to those who have resisting being as their
> natural way of being

(and here we see where Stein places herself)

> an object is it itself to them, the meaning, the use, the
> emotion about it, the beauty, the symbolising of it is to
> such of them a secondary reaction, not altogether at
> once as in those having in them attacking as their
> natural way of being. (348)

> things as they are   Q.E.D.   this is to be a constant theme
> running thru all of Stein's work   "How do the words you make
> inside you compare to the words you make outside you"   but
> there are no value judgements here   Stein is not interested in
> saying one kind of being is better than another

> Well then that is true then that of each kind of them
> there are nice ones and nice enough ones and not very
> nice ones, and not at all nice ones and very horrid ones.
> This can be in them with any strength or weakness of
> their kind being in them, it is from the mixing and the
> accenting and the relation of parts of their kind of
> nature in them. (466-7)

everything is relative

i cannot say too much more about how
Stein SEES   it is there in *The Making of Americans* & she asserts
that it has "real meaning" that she is talking about actual things
     years later in *Lectures in America* she reasserted this saying "Of
course you all know that when I speak of naming anything, I
include emotions as well as things"   in *The Making of Americans*
she states what she sees because her honesty her commitment to
the process demands it but it is with temerity that she does so

> ... you write a book and while you write it you are
> ashamed for every one must think you are a silly or a
> crazy one and yet you write it and you are ashamed, you
> know you will be laughed at or pitied by every one and
> you have a queer feeling and you are not very certain
> and you go on writing. (485)

so this will have to do for now on Stein's seeing
                                        we will clarify
one more thing about attacking & resisting being   in speaking
of Clara Dounor (it is Phillip Redfern's attraction to her brings
an end to the marriage between himself and Martha Hersland)
Stein says

> To understand the being in her there must be now a
> little realization of the way beginning is in very many
> persons having in them a nature that is self growing and
> a nature that is reacting to stimulation and that have it in
> them to have these two natures acting in not very great
> harmony inside them. (458)

this statement makes clearer what we were talking about earlier
about a type of personality the stimulation had to be "remade out
of" which Stein here calls "a nature that is self growing"   this is
as we have seen a quality of the dependent independent who
have resisting fighting as their natural way of winning   such
people are at their extreme only motivated by interior stimulation & have to re-make any stimulation that comes into them as
if it were their own hence "self growing" self-motivating &

expanding   those who have a "nature that is reacting to stimulation" are of the independent dependent kind who have attacking fighting as their natural way of winning   but these are absolutes & in the above statement Stein is once again asserting that nothing is that absolute   Clara Donour has both dependent (resisting) & independent (attacking) being inside her "acting in not very great harmony"   but to clarify further what the term self growing (stimulation having to be remade out of them) means

> I will now tell a little about what I mean by self-growing activity in such of them and reactive activity in such of them. As I was saying a long time back when I was describing the dependent independent kind of them, reaction is not poignant in them unless it enters into them the stimulation is lost in them and so sets it, the mass, in motion, it is not as in the other kind of them who have it to have a reactive emotion to be as poignant as a sensation as is the case in the independent dependent kind of them. Miss Charles then as I was saying was of the kind of them where reaction to have meaning must be a slow thing, but she had quick reactions as mostly all of them of this kind of them have them and those were in her mostly attacking being as is very common in those having in them dependent independent being. (459)

self growing then means just that   in the reactive (attacking fighting) personality stimulation is fed back immediately almost in a way mirroring it   in the self growing (resisting fighting) personality stimulation sets the person's mass (his bottom nature) in motion & the response grows out of that activity within the person that self growing activity within them

resisting being then is the dependent independent way of fighting that is winning for them   such people tend to re-make the stimulation put into them (are self growing)   they are interested in things as things in themselves & only secondarily in whatever qualities they may possess   attacking being is the independent dependent way of fighting that is winning for them   such people are re-active & respond directly to stimulation   they tend to be interested primarily in the qualities of a thing or the feelings engendered by it & secondarily in the thing as itself   everyone can have a mixture of both types of being in them   it is in fact fairly common that a dependent independent person will have quick reactions to some things & that these will manifest themselves as attacking being

a review of bpNichol's "some beginning writings on Gertrude Stein's Theories of Personality" as published in *Open Letter* 2/2

1972

it's interesting to see in Nichol's beginning writings on Stein the same indefiniteness that one encounters in *The Making of Americans*   Stein's major novel begins as a study of the shifting forms of human personality   in the course of it she is led more & more to consider simply the surface of the reality of things as they as are (Q.E.D.) to give up the didactic for the tentativeness of this statement

> Family living can go on existing. Very many are remembering this thing are remembering that family living living can go on existing. Very many are quite certain that family living can go on existing. Very many are remembering that they are quite certain that family living can go on existing. (925)

> Any family living can be one being existing and some can remember something of some such thing. (925)

Nichol in his article in the form he chooses to use reveals the same indefiniteness the same tentativeness as Stein   he starts out proposing to extract Stein's theories of personality   his presentation is incomplete (acknowledged in his use of the word "beginning") leaving us unable to judge whether or not he has succeeded & yet the fragmentary nature of these notes gives us clues as to whether any ultimate success can be expected

b e f o r e taking this further let me point out that failure to achieve a professed goal does not mean failure as a work   Stein had the greatness & the humility to allow *The Making of Americans* to stand as it is a record of an attempt & the results achieved   in the course of writing she achieved more of her goal than she has been given credit for (for which reason it is to be hoped Nichol does finish *his* undertaking)

Nichol has attempted thru the elimination of punctuation as a visible series of periods commas semicolons etc. to arrive at a syntax that depends to a greater & greater degreee on the placement of each word   he is out to find his own voice to find an outward form for a very real inner insistence   in beginning writings on Stein he has failed   in his substitution of visual space for a period comma etc. he takes off from the work of the German typographer/poet Hansjörg Mayer who used varying sizes of space to indicate these signs

the problem with Mayer's system is that it merely substitutes one set of semiotic conventions for another without attendant alteration of sentence structure   Nichol has taken what he was doing in *For Jesus Lunatick* & extended it thru the incorporation of hints gleaned from Mayer but he has not taken it far enough

the text is too often simply confusing   some of the confusions are obviously compositor's errors (there are at least three instances that could've been caught by a more careful proofreading) but the responsibility for the others remains with Nichol

in this i can see his (at this point) failed attempt to express how his perceptual system has been altered by his encounter with Stein's perceptual system (surely this is what we mean when we say one writer has influenced another)   i know for a fact that these first notes of Nichol's were written in the spring of 71 & submitted to *Open Letter* without revision   obviously enough came through to the editors that they saw fit to publish them without insisting that Nichol make his intent clearer   seeing this we can say that Nichol has partially succeeded   but the hesitancy in & tentativeness of these first notes shows through in his lack of mastery over his own structures (he is (for instance) still wrestling with how to handle the differentiation between commas & periods   he has set out to create punctuation anew to serve his own ends & has not succeeded)   writings of his done since this time suggest that he is coming closer to achieving

his intent   call it my bias but i hope he continues with both
projects & that we eventually see the end products

pbLichon
toronto
september 16/72

Review of *Typewriter Poems*, edited by Peter Finch

1972

in the demarcation lines which exist between various approaches to concrete poetry (that term everyone is decrying as being hopelessly inadequate to define anything which you have to admit does bring up the interesting question of how any movement interested in freeing itself from the strictures of the ordinary semantic & visual structures of language got stuck in such a cement straitjacket) one of the best ways to figure out the differences is by going back to the roots the individual poets came from   thus hansjörg mayer with his origins in typography will always have an interest in a cleaner visual approach than say the late d. a. levy or bill bissett or (one of the best poets & some of the best poems in this collection) bob cobbing who came at concrete by way of the poem & the mimeography machine mimeograph being the best expression of pure typewriter concerns allows you to carry over the typewriter's tremendous advantage (that each character occupies exactly the same space as any other character which allows for the permutational nature of such approaches as the DEVELOPER method of the czechoslovakian concretists of which in this anthology meic stephen's poem is an example) into a context in which you can use overprinting & reverse printing & all the techniques that levy bissett & cobbing have used

now i've gone into this to give you some background for what i want to say about finch's *Typewriter Poems* which is an anthology of current british concretists working with the typewriter   it is important to realize that the equal space value given each character by the typewriter means that the poem is in a literal sense not the same poem when set in type   thus the most successful poems as far as any definition of typewriter poems in particular goes are those which acknowledge & work with this fact   this is one of the bases for formulating critical judgements about concrete poems of this nature   the other basis is well stated by michael gibbs in his contributor's notes to the anthology when he says

> dissatisfied with tendency towards typographical decorativeness and simple typewriter games

which j p ward (another contributor) amplifies further when he states

> the typewriter lends itself to geometry, abstraction, and therefore, perhaps, to the infinite, the deep truth that "number holds saw above the flux." Sadly we all too often reduce this to the level of typing pretty patterns of very elementary nature, and feel pleased with ourselves for doing so, but more elaborate patterns, including semantic ones, of greater intricacy and intelligence are possible — requiring only the poets with the patience to find them.

given these additional considerations & the recognition that we are dealing with a particular field of activity within concrete poetry (particular because of the particularity of the typewriter & its effect on the perceptual field of the writer) we can make some assessments of this anthology

the most successful poems for me are lloyd's houedard's cobbing's ward's (particularly his "but i say unto you") mayer's zurbrugg's & mccarthy's   ward is an interesting case in point since the successfulness of his piece "but i say unto you" is achieved by working against the geometrical exactness of the typewriter   using a deliberately disturbed typing in which lines weave across one another in broken fashion phrases beginning & stopping prematurely words misspelt errors left intact & any aesthetic of design deliberately avoided   one gradually uncovers in reading the phrase "but i say unto you he has already committed adultery with her" the semantic the emotional & the visual are wedded in a gut statement of reality   the further innovative strength of ward's piece is the fact that he is the only poet in this anthology to include & work with a syntactic element all of which makes his piece the single most successful poem here   bob cobbing's duplicator pieces (reproductions of his mimeographed texts) can only be understood in light of his attempts to notate his multivoice sound poems   his sense of notation is similar to that of many of the contemporary composers included in john cage's Notations in as much as he is not trying to give you a strict text to follow but rather to   as he puts it

> [by] superimposition by means of stencil & duplicator
> enable one to dance to this measure

    thus his texts are movements in space   attempts to graph pictorially sonic clusters & as such they achieve their goal magnificently   similarly andrew lloyd's "5th dolphin transmission" is a beautiful poem in its own right   dom sylvester houedard takes a different approach   for years now he's been working with his typestracts   pure iconomic typewriter statements using the full range of characters available working with & against the typewriter's limitations to achieve his concise meditative statements
    i could go on   each of the other poets mentioned achieves what he sets out to do exploring the typewriter & the semantic of the pieces involved
                    the failures are also interesting   typing this i'm aware of the difficulty of talking about these pieces without your being able to see them so it is to be hoped you'll go out & buy this anthology because i do think it's well worth the money & is the first really NEW concrete anthology to appear in a long time   too many of the recent crop of anthologies & indeed the magazines themselves have been rehashing the already too familiar pieces   thank you peter finch for getting a relatively new body of material in print   now about the failures
                                                  p e t e r
finch's own contributions to the anthology don't work   his "texture poem for the moon of stars" is pretty & that's it   it's the old problem of being too pictorial   the fact is one's initial response is "how about that a moon with two clouds floating in

front of it done with the typewriter" which means the poem is robbed of any impact   a hand drawn moon with two clouds in front of it would've conveyed the same information   it is a bravura demonstration of technical control which i hope he'll apply to something more challenging   his "music for cloud song" tho not as pictorial suffers from the same feeling of sub-stancelessness   compare what finch is doing here with steve mccaffery's *Carnival* (forthcoming from the Coach House Press) for an idea of what can be done with masking in this whole approach to the poem   alan riddell's "the honey pot" also suffers from an oversimplified pictorial approach   what is the value of having a bunch of b's floating around a tightly clustered bunch of b's   i feel it is important to realize the difference here between what emerges in this approach & say garnier's *Spatialist* poems in which he freed the single letter from any specific ties to semantic syntactic or visual criteria & left it free to dance with other letters as it would   riddell has tied the letter to a specific aesthetic a specific grouping of associations just for the sake of a visual pun which in the end is not strong enough to carry the weight put on it   the pun is in danger of getting overused in concrete   not enough poets realize the skill needed to handle it effectively   take for instance michael gibb's poem "avenue" in which he repeats the word cluster "treestreetree" one above the other so that one is left with you guessed it a tree lined street   need i say more   john gilbert's "eve" poem (masked to the shape of an apple with a bite out of it with the word "evil" repeated inside it) is corny   michael gibb's other poem in this anthology "proverb" works however   embedded within a square composed of the word "tree" repeated over & over again lies the word "wood"   his point is made   the pun here is funny & working within what is literally a cliché form in concrete gibbs pulls off his pun   & this is the way the whole anthology goes   the successes outnumber the failures   whatever specific poems may lack there are others that cover those gaps & leave you feeling satisfied when you put the book aside

as much as anything i have tried in this review to give some criteria for evaluating such work since at this point in the history of the concrete movement we have a substantial body of theory pointing towards this place we've reached & too little that critically examines the limitations of the conventions we still take for granted or the new dogma we have brought in to replace the hated older dogmas

the brazilians were wrong when they said in their *Pilot Plan for Concrete Poetry* that the historical cycle of verse was closed

nothing is ever closed in that sense   more & more we become aware that verse had been in a straitjacket which was slowly strangling it until the advent of mallarmé stein the dadaists olson & the concretists   we begin to catch glimpses of the other side   what none of us suspected may yet come to pass

that everything we've done is merely the prelude to a poetry that is beyond conceptualization at this point in time   it is our own poor minds that set up these dogmas these limitations

finch's *Typewriter Poems* suggests even more than it says therein lies its power   i'm glad i've got a copy on my shelf

```
        asea ease   ease
         ease seas   seas
         seas asea   asea
         asea ease   ease
          ease seas   seas
          seas asea   asea
           easease ease
           aseas  seas
           aseas asea
           easeasease
          seas aseas
         asea  aseas
        ease  easease
       seas  seas asea
      asea    ease seas
     ease        asea ease
   seas          seas asea
    ease          ease seas
     asea          seas   ease
      seas     asea        asea
       ease ease          seas
        aseaseas            ease
         seasea            seas
          ease            asea
           as            ease
                        seas
                        asea
                      ease
```

Sound and the Lung Wage

The wild wolves are almost gone.

This may not immediately strike you as tragic. You may believe — as so many do — that wolves kill human beings. And yet there is no authenticated report of a human killed by a nonrabid wolf in the North American continents ...

Our terror of the wolf is superstitious and magical. It comes from his seeming invisibility; we know he is there because we hear him and see his tracks and his kill. But we seldom see him because he avoids us.

And it comes because his wolf howl sends chills of fright through our minds. We feel threatened ...

If we are killing them off not for what they are but for what we, in our fear, imagine them to be, then perhaps what we fear is something in ourselves.

man has a strange fear of vowel sound   nowhere is this better illustrated than in the tragic story of the gradual extermination of the wild wolves   what we know of the wolf comes from the SOUND of his howling & our feelings about it   & it is our FEELINGS about it (the terror & loathing) that governs our handling of the wolves

howling screaming & crying   let's just pause for a moment & consider two things   1) when a baby cries we always ask "what is he trying to say" or "listen he's trying to say something"   there are no words to consider only SOUNDS   there is probably not even a faculty for word for-mation developed   but there is communication   usually we understand   2) sound is an expression of the total organism

much of what we know about a person we know because of the sounds he makes   there is a close link between body & breath between breath & sound between sound & articulation (which can mean conceptualization)   Dr. John C. Pierrakas pointed out

> Children who are not permitted to vocalize freely and
> are shut up develop severe disturbances in the breathing
> pattern and their voices then become mechanical and
> dry, or limited in range.

how many of us have not encountered mothers who become ter-
rified when their children cry & immediately attempt to quiet
them or who when their children shout in public (for whatever
reason) look embarrassed & get angry at the child for drawing
people's attention to them
                              in the Hopi indian creation myth the
story is told of the creation of spider woman shortly after the
world was created   spider woman gave birth to two sons one of
whom was called palongwahoya   it was his job to go forth &
praise the creator to open his mouth & sing   when he did this
he set the vibratory axis of the earth in motion so that the earth
vibrated in tune with the vibratory axis of the universe   as long
as men sang the creator's praises everything vibrated in tune &
the universe was in harmony   then men ceased singing &
retreated into their homes & began to use speech only to communicate between themselves & the world began to vibrate out
of tune & the creator destroyed it   thus it has been thru four
worlds & this world we live in now is the fifth the creator has
made for men   Pierrakas (in the article i quoted from earlier)
speaks of "excitatory waves from the cores of the organism" of
how "each person has a specific vibratory state" & of the CRY as
"the basic pulsatory movement of the entire organism"   it is
not difficult to see that he is speaking of the same thing as the
Hopi for what is their creation myth telling us if not that man as
an organism must be in harmony with the organic universe he
lives in & that the medium thru which that harmony can be
achieved is human sound
                              two of the most commonly seen phe-
nomenon in psychic disturbances are people who use words to
push away (compulsive talkers are a good example of this) & people who use words privately which is to say do not attempt to
communicate anything to anyone exterior to themselves (autistic
children being an extreme example of this)   in both these cases

sound tends to be used in a minimal clipped fashion   the full range of human voice is neither explored nor expressed   as a result the full range of the organism is suppressed   one is literally holding sound in muscles tight the whole body in a constant state of contraction   one can read the Hopi creation myth as a description of the origins of mental illness & it reads accurately

but the fear of sound shows itself in even more obvious cases

one only has to let out a yell in a subway station or on the street corner of any city & watch the reactions of hostility & fear to realize how general it is   thus our slaughter of the wolves as the ones who howl becomes clearer   it is not too different from our reaction to mental illness for the social or popular conception of an insane asylum is of a place of screaming   & the people we put there are those whose cries of anguish we can no longer bear to listen to feeling as we do helpless to deal with them   thus we lock them away & view with fear & suspicion those we pay to take care of them for us   we criticize on linguistic or philosophic grounds "theories" of mental illness when our inability to handle such people lies in the fact that there is no logical or philosophical system that touches or comforts them in their anguish   their vibratory state is disturbed   their world (their perception of it) is destroyed   they scream to let the pent up sound out

why was the emphasis on sound dropped   the acoustical perfection of greek architectural spaces is still a marvel in this century   there is no problem vexes architects more than how to create a perfect acoustical environment   one theory to account for this is the belief that greek & earlier architectures were based on the ear as opposed to (as is the case in the 20th century) the eye   this eye ear differentiation is an important one   our alphabet is a visual one which developed much more from the pictograph than from any phonetical base   to speak the name of a letter like "T" we actually combine two sounds thus phonetically we spell the letter "T" as "Tē" or more simply "TEE"   print with its emphasis on the eye in reading as opposed to the speaking of words dealt a decisive blow to the oral culture   the eye (print) & the ear (the spoken word) became split to the point where Charles Olson in attempting to unify them again in his poetry by treating print merely as a score for vocalization was castigated by the already firmly entrenched (in less than 5000 years) print culture   so that in this ascendancy of the eye over the ear we have reached the point where a question we must ask ourselves is is there a real gap between the eye & the ear   is Charles Olson for instance attempting to combine two dissimilar modes of perception or is the problem now that we THINK of them as dissimilar   i.e. is our formulation falsely based   it is an important question for the eye & the ear are our two major instruments for taking in language information

   the si–milarity (let's approach it from this angle) is that both the eye & the ear obtain information thru wave phenomena i.e. light waves & sound waves   but light waves & sound waves exist at different frequency levels & light travels faster than sound   for the purposes of what i am about to say realize that a fast moving object makes more of an impact than a slow moving one   it also reaches us sooner   "i believe what i see not what i hear"   "hearsay is inadmissible as evidence" (think about what is being said there)   thus the visual culture within a few years of its inception (& by visual i mean print) overwhelmed the oral one   with the ascendancy of print comes the move out of the "dark" ages into the age of "en*light*enment"

   the great disciplines of our times are born   history is a visual phenomenon   myth is a sound one   science is a visual phenomenon   magic is a sound one   i.e. the emphasis in history is on the visible artifact as proof   myth is transmission of an oral culture (no or little visual proof)   in science the burden is on print on the recording of visible phenomena (including measurement of sound phenomenon) or on the proving of relationships between a series of signs which stand for invisible phenomenon (mathematics) in a visible print fashion   in magic (as in religion the base is chant i.e. oral ritual)

   in the formation of the alphabet as a visual code (remember its base is pictorial & not phonic) we see an example of the ascendancy of the eye over the ear that lays the groundwork for the eventual domination by print (the eye) in our culture   the problem then becomes the lack of any middle ground between the eye & the ear   we have allowed them to become polarized   at different historical periods the one or the other dominates   this is our folly because both are vital   the sound waves (myth & magic) affect us in a deeper way than the eye or (and perhaps this is a better way to phrase what i am trying to say here) disturb us more because we have cut ourselves off from the effects of sound from that expression of the total organism that sound can be   you can take as proof of this that both myth & magic ritual have survived thru periods where no visible artifacts as either science or history can be pointed to   remember also that the impact of history & science depend on quantity of proof & not just quality   a high amount of information is needed to make the visual impact clear   myth & magic are in fact incorporated into the visual to give it "depth" or "deeper meaning" i.e. greek myths & all other incorporations of oral tradition into the visual

i am aware that much of what we know as myth exists only because someone a long time ago took the time & trouble to scratch them out in clay or write them down on papyri   but i am talking about the imbalance that has dominated this century because it is the correction of the imbalance that i see as our primary task at this point in time   not to eliminate either the eye or the ear but to find the point of balance   the centre

there is more here to consider   one of the more powerful uses of language is the pun   there is a curious duplicity about this for consider the following two facts   1) the pun is always referred to as "the lowest form of humour"   2) both linguistics & philosophy tend to attempt to make language more & more concrete to remove ambiguity   further there is an emphasis on a ONE STATEMENT = ONE MEANING dictum which the political & educational structures foster   a re-reading of the gorgon myth (the story of the head of many TONGUES whose EYES turn you to stone) reveals the concept TO SPEAK MULTIPLY MEANS DESTRUCTION   but i spoke of duplicity so let us examine the social paradox as it exists

1) concretion is forbidden   consider words like fuck or cunt or any which refer specifically to either the genital organs or their functions   when

speaking of such things the concrete words are taboo and the pun
is acceptable   it is important however to mention that here the
pun tends to be used more to conceal than reveal   it is misused

2) the level of multiple meaning is taboo   for instance if i
am prime minister of canada and say "such & such is true" you
should believe that it IS true whether it is or not   if i say one
thing & mean another you should concentrate on what i say &
believe it   if on the other hand our enemy says something well
that he doesn't really mean then HE IS BEING DECEITFUL &
really means something else   hence experts in world affairs &
interpreters of political statements   or if i as a parent or teacher
say I LOVE YOU you should believe it whether or not you sense
differently   after all doesn't the very fact that i am your teacher
or parent show that i love you

psycho-analysis rediscovered the
multiplicity of tongues   it put the emphasis back onto the fact
that one can say one thing & mean many things   the pun
because it links sound & meaning (uses similarities in sound to
pivot between many meanings) is the place in language where
this is revealed most clearly   but language always embraces the
mores of the dominant social group & in our time the emphasis
has been that THE ACTUALITY OF LANGUAGE IS ITS
SURFACE   extensive use of sound & hence awareness of multiple meanings is looked down upon   take the classical case of
your lover saying to you "i love you"   meaning here is not conveyed by the words but by the feeling within the words by the
nuance & tone   the words themselves have become hackneyed
& meaningless   it is what the sound conveys that gives them
credibility   here the sound could convey the message "i hate
you" even when the words are "i love you"   but in our time to
behold that man has many tongues (& here i take the gorgon
myth as revealing the primitive underlying fear) leads to death or
insanity   in our insecurity we cling to the surface of words &
listen no further   the multiplicity of tongues is seen as evil &
associated with lying   "he speaks with a forked tongue"
   insanity = the man with many ears

it is no secret that what happens in a psychosis is that the psychotic is overwhelmed with sensory data & his mind cannot distinguish its sources   in its extreme the whole world is a threat because he experiences anger for instance as a natural force threatening him & cannot sort out the sources of the anger or who the anger is really towards

thus passing any person who is angry he immediately senses it & feels it is directed towards him   language because it is the tool of self-definition and conceptualization helps a person sepa- rate out sources   this is what Freud meant by ego i.e. this is my feeling & that is your feeling   that sense of acknowledging the sources of human emotion & of taking responsibility for your own feelings (in current jargon "ego" is used to mean "narcissistic self-involvement to the exclusion of others" which was never Freud's concept)   but at some point this use of language turned against man   in the filtering out & classifying of sources the phenomenon of censorship took over & gained the upper hand

which is to say that somewhere the idea crept in that if this particular way of using language enabled one to locate the sources of one's fears then extended use would eliminate them entirely   as we have seen this wasn't true   all this did was eliminate conscious acknowledgement of the feelings to the point where the society looks with fear & suspicion upon a real use of vocal sound & hence multiple meaning   the ONE STATE- MENT = ONE MEANING dictum is the straitjacket upon our social madness   both the arts & insanity are attempts to break out of this trap   here we can see why historically political & social institutions are suspicious of artistic endeavours because by their very nature they threaten existing structures   mental ill- ness (people snapping under the strain of the artificially imposed ONE STATEMENT = ONE MEANING dictum) threatens the fabric of the society

the emergence in the 1950s of television the tape recorder the 45 rpm & the long playing record heralded the re-emergence of sound of the ear because of a technology that 100 years earlier would have been impossible   but it is not human sound   just as print was not the voice put on a page (remember that Olson's attempt to treat print as merely a score

for vocalization was a REVOLUTION)   what this new technology afforded were wave patterns that DUPLICATED the
human voice but that also amplified it distorted it & which were
simply not HUMAN   an interesting part of this phenomenon
is the level the volume at which most contemporary popular
music is listened to (which is to say LOUD) indicating the degree
to which the print dominated culture has been a desensitizing
one   it has been necessary to literally bombard the nervous system in order to activate a response   thus what first appears to
be a return to sound is NOT a return to human sound but rather
the creation of a technology as potentially imbalancing as print
ever was   it is as if in a strange way we have dissociated ourselves even further from our own voices   the belief which an
african tribe is said to have held that to have your picture taken
was to have your soul stolen does not seem so farfetched   what
the microphone does is remove the necessity for the entire
speech apparatus which is to say the whole body to exert itself
     the microphone begins to supply the nuance & tone the
emotional shading   movies & television & records take it a step
further removing even the necessity of the speaker's actual presence as an active part in the communication   now in the 1970s
when it would appear that sound was never more present as a
factor in our lives in another way human sound was never further
away   what fills our lives now are electrical & magnetic forces
whose effects on the hearing on the entire biological energy field
we call the human body is little understood if in fact it is understood at all   we have parlayed our fear of human sound into a
technology which screams at us justifying to ourselves our sense-
less search for silence
                    there is little more to talk about   what i've
been pointing out here is the problem as i see it & it is admittedly
one man's opinion   to me the choices seem obvious   human
sound minus the technology it leans upon too heavily must be
released again & the full potential explored   if language has lost
its credibility in our time surely it is because the emotions which
supported it (conveyed thru the sound (nuance pitch & tone))
have lost their credibility   in the final analysis language is a tool
which serves us only for as long & as well as we take care of it

there has certainly never been a time in human history when we have needed it more & yet we use only a fraction of its potential & if we are to believe the Hopi myth this could be the fifth world's downfall   the struggle will at times seem pointless but perhaps the words that Hugo Ball wrote in his diary in June of 1916 will cheer you on

> People may smile, if they want to; language will thank us for our zeal, even if there should not be any directly visible results. We have charged the word with forces and energies which made it possible for us to rediscover the evangelical concept of the "word" (logos) as a magical complex of images ...

A Letter to Mary Ellen Solt

1973, 1985

dear mary

this is an essay in the form of a letter which very loosely i was going to title "Autobiography of a Passage" to illuminate in some sense my course thru the language since it does seem to be motivated by a number of disparate senses of language & (for me) a continuing process of discovery so that most of the poems i have included here function as illustrations of what i am talking about

from the beginning there has been an obsession with the messages concealed within language the sense of both crypto graph & the literal many levels of speech thru the use of small letters & capitals this was quickly supplanted by poems like "to the memory of su t'ung po" in which the poem billows out from the primary statement the language is the landscape of the poem the reference back to the chinese poet acknowledges my debt to the chinese literature in translation that was/is a large influence on my work by the time of the *Still Water* poems (the original title of which was *The Chinese Poems*) & proceeding from Pound's sense of the ideogram (via Fenollosa) i was attempting thru visual placement of the words (involved with nouns only) to evoke the power of the thing named — to reunite the signifier & the signified

for a long time parallel to the concerns i name here i had been drawing comic strips & working with ideas & syntax & narrative as they are present in the comic strip realizing that the individual frames tended to function as paragraphs with the linear narrative proceeding from frame to frame (i say "tended" because many current comic strip artists have broken with this particular traditional usage & are making incredible breakthrus in the area of narrative) within the frame however the narrative was not linear or, rather, did not have to be thus in a strip like Herriman's *Krazy Kat* the landscape or setting changes from frame to frame making each frame a unique event

& our involvement with each frame non-linear   as well as drawing the comic strips i was doing a series of poem/drawings in order to express certain concepts re single letters re language that came into my mind constantly that i had no way of expressing thru my writing as a typewriter/print phenomenon   & in these poem/drawings that sense of things concealed within other things comes thru clearly in pieces like "Door 1" & "Door 2"

in a period of about six months from fall 70 to spring 71 i made a breakthru   in the series i called "Frames" i focused on the single comic strip frames & began to replace the drawings of things with the names of them much as i had done in *Still Water*   thru the poem/drawings & the comic strips i had worked on building up a stock visual vocabulary & allowing it to insist itself over & over again   thus there was for me no ambiguity in replacing the thing itself (for instance the drawing of the cloud in "Frame 16") by its name (as happens in "Frame 11")   for me they were one & the same   thru play as Gomringer & Stein had both suggested it there was recreation & hence re-creation   i was making the language anew for myself & because i had re-discovered that conviction in the words i used i was re-investing the word with its own logos

two different things happened at this point

the poem /drawings changed   in the series "Allegories" i compressed story into one image in which there was no narrative succession

we should not be bullied by the cultural preference for "the book" as a certifying object. unless approached carefully, which is to say knowledgeably, the book has a tendency to homogenize our work & an essential heterogeneity can be lost.

of frames & indeed no frames only
the cluster of images   thus no
linearity to the narrative but rather
a grouping which the "reader"
must "read" into a linear sequence
        i was freed up   i began to
consider a serial development of a
primary drawn text (much in the
manner of the "su t'ung po" poem
mentioned earlier) & in doing so
the emphasis began to shift from
using drawing to express ideas
about language (hence poem/

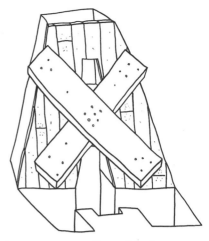

drawings as a naming) to the point i am at now of considering
drawing as drawing — line as line   you can trace this development chronologically in the three series "Aleph Unit" then "Love
Affair" & then (most recently) "Line Telling" (in which H is used
as a point of departure & tension)

        the other thing that happened
was a sudden integration of my breath line poetry (my belief in
sound) and my literal obsession with the single letter & what it
contains as element of word as sound unit & in terms of its own
history (vis-à-vis Alfred Kallir's *Sign & Design*)   i had in my
comic strip drawings frequently included letters floating in the
sky or simply standing in the middle of the landscape   since
"Frames" had shown me i could replace things with the names of
things & still retain the power i suddenly realized that i could
simply include the single letters in my poems   in this case the
name & the thing were the same   the alphabet is runic   i
began to write *Love* climaxing in a long 49 section poem titled
"Trans-Continental"   love poems because they expressed my
feelings about the alphabet celebrated my wedding to it (i wax
romantic but it's true — the burst of feeling when i wrote them
was incredible)

        then i lay fallow   i had brought these things
home together at last & yet something was missing
        always that feeling there was something more bothered me
        this past February it came to me in writing the closing section

of Book 3 of *The Martyrology* (the final book of my journal/record of my struggle thru the language/life to this point in time)   the key word was women   i looked at it & saw "w's omen" & it struck me that W's omen was that it contained more than itself that it flipped over to become M   but it was more than that   the omen or portent was that i was reading words as sentences that said things about single letters   thus (for instance) "time" becomes "t i'm e" etc etc   another door had opened & this time it was speaking to me telling me things that i could build anew on   at this point "Mid-Initial Sequence" feels to me the most important thing i've ever written because everything is there including the dreamed palindrome

i had first gotten into what i later learned was called "concrete" because i had thot myself too arrogant had found myself trying to dominate in the act of writing the language i was using as opposed to letting myself simply learn from the signs themselves   ten years had passed & the fresh illumination was there   thus the closing lines of *The Martyrology* (the seven referred to being the period of its composition)

> the emblems were there when i began
> seven years to understand
> the first letter/level of
> > martyrdom

> best
> bp

> Spring
> 1973

clouds

a bird

mountains

a river

something is moving

1973

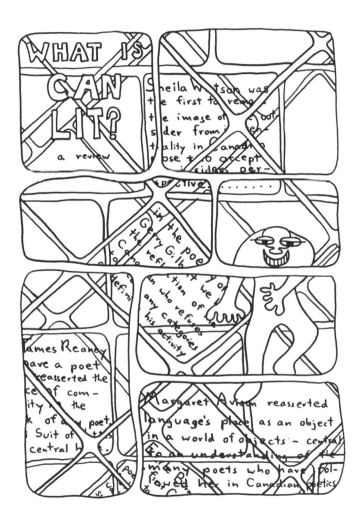

Interview: Raoul Duguay

1973

rd: what's the idea of a typewriter

bp: the actual idea of one? — you got me there (laughs) — actually that would be a very interesting thing to know the history of

rd: but you tell me that you use the typewriter now much less than before

bp: yes

rd: & you're starting over again to write by hand

bp: well what i like about that is it's a much more — it feels like for me it's a more direct connection with the body — i'm actually shaping the individual letters with my hand — essentially when i'm typing each letter's the same as an experience with fingers — it's just a pressing down — when i'm writing it —

rd: you have a feeling of the form

bp: that's right — the form is moving into my body — it's moving into my own muscalature — it's like an intimate involvement with the architecture of the single letter

rd: do you have the feeling when you make a letter — i mean like let's say *b* or *z* — off the end of your pen —

bp: that's right — it is like i fly off the end of my pen onto the page

rd: yeah — down there (gestures) & it makes that — *b*

bp: robert fones has been working with what he calls continuous forms — which is just writing words — he's just gone back to writing so that letters flow one into another — just playing with the way that — in writing as opposed to printing — you can simply continue the flow from one letter to the other — so that the flow is like a speech flow where there's absolutely no silence between the letters — the letters are all linked by line

rd: did you see — henri michaus — he made a book only with the — he started with a word — the noun he used — i didn't know — it's a horse — just by the design — he makes that the the visual aspect & the manual aspect & the gestural aspect of writing — because — what did you say before — you write & you have the feeling the word comes out of your body — you're really involved in it — & the idea — in your poetry the way you figure letters & concepts — forms & concepts — is there — before you start to write — an idea of what you want or do you discover it at the same time —

bp: well i discover it at the same time

rd: & you can perform — you can develop it —

bp: oh yeah — for me it's very much a sense of learning from the language — this is what for me is endlessly exciting & fascinating — since i got over my arrogance of trying to impose myself on the language & have simply played with it — gone back to the point before language when i was a child & i was just discovering the forms

rd: i understand you very well — i feel exactly the same — you feel like a child but you are — it is like you were your own teacher

bp: right

rd: nobody teaches you but your body teaches you

bp: that's right — in a way you're following — it's almost like you're following a path up out of the trap you've been in being an adult who's had a certain cultural view put on top of him

rd: yeah

bp: instead you say okay when it comes to the language i'm a child — i'm not in any sense a master — i'm not a poet in that master sense of the word — i'm like the disciple who comes to learn who covers himself in sackcloth & ashes & says "i just want to start over again teacher" — but my teacher is language — so you're starting at the bottom but it's like you're starting at the beginning — you're starting at the end — you're right there at the heart of the creation — like when you said for you the letters are creation that's the way i see it — when i began to look at words as being sentences it was like another world opened up — just another complete world — & it was just like revelation after revelation

rd: do you feel sometimes when you write — because for me all the poets are conscious of the inner side of the word — it's like you were opening the stomach of the word

bp: oui

rd: i loathe this part but i'll use it — good — this i won't use — you know — you feel that when you work with the sounds

bp: yes it's like being a doctor a surgeon — in a way it's a very old thing that's being done — you could call it revolutionary poetry but it's not — it's the most primitive the most basic

rd: the most simple

bp: it's the most simple thing

rd: it is — i think because it is it looks complex

bp: that's right — i find that some of the poems i've been writing recently have been the most complex poems i've ever written but they're about the simplest things or they proceed from such a simple premise from such a sort of simple point of view — like looking at words as sentences — it's such a simple thing but i never saw that until about six months ago when i looked at the word "word" — it said to me "w or d" — the word "word" was saying to me there's an option there's a choice — you've got a w or a d — everything is balanced around a focal point — not only that but the w is in the fourth position from the one end of the alphabet & the d is in the fourth position from the other end of the alphabet

rd: oh yeah i never saw that

bp: so it's like you've got a double balance point

rd: in the word "word"

bp: in the word "word"

rd: ah that's good — usually i think in french but maybe there are words in all languages that are bp: i'm beginning to think that

rd: specific eh

bp: that's right

rd: for the writing &

bp: it seems there's something about — i find the alphabet the most mysterious system — because it's so amazing — why those 26 letters — what is there in them — it's like i'm looking for hidden content — they're like a doorway into another universe — & i want to go down into that doorway & i want to find where it leads — it's sort of like *Alice in Wonderland* where she falls thru the opening in the foot of the tree — well it's like the foot of the tree & i'm tumbling (laughs) — i'm spinning over in space & there's a bottom there somewhere & there's another thing on the other side — i feel that — & you can get there thru the sound & thru the visual both — i think both things lead you there — & that other world is really this world — it's really this world in the most basic sense

rd: do you think sometimes that words are really empty — sometimes do you sit there & look at the poem & say what have i done there — you know rationally it's perfect — what does it mean — why is it there — for whom

bp: i find that happens — you reach a certain point where — what i found about a point like that when i'm looking at a poem in that way is that i'm seeing it both for the meaning the feeling i was getting out of me when i was writing & then suddenly i start to see the words as objects — they're also just words — & the meaning is emptied out of them like if i write the sentence "the dog has measles" or "the dog is sick" that has content that has meaning — but if i empty it of meaning & look at the sentence "the dog is sick" it doesn't have meaning on another level & i think well i would like it to mean on both levels — so if i empty it on one level it fills on the other level — & i do want that balancing point — so palindromes interest me — words that spell the same things frontwards & backwards or sentences that do

rd: it's hard to do

bp: it is yeah but when they work that way i find them just amazing — sometimes i spend an evening just working with palindromes trying to get palindromes — finding working with the letters that look the same forwards & backwards

rd: for you what is most important about oral & scriptural poetry — you write books & you make sounds — what is the difference & what is the identity the correlation

bp: well in a way they're exactly the same — there's one way in which they're exactly the same — i do have some poems — & these are the poems i like the most right now — where you have to really hear them & see them at the same time — i think in a way that's what i'd like to move towards — poems you would have to hear & see at the same time so that both senses are in use — both the eye & the ear — when i'm doing a pure sound poem i'm the visual element — me & my body — i'm the visual element — when i do a pure visual poem — well in a way i'm no longer there — i've destroyed myself in making the pure visual poem — pas d'existence pour l'auteur.

rd: how do you figure this with your perception of life

bp: well — the way i see it is something like this — i was saying this to you earlier — i used to think that in this art which is poetry one would achieve some sort of master status around the age of 45 — now more & more it comes to me that one is simply an apprentice all one's life — that one is always & forever learning — so that one continually reaches the point where one is full — one thinks one has really gained a totality of meaning then the next moment one suddenly becomes aware of a greater meaning beyond that which suddenly empties you of the other thing — it doesn't take it away

rd: it puts it into

bp: perspective — it gives you your balancing point again — you're balanced between what you know & don't know — & there's always more that you don't know & you're always learning more & hopefully what you learn helps others — so that i want to do the two things — i want to as much as possible thru the writing bring in as many of the senses — the meaning both in traditional terms and also the forms of things the sounds of things etc — all these types of meaning i want to bring together into one thing so that i can present it in its totality — & i want to keep on learning

rd: what is the use of poetry

bp: i think poetry is language raised to its highest power & its joy — & language for me is an expression of the total body — & i think really everybody should be doing poetry because everybody should be using language raised to its highest power — this sounds sort of simplistic but i think everybody's better off for that — if everybody's using language raised to its highest power then they take what they say more seriously — they don't play cheap in conversation — they really say what they feel — because language is not a cheap thing anymore — it's a felt thing an important thing

rd: but for you i'd like to know what the idea is of making sound poetry

bp: well it started off because i had sounds inside my head that weren't words they were just sounds & i had to have an outlet for them — initially i had some fear of making a fool of myself but i thot well i have these sounds i should express — i knew the dada poets — i knew about hugo ball at that point — & i knew that they had done sound poetry but well that was years & years ago — & i thot well somebody's done it — they had the courage to do it — why shouldn't i go ahead & do it

rd: how long have you been working on that

bp: sound poetry i've been working on for close to nine years now — since about 1964 or early 65 — & then what i discovered was when i started to do sound my voice changed — my breathing changed — poetry readings really changed for me — i became much more aware of the people i was reading to — they became much more aware of me in a really good sense — readings became a real energy exchange — i was giving them something & they were giving me something — suddenly it became a living situation

rd: but how do people figure what you do

bp: well it's hard to measure — i think from what you've told me i'd say you've found a similar situation to mine which is — you get a lot of people who simply laugh at it — there's something about a really simple thing which seems to be difficult for people to accept — i mean there's a complex aesthetic & philosophic base or a theoretical base which i could defend & expound on for hours but the fact is it's very simple

rd: i wanted to know about that point in relation to your public — do you figure if you work on that context of voice & sound — the inner side of words — that you can have a kind of pedagogic attitude — or you do not become a teacher but you are like a lake where the fish are — anyone can come you know — you are a kind of a reservoir — & some people come & hear you & they say AHH in this part of the lake we didn't know there was that fish

bp: right

rd: & they come & see what's going on there

bp: i know there has been recently — well recently i've found myself writing a lot of articles about writing — i've started to write about writing — & i've found it very good — because it's clarified a lot of things for me — but the way you put it is very good because that is much more the way i see it — i know my idea behind publishing has always been not that these things are completely finished or they're the best i'm ever going to do or anything like that but that i should put it out there & then the people who are going to get something from it can get something from it — there're many things i like — well bill bissett's idea of publishing i very much agree with — he pursues it more totally than i do — he doesn't quite publish everything but he publishes pretty close to everything he writes — & he writes a tremendous amount — & he's saying here is the total man — he's not writing specifically for an academic audience — he's writing for everybody — so he's putting all of himself out there — he's saying you respond — the parts of me you like you can pick up on — the parts of me you don't like you don't have to read you don't have to listen to — but it's all of me rd: do you feel like that — if there are some people who don't understand what you do

bp: oh yeah — and i don't mind talking about it with people — i have never minded talking & saying how i see it because i think what another person gets from it will always be slightly different — i will talk about what i am consciously trying to do — but there's a lot that i don't think i'm conscious of in what i do — it just comes out of me — i've really worked to get as much — to establish techniques & formal discipline — but it's just to improve the vehicle thru which the poetry passes — i am the vehicle

rd: you figure that you are

bp: i'm like a tap — something like that — because i know when i'm writing it's like a different frame of mind

rd: the medium

bp: thru which it passes — that's right

rd: on that point do you think your writing is a kind of a yoga

bp: in a certain sense yes

rd: if we call a yoga the experience of getting acquainted with knowing who you are & what are things — what is everything — knowing — connaissance

bp: oui — oh yeah — very much so — i think that as a writer i work to master the disciplines that i see as essential — to achieve formal control — to examine the tools i use — the book which is a machine — the typewriter — my voice — to understand the tools that i'm using — but when the moment of writing comes it's something else that's happening — i've got all those things there & they're at the service of the writing then — but the writing itself is a different thing & i can't explain the writing — why i write — what is the inner urgency that drives me — that i can't explain — and i can't really explain — i mean i've explained why i pursue the things i pursue but there's something in all of that i can't explain — why it should obsess me as much as it does still intrigues me — i don't know (laughs) — i'm a man obsessed with language

Letter re James Reaney

1973

dear Frank

what i'm trying to set down here is what i see in James Reaney's
work since i find myself constantly in this position of people
looking at me with slack jaws when i tell them that i get a lot out
of what Reaney does & that i think he's one of the poets everybody has to read if they're seriously interested in what's happening period (rather fascist of me)   if we take off from Frye's "all
literature is made from other literature" what do we get   well
standardly we get mythopoesis   now if i use reference or "classical images" what do i do   i stack information   it's the pun in
a different guise   one image or phrase breaks different ways   i
slow the movement down   the ongoing flow of the poem has a
whirlpool within it   i am taken into the centre to focus on one
thing   here a type of historicity is used to eliminate time   a
cancelling out by insistence   it was then it is now it will always
be   thus the reading becomes a slowed down meditative experience   but Reaney's concern is also with language with the
materials of language   you can see the jump in consciousness in
the difference between *12 Letters to a Small Town* & *Emblems*   in
12 the drawings illustrate the text   in *Emblems* the text & the
emblem are inseparable   the materials of the poem are no
longer external   it is the object it describes   no more duality
here Reaney comes close to writing writing   he has finally
done in his poetry what he has done in his plays which is to say
he has made them self sufficient   they exist as real objects in the
world
    now strangely enough this all grows quite logically out of
Reaney's much touted background as a Frygian scholar because
the basic material of all literature IS language   Reaney's work &
growth as an artist illustrate his awareness of this in   *Colours in
the Dark* the blind man's eyes are his ears   sound the vehicle of
language   & tho Reaney's poetic may not be a breathline one

he is obsessed with language as sound   his plays build up textures of song & chants a vocal insistance

Reaney once called bissett a one man civilization   the same could be said of Reaney   having been stuck with the tag of being of the Frye school (surely as crippling a naming as Black Mountain ever was) Reaney tends to get dismissed by younger writers   he is an explorer & an innovator   as an artist he has shown constant growth & change a willingness to abandon earlier positions if subsequent searching shows them to have been wrong   a statement one can make about only a few writers

i think part of the dismissal comes as a result of the old content/form argument Wilhelm Reich said a long time ago that there was no point in bemoaning life inside a trap or describing the beauty of life outside a trap while still trapped inside it if all we had to do was turn around & walk out the door in order to be free   most of the poets who see form as one of the vital issues that has to be tackled in writing are involved in that search for the door to walk thru into a life beyond the trap language has or can become

for these people their art is the manifestation of that search is that process that action necessary   the point here being what's so vital about content that simply delineates a trap if it doesn't simultaneously seek an exit   Reaney remains to my mind one of our handful of real seekers but the path he's chosen probably seems strange to most   he has mastered & then discarded more of the forms in which a poet traditionally served an apprenticeship than just about anyone else in the history of English Canadian literature   after all let's remember the old celtic bardic tradition & the mastering of the various metrical systems necessary   this makes *A Suit of Nettles* completely necessary in his personal growth as an artist   what better delineation of WASP Ontario than a bunch of dumb geese talking in an archaic syntax proof of their colonial bondage   but even the poets most concerned with form (& i'm thinking here of form as a notational system & what lies beyond it   that recognition of how the form chosen or the one that insists itself delineates & limits what is said physically which has to mean in terms of content as well) have tended to dismiss Reaney   it seems well to quote from the most neglected statement in Olson's "Projective Verse" essay

> (and I say this carefully, as I have said all things about the non-projective, having considered how each of us must save himself after his own fashion and how much, for that matter, each of us owes to the non-projective, and will continue to owe, as both go alongside each other)

that was 21 years ago   the message Olson was proclaiming in his essay about the necessity of the projective tradition has been heard by many of us & the balance the focus of the quest (if you like) has shifted   it is necessary if we are to continue fruitfully that we open our eyes & ears once more to that non-projective tradition of which Reaney is perhaps the leading innovator in Canada   & certainly for us as writers in Canada at this time if we in fact take seriously the idea of a Canadian literature we can surely see that its ascendancy will come not thru a common thematic concern but thru a common voice which will be identifiably Canadian   a language which is neither American nor British but a joual of our own & really need i say anything more about why i think James Reaney is important to ANYONE writing now

love
barrie

Two Pages on the Nature of the Reality of Writing

1973

the nature of the reality of writing on two pages

transcends the nature of the reality of writing them

Interview: Nicette Jukelevics

1974

Nicette Jukelevics: Initially, you began to get into concrete on your own, and later became aware of others who were doing the same thing?

bpNichol: Yes, initially I started to do it by myself, and mostly it was bissett, his influence too. Just seeing him busting out, and I said to myself I can bust out too. And Michael McClure, his work opened up new possibilities for me. So there were influences, but I did not set out to copy someone else's poems.

NJ: What aspect of Apollinaire's work and the Dadaists' influenced you the most?

bp: I remember what impressed me most at the time was Kurt Schwitters' "W" poem. He had simply taken the letter W and made a poem from it. The poem was the letter W, and that blew my head really. It was a minimal statement. You don't get much more minimal. And when I thought about it, I realized that there was tremendous power in that simple letter, and that was very exciting. So that sort of opened up the idea. At that time I couldn't think further than the excitement of that poem. So when I think of the Dadaists I think about Schwitters, and specifically about the sound poems of Hugo Ball, and about the typography that some of the Russians were exploring. At that time I called it all Dadaism, so that's why I still refer to it as Dadaism.

And with Apollinaire, it was two things. I did some translations of his poems, there was the experience of the translation itself, and in the process of translating his poems I discovered his Calligrams, his visual use of the page, which led me to Mallarmé and what Mallarmé was doing. At that time I was in Vancouver and sitting in on a bunch of workshops that some people from *Tish* were conducting, heavy discussions about the relationship of form and content. At that time this was very new to me, I used to sit there and shudder at the implications of what was discussed. Anyway, this opened up another dimension for me. And when bissett once again came out with the *Blew Ointment* issues, I got a sense of inspiration, the kind of inspiration that comes from a person who is also interested in the same thing, the inspiration of somebody communicating exactly what you are interested in and are doing.

NJ: Are you saying then that concrete in Canada started on the West Coast?

bp: In a way it started with Earle Birney. Birney was interested in specific notations, that is to say the rise and fall of the line on the page which approximates the human voice, or which approximates the action of something falling. It's simple in a sense. That did not particularly influence me because I wanted something different, but it was there as an idea. Other than that, it began with bissett and Lance Farrell. I was out there doing those things, but I didn't know anyone doing the same thing at the time. I didn't know bissett at all at the time.

NJ: Were you responsible for bringing concrete to the east then?

bp: Yes, I guess so. I don't really know in 64-65. What happened was David Aylward and I started *Ganglia* about this time. And my specific thinking was to get some of the West Coast people like bissett and others into the eastern scene. The first issues of *Ganglia* were not pure concrete, as I later began to understand the term.

NJ: Which brings me to the question, how do you define the term?

bp: Well, it's really a tough thing to answer. It would be simpler to say that I define it in Dom Sylvester Houédard's term, "borderblur." That poetry which arises from the interface, from the point between things, the point in which poetry and painting and prose are all coming together. That's what is referred to as "borderblur."

The term concrete, see if you get into Eugen Gomringer's very pure sense of the poem which he calls "constellations," he has very specific definitions of what the concrete poem should be. So in a sense I can't really call all I produce concrete, at least not in the terms that the guys who started the movement call it. That's why, in a way, other than using the term humourously, as I did in the title of *The Cosmic Chef: An Evening of Concrete*, the Oberon Cement Works, and all that thing, I never thought about my poetry as concrete. I thought about it using the fact that the page is a visual field to do visual things.

NJ: Would you consider your visual poetry, poetry?

bp: Well, yes, I would, in a way. Some of it I would and some of it I wouldn't. Steve McCaffery and I did an essay as part of the TRG (Toronto Research Group) thing, on why you would call concrete poetry, poetry, and why it is a valid term. It's because the left hand and right hand terminal points, like in poetry, the left hand margin and the right hand margin have a function based either on the breath prosody or metrical prosody or whatever, but it has a function. It is important where the poem breaks off and where it picks up again. It's very important in poetry. It's not in prose. In prose it's simply because you can't have a book that runs out. In prose, the line is a horizon upon which words stick out.

In concrete or visual poetry, in the constellations or whatever, the left hand and right hand terminal points once again are functional. They are there for a reason; therefore, I call it poetry. As you know, one of the hoariest questions has always been the difference between poetry and prose.

NJ: Would you say then that the basic difference between poetry and prose is the function of the terminal points?

bp: Yes, the essential difference. Then there are things like rhythm, intensity of image and so on. And then you get into the long poem. Now the long poem is very close to prose and very close to story. One tends to think of poetry as imagistic and prose as story, but I think those terms are arbitrary.

NJ: How would you define the term "concrete"?

bp: The same way, the importance of the left and right hand margins, the terminal points. From the sound point of view you see, then that goes into what my values are in writing. My values in writing tend to be governed by sound and the music I hear in the spoken word. In *The Martyrology*, for example, the page becomes a printed score, and the right and left hand margins as it were are important as notations for breath pauses for emphasis, and so on, and so on. So yes, I would still think of sound poetry as poetry.

NJ: Is there a particular national characteristic that is typical of what is being produced in Canadian concrete?

bp: Well, I used to think there was. I don't know if I still do. But the most underlying basis of most Canadian concrete seems to be sound. There is of course the visual and rhythmic kind of poetry too, but Canadian stuff tends to be — I think it was Stephen Scobie who used the term — "dirty-clean." The visual stuff I mean, say in relation to Hansjörg Mayer's work which is super clean. Whereas if you take somebody like bissett, or someone like d.a. levy, who use the mimeo look, this is what Scobie was referring to as the "dirty-clean" look in Canadian concrete. He called me "clean-dirty-super clean." But that's the underlying characteristic of visual concrete here.

NJ: In one of your *grOnk* mailout sheets you wrote that it functioned as a "free information service to get stuff into print from the language revolution in this country back into the general stream." What did you mean by the "language revolution"?

bp: Well, I simply meant to provide as many entrances and exits as possible, to alter consciousness. To reconsider the value of words, the value of translation, a total reconsideration of language.

NJ: In the same mailout sheet you also mentioned that you were planning to give away Canadian publications by David UU, John Riddell and others to people outside of North America because they simply had not sold here despite appearances on various book racks. How do you account for the lack of interest in this kind of medium in Canada?

bp: I really don't know what it is. I haven't reached any conclusions yet. All it seems to me is that there are a lot of questions that people don't seem to ask. There doesn't seem to be a big audience

 in Canada in the sense of considering some of the basic issues that are being raised about language,

about prose and poetry. Even among writers the interest seems to be negligible.

I know that when Steve and I worked on the TRG we sat down to try and tackle the issue of what is narrative. It's a term for which there is no useful working definition. It's a vague term which gets used and used, it's confused with the idea of plot. It's not plot, but people just don't seem to be interested in asking themselves these questions. I think it's because once you start to ask yourself these questions, you have to ask yourself why you write.

There is also a kind of freak element in some of the things that bissett or I do. I remember when I first began to do sound poetry, I did it because I had something to say. But I remember the first time people were shocked. It was total shock. The audience was not prepared for someone to forsake the traditional role of the poet-reader as someone who stands and reads or does monologues. They were not prepared for that. Now that attitude has changed. Now people are not as shocked. They are more open to that kind of experience.

NJ: To those who are not familiar with its basic principles, concrete is somewhat enigmatic. Are you at all interested in making your poetry more intelligible to your audience?

bp: Well, sometimes it's just a result of a bad piece of writing on my part. I think it's a kind of thing which raises questions by its nature. I think sometimes that's part of the problem. In a way, what I am into is research. I know that, I am into research writing. I am not, say, in *The Martyrology*, which is a completed piece. Actually, everything that I publish I see as complete, but it's research. Whereas in *The Martyrology* I have taken everything that I've learned, I've incorporated it and now it's coming out. So there is an element of research in most of what I do. So in a way I have no anticipation of what an audience reaction would be.

NJ: Are you interested in making your audience understand what it is you are trying to do, or does it not matter to you that much?

bp: Well, I would be a liar if I said that I was not interested in communicating with my audience, that I didn't have the desire to please. But if I was mainly interested in pleasing and making a name for myself as a popular author, I certainly chose the wrong kind of work to get into. On the other hand, I have had two feelings. One is I always like to be two jumps ahead of what I write, so that by the time I publish it it is a phase that is behind me. And I think if you are growing as a writer you are always ahead of the last piece of work that you did. There is an element of wanting to please, but in the end you can't let it govern your life.

NJ: There is very little theoretical or critical work being written on concrete in Canada, and for someone who is interested in knowing more about it, there is little material available.

bp: That's why Steve and I are into the TRG. See, I don't think there is anything to explain, because there is a way in which visual and sound poetry is completely reactionary. There is a way in which it is not evolutionary, and that is, it is a return to such basic principles that people often are looking for things that are not there.

I have done some theoretical writing in which I outlined what I understood to be basic principles behind visual and sound poetry, but there is a point at which the thing itself says it better than any explanation ever could. I think it just makes people more secure, in a way; not that it makes them understand it better. Where I thought I had something of general value to say I tried to say it. I don't believe in theory for its own sake.

In the work that Steve and I are doing, we are doing research. We are researching writing, trying to get at the basic understanding of some of the labels. In fact there is so much weird categorization that most people are confused about the different kinds of writing anyway. I guess at the back of the question you are asking if I am interested in communicating. The answer is yes. It's a question which I've often heard before. But the whole thing is that people come to concrete with so many expectations. In a way, what I am saying is, look, abandon those expectations, play a while, and see what emerges from that. Basically it's a game which you have to play. You can't read down line by line and come to a satisfying conclusion.

NJ: What is the significance of concrete or visual poetry as you see it?

bp: By getting into the visual or concrete poem you are forced to play with it. To discover new meanings for words, to reevaluate the use of language in general. The only way to get into it is to play, to examine the structure, to evolve new meanings and new relationships. When you are writing ideational poetry, the emphasis is on thoughts and symbols not on language. For me the importance of sound poetry is that it takes poetry back as a spoken art, as it was meant to be. It brings poetry back to its aural tradition. In visual poetry, it is more or less an assertion of different values which say that since the advantage is not of reading but of print, the whole iconicity of language comes out, the meditational aspect. I can take this page, I can meditate on it, it's not a quick thing, it's not an instant high. Its value lies in exploration.

Overwhelming Colour: Review of *White*, by Douglas Barbour

1974

I open my heart to this boundless space;
Above and below there is nothing strange.
Here there is a special quality,
Whatever you gaze upon is always delightful.
My spirit was noble and pure,
Falsely separated by earthly dust.
This earth was to me unknown,
I did not know such a spot could exist!
   —Su Shun-ch'in 1008-1048 ad

so landscape is all
it can be,
a limitless pattern of
ascent and descent

(descants on
the song of a sphere.
   —Douglas Barbour, from *A Poem as Long as the Highway*

for a long time i have looked for some way to explain what it is
that i see in the poetry of Douglas Barbour what it is that draws
me to read it again & again beyond the simpler act of friendship
(being as he is after all a friend of mine) because if it's only
friendship then you read the book in a cursory fashion & grunt
something fairly non-commital (if you're afraid of hurting his
feelings) but don't go back & read it again & you don't find yourself saying to other people in conversation "well i think you're
missing the point" when they launch into a criticism of his work
(which missing of the point i have never been able to articulate
clearly enough to have my words carry conviction) so that it was
in mulling over in my mind my sense of his most recent work

White that i happened to pick up my copy of *Moments of Rising Mist* (a collection of landscape poetry from the Sung period of Chinese history) & the two things came together in my mind
i'm going to try to make this as clear as possible   to my mind Doug Barbour's poetry is concerned with landscape in a way i have seen no other Canadian poet be concerned in as much as it is not for him a hostile force but a reality greater than the reality of his own existence   for him the landscape simply is

> this poem is full of facts:
>
> ...
>
> These are not metaphors:
> they are facts
> of life / of death

& it is not the landscape that disrupts him or alienates him but (& this is the essential acknowledgement) the fact that he is out of touch with it disturbs him

> Walk in thick fog. Why
> can I see   nothing

from his first book *Land Fall* you can see the sense of struggle with the landscape coming to the fore in his titling   that sense of discovering the edges of a thing as one who has been lost from sight of land for years   then *A Poem as Long as the Highway* as the poem becomes literally an attempt to carve a road thru the land around him   & now *White*

> the many names of
> colours in a single spectrum

that sense of nature of the season change of (then) the canadian writer   that overwhelming colour in the mind's eye
it is the chronicle of a man not at peace with the land around him but acknowledging himself as stranger   the uneasiness

shows up in many formal aspects of his poems   he has a tendency towards easy images as a way out of dilemmas he cannot solve

    a great grey cauldron
beginning to bubble

   ...

Colgate purity

   ...

sepulchral city

the trouble with conclusions is that they conclude. ideas have side-effects too. you have to keep an idea open as long as possible in order to get a feeling for, a notion of, all its possible side effects. the history of ideas teaches us that one life-time isn't a long enough testing period for any idea.

images that convey only his own sense of uneasiness with what he encounters

there is, too, a complete lack of surety with assumed forms as in his spelling of the word "your" as "yr." where the period functions as a sign of his alienation from such usage

he has not achieved that yin-yang balance the Sung & the earlier T'ang poets strove for that sense of oneness with the earth yet his writing is obsessed with it   & it is i think that sense of the struggle that draws me again & again each time more critically & yet each time more appreciative of what he attempts   he assumes a goodwill on the part of his readers that borders on naivete as in the poem that ends

> White emptiness, the page
> you read / I write
>
> the page / filled
>
> and your hearts.

yet i believe him
                    there is one image recurs again & again as i write this down which is of Doug talking endlessly and excitedly of all that he has read or thot or felt   talking against perhaps what Mike Ondaatje described as "the perfect white between words" i think that what he is truly capable of as a writer lies there in that white silent landscape where the minimal gesture expands sounding explosively over the frozen whiteness the cold inside & outside we are all building against where the words he has so far used fall away & only the bare unstated nouns are left

Review of *Lists*, by Jean-Jacques

"To adduce lists, to enumerate or imply the
enumeration of their elements and then to
permute and combine these elements -- this,
Joyce seems to imply, is the ultimate re-
course of comic fiction."

Hugh Kenner ART

IN A CLOSED FIELD 1962

ELM ROAD

434	Diack, Mrs. Margaret,-	109
433	Vahtula, Mrs. Voltema, retired	110
433	Vahtula, Mrs. Hilda,-	111
432	Brown, Mr. Milliard, retired	112
432	Brown, Mrs. Irene,-	113
431	MacMahon, Mr. J. Clive, teacher	114
431	MacMahon, Mrs. Gloria,-	115
430	Grant, Mrs. Laura, widow	116
430	Metcalfe, Miss Ruby, retired	117
429	Olley, Mr. Robert, trust officer	118
429	Olley, Mrs. Muriel,-	119
428	Rorke, Miss Victoria, post-grad. stdt.	120
428	Lane, Mr. F.E., retired	121
428	Lane, Mrs. Carolyn,-	122
427	Jones, Mr. Russell E., engineer	123
427	Jones, Mrs. Sylvia, comp. programmer	124
426	Campbell, Mrs. Donald B., accountant	125
426	Campbell, Mrs. Verna,-	126
425	Renner, Mrs. Bertha,-	127
418	Gorman, Mr. Michael, manufacturer	128
418	Gorman, Mrs. Helen-Sue,-	129
417	Morton, Mr. William, supervisor	130
417	Morton, Mrs. Frances,-	131
416	Jennings, Mrs. D., Evelyn, sec.	132
416	Bamlett, Mrs. Daisy,-	133
414	Peterson, Mr. David H., retired	134
414	Peterson, Mrs. Janet E.,	135
413	Finlay, Mrs. Leilani, sec.	136
413	McKinnon, Miss Margo, revenue clerk	137
412	Smith, Mr. Leslie A., retired	138
412	Smith, Mrs. Adele,-	139
411	Bookalam, Mrs. Mabel,-	140
411	Bookalam, Mr. Bill, trucker driver	141
410	Ritchie, Miss Alison M.,	142
410	Ritchie, Mrs. Mary A.,-	143
409	Dickinson, Mrs. Martha, bookkeeper	144
409	Dickinson, Miss Louise, secretary	145
408	Ritchie, Mr. Hugh S., retired	146
408	Ritchie, Mrs. Marjorie,-	147
407	Kalnins, Mr. Ernest, maintenance wkr.	148
407	Kalnins, Mrs. Emma,-	149
406	Turnbull, Mrs. Agnes,-	150
405	Carruthers, Mr. William, architect	151
405	Carruthers, Mrs. Geraldine,-	152
403	Doherty, Mr. Archibald, retired	153
403	Doherty, Mrs. Margaret,-	154
400	Boal, Mr. William R., theatre mgr.	155
400	Boal, Mrs. M. Eleanor, sec.	156
400	Boal, Miss G. Jean, student	157
399	Bolton, Mr. George, retired	158
399	Farthing, Mrs. Grace,-	159
398	Gray, Mrs. Myrtle, investment broker	160
397	Bailey, Mr. Albert, electrician	161
397	Bailey, Mr. Robert, student	162
397	Bailey, Mrs. Edna, clerk	163
396	Clark, Mr. W.R., manager	164
396	Clark, Mr. Campbell, student	165
396	Clark, Mrs. Elizabeth	166
395	Davey, Mr. Frankland, univ. teacher	167
395	Davey, Mrs. Linda,-	168
394	Kemp, Mr. Murdo, lather	169
394	Kemp, Mrs. Rosalie,-	170

What it is
Why I need it
What are the benefits
Who can join
How to enrol

(please print)

Interview: Pierre Coupey, Dwight Gardiner, Gladys Hindmarch, and Daphne Marlatt

1974

Edited by Daphne Marlatt and bpNichol

An Introduction in Which the Author Covers His Tracks with Some Fancy Footwork

There seem to be a few views when it comes to the transcription & publishing of interviews with authors. One has it you should leave every burp & belch intact to preserve the actuality of the event. Another has it you should tidy the whole thing up to make good prose. Me i stand somewhere between the two. The facts are that belches, burps & laughs don't come across in print. "HA HA HA HA HA HA" reads quite strangely mostly because it lacks the intonation & the context of human contact that occasioned the laugh. Also there's little distinction made between the belly laugh & the chuckle. On the other hand, why pretend that every writer speaks flawless prose? I don't. I use a tremendous amount of slang when i talk, tend to gesture with my hands a lot, & depend on facial expressions & intonation to get my point across. Thus i can't pretend that i'm one of the masters of spoken english. On the other hand, when i first read thru this interview i was appalled at the number of times i said "you know" & "sort of" & various other qualifiers & verbal shifts. I had to face the unpleasant truth that though i said what i believed i put a lot of padding around it almost as if i were saying "here's what i believe but on the other hand don't take me too seriously folks." Probably this is a kind of tribute (there i go again) to the respect i have for the writers i was talking with but it harks back to the timidity that made me (as i remark in the interview) hide out for a long time. Being a firm believer in learning from one's errors or sins of omission i decided to edit the majority of these qualifiers out of the printed interview but to acknowledge them in this introduction. I have left some of them in to retain the flavour of actual speech but there remains the fact that by doing so i have created a fictional conversation in as much as in this version i appear more definite than i sounded then ...

bpNichol
Edmonton/February 21/1976

[H]

Daphne Marlatt: I copied down a couple of lines from *The Martyrology* which I was interested in asking you about ... You say "we must return again to human voice and listen / rip off the mask of words to free the sounds." And in the little thing you wrote as — I don't know if it was an introduction or a postscript, but it's a fold-in — you also talk about "a future music moves now to be written / w g r & t ..."

bp: Well okay, the actual line comes out of the feeling that I had at that time which was that the importance of sound poetry — for myself, say, and you can make an even wider application — was to free the emotional content of speech from ideation or from words, necessarily, and to just be able to let out the voice. And that once the voice had been let out, then the words would follow. I always go back to that Palongawhoya legend, you know. Palongawhoya's job was to open his mouth and to sing the praises of the creator. And that if he did that, then the vibratory axis of his body vibrated in tune with the vibratory axis of the cosmos and everything was in harmony, see? But then people got tricked by Raven and they began to use speech as a way of talking inside their teepees to each other. And this was a false use of it. Eventually he who creates everything comes down and bumps them all off for misuse of voice. And that's happened about four times according to the legend. So that's really what I was thinking of in that line — just that necessity to not use words as a masking, which a lot of people do in conversations. Like you have a lot of different types of conversations. You have, say, the make-out conversation. This is where two people are talking about something — I'm sure you've seen lots of these — but they're not really talking about anything other than they're sort of, reconnoitering — when they're going to hit the sack and all that. That's one type of conversation. You have the same sort of thing in a business situation which is filled

with all sorts of pleasantries and underneath this is this other rip-tide going on, you know. So it was also an awareness of those sort of uses of language and saying, okay, let's get rid of all of that and just let out the sound and see what's behind it.

Gladys Hindmarch: And you've evolved a character in some sense now and let out the consciousness like you were doing in *Journal*. And it's going to be living out another side of that really.

bp: Yeah. Well you see, in the work I do, which is working for Therafields as a theradramist and seeing people and talking with them about what's bothering them, what you're doing in the situation is not imposing yourself on the person but basically being a catalyst: to ask questions they can't formulate, to put them in the situation where they're going to have to deal with the material themselves and where you help them as much as you can. It negates a certain type of writing. That is, if you're doing it all the time it negates the traditional psychological novel, in which you simply describe a character. It becomes very uninteresting to write that type of novel when you're sort of there, articulating it on a daily level in your life. So the problem for me, or the way I saw it was, okay I wanted to write novels — and I saw this about ten years ago — which reflected accurately the processes of the way the mind works. I keep going back to this, of how consciousness works. Like in *The Martyrology*, I would bring in names very briefly, or characters very briefly or faces very briefly. Because it felt to me like that was the way you encountered people in real life. You're walking down the street, you're feeling things all the time, you see somebody you meet very casually, you know their name. You might never meet them again, but for that moment, they're there, and that's all you know about them. Whang — they're gone. So I let all that stuff into the poem, I let in a bunch of maudlin things because it felt to me that it was all part of the process of moving through something. All those things actually collide with your consciousness, so I left them in. But it makes for a very strange poem.

Dwight Gardiner: It always seems to be a bringing-out, a calling-up, in terms of memory or consciousness. Does it ever approach myth? That seems to be the other end of calling things up.

bp: Well yeah — it's always seemed to me that there are real mysteries and then there are false mysteries. For instance, the reason I never got off on C.G. Jung was, in his language he is obsessed with mystery. He loves mystery, and that's kind of the level he wants to leave it at. This is what I always feel when I'm reading Jung: he loves mystery and he's more interested in rolling around in mystery than in explication, in trying to solve mystery. And getting beyond what is the false level of mystery and what are the real mysteries — this is always the issue that intrigues me.

I think there are real myths and then there's the process of mythi-fication that goes on that's completely phony and completely artificial, which I'm not interested in. When, for instance, The Four Horsemen started, the first thing we had to overcome was that everybody knew my name and nobody knew the rest of the group's names. Okay, so what you have is "bp Nichol and The Four Horsemen." It sounds like I got this back-up group of Motown singers snapping their toes. So we worked very hard; literally we had to work at it consciously, we had to see the posters and say (you know cause this was what they kept trying to do), no way — group, group, group, group, you know, think of it as a group. This was a very hard process. People don't want to think of writers as groups. They're fixed on writers as the single consciousness, because for years that's the historical position of writers. Even though it's not our antecedent, that's our position in the 20th century. So there's a process of breaking down that old myth — this is what I'm talking about — around the individual sort of superstardom and what that means. I even remember hav-ing a dream years ago about a gigantic robot mummy wrapped in cloths and stuff, that was pursuing me. And in the context of the dream at the time it came, it was very clearly audience; it was my sense of audience. I was sort of whipping through the back woods trying to keep ahead of audience. It was just a paranoid dream but I realized what it meant at that time was that in this sort of context people are encountering you through readings or through your books and they're not encountering you as a real human being in your living situation. You try and bring as much of you as possible into it,  but it's still different from the live human being. You're fighting a mythification process really; you're fighting the attempt to make you something you aren't. From time to time I get strange about it. From time to time it's not even an issue. It's been there. I don't know if that answers the question.

DG: I remember you saying to me a long time ago about the fact that you couldn't take myth, so you were creating your own personal mythology which is the calling-up.

bp: Oh yeah, right. Well I remember at the time feeling (I think I remember that conversation) that the Greek and Roman myths had no currency for me as a human being. I like them, but I learn them when I'm 23, so they're not a living part of my existence particularly. The Gilgamesh epic always had more punch for me. I sort of encountered it on my own: it was really a part of my experience. The comic strip characters — I mean Dick Tracy was always a vastly more mythic figure for me than anybody else to this day. And you know, the haunting quality of Little Orphan Annie — things like this. These all had a much more powerful mythic content. And the saints! I mean, the saints essentially came out of that whole perception of when I was a kid and thought that the real people lived up in the clouds.

GH: I heard that they were in a hole in the sky.

bp: Well it was sort of like that. I looked up between the clouds. I always thought it was like the edges of a lake and that we were living at the bottom of the ocean and the real folks were up there. That's where we were going to go someday. Heaven. I always thought heaven was the clouds, because those are the drawings you get: in the United Church you get a little Sunday school paper and everybody's walking around on clouds.

DM: We've talked about naming, and you talked about calling-up, and you talked about nouns the other day. But I'm still sort of stuck back with the question and I don't know how to ask it. It's something very naive like, how do you feel about verbs?

bp: How do I feel about verbs? Well no, it's actually a really interesting question because, in a sense say, in a novel like *Journal* or a novel like *For Jesus Lunatick*, nothing happens essentially; nothing happens in terms of external action. Most of it happens in terms of internal action. *For Jesus Lunatick* is a real bummer because the character just gets into this thing and he never gets out of it really. He just rolls around inside of this madness of his and he bumps up against other people who seem equally mad from his point of view; and the whole thing ends with the thing of the river. So there's that sense of action. Now in terms of verbs, other than saying I like them — the thing that I tend to dislike intensely is adjectives. I dislike them because it always seemed to me the premise of an adjective is that the noun doesn't say enough. And I always think of nouns because it's sort of like a very strong sense of the objects that are there, you see: and then the actions will define themselves.

DG: They carry their own action.

bp: That's right. So, in a way, the verb is generated by the noun. What happens is generated by what is there in the noun.

DM: I've always thought the difficulty of naming a character or naming anything was that in fact nouns do not exist in the world, that nouns are simply ways of designating ongoing processes. You know, you fix it, you freeze it for a moment with a name.

bp: Well, there's that. But I mean if you take the really early Runic sense of language, that if you put the alphabet — if you put a mark on a thing — to name it was to call it forth — you're actually calling forth the spirit of the thing. So in that sense the noun contains the action.

DG: And you personify it.

bp: That's right. Once you put the name on the thing, then you're calling up that deity: if you put the mark on the wood, you're calling forth the spirit that's in the wood. Then it speaks through the mark, see. So what I'm saying is that the noun has all the power if you line the nouns up right; if you line the nouns up inside the sentences right. If you make the syntax a vehicle which releases them as opposed to a vehicle which straitjackets them and lays them down flat.

DM: The fact that Adam's task was to name the animals seems like some kind of outering process that goes along, a separation thing. If you can say that that's a "buffalo," you know you're not a buffalo. *That's* the buffalo out there.

bp: That's right. Yeah, it does, it's a process of distances. It's always the way it seems to me, anyways. It's a way of not having your skin quite as porous.

DM: Right. But then the naming, I mean the calling forth by name, is the reverse of that.

bp: Uh, hold it. I think you left me at the last turn.

GH: That's because of the way you're saying that's the way verbs are, that if the noun itself contains the energy, then it's the reverse of the process that she's talking about; that once you identified "buffalo" then buffalo is there on the hill.

DG: It simply *is*.

bp: As a distancing — oh, I see what you're saying there. It doesn't have to be though. See there you get a split between the way ...
END OF SIDE ONE.

bp: ... I think what I was saying there was that, okay, you have the traditional or let's say the last 500 years of language in which, say, the noun is used for categorization and lists against an earlier usage of language. And that's what goes back to the Williams quote I was mentioning which is that if all the words are either dead or beautiful, then they're no more use to us as writers than a dead abstraction is to a philosopher. There are only two things you can do at that point: strip the language bare of beauty (which is more or less what he saw as his approach) or break the words up and start over again (which is what he saw as Joyce's approach). I disagree with that because Joyce was keenly interested in cryptography and was actually into concealing. He was into concealing; he was not into explication. Now that's where I felt

Stein did that. Gertrude Stein has done that. Beckett has done it, much more than Joyce did. Proust — all of Proust's novels are about nouns. I mean that whole fantastic section in *Remembrance of Things Past* of place names, the place. He goes on and on naming things and evoking every memory he can remember around the name. My God, he's full, full, full. But it's an interesting approach to adjectives. It's really interesting reading Proust; it's the most slowed-down reading you can do on God's green earth — lying in the sun somewhere so that you can fall asleep at every fifth sentence, so slow. The thing is, he uses so many adjectives in a way he goes beyond that whole thing I was saying about adjectives because he's no longer trying to rush the process. He's in fact trying to evoke absolutely every goddamn nuance he can think of. It just goes page after page after page around one object.

GH: Filling the scroll on the lamp. You can just see that lamp so clearly.

bp: That's right. And that's what Francis Ponge has done. Have you ever read his book, *Soap*, in which he just takes soap and *everything* around soap, you know. Ponge is the clearest successor I can see to that thing in Proust.

DM: Ponge also has that theory about the chord. ... He has this thing about language, the way language stands to an object. If you strike the right chord in the language, you'll hit the chord in the object. Everything has its own musical resonance, okay. And you can see it happening in like "The Carnation," where the words are coming up and you can't even see the connection until he checks it out in the dictionary. And he says Oh wow! Yeah, you know, like that's where language is really carrying it, carrying that presence.

bp: See, that's what Stein did too with the *Tender Buttons* sequence. Like if she said vase, it was not a vase. It was a vase in language, it was all the words inside her at the moment of perceiving the object, and therefore they are connected with the object. Because those are all the words inside her when she sees that object.

DG: Yeah. That reminds me of what Sapir says in *Language* about house: that house is not simply all of our individual experiences of house, but it is everybody's experiences put together to form a concept, you know, of what it is.

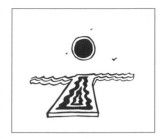

bp: But it seems to me that my obsession in a sense, and I can see that as we're talking about this, (I hadn't realized it before this moment) has been to take the noun (and I really think in some ways that some of my books are just about one thing, just one thing) to take the noun and to kind of bring it back to its base — like the thing in *Still Water* with just the single noun on the page — and precisely to let it regain its own resonances. Stein said that really nice thing about "a rose is a rose is a rose." She said that when she wrote that way, she thought she had written truly about the rose for the first time in hundreds of years in the English language. I think that in a way, it's a whole other thing which Steve and I came across in writing the TRG thing, the Toronto Research Group, which is Steve and I (another convenient name that allows us to operate). Our perception of it was that 20th century writing has gone through an unacknowledged present; that is, there is a whole tradition which we can call the avant-garde tradition, for lack of a better word, which is Stein, which is Dada, which is the Russian futurists like Klebnikov and so on — all those guys. There's a whole tradition that went through, which up until very recently, up until the last five or six years, was literally undocumented. I mean the stuff existed, but in private libraries all over the place; it was not accessible. Therefore, we were operating much like amnesiacs would. That is to say, we were operating out of a necessity to first of all regurgitate the history of 20th century writing in order to get beyond it. Like when I look at a book like *ABC*, the Alephbeth book of mine — which I like, but it's an early piece, I mean it's even earlier than me. In a way, it belongs about the 1930s: it's ahead of what the futurists were doing, but it's behind what some other people were doing. But for me, it's an important book. If you're just thinking Canadian, then I haven't seen it done Canadian. And I certainly wasn't aware of those writers when I wrote it. But knowing what I know now, I know it's an early work: it predates me. And it's because this material has not been present to our consciousness that we've had to take all this material which is there and regurgitate it in order to get beyond it. Like we have to bring it up out of our collective memories.

DG: Do you feel that you're restoring language to its original meaning or are you inventing a new use of language?

bp: I don't really know. Sometimes in my revolutionary zeal I think that we're doing all these things. Well my sense of it is simply what Pierre was saying about research writers. I obviously have a belief in writing as a kind of process which can lead not only the writer but others into new perceptions. Rafael has said many times that we have a perfect time machine which is the human mind, and it's a question of learning how to tap it. And I really believe that, because of déjà-vu experiences and so on. We usually exist in time warps and it's a question of finding the modes in writing which free up the armouring. The whole reason I got into concrete — I've said this many times, but I'm going to say it again — was that I thought I was being too arrogant, that I was sitting down and I was writing and I was coming to the situation obsessed that I had something to say per se: a very didactic purpose as opposed to simply giving myself up to the process of writing. And as a result, I was not learning anything from the language, you know. And the fact is, the language is there before me. I'm born into the language community. The language has a history of its own. I have things I can learn, if I sit down and let myself play with it — which is more or less the motivation behind getting into concrete, getting into sound. As well as having things to say that I couldn't simply put into those forms. Now, what strikes me about this whole thing of naming is that there are two ways of looking at it: you can look at the noun and at naming as a way of putting distance between yourself and the thing, or of treating it with respect, allowing its own existence, not simply consuming it as part of yourself — allowing it its own separate existence so that there can be a real marriage between you and the object, person, whatever. That's the two ways of looking at nouns. It's the second that interests me.

GH: That's a release of spirit.

DM: It's very hard, though, to get away from the implications of that Sapir quote of yours.

Dwight: That every word carries with it this huge accretion of concepts about the thing, and that that is what's been called up, rather than the thing.

bp: Well that's why, for instance, adjectives are so directive. Adjectives say to you, okay, here's the accretion I want. That's why Proust goes beyond it. Proust brings in so many adjec-

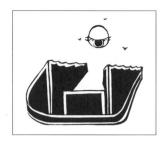

tives they're buried under a man-mountain of them. And in the end, in a way, you just end up in the midst of every possible memory you could have of a name. But what the concretists have done, in fact, in releasing the noun, in releasing it into the field of the page (and releasing the letters too, I mean if you want to go below that into micro-syntax), is to allow them their own existence again; to allow them a chance to re-group and a chance in a way to shed all that extra fat and see what they're doing by themselves. And in fact when you just write the word "moon" on a page and look at it, you find a lot of that accretion drops away. You're up against the elemental word which means you're up against the elemental thing. Except a lot of people get … I don't know, it's not exciting to them for some reason. Like they want those signposts.

Pierre Coupey: I'm struck by the tremendous variety of processes in composition that you utilize in order to discover new forms. It seems to me that your final interest is the form of the communication.

bp: Well, I believe two things about forms. I believe that form follows function as Louis Sullivan said, or that form is nothing more than an extension of content as Creeley said. But I also believe that form by itself says a lot about what the content is. So I believe both things are true, you see. It's like one of those chicken and the egg things that you don't bother separating.

PC: In a sense you're investigating form as content in itself.

bp: Right.

DG: Do you know the quote from Gertrude Stein about composition? Robert Duncan quotes it in an essay that's in the first *Caterpillar*. But carrying the sense that "composition is." Simply is.

bp: Right. She said that a lot — more or less that the reality of the situation was that the situation was. Like that quote that I use in *The Martyrology*: "let me recite what history teaches / history teaches." See Stein did not believe in the unconscious. She said she had no unconscious and she was constantly insisting on the absolute of the experience itself. Really, she was saying, all this thing is, is what it is.

DM: Well she was the first great stresser of process. That favourite quote of George's — help me. I can't remember it.

GH: "Composition is how we compose."

DM: Right. "Composition is how we ... " But there's a connection there in that talk about form, that little bit you just said,

```
what i do is i just keep shuffling ideas
around.
```

with the kind of identification that's occurring in your sense of naming as calling forth.

bp: Well Chomsky makes that distinction between competence and performance in language. It's essentially the same distinction that Sapir made about the difference between the actual life of language and the study of linguistics. And I don't know if this relates or not, but I have found that my interest is in the actual life of language or in what Chomsky calls the performance, as opposed to necessarily in the competence of the linguistics area per se. That what happens inside the psyche, or the human being's relationship to the materials he uses — which are language, the book and all those things — is I find the most important thing.

That relationship of human being to material used.

DM: Well, in fact, the language becomes the thought. There is no thought outside of it.

DG: If there wasn't language there can be no thought, that's his statement.

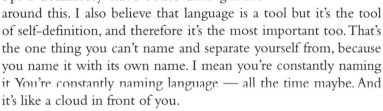

bp: I definitely have some ambiguities around this. I also believe that language is a tool but it's the tool of self-definition, and therefore it's the most important too. That's the one thing you can't name and separate yourself from, because you name it with its own name. I mean you're constantly naming it. You're constantly naming language — all the time, maybe. And it's like a cloud in front of you.

GH: I really believe, though, there's thought without language. I mean I disagree with that.

DG: I don't.

DM: I think there's *sensation* without language.

DG: But there isn't thought.

bp: You get into one of these really incredibly well-argued areas in which nobody's really reached the definitive conclusion of it yet. I don't know which I believe, actually, to tell you the truth.

DM: Collingwood did a nice bit on that, on that whole thing about thought and language.

PC: R.C. Collingwood. Where he says all history is the history of thought. And the other translation of what you said is that there is no history, except in language.

bp: Right.

PC: One thing I wanted to ask you, when you were talking about the process of repetition or insistence in *Journal*, as opposed to Gertrude Stein's use of insistence as a medium for intellection.

bp: My awareness of it was that Stein only occasionally used it for emotional insistence. She was using it to just let the materials themselves, the materials of language, repeat themselves. Whereas my use of that thing of Stein was to allow the materials as emotional charges to insist themselves. And that was the distinction.

157

And that's why I feel that *Journal* is radically different from what Stein was doing.

DM: In fact, you spoke of it as emotional syntax yesterday.

bp: Right.

GH: That's where I find you much more interesting than Stein.

DM: Well it moves, it really moves one, in that emotional way that Stein doesn't. And in terms of any kinetics of language, that's where it is.

PC: "Only emotion endures."

bp: You'll be remembered for that one.

DG: That's Ezra Pound.

bp: Well Wittgenstein — here we are, chucking big names around — ah, Wittgenstein had the sense of language games, which is also a really nice way of looking at it. They're all just essentially different systems which say different things at different times, you know.

GH: What, language does?

bp: Yeah, language games. He means game in the sense of play and he just keeps proposing different systems. Suppose I mean this by this, what's the implication of that? You know — 50 pages — suppose I mean this by *this*, you know. Actually Wittgenstein is very funny to read.

DM: That gets back to the noun thing again. Because what that's saying is that to be always at the edge — like writing letters at the edge — is always attempting to bring in more of what lies *outside* the system, which you can't get at except *through* the system, which is language.

bp: Right. So really, writing by its nature, in my opinion, writing is always out on the frontier going out a bit further. I think it depends. I think there are writers who are like that. I think there are research writers and I think there are synthesizers and I think there are simply popular writers (I don't mean that in a bad sense). I mean there's the person who gets out there on the edge and gathers in the materials. There's another person who'll take that material and synthesize it and do incredible things with it, and there's the popularizer who'll take the same ... eventually it filters right out into the mass market thing. Like, you know, stream of consciousness: you almost can't read a novel without stream of consciousness anymore. But on the other hand, that's a radically new development in popular literature in the last 20 years or so.

DM: But by that time it's become a habit of thought rather than a new perception.

bp:Yeah, by that time, you're all ready to move on.

Interview: Nick Power and Anne Sherman

NOT WHAT THE SIREN SANG
BUT WHAT THE FRAG MENT

1975

 On the whole I believe the form should arise out of the occasion of your writing — that you shouldn't be enforcing it on it. I realized early in 63 I was just plugging into form. I became intensely dissatisfied with that so I began to play with the language and that's how I got into "concrete" poetry.
— bpNichol

Anne Sherman: The judges awarded you in 1971 the Governor-General's award for your impressive output in concrete poetry. The rest of Canada as represented by several MPs judged it bad pornography (see *Hansard* where, as the interviewers note, Nichol was called "an affront to decency"). What was it about your poetry that was so unacceptable?

bpNichol: The actual thing that was bad pornography was *The True Eventual Story of Billy the Kid*, which was about this guy who had a short dick and who went around killing people. The encouraging thing about that was to see that language still had the power to move a few people even if not in all directions at once. It made them angry, at least, and when I wrote the piece it was an angry piece. It was about myth.

Nick Power: At the time, most of the reactions were to the so-called porn; no one talked about the development of concrete poetry.

bp: They got stopped by a couple of four letter words. I'd say if a guy with a short dick is sexually stimulating I'd say you've got some pretty weird MPs on your hands. Actually only one of the four books (for which the award was given) was specifically concrete — *Still Water* — and then I edited the anthology of concrete *The Cosmic Chef.* Both of these are types of poetry which are on the whole more meditative in that they demand of the person that you sit there for a 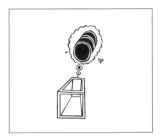 while and kind of get into it. They're not as immediately accessible as some forms of poetry. On the other hand they're so immediately accessible people think they missed the point, because it's too simple. So that all the things which people generally recognize as content were absent; so, much like the dog deprived of the stimulus who can't salivate because he doesn't hear the bell, they don't see the thing they recognize as content — "concrete content," they don't know what they're looking at, in a sense. A lot of it *is* conditioned response.

But there was no real coming to terms with the work, there has been very little. My work as work has had notoriety — I'm often regarded as the weird performing monkey in Canadian poetry. That's really a way of distancing something that people don't know what to do with.

AS: You don't think you've had good critics?

bp: Recently I've had perceptive critics. On the whole I've not; I'm partially responsible for that. Partially I was hiding behind the concrete myself because I frankly knew more about it than just about anyone I knew at the time, so therefore I could talk a theoretical blue streak and keep people at a certain amount of distance.

I was doing that basically out of a fear of being devoured by my audience — a certain danger I felt was possible on the Canadian poetry scene. It's become even more possible recently because of the craving for national heroes. Everybody wants a national figure and they want a literature they can seize on and call their own.

NP: Is that why Margaret Atwood must be self-protective in the face of people who want to make her into a cult figure?

bp: Right, I hope she avoids it. I don't think she's been successful; in fact, I think she has been made into a cult figure and I think she's personally feeling the effects of it because I think it's a horrible position to be put in, I don't envy her at all, it's a frightening thing to be. Unfortunately her book of criticism — *Survival* — helped to put her in that position. Despite her disclaimers at the front about it merely being a guide, it's being taken as a textbook and guys are actually writing poems — "Homage à Survival."

NP: How do you see yourself relative to the mainstream of Canadian poetry?

bp: I'm writing out a whole bunch of things that are immediate personal concerns for me and a lot of them have to do with language. A lot of what I do when I write is about the effect of being involved with language. *The True Eventual Story of Billy the Kid* was about the effect of the mythifying process of literature on a figure and what happens to him and the whole set of bullshit that goes down. Here's this stupid punk who goes around shooting people and he's a hero! It's weird!

AS: To most of us now it looks as if back in the 60s there was a group of people out there on the West Coast — like bill bissett and Judy Copithorne — who were experimenting with language; and then you came here to Toronto. How do you see yourself in relation to them?

bp: Obviously that's not a complete picture. The first thing I saw about concrete poetry in Canada was Pierre Coupey's "The Alphabet of Blood" in *Delta* magazine. I sent a fan letter to him at the time. I was familiar with bill bissett's work though I didn't know him then. And of course Raoul Duguay has been doing very similar stuff in Quebec for a long time. So the picture is very scattered. Of course part of that has to do with the artists themselves who have been working in a type of isolation.

I have a lot of sympathies obviously with what bill, and Judy, and Raoul are doing but that all grows out of us having a similar concern with languages, what happens when you put language on the page, the effect of treating the page as the field in which language activity happens in a book; or, alternately, the effect of language when you speak it — which is the sound poems.

bill and I have had the same treatment. He has been seen as an "idiot savant" — an eccentric. Yet, in his readings he's had a very powerful effect on people. The medium where people seem to become convinced or really interested is the medium of the reading.

NP: In order to get people interested in those early days you did a lot of your own publishing. Why was that?

bp: In the early 60s who was there to do it except me? David Aylward and I started *Ganglia* magazine because I wanted a forum in eastern Canada for those like bill and Judy who were doing concrete. We put it out free eventually. We had a mailing list and were sending it to people in Canada, United States, and Europe. It has since become *grOnk* and there are about 250 people who get it. Victor Coleman has called *grOnk* the limbo of Canadian publishing since so few people have seen it.

NP: Are you interested in publishing on the large scale?

bp: Several of my books have been published, never in runs of more than a thousand, mind you; but, *Still Water* (Talonbooks) is out, *Love: A Book of Remembrances* (Talonbooks) is selling.

NP: You and bill bissett talk of "breathing together" with people. There's a sense of a unity being sought but it isn't really a nation-alistic scene …

bp: It's a very hard thing to define Canadian Literature. We're in a period where something is definably growing which could become an "English Canadian Literature." What you're getting is a lot of premature definition of it. Now it's true, when I was in the earlier stages I was laying down a lot of rhetoric about the language revolution, a lot of shit-kicking phrases about "breathing together," and that came out of conviction. I was very much into sound poetry at that point; I still believe very much that if you're going to do a reading the occasion is very much one *for* sound. I like variety if I'm doing a reading. I find it more interesting, people find it more interesting if there is tonal variety, if there is change; which should be part of the human occasion of being together with people. So a lot of that "breathing together" has a broader application but was directed specifically at the poet and what should be made of that occasion.

NP: There's very little mass impact of poetry in Canada. You've had some public success with the sound poetry ensemble of The Four Horsemen. What is developing within that group?

bp: The Horsemen was Rafael Barretto-Rivera's idea. Steve McCaffery and I had a reading at the St. Lawrence Centre (some bomb!); they were hoping to make a cash deal out of us by this evening in which 20 people showed up in this huge hall. So Rafael was there and really enjoyed us so we got together with Paul Dutton and we all jammed. I was very interested in getting into that because I was very bored with the limitation of one voice. What four voices allowed us was more choral, more theatrical possibilities — in short opened up the whole ball game. As a writer this was a tremendously exciting challenge to me.

In fact, The Horsemen as a performance group have been very successful in what we were trying to do: reaching people. We've had difficulty ourselves personally, in knowing what we want to do when we finish a reading. There's been a tremendous input into the audience, the audience has usually been very responsive, we get a lot of feedback just in terms of attentive listening and applause (people also join in on some of the chants that are part of the sound drama); and then, there we are, we're no longer a group and we're just individuals and it's often a very dislocating time. That was something we were never quite able to get a hold of.

At this point the energy of the group has moved off into collaborating on writing a novel; we aren't doing performance any more. It's totally fresh, it's unmapped territory, it's never been tried except with *Naked Came the Stranger*. In Sci-fi and detective novels there are teams — like Ellery Queen is two writers. Four is different!

AS: If one looks at the international concrete poetry movement it looks like it's going in two general directions: on the one hand there are writers who believe a work of art should be cut off from life and then there are people (like the Brazilian Haroldo da Campos) who believe the poem should have a political impact. Where do you see yourself?

bp: Usually by the term political they mean ideological, that is to say there is a very specific point of view being expressed; now I think any poem by its *nature* — if it works on the emotional systems of the individual — is in that sense revolutionary, it is in that sense political. I think poetry by its nature is a political activity. Now, as always, the arts have never been able to justify themselves in terms of putting bread in people's mouths. In fact, most of the studies of the arts tend to show them as being elitist activities. That is why when you get writers or painters who get very much into a Marxist ideology, they find themselves on very dicey ground as to what to do about their writings: like Mao publishes his poems with an apology for these old-style revisionist things.

As far as a specific political ideology it's not present in my poems. What is present is my own personal belief that the language you use, which includes the emotional content of the language, has a tremendous effect on the world and that I've always seen these things more from a personal point of view. That is to say the individual working his path through the thing and if the individuals claim a ground in common and if the struggle is together, they will build something.

A Letter to Michael Gibbs

1975

dear Michael Gibbs

... i was troubled by Felipe Ehrenberg's review of Edgardo Antonio Vigo's book (see *Kontexts 5*) because it is a type of criticism i find almost intolerable
1) it's simple to make from outside the country   since Ehrenberg reveals no depth knowledge of Vigo or what his political/emotional commitment is to Argentina etc   on what basis of fact is the criticism made   obviously on the groups that back the organizations the publications were backed by (the usual torturous road of 3rd world intrigue)   big deal   *Das Kapital* is published by all sorts of big capitalist publishing houses & Bantam Books in the states published Mao's quotations   it's the old guilt by association number
Ehrenberg reveals this with the quotable quote that the book "could easily be liked, even praised, were it to have been produced in Europe"   doesn't that line bother you a bit
2) it makes inherent assumptions about what is revolutionary art & continues the old elitist myths about abstract and minimalist writings (concrete if you like   whatever the tag) which (god knows) lots of people who are doing the stuff these days are probably into but hopefully is not believed by everyone   i mean isn't the operating premise that a man is shaped finally by the language he uses the categories his thinking gets trapped into whatever the level of language those categories operate on   i could posit the opposite from Ehrenberg (i don't know what the facts are so this *is* a probable not an actual) & praise Vigo for his revolutionary zeal in undermining bourgeois notions of language as commodity & in sticking it to the OAS by having them actually publish it   a poetic coup   i am left you see with the distinct feeling that Ehrenberg sees "concrete" et al as fashionable & not revolutionary   ah history
but that does touch on the thing i was going to first write to you about which is that element of fashion   d.a.

levy who seems to have been at the moment largely forgotten could never have been fashionable precisely because his work was more tied to language to poetry than to painting & it is that element of the art gallery the exhibitions that gives to concrete the big marketplace feel   what has been an albatross for the painters and sculptors et al overlaps into an area where it has never been before & i have heard so many judgements made on works by various people not on the basis of what they are doing *with* language (in fact i read almost *nothing* on what they are doing with language) but as picture & worst of all a judgement on them as "pretty" pictures   people do seem to have forgotten the title of that first exhibit in London "between poetry and painting"

even most of the people working in the field   that's why it was nice to read Jiri Valoch's comment   or yours (i think it was yours   the one in *Typewriter Poems* about being disturbed about the tendency towards "pretty" pictures)   on the other hand you get rejections of Ian Hamilton Finlay's work because it's pretty without anyone bothering to go into the language revolution that's involved in what he's doing (i try to avoid Stephen Bann on Finlay because for me he does not elucidate but obfuscates but then that's just me)   the whole situation is screwed up

... a little note further on "pretty" pictures   my judgement is of course based on the sense of language i have   it's not that there's anything inherently wrong with a pretty picture   it's a question of where i see the struggle as being & i think that someone who just makes pretty pictures with his typewriter or his letraset is missing the point of the struggle

it is a struggle & we are up against one hell of a lot of conditioning a hell of a lot of fear in people

people shouldn't get sucked in to thinking concrete is fashionable because that's just a way of dismissing it of not having to come to terms with what it's attacking   the whole statement that is being made   & when i make a judgement on them as "pretty" pictures i mean this relative to the current aesthetic mode   they are judged as graphics with all the other assumptions that it involves & almost never as language pieces

best
bp Nichol

Interview: Caroline Bayard and Jack David

1976

Caroline Bayard: As a teenager, what kind of poetry did you feed on?

bp: My favourites were Walt Kelley's Pogo, Dr. Seuss, Wilfred Owen. I loved Keats. But the teachers I had always thought he was the most shallow of the Romantics. Up to 17, those were the people — and D.H. Lawrence. Dave Phillips and I used to read Lawrence and Kenneth Patchen. It was about then that I started to get into Creeley and Ginsberg. The person who particularly impressed me at that time was Lew Welch and some of Philip Whalen's things. I was into the visual thing from Patchen — through his poem-drawings — and around that time, a friend of mine, James Alexander, introduced me to some of the Dada people and Apollinaire. I was reading a lot of Chinese poetry in translation. I was reading a lot of West Coast Indian poetry that I could find. All that stuff. Chinese poetry I was very stirred up by at that time — more Chinese than Japanese. I wasn't really that into Canadian, strangely enough.

Jack David: In 1963 you were hauling books at the U of T Library. In what sense was that a valuable experience for you?

bp: It impressed me with the narcissism of much literature. It took away from me the illusion that I was simply, by writing books, going to change the world. In fact, writing a book was not necessarily the vehicle to use to change the world; there were probably much better vehicles for it. When you spend day after day under the dusty stacks of the well-meant words of millions of people, it changes your view of literature and what the point of it is. I ceased, at that point, to have a view of myself as reaching out and "changing the masses." In fact, I became very suspicious of the term, "the masses." Because it seemed to me a convenient coverall for all sorts of megalomaniacal fantasies. It also made me unable to read for a period of time. I had a surfeit of print. It was also the feeder of much of my reaction against a lot of traditional books. I just felt, well, most of it had been done, in a way.

JD: In 1951 Eugen Gomringer said that he had written a lot of Shakespearean sonnets, and then had come to a dead end. He didn't write for a couple of years, and then snapped out of it. Was that the same kind of experience you had at the library?

bp: Surprisingly similar, which is to say I was writing lyric poems — the sort of stuff that is in *New Wave Canada*. I reached a point where I was sitting there — and I was feeling in a pretty good mood — but I would sit down to write and I'd write this o-u-t out lyric poem. I realized at that point that I was somehow simply plugging in. And I've always believed that content takes care of itself. If there are things you have to say, you will say them. So the question becomes one of form — how do I get that out as openly and as clinically as possible? So my focus shifted onto form and I stopped writing lyric poems and began writing what I at that time called "ideopomes," which were just these little ideogram type things. It came out of my sense of Chinese poetry. Eventually I tied in with the things that were happening in other places. So that I, in essence, abandoned "straight" poetry for a period of about a year and a half until I heard about the *New Wave Canada* anthology through Margaret Avison. So I roared home and literally sat down with everything I'd learned in a year and a half of focusing on form and on the page as a field of play, and rewrote those poems. My ear was better. I could hear better after that year. I had a much better sense of rhythm, of music. I was better able to listen to the words and less concerned with imposing some sort of preconceived notion of wisdom on the occasion of writing.

CB: You dedicated *Love: A Book of Remembrances* to Avison and Birney with the following: "Where one or two have won: / (The silver reaches of the estuary." Have these two people helped you to find the silver reaches?

bp: I realized later that I was on dicey ground because Avison meant death there. What I meant by that was literally the breaking through to the other side. And I would say yes. I would say that Earle, not through his visual poems at all, but through his "Near False Creek Mouth" — the rhythms of that poem, which are so much like British Columbia, to me anyway when I heard it, had a tremendous influence on me. The sound of the thing. I found that poem quite exciting. With Margaret Avison she was a tremendous influence. When I got into *Winter Sun* and read those poems — once again it was an education to the ear. The same sort of education Sheila Watson was to me. I heard better after reading those books. It extended my sensibility of how language could move.

To a lot of people, that would appear to be a curious book to dedicate to them. But in fact it was because at that point I had been able to take the letters and incorporate them into the breath-line poem. To me, that was a very big breakthrough and it allowed me to reach into a whole other region which has just begun flowering this last year. That book was a really important transitional point. So, a heartfelt dedication.

JD: In *KonfessIonS of an ElizAbeThan Fan Dancer*, you thanked Bob Cobbing who first published you. When did he publish you, and did it take guts for him to do so?

bp: Well, I think Bob Cobbing has guts, period, because he's been publishing visual poetry for years, in England. In essence, *KonfessIonS* was the first selection I had published. And that's the only selection of concrete stuff I've ever had published — other than *Still Water*.

JD: In retrospect, what do you think of your early typewriter poems?

bp: The structure of them visually owes a tremendous amount to the carriage limitations. You know the standard limitations that you're into with the typewriter. When I was into typewriter concrete, it was as much that I was into the typewriter as a tool of the writer — as an extension of the writer. In fact, I just use the typewriter now to type up a poem when it's reached the stage where I'm thinking, how will it stand the transition to print. Other than that, I write by hand. I do very little composition anymore on the typewriter. Whereas at that period, I did all the writing on the typewriter, so it was logical that I would explore the limits of the typewriter. Now I do most of my writing long-hand. When I started writing — God, I've been writing since I was 13 — when I really got into the typewriter it was because there was so much stuff in me I could not keep up with the words in my head. I needed something faster than my hand. And I'm not a good writer — I tend to defensively print. I needed something very fast that could keep up with my thought process. As I got more control over that and became less panicked that I would lose the gem of the century by hand writing, I began to write again. And began to use notebooks a lot.

CB: When did you first become aware of the international concrete movement?

bp: Andy, of *Andy* fame, sent me the *TLS* article and an issue of *Image* magazine. Now that was in January 1965. I was already doing these simple little things at that time. But I was doing these things and getting nowhere. No one was publishing them.

CB: But they were good …

bp: I don't know. I was a very unselfconfident writer at the time. I was a very secretive writer for the first six or seven years of my writing. Dave Philips and I used to show each other our stuff in Vancouver. Then I moved to Toronto. I knew nobody who wrote, literally nobody. I was working away on these things. I met Dave Aylward, who thought it was all bullshit at the time. James Reaney was the first person to take some of my initial stuff for *Alphabet*. That's one of the reasons I've always had a tremendous respect for Reaney. I think he's a very inventive and a very creative man. Until his plays, people had an unreasonable bias towards him.

I sent poems to Bowering's *Imago* after the first issue because he published Ian Hamilton Finlay. I thought, if he'll publish Finlay, maybe he'll publish me. I sent them to him and he said, "I don't like this kind of stuff. I only published Finlay because they were like lyric poems. But, why not send them to Cavan McCarthy?" So, through Bowering I found the European underground of concrete.

JD: In your opinion, were the *Noigandres* poets in Brazil the most influential theoreticians of the early concrete movement?

bp: Who can say. I can't actually answer the question because I come into it in 1965; I come into it from my own angle; I come into it through Stein, whom I'm reading at that time; I come into it through Dada. And really, I come into it through Patchen, through bissett, and Birney, and Pierre Coupey. I'm doing it with my own biases, and from my own point of view, and then I find this thing happening. So I'm doing things that are similar, and I'm learning things from what I see, but don't encounter theory until I'm already doing the stuff. You see, theory tends to be after the fact. When you get so interested in the theory, it really influences the head to a crippling degree. You read the theory, and then you have to almost completely forget it, and just absorb it, and see how it comes out. I would say yes, inasmuch as people read it, got very influenced, it paralleled thinking other people were doing — on that level I would say yes. In my own experience, no. I can't keep up with these other things, and I can't read Portuguese. Occasionally Alvaro de Sa sends me a translation of something and I read it and I'm fascinated. Even then, at this stage in my life, there are still things in my writing that I am following through that are my own obsessions — my own vision of things. So that these things come in in a different way than when I was 24.

CB: This is something that's been bothering me for a long time. You seem to look at the traditional dichotomy between prose and poetry as misleading. What do you think is false about this dichotomy?

bp: Well, as far as I can figure, it's actually a visual distinction. And it has to do with the type of line, that is to say, prose tends to be a much more talky, much more discursive, less imagistic, less tightly imagistic type of writing that visually is arranged in a particular way on the page. Now there's no reason it has to be arranged that way. The main reasons are typographical — they have to do with the limitations of the book and not with the writing itself — it's imposed from the outside. Thank God, we wouldn't want to read Proust like a ticker tape. Poetry, on the other hand — the way Steve and I put it in a TRG Report — there's a reason for the left-hand margin and there's a reason for the right-hand margin in poetry. It has an exact and purposeful reason. It doesn't matter whether you're writing sonnets or a more breath-line or a Steinish type like Clark Coolidge, the American, the left and the right have a syntactic point. There is a very real reason for having them there. Now, when a writer starts to get tightly imagistic in his writing in prose, and tends to get led by the ear, they start saying, Well, he writes prose-poetry. Which is one of the strangest terms of all time. What it says is that there is this middle ground between the two things. It's convenient — you can say this is prose and that is poetry. And it's useful — I use the distinction from time to time. But I don't think it's all that vital or important. A lot of writers say, Well, I can write prose, I can't write poetry, or vice versa. And what are they actually saying? What they're saying is, I can't write a certain type of writing.

CB: OK, this is true. But then, isn't there a contradiction in the fact that when you got into the TRG Reports with Steve, you were very careful to say "TRG Report I — Narrative," and "TRG Report II — Translation." So that, in a sense, you've upheld these differences at the same time that you're criticizing them.

bp: Well, in a sense, yeah. What I'm saying is it's there, it's useful, you can use it. But it's not big and major, it's not important. It's a tool, you can use it if you want to, or you can ignore it if you want to. Really, the reason for making the point is to say, Here's something you can ignore. Now what in fact I've seen since then — I was reading B.S. Johnson's excellent book of essays —

JD: I have to interject here. Brian Henderson and I, when we read that in the TRG Report, thought that B.S. just meant bullshit — there was no such person.

bp: Excellent writer, fascinating writer. He's dead now. I was reading this book of his where he was discussing the shift from the narrative poems — Walter Scott he saw as a seminal figure because he was writing narrative when the novel suddenly became big, he shifted gears without effort and went into the novel. There he was writing novels, and for a while the novel was the popular form. Then along comes movies. Movies take over the burden of narrative. Straight simple story-telling becomes the property of the movies. Along comes TV. TV takes over the property of straight story-telling and the movies become more and more concerned with other things, just as the narrative poem starts to seem like an anomaly. Now what I realized, reading Johnson, was that when you stop and think of how the long poems have had an incredible resurgence in the last 20 years — everybody and his mother has written a long poem — that we have reached the point where, in essence, poetry and prose — in the sense of the novel — were moving into exactly the same sphere. And you can move from one to the other with ease. Formally, there was no longer a usefulness in the distinction — they were simply modes of writing that you could move back and forth with. The only thing was how you made the change, the transition point, and how you handled them technically. That's the only limitation. How you ease the reader from one into the other. It becomes a tool that the writer can use. It frees up, once again, another area in which you can move. It therefore increases the range of content that you can explore.

JD: TRG defines content as "the particular movement of a text, the sum total of referential thrusts."

bp: Yes, that's a McCaffery-ism. It's really quite simple; I don't know why Steve insists on these $10 words. OK, in any text you build up a lot of different references, a lot of signifieds where this word refers to that, that word refers to this. So that this lamp and this candle that we have sitting here on my right become then the sum total of those thrusts or what happens in that crossover becomes the content and that's what I'm writing about. So, in essence, the sum total of everything I refer to is the content. In a way, the talking about it opens up your thinking so that you can look at the text more abstractly which is why Steve tends to put it in what would be regarded as a more scientific language.

CB: Are you always very much aware of the signified outside of the text? Like of the lamp as a reality that you can touch, that can break?

bp: Not necessarily. In good fiction writing you're aware of the lamp as a lamp inside the book, and hopefully you're no longer thinking of these things as a big conscious connection. Though it's obvious that any reader reading the thing brings his own referent to the word "lamp" unless it's described. So that, no, on the whole people aren't, unless the writer makes a big point of it. Now a lot of Steve's work, for instance, takes it even further so that not only are you not aware of the lamp outside the text, it doesn't have anything to do with the lamp outside the text. The same sort of thing that Stein was working with in *Tender Buttons*.

CB: Barthes defines the reader not as the consumer but as the producer of the text. Doesn't the quality of the production depend upon the reader's ability? Would you say that there is a democracy of readers?

bp: I would say it depends on the reader. It depends on his ability to have sympathy for the text. A lot of stuff doesn't interest me. I mean this is where you get into the area of personal tastes. I know there are people who loathe my writing and what it stands for; there are other people who really like it. But that is taste.

CB: If they don't like it, then there is no production.

bp: Yes. They're not going to produce, because they're not going to interact with it. The production demands an interaction. I think later in the TRG article we point to Brigid Brophy's statement which was that a lot of writers throw the book at the reader and it lands there, legs akimbo, saying do with me as you will. You see from 1968 on we really got obsessed with trying to get to a non-narrative prose. Was it possible? Steve and I finally came to see that, no, it was totally impossible. In fact, anybody looking at something takes a path through it, and that creates a narrative. So the best you can hope for is to present a text which demands of the reader that they organize it themselves. What do you gain from that? A minimal amount. How many readers want that kind of democracy? So you see here you are fighting a war for freedom and nobody's noticing they're enslaved. In a way, it's an issue that's probably of more concern to writers. In fact, when we worked on the TRG essay — I mean, we're talking about readers, we're talking about a very specific type of reader — that is to say, a writer-reader who is obsessed with issues of writing. Right?

He's the guy who's really going to get off on this sort of stuff. And with TRG, Steve and I were super-conscious of the fact that the audience for TRG has got to be one of the most minimal ever spoken to in Canadian literature. It's going to be a specialized group of readers. This is not exactly popular literature. My sister-in-law wouldn't read it, I can tell you right now.

CB: You said that "there's a new humanism afloat that will one day touch the world to its core." Have you witnessed any signs of this new emerging humanism?

bp: I was talking about my experience with Therafields at that point and the attempt to deal with emotional disturbances, creating a human context of community for people where they could live, where they could function, and where they could …

CB: Are you saying that some political revolutions are not really touching the individual at all?

bp: No, I'm not saying that at all though that's undoubtedly true. All I'm saying is that eventually these things tend to run afoul of a restrictive element in the individual which leads to a type of dehumanizing process. In fact, if we look at the Cuban revolution, we see that it's been successful. I think there are elements there that are not as successful.

CB: So not all revolutions lead to this de-humanizing process. Some do.

bp: A fair number do, historically. Usually there's a swing back to fascism — to police control. It doesn't matter if you've got a socialistic or a fascistic government, eventually police control is utilized. Now I think it's obviously naive to think that the world is made up of angels. In itself, some type of police control is not to be shunned. It depends on the quality and the level of what goes into it.

CB: Do you think there is a connection between world order and revolutionary writing — between world order and word order?

bp: Oh yes, because I think syntax equals the body structure.

JD: Stanley Berne refuses to refer to new writing as experimentation. For him, new writing is a finished product which investigates areas that have never been investigated before.

bp: Right. He's reacting against the thing that if you look at it as an experiment the very term suggests unfinished. And what he was arguing for was the position of research. Research is, in fact, not unfinished in that sense but is rather regarded as being complete in itself. Because it leads on to something else does not mean that the thing itself is unfinished. Which I agree with. A lot of my writing and my publishing has been from a research point of view. I've published things because that's the point I've reached and maybe somebody else can pick up on it. As opposed to the finished polished artifact. I revise like crazy and rewrite like crazy and polish, polish, polish. But I don't put it aside for 20 years and see if it's stood the test of time. In fact some of the stuff I've published hasn't stood the test of time. I used to believe that when you turned 45 you automatically became a master. It seemed a long time away, at the time. As I crawl through my 30s I see that that is wrong. All of one's life in fact one is simply in the process of learning. It's sheer madness to think that you arrive at some complete point in your lifetime. In fact you die. Hope lies in what happens to the race as a whole. Each of us personally chooses the path that will ultimately affect the most things for the most good. Of course you get into a lot of disagreements about what that path is, but you follow through.

CB: You've also said that formal constraints limit your ability to develop exits from the self.

bp: Syntax and the way you structure the sentence limits the content you can put out. I have seen this over and over again. The reason I have moved between styles of writing is because I have always seen the connection between form and content. You can't divorce the two things. I have chosen to talk about form simply because I don't see any point in talking about content. Content is self-evident there in my writing. If you want to know what I think all you have to do is read the works. Why should I bother jazzing on about that? The form — and the need to free up form — to unarmour the poem. You know how the muscles can get tight and constricted, and therefore the body. I have this arm — let me demonstrate. My arm floats above the floor, you see. Now that's because of the muscles that are too tight up in here which depends on all sorts of tensions because of all sorts of other things. This hand does not actually relax onto the floor. I can force it down, but if I just let it go, it just floats above the floor. Same thing happens in poems. Depending on what structures you put in, you limit what can happen, you limit the flexibility of it, you limit what you can do.

JD: Sometimes they're accidents of birth, though. Same thing in poems?

bp: Yeah, but you're the one giving birth to it. So you should try and have the healthiest body making use of it — the most flexible body possible. If you know that smoking cigarettes is going to give your kid cancer when it's born — you stop smoking cigarettes. You know that constantly using end-rhyme is going to restrict what you can say — you stop using end-rhyme. Not that end-rhyme is bad, maybe you don't need it for that thing. I've used end-rhyme — sounds like a drug — "I've mainlined end-rhyme!"

JD: The great emphasis of contemporary poetry is on the ideational and not the emotional. Some of your books are ideational — *KonfessIonS* and *Captain Poetry* — while others are emotional — *Beachhead* and *Monotones*. Do you find it difficult to integrate the two — ideational and emotional?

bp: I would say the integrative work is *The Martyrology* which becomes particularly clear in Books III and IV. There have been times where I've found problems with that, except how it reveals itself in the emotional is through formal things. That's where the ideas influence the structures — free up the structures — and I find myself able to say things I'm simply not able to say before, because I did not have the language, I did not have the formal ability. I am still learning. I've got a tremendous amount to learn yet. It's really funny because people develop expectations towards you. This is one of the things that you are constantly fighting when you are writing. If I was interested in doing the big Grabbing-Ahold-of-the-Public-Media number, I had the ideal chance when I got the Governor-General's Award. Because there was so much stink about it. I was approached by a suitably big publisher who wanted to put out *Billy the Kid*, splash it all over the place. I could have been big, big, big. I could have been the pre-Margaret Atwood, on that level. But I wasn't interested in that because it was a mis-reading of the text. Why let the piece get notoriety for something which has nothing to do with the piece? If I was going to be true to the text, to the content of what I had written, I couldn't do that. So I just ignored the whole thing. In fact, the book had one printing of 350 copies. It still hasn't been put back into print. With the emotional things, and with the expectations that go towards you, when I had written reflective poetry, a lot of people didn't like it. The reason they don't like it is because other guys are writing reflective poetry that's very similar. Guys are snappin' it off, saying this is the hottest thing to come out since sliced bread. But a lot of it has to do with expectation. I had one manuscript — which was, God knows, heavy — which was called "Dark Night, Secret Room," and it had a lot of the poems in it that ended up in *The Other Side of the Room*. It was rejected, and the rejection letter read: "Lacks the humour I usually associate with your work." So if you start exploring something different, people are generally back in the frame you were in before. It's not simply that I can't bring them together — it's readers that, in a sense, can't bring them together either.

JD: There's a difference, though, if you're moving into an area that has already been habituated by other people as opposed to moving into an area which is "new," in a lot of senses. Then you wouldn't get the same kind of rejection from the readers.

bp: Well, you get a more cautious approach. It isn't that you really get an acceptance. I didn't have any big illusions when I started getting a "reputation." A lot of it was that people didn't want to gun it down in case it turned out to be big. That was the level at which I got acceptance initially. Now it's not true at this point. I think a lot of what I've gone after and a lot of what I believed in, people have heard and I have sympathetic readers, as it were. People who hear it, and feel all of it, some of it, part of what I'm saying. That was not the situation in the early stages. I've had a very interesting career that way because *New Wave Canada* — that was the lyric poems I got in for — and the next thing I was known for was the visuals, the concrete stuff. Then my reputation was for the sound poems. The last few years it's been really for the collaborative stuff with the Horsemen. So I've literally had these different phases for which I've been known. And depending on the period of time people look discomfited when I read some things, and really happy when I read the stuff I'm known for at the moment. Doesn't matter. Partially I agree that if I'm out on some kind of frontier — as it were — or what appears to be a frontier at least — then people sort of feel excited and opened up. If you go into something that's more introspective and more moody, they tend to feel more closed out so they're not as excited about it. Fair enough. *The Martyrology* is where all that stuff comes together. It's where everything comes into focus. In all four books, which represent different stages. By the fourth book I had managed to bring together the eye, the ear, and everything.

CB: The five senses?

bp: No, my two obsessions. The eye — the page as a visual field — and the ear — I've always been lead by the ear in my writing. Stuff which is not visual, my structure has always been sound. That's why *Love: A Book of Remembrances* is so important, because that's the first place I've managed to bring together the eye and the ear. I don't know if it works as well for the reader, but it works really well for me. In "transcontinental," the letters exist as themselves, they're visual entities, the shape is right there in front of you, but the line is a breath line, and it moves quite well. I've read that poem at a number of places and it always goes over surprisingly well.

JD: In your opinion, new writing mirrors new realities. How is this different from the Elizabethan theory that art imitates reality?

bp: Well, the difference probably lies in the words imitates and mirrors. The one reflects something back at you; the other suggests Williams' distinction — not to copy nature, not to imitate …

CB: Just to imitate nature's creativity.

bp: But to dance two and two. The idea of something paired.

CB: You create the way she creates. You only imitate nature inasmuch as you create as nature creates.

bp: That's right. What happens with new writing is that if you create a new reality — and this can be formal, this can be content — a damned good novel — in that thing, you create something which mirrors a new reality. Science fiction mirrors a new reality to the reader. One which does not exist. Hubert Selby Jr., in a much different way, mirrors life. "New" is so relative to your experience, right? Imitation, for me, has more of a feeling of artifice about it. I'm less interested in artifice than in the actual event at hand, the writing, and what it's creating, the actual event of what is going on. So I don't really want to imitate. Actually, I wrote this in a notebook at one point. This hit me one morning in Vancouver. I was staying at Warren Tallman's place because I was in town for a reading. And I was walking down the street at seven in the morning to clear my head and there were crocuses coming up through the ground. I realized that I never had the urge to rush home and write a poem about crocuses. Rather I wanted to literally create poems that were crocuses. That had their own thing, that burst forth and were brand new in themselves. But I've never wanted to describe a landscape. I've wanted to create landscapes. So that's my argument with the word imitate.

JD: That notion is pretty close to the way that Modern Art gave up representational drawing.

bp: Yeah, but it doesn't mean that you can't do representational drawing. But it absolutely changes your point of view about it. It changes what you're doing with the poem. It's a change in consciousness which may not appear on the surface of the writing. But it makes a hell of difference to the writer.

CB: You've said that "writing writing means that the materials of the poem are no longer external — it *is* the object it describes." Is this an outgrowth of Black Mountain theory?

bp: I can see a logical connection with it. Because I see a connection between Olson and Stein. Because both of them wanted to take the language and absolutely re-make it. And yet they were both using the materials of language. I can't really articulate this well, at the moment. There have been moments in my life when this has been very clear to me. This is not that moment. For me, probably much more of that had a connection with Stein and

Stein's love of Cubism. She wanted to make a thing pure unto itself. There was a period when I wanted to do absolute things which were totally independent, which had nothing to do with me, nothing to do with anybody, except that they were themselves and they existed as objects. *Still Water* is like that. *KonfessIonS* and the *Aleph Beth* book are very much like that. Those are my purest expressions of that concern. I've become much more interested in taking that tendency and incorporating it and pushing the whole thing that is writing even further now and just seeing where it takes me. Formally, that's what I'm interested in. I say I'm interested in it because I find that's what I do and like. But that's where things have lead me. So I can see a connection with Black Mountain, yeah, because if you actually get into following the ear, then sound itself can become intense pleasure. And Stein talked about that at one point. She talked about how, at one point, she became quite intoxicated with the words and then she realized that was a very dangerous thing. So she withdrew from it. I wrote an essay about bissett in which I said that was the difference right there between Stein and bissett. Because bissett plunged right into the middle of it. bissett absolutely plunged into sound and got intoxicated with it and just let the high carry him. Whereas, Stein, who was much more intellectual, withdrew.

JD: In 1915 Hugo Ball wrote that he had invented a new species of verse, "verse without words," or sound poems in which the balancing of the vowels is gauged and distributed only to the value of the initial line. Has contemporary sound poetry moved beyond that point?

bp: Yes. Here you get into some wildly differing theoretical schools. Henri Chopin would say that what I do has not moved beyond that point. He said this to me. He said that what I do is *poésie phonetique* — phonetic poem — and that that type of poetry is good where you have a good reader. And he said he thought I was a good reader, with a good voice, and therefore the poem lives. But he felt it dies with the poet. He feels that where poetry is now — *poésie sonore* — is with the use of the tape recorder. Now I eschew the tape recorder because it's a machine, it's not the human voice. He sees it as a tool which can be used to change the human voice, to reshape it, to restructure it. So that the tape recorder, in essence, is the pen. The microphone and the machine are the pen with which he writes. I find the sound too mechanical. I'm much more interested in that blood-guts-sinew connection but then it's less sound poetry that I'm interested in and more in the relation between me as reader and the people who came to hear me. Through sound I could affect them and reach them and I could change the dynamic in the room. And that, as much as anything, is what got me into sound. I've come to realize that in retrospect, in a way as I've had dissatisfactions with readings in recent years. I give very few readings now.

JD: You said that "I suppose if I have a theme, it's the language trap and that runs thru the centre of everything I do."

bp: Well, that was a very particular view I was into at the time which was that same thing about forms and the lack of exits; that the language trap is really sticking within the confines of specific fatalistic uses or historically established usages rather than trying to attack those. Whenever I have gone to the opposite extreme, it is not out of the belief that one would never use that theme again. Rather to completely open up the sense of what is language — in this particular case, what is written language. In sound poetry — what is spoken language, what is the meaningful utterance. Is not the scream as meaningful an utterance as quoting Wittgenstein. Quoting Wittgenstein can be as meaningful as screaming, depending on the context. So the language trap is not so much a trap of language as it is a trap of cultural usages of language. My view of language tends to be as a tool. I get a lot of argument from people about this because they say, after all, it's how you see yourself. It's the world. It is what you are. It is a huge philosophical problem. My view of it remains, nonetheless, even though it is the tool through which we view ourselves; the process of thought might be something else entirely, but language *per se* is a tool which you can put to various uses. Depending on how wide the range of those uses are, to that degree you are free to move. So consciously, the image I have of myself is one of working to free up the uses of language. Do I think I'm reaching a very big audience? Probably not. I think that there are many types of writers. There are those who do the basic research — those who get the spadework done — these things tend to filter out. Until stream-of-consciousness was established as a technique, it never appeared in the popular literature. Now, nobody writes a novel without stream-of-consciousness. It's a valuable contribution. So I think there's room for everything, really. I don't negate one thing by what I do. I do what I do. And I do it because I believe in it. But I think that what I am doing, and the attack I pursue, eventually has that broader application. But I don't think that broader application necessarily is felt in my writing because of the nature of my writing.

WHAT IS NECESSARY IN ORDER TO UNDERSTAND IS A

TOTAL
ASSAULT

9

```
  A    H
  H    V
  V    A
       H
       V
       A
       H
       V
       A
```

```
A A A A
H H H H
V V V V
```

A A

A A A B C

A A A B C

A A A B C

A A A B C D D E E

WHY? (this one?)

ORDER  YES

alphabet soup

IRONY?

```
1 1 1 2 2 3 3
4 4 5 5 6 6
7 7 8 8 9 9
0 0 0 0 0 0
```

standardized systems
of communieation?

O Q O

P R R R S

P R R R S S S T T T T U

S S S T T T T U

```
        MONEY
     N U M B E R S
   A L P H A B E T
     N O T A T I O N S
 M E A S U R E M E N T
```

T T T U

T T U

begin again at the beginning
what was in the beginning ?
wha t was spoken?
          what grew?
name a goddess of norse religion.
name a rabbit.

T U

ST. REAT I HAVE FORGOTTEN YOUR OTHER NAME.

        Y O U R O T H E R N A M E

Some Notes for Jack David on Earle Birney's "Solemn Doodles"

1977

Reading your essay in *Studies in Can Lit* of "Visual Poetry in Canada" i wanted to shove some quotes at you & then some observations (maybe just as a basis for future appreciations of this aspect of Earle's work).

Speaking of the Pythagorean underpinnings of the aesthetic behind the pattern poem in the middle ages, Dick Higgins, in *George Herbert's Pattern Poems: In Their Tradition* (Unpublished Editions, Vermont, 1977), says "sacred power was attributed to letters, which were not seen as mechanical components of the written word, but as essential and autonomous instruments expressing the process underlying them, analogous therefore to numbers and proportions. The process of forming words became, then, a very sacred one indeed, part of the divine game of realizing things out of their underlying numbers or letters."

Birney, in the intro to his section of *Four Parts Sand* (Oberon Press, Ottawa, 1972), says "tell it (the printing press in this case) to adjust to our hands once more   to our freehands   so we can get close again to the ideas and the sounds behind the deadletter shapes   let the photo–offset solemnly assist our doodles   our solemn doodles   our spontaneous leaps into magical play."

And Vachel Lindsay, in his introductory note to *The Candle in the Cabin* (D. Appleton, New York, 1926), begins with a discussion of the Spencerian System of Penmanship & then points out that "Spencer was the only man in the Anglo-Saxon world who taught the public to build up handwriting into birds and flowers. If he had used the natural autograph of each man, instead of a watchspring curve, as the basis of his system of teaching, it might have become a school of art, instead of a discarded curiosity." Lindsay goes on to point out how the Arabesques of the Arabs, various schools of Chinese & Japanese painting, &, in Lindsay's opinion, half the history of art, all proceed from forms of handwriting. Speaking of his own work he says, "In all the pictures in this book I have used the letters of the alphabet, capital and small letters, upside down, in circles, on top of one another, and all sizes. In short, these pictures are written, not drawn."

Birney, once again in *Four Parts Sand*, says "the excitement and fear of the alpha betas have been shoved aside by the dumb march of the letters   there's no emotion running out of the shapes in the linotype   not even a glimpse of the thing or the idea of it."

And (to round this off) near the end of his already referred to essay, Dick Higgins points out, with regard to the pattern poem, "its unsuitability for any sustained argument of emotional persuasion. Its appeal is immediate and involves the recognition of the image. Thus the Aristotelian rhetorical goal of persuading and convincing a reader is unlikely to be achieved within a pattern poem. And an Aristotelian age — such as followed the Baroque — would, and did, find the pattern poem essentially trivial or eccentric."

 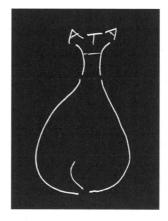

i think this grouping of quotes suggests, certainly to me, the necessity that any reader or see-er approaching texts like Birney's "Bilingual Cats" or "Figure Skater" must do so from an awareness of the importance of the individual letters involved in his writing of the poems. For these poems & others like them are more truly "written" than any others in his can(ada)on. The "content" lies in the gesture not in the result, lies in the importance of this activity to Birney as a member of the human tribe. One could, & hopefully some day somebody will, write a major essay on Birney based entirely on these handwritten poems but only if the belief system inherent in the gesture is seen. The thematic content of them is transparent, & it is that very transparency that distracts Birney's traditionalist critics & makes them either overlook or dismiss this aspect of his work. The content in the gesture that produced these poems lies at the absolute centre of his concerns as a writing human being.

One Further Note

In "Figure Skater," using the handwritten shapes of the letters, Birney gives us the perfect parallel to the "gesture" & "result" i am talking about.

If we criticize a figure skater we do not do so on the basis of the result, the marks his skates make on the ice, but rather on the basis of gesture, the feelings, thots & movements that have gone into making those marks. But in "Figure Skater" we are not present at the "performance," the actual writing of the piece, we have only the result to consider. It is, nonetheless, important for us to appreciate the gesture, otherwise the result is not meaningful.
Birney is, after all, the figure skater who produced "Figure Skater." The gesture is autobiographical & tho the thematic content of the poem appears transparent the belief system behind it has deep historical roots & forms part of the larger "content" which the text both draws open & refers back to.

A Contributed Editorial

1978

Frank Davey approached me in 1972 to become involved in *Open Letter*. He and i had never met before that first restaurant talk tho we had spoken briefly on the phone and had even had occasion to exchange disagreements in the first series of *Open Letter*. Frank offered me carte blanche — a section in each issue of *OL* in which i could do whatever i wanted. This was a tempting offer. In the meantime Steve McCaffery and i had been looking for some way and where to launch the Toronto Research Group. Our idea was to begin publishing theoretical writings (research as we preferred to call it) because it seemed to us there were all sorts of questions that should concern writers that were not being addressed in any of the magazines etc. that we had access to. We were not interested at that point in criticism per se but very definitely in theory as it actually affected and impinged on the writing life. *Open Letter* provided the focus and the forum. To this day i'm not sure how many writers read, enjoyed, hated, agreed, disagreed, etc. with the TRG reports Steven and i published and hope to continue publishing. Certainly along the way much of our own thinking has been modified by the discipline of bringing our theory into print and by the actual content (and hence form) that has arisen in our individual writings. It has been our disagreements that have fueled and modified the reports and we were genuinely hoping other writers would feel strongly enough about these issues to offer their thots and discoveries. It's happened occasionally in conversation but never in print.

But what has crept up on and surprised me is my own desire to articulate for myself a way of replying to other writing that honours my awareness of it. By this i mean then not a criticism which presumes to know more than the writer of the text, taking for oneself the role of the superior and benignly indulgent uncle who says "what Al Purdy really means here is (etc. etc.)," but rather an articulation of a particular (to this writer) understanding (and i'll take that literally as standing under or subservient to the text) which may offer a way in for others if they choose to take it. That free choice option as opposed to a critical dogma strikes me as crucial. I know, as i have said elsewhere, i have always stressed form and perhaps that has been a mistake. But from a writer's point of view that question of form(s) is paramount if one is to be open to the moment when the writing comes, if one is to have at one's finger tips the possibility of moving fluidly within the options that any impulse to write can open. Not to allow the material to move where it wants to because of one's own formal limitations is to beg off the whole issue of craft in writing. Thus the whole point of discussing form for writers (and i oppose them here to critics because the opposition does exist) is to expand the possibilities for the release of new contents. Content i have always taken as a given. One writes about what one writes about. Hopefully that expands, gains new depths of insight and feeling, as one's own life expands. Indeed the best place to work on content is on a day to day level in your dealings with other human beings. Then the gap between the content (insights and feelings in your writing) and how you live (your day to day life with other human beings and the society at large) will narrow and, hopefully, disappear. Thus my response to another writer's work must deal not only with a response to the content of his or her words but a response to their gestures as i see them writ large on the page within the form the pieces take. It is this articulation of gesture and the content as gesture which i see as the important ground between the daily life (autobio and bio/graphy) and the content (meaning per se of the word group-ings), and it is my response to it (subjective and from my own ground but interjected with that objectivity that i struggle to attain) that i hope from here (December 1977) to more and more articulate in my own writings on others and in any pieces that i may have occasion to solicit for *Open Letter* in the future. As the third series ends and the fourth series begins and my own involvement with *Open Letter* passes its fifth year it seems important to speak of these awarenesses.

Tabling Content: writing a reading of Shant Basmajian's *Quote Unquote*

1978

CONTEXTS ONE

If we begin with an overview, an attempt at glyphing the entire work, two things strike us without even opening the "book":

> 1. impermanence — there in the fact that the book is not bound but rather held together by a paper clip so that the author's preferred order is there, but only barely there, it has taken sequence for an instant but could as easily slip away &

> 2. negation — what forms within the poems, among the words, within the interplay between poems suffers from that same impermanence & quickly negates itself. This is visible on the cover where the author has deliberately crossed out what he set out to say & the only clear signs that are left are the opening & closing quotation marks & parentheses.

QUOTE UNQUOTE

It rises out of the thot process, is not necessarily the quoting of some other author, is, in fact, specifically, the process of thot, of print speech, the opening & closing of the attempt to articulate & when all the words are gone, erased or crossed out, then only the process can remain, carrying within itself its own content, a signi-fier that the punctuation signifies if we let it.

The title page sets us up for what is to follow. An original (?) titling of "Quote (and) Unquote" changed to "Quote Unquote" by the scribbling out of the word "and." Three levels of activity are pointed to. The "Quote Unquote" functions like parentheses or quotation marks around the crossed out word/phrase. Thus it is these areas of error we will be dealing with in the actual texts, what the texts are

 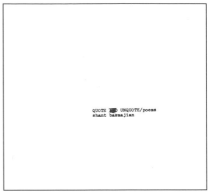

about, not in the sense of concealment but in an attempt to understand the interplay. Alternatively we realize that words, articulation, simply frame the unsayable, that what the author is attempting is to deal with it all. Thirdly we recognize that the "and" does not in fact carry the author's real intent since what he is not attempting is categorization & what he is attempting is a focusing on process & its relationship to content, to what is said.

The front cover, the way the "book" is held together, & the title page, should give us the clues we need to gain access to the texts that follow.

TEXTS: ONE

THE SAILOR AND HIS STARS

Basmajian uses titling to point to the context in which he sees the poems as most profitably occurring. Often these titles are romantic or have a beat or hip ring to them. The texts float below the titles almost oblivious to them. The relationship between the two seems thin & shimmers with that same impermanence we have already referred to. Basmajian's titles are definite in a way the poems aren't, specific where the poems seem almost universal. The effect is, in turns, of a latter-day Keats or Blake, a Ginsberg or a Corso, suddenly focusing all that energy into minimal utterances where only the titles remain as a memory trace of earlier poems he/they might have written. In this way the titles function as contextual quotation, referencing specific, but shifting, sensibilities.

In the poem the o, the zero or nothing, floats above

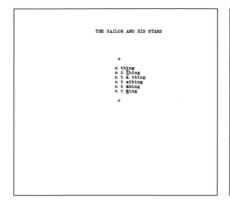
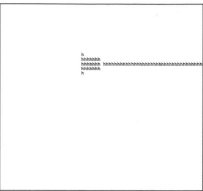

and below the emptied word it mirrors: n thing. In the second & third lines of the poem an underlined i & t bring a mysterious "it," a something, briefly into focus. As the line lengthens (n t a thing) "it" disappears again. At this point the movement of the poem changes. The "thing" comes back into focus & begins to move closer to the a (the beginning obliterates it in the 6th line, the t piling on top of the a, &, in the 7th, begins to consume itself, the h piling on top of the t on top of the a. For the first time since the 2nd line the actual word "n t hing" is restated within & behind which an a & t float, memories of "a thing." The underlined h in this second last line pushes us forward to the second page of the poem where precise rows of h's float, breath sounds, a noise emerging from a void. This is the sea the sailor sails, the voids & the terrors, the shifting & impermanent stars he must depend on to guide him.

THE PERFECT CONTRADICTION
A title only. A blank page. A page which is not blank since it contains a title. A title which suggests a text which is not present. A text which is present as a blank page. "I have nothing to say & I am saying it." A second take on nothing.

POEM
Almost a rock song. "i found a love today / in the san diego freeway." The same movement present from the impermanent "i found a love" to the focused "i lost my love" to the final antipoetic & despairing "she made a right turn / and i forgot." The

THE PERFECT CONTRADICTION

POEM

```
i found a love today
in the san diego freeway

she was in her 67 chevy
and i in a 69 skylark

i lost my love at a
busy intersection in
inglewood

she made a right turn
and i forgot
                inglewood california
                august '70
```

song slips away with the girl, the whole rock & roll sensibility ("Help Me Rhonda") beginning to shatter in the third stanza, where the line becomes jerky, grinding to its final halt in the fourth. Poem. The classic theme laid out in the late 60s rock rhyme schemes & thrown away like the era. A focus on infatuation as opposed to love, infatuation which is so often taken as love, emoted as such in the rock & roll radio wave world we live in. "Infatuation," with all that emotion's impermanence, where the signifieds slide below their signifier. Poem written in Inglewood, California, August 1970.

SIGNIFYING THE UNFINISHED POET

Here Basmajian uses quote as sign. "mary had a." The uncompleted beginning of the classic nursery rhyme. But tho it is the quote that is unfinished Basmajian tells us that that isn't what's important — what's important is that it's the poet that's unfinished. Quote then out of context? Or the beginning of a new context, the placing of the found text into a larger whole, which is the poet's work? What larger whole if the rest of the page is blank, is that nothing we have already referred to? The poet then as an accumulation of quotes, of things he has heard, so aware of the absurd nothing in which he moves attempting to speak, moving back further even than early rock & roll memories, back to the nursery rhymed beginnings, signifying the unfinished poet, the beginning of his sail upon the sea of language, the looking for stars or words to guide him from the quote to the unquote, thru the impermanence of being.

<table>
<tr>
<td>

SIGNIFYING THE UNFINISHED POET

mary had a

</td>
<td>

BUT

i miss you
i like you
i think of you
but

</td>
</tr>
</table>

BUT

A memory trace. First the title functioning as the exception to all that's gone before. "Yes all that's true but ..." And then the text. A movement of memory in time, the diminution of pain, "i miss you / i like you / i think of you / but," the emotions losing focus, becoming less & less distinct, moving to the final "but," the dismissal of what's gone before as one way of handling the pain, a stepping into the nothing & embracing it out of a desire to escape or, the nothingness that waits at the end of any playing down of feeling.

AS THE LETTER K TAKES ONE STEP BACK INTO OBLIVION

K now. As we dismiss knowledge we end up standing on the now ledge, placed squarely in the present, outside of memory. The movement here is from the "but" of the earlier poem to the "k now," a move out of missing, a longing for the past, into the present. But it is an absolute present in which there is no room for knowing, only for reacting, possibly even in the sense of re-acting (prefacing the intent of the second half of this collection — the re-collection). It is also a move into lettrism, a fractioning of the word which takes the letter, the writer & the reader "one step back into oblivion," that place is lived on the edge of all the time. Words & worlds. Both are impermanent.

THE DAY MISTER JONES REALIZED HE LEFT HIS SLIPPERS ON THE WRONG SIDE OF THE BED

A gestural drama in six movements, each like the frame in an absurdist film, the first gesture finding its opposite but equivalent gesture in the last, the second in the fifth, the third in the fourth. For Basmajian punctuation takes on a processual &/or gestural definiteness that words never can. The incident itself is minor, everyday & absurd. A man is thrown off because he cannot find his slippers, does not know where to find them. We trace their search & discovery. We do not see him, nor do we hear what he says to himself, we are aware only of his two conflicting emotions, amazement & puzzlement, & even there we're aware of a shift in tone. The first "!" does not mean the same as the last "!" & so on. Memory does not always function as it should. Here too the first word (words?) in the title are crossed out. Something is not explained, is not clear. The "?", the puzzlement, leads us on into the next text.

"LUCKY" SEVEN — riddle

"Lucky" in quotation marks signifying irony. There is nothing "lucky" about it or he is quoting someone else & doesn't necessarily believe it. A sense of starting over since what actually happens is that each of the first seven letters in the alphabet (a to g) are given their numerical place value (1 to 7). Superstition since if seven (g) is "lucky" then what about h, the last letter he writes down? He gives it no numerical equivalent & in fact stops there. H. 8. Also the infinity sign if turned on its side. One away from

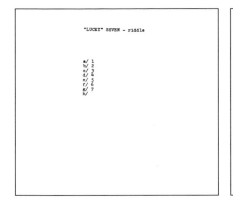

the i, the self of the poet. Infinity which is another name for the unsayable, for the void in another sense. The riddle is for the poet to solve, not for us. He is at the k, on the brink of oblivion. He has moved thru the gestural attempt to reassert even the simplest knowing & is now starting over again, hung up at h, puzzling the next step & where it takes him.

TODAY A POEM …

Shift gears. The "poem" as the "i" personified. Personalist. A step away from oblivion into a total identification with the poem. Poem / poet too as a shifting signifier of which the author is only one of the signifieds. The whole of this in dismissable journalistic tones. Sensationalism when it is sensation itself that is searched for. Like a news broadcast in an empty room where the poet sits creating texts on nothing. This "poem" then is not the poem but a poem coming in as an intrusion from outside, another sensibility placed between the "'Lucky' Seven — riddle" and

SOMETHING RUNNING UP YOUR NOSE

Thirty dots or periods. An elision. A continuation, perhaps, of the dots that follow "Today a Poem …" Thirty points of stillness, 30 periods in time. Intrusion. The something coming into focus again from the void. A something that is never clear. But the something of the title moves up and the text moves across. The title then referring to an event separate from the poem. The poem not a simplistic graphing of the title but in tension with it.

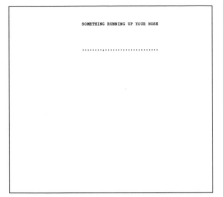

Take it then as two separate events occurring simultaneously. The "something" passes from the text into the title, out of the void of the page into the reader's ("your") world. An absurd moment. The bird of paradise. Hickory-dickory-dock. And below it the text floats. Thirty precise instances in time that begin with the S of "Something" & end with the E of "NOSE." Except for one thing. In the ninth position, where the i should float, a possible comma, blurred & indistinct, as shifting & impermanent as anything else in the world Basmajian charts &, further down on the page, a mark, a something which is nothing at the same time, a seemingly random & imprecise scratch, catches the eye & leads it on to the next page, the next text.

THE POEM — "FIVE YEARS ALWAYS TOO LATE AND TEN YEARS ALWAYS TOO SOON"

Out of the hesitancies, the jerky stops & starts that have preceded it, the despair of saying in an impermanent world where even the words shift, out of the final scratch of the text before, so tentative that even what had seemed the more fixable gestural language of punctuation had been thrown aside, out of all this Basmajian starts again, focusing in not on the universal POEM or the general A POEM but on the specific THE POEM, lamenting even as he does so that it seems too late to do it or perhaps too early to begin. He fixes himself in the flux, at the crux of his hesitation & proceeds anyway. THE POEM because there is a content, a specific set of words, he is attempting to say.

The first page of this four page text prepares us for what is to come. A darker black text

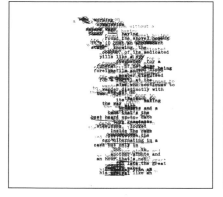 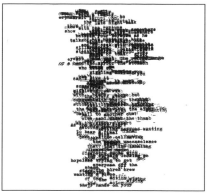

floats above a lighter one, so light it is at times almost imperceptible. The darker text comes out of the lighter one, appears at first to be simply a darker duplicate of it, but as we read it, as we struggle, literally, to understand it, we realize some of the words are left behind in the lighter text. Words are repeated, sometimes once, sometimes twice, sometimes in both the light & the dark text, sometimes only in the light text, but repeated, like the old trick of writing with two pens at once, you read the history of a double intention. Some words get crossed out, usually those in the lighter text. Sometimes the words that are crossed out in the lighter text re-appear in the darker one. The effect is of watching all the hesitancies, the imperfections, the stops & starts, being caught as in a still photograph, a picture of the impermanent world, but one, too, that operates like Alice's looking glass, inviting you in to cross out words you don't approve of. We are looking at a final draft that is not a final draft, that never achieves that neat safe look of permanence but instead floats there, shifting & changing before our eyes. For here the yellowed page (yellow as aged paper is) functions as a level of content, as the void out of which the words, the thots, float, coming together into meanings without ever really congealing. As you turn the pages the process accelerates. Darker texts are laid on top of darker texts till by the fourth page the words are almost unintelligible, the layering having become so thick. The crossing out of mistaken words, of false starts, increases in intensity too, moving from a single line drawn thru a word, to a more frenetic scribbling &, finally, an almost completely obliterated word or words.

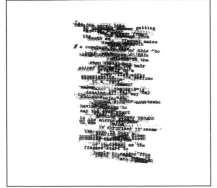 

These physical actions are the content. Within the text Basmajian declares the futility of speaking, of singing in the world: "the lung can get so corny" & later "words that already know him better than any song he's sung." Nonetheless he is trying "no matter how hopeless," for "the heart is still itching still trying to get a final shot." The poem meanders thru various scenarios, guises the figure in the poem assumes, always conscious, it seems, of an audience he, & everyone, is playing to. As the inability to communicate grows the paranoia increases. The drama itself takes over, "the curtain looking so / hopeless trying to get / everyone off the / stage." The poem pushes forward, "having nothing to / say the eyes start / getting closer caught / in the mirror everyone / being / surprised it seems / the nose is busy / staring like a clown / pounding the rhythm / of the drums as the / fingers start to / juggle to escape from / the one who (pushes them?) on."

It is unclear what the "one," the writer, does with his (their?) fingers. Most obviously the fingers have revolted, obliterating almost completely the third & second last words in the text. Impermanence even in the body then. The eyes, nose & fingers going their own way, despite or because of, it doesn't matter, the writer. The text obliterating itself. Not content to be simply content in a passive way, more solid really than the one who tried to spawn it. The gesture more permanent than the gesturer/jester/clown.

"… LATER ON"

The final obliterated word (words?) of "The Poem" — leads on into this text where the obliterations outnumber the words 12 to 6. The words that are there in each case occur twice, one overlapping the other. Below the text a line scrawls like two huge run-on S's, the scrawl itself fading & reappearing as if it looped in & out of the void it cannot describe.

The title with its three dots (…) echoes the end of the earlier title "Today a Poem …," while the visual appearance of the text, its position in the collection, suggest it as a continuation of "The Poem." But why the quotation marks? Who is it speaks or is quoted? Is it that the text is finally quoting the writer? "… Later On" the writer tried again "sitting on" "while" "stays" "looking (   ) at," the final scrawl signifying the loss even of intent.

MY LOVE SONG

What is left? Out of the almost unbearable struggle to articulate what is left? Basmajian abandons the attempt to stay in the present & returns to an earlier time (1968) when he spoke with more surety. This is only the second dated poem in this first part & its placement, the fact that it is the earliest of the dated pieces, weights its significance. He has come full circle. "for you / i could write / a million poems / to show my love." Remember he has already declared "My Love Song" is what he is singing. "but i won't" he says. The silence then is his say. He has tried to speak out of it & failed. He is left only with the earlier realization,

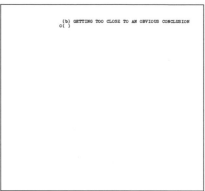

forced to quote himself because he cannot unquote, cannot articulate the present moment.

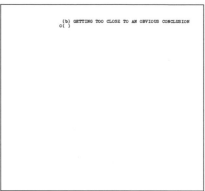

CONTEXTS TWO

Impermanence & negation. The record of the struggle to articulate. A focusing in on error, on the starts & stops along the road to speaking, to finally putting into words *POEM, A POEM, THE POEM, MY LOVE SONG*. There is then a kind of triumph, the staking of a claim, the ability to say that "this struggle, this voice that struggles in the silences, in the void, these words, that never do achieve permanence, they are, nonetheless, my love song." At the end of the first half of "Quote Unquote" Basmajian has claimed all these experiences as his. Error is his life. Process, which includes error, includes the unsayable, is his life. He makes a leap of faith. He begins, at this point, an examination of memory. If he cannot "Unquote" then what is the "Quote"?

The title of part two is "1/ Re-collection/old poems (1963-1972)": "1" because he is going back to the first beginnings, 1963, the pieces that preceded the first half of this book. "Re-collection" because it is not simply a collection of them as they were then but rather as they occur in memory, are recollected. "old poems" to emphasize that they are of the world of memory, not of his present life.

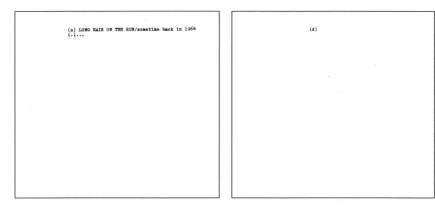

Texts: Two

(a) OUT OF LINE

This is the first of eight texts lettered a to h. The lettering of the series echoes the "'Lucky' Seven — riddle" of the first half. Only two of the texts are dated — this one (1969) & the third one. Within the series only two words occur — the word "line" in this text & the word "mind" in the h text.

In "Out of Line" we encounter the word "line" floating above a line of run-on "lines," floating above an empty space in that line it does not quite fit into (three spaces where it needs four). The third line of the poem is the word "line" once again floating above a line of run-on "lines" & this time room is made for the floating word (four spaces) but at the expense of an e in the last "line" in the line, forcing the e to the front of the fifth line where it sits one place further to the left than the lines above so as not to spoil their vertical alignment. The same problem at the end of the fifth line forces the same action at the start of the sixth line with the carried e's beginning to form their own vertical alignment. But within the sixth line the words begin to move, the e of each "line" being overlapped by the l of the "line" following it. Even with this, even tho there are more "line"s in the sixth line (17 as opposed to 13), there is still not enough room in the 51 character line Basmajian has allowed himself to include the final e & it is carried to become the complete seventh line of the poem, aligning with the e's above it.

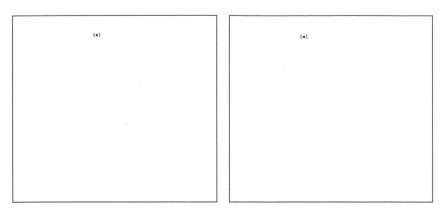

Beginning then with "line" & purely with line. A line of poetry. & the question being "out of line comes what?" Basmajian is obsessed with what is out of line, does not fit in, is not fitting in because of limitations we put on the poem (in this case the 51 character line — a wholly arbitrary measure). He is re-collecting all the lines he has written, placing them into one poem, the year 1969, taking what is out of line as what can grow out of line. Seeing that these "errors" form alignments of their own.

(b) GETTING TOO CLOSE TO AN OBVIOUS CONCLUSION

The re-collection moves forward. Basmajian totters on the brink of an obvious conclusion, i.e. "i have nothing to say."

Below the b of the title the parentheses are repeated but this time they enclose nothing. To the immediate left of the parentheses an O sits. The zero, the nothing, is not yet an aside, tho the aside (the parentheses) truly enclose nothing. He is saying the nothing but fears that even that may ultimately become an aside, that the nothing that is unsayable will come forward & overwhelm even these minimal & impermanent perceptions of nothing that are his, that the he, the being that perceives & records the no thing, will be swept aside by the nothing.

(c) LONG HAIR ON THE RUN/sometime back in 1964

The re-collections shift. Basmajian's mind casts back to 1964. "Long Hair on the Run" is ambiguous as a title referencing

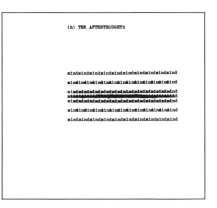

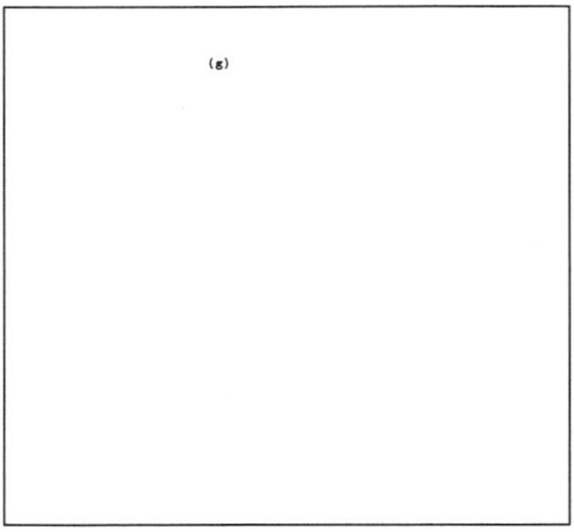

(g)

(h) THE AFTERTHOUGHTS

mindmindmindmindmindmindmindmindmind
mindmindmindmindmindmindmindmindmind
mindmindmindmindmindmindmindmindmind
mindmindmindmindmindmindmindmindmind
mindmindmindmindmindmindmindmindmind
mindmindmindmindmindmindmindmindmind

either someone he knew or saw or a self-ironic reflective sensibility. The text picks up on & expands two earlier themes. Once
again the parentheses surrounding the letter (c) are repeated
immediately below it. Three dots are almost enclosed by the
parentheses. In fact they pass thru the centres of the first & third
dots. The three dots are part of an evenly spaced series of six dots,
three enclosed by parentheses & three not. c is the three. Its count
or number is repeated then below its alphabetic representation.

(c)

(.)

But here we see the parentheses do not enclose. They intersect.
And in that intersection they echo the original (?) titling "Quote
(and) Unquote" where the middle dot becomes the deleted
"and" & the (stands for the "Quote" & the) the "Unquote."
Basmajian points to or suggests then that the letters themselves
become an aside, are part of, or can become part of, an unnecessary categorization, are merely what we choose to focus on or
thru. He underlines this beautifully by repeating the three dots
immediately afterwards but without the parentheses. The parentheses, the "Quote Unquote," as an eye then, Basmajian's eye & i,
imaged in the (.) formation, fixing in transit, ON THE RUN, on
the transient, floating world.

By this very focus he refocuses our
reading of the three dot formations of the earlier "Today a Poem
…," "Something Running Up Your Nose" and "… Later on." The
30 dot sequence of "Something" (10 x 3) enclosed by the three
that end "Today a Poem …" & the three that begin "… Later

on." Levels within levels.

     … to be read as (or (&

     … to be read as) or)

All is one & all is nothing. ( ) enclose nothing and 0 is still something. He goes on.

(d), (e), (f) & (g)

The next four texts appear the same — blank pages lettered to form part of the larger sequence. In a strictly phenomenological sense they are, of course, completely different. The nothing of (d) is different from the nothing of (e) is different from the nothing of (f) is different from the nothing of (g). Basmajian moves to an increasingly subtle examination of the void. From instant to instant the mind perceives differences. The absence of content, of any meaning whatsoever, still does not stop the awareness that from instant to instant everything is still changing. Even the nothing changes. And it is this basic awareness, the central one in "Quote Unquote," that allows hope. All is process. Everything, including the nothing, is in flux. Within the void the perceiving mind, as he goes on to show, continues to operate. The letters, operating, as we have already seen, as ANDs, achieve a dual function of sequential categorization & shifting signifier/signified sign /objects.

     d is AND

     e is AND

     f is AND

     g is AND

is d

But AND

	is e	is	many things
	is f	is	one thing
	is f	is	on thing

&.&.&.&

(h) THE AFTERTHOUGHTS

All the lines, the dots (a line is a sequence of dots), meet finally in the mind. One letter forward at the beginning (i to m) & one letter back at the end (e to d). Within the "mind" the *i*. M in d. L in e. *i* in both of them. And the movement of the *i* here is significant. 10 in the first & last line. 13 in the second & sixth. 19 in the third & fifth. 28 in the fourth. An increase & decrease in *i* (i's) based on a pattern of threes: 3, 6, 9, 9, 6, 3. Three evenly spaced lines before the crossed out middle line. Three evenly spaced lines afterwards, after words, after thoughts. Quote and Unquote. The mind is both the container & the contained. The *i* increases the closer you move to thot, to words, to "and," to all the confusions & struggles we have already discussed & the increase is the "and," the move towards categorization. But the *i* is there even at the edges, even, as we have seen, in the void. Not the *i* of Narcissus, but the *i* of being. *i* which follows *h*, comes after thought. *h* which is the breath of "The Sailor & the Stars," comes from the body, which is the conclusion drawn from this sequence & the answer to the "'Lucky' Seven — riddle." (h). The mind & the body (breath) together. A solution of a kind.

THE RAILROAD STATION

All the lines, the dots, meet finally in the mind, the lines of movement in "The Railroad Station." 18 dots stopped by an exclamation mark followed by another dot. The end of one line but the beginning of another. Things are stationary but carry within them the potential of movement. He is following a train of thought & the (!) references us back to the preceding sequence, carries within it the underlining of the recognition, the solution he arrived at to the problems posed in part one of the book. & then the new dot. Identical & not identical. A new movement in the void.

QUOTE,,*UNQUOTE*

The poet as an accumulation of quotes, of things he has heard. In the long title piece (eight closely typed pages) Basmajian attempts the ultimate "Unquote," an emptying out of all the "Quotes" that still enclose him, fill him with a void of things, phrase objects, sayings that are not his sayings, things which are nothing & blot out the nothing that is a thing, a thing he has come to terms with.

At the top of the first page an O. An emptied period? as a period could be a full O? The O of speech, of surprise? The O that is a sign of despair? The O of hope? I would say it is all these things & is, as well, as we have come to see, the zero, the nothing which is a thing. And Basmajian proceeds to remove it almost every time it appears in the eight pages that follow, to remove it from the chain of cliché, of sloppy imprecise usage he has been

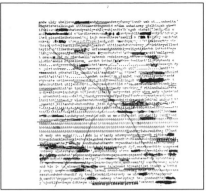

inundated with & is now emptying out. Voices mock him:

"watch your language"

"who do you think you are"

"if you ask me i think it's stupid"

         & in the eight pages that follow the only word he manages to slip into the conversation boiling around him is the word "and" that separates/joins the quotes. But it is not really his voice but rather the marking of time, the taking of a breath &, as we read thru we realize, delays the "Unquote," prevents the resolution of his dilemma by literally inviting other voices to have their say. "And" then as equivalent to, for Basmajian, the passive mind that accepts things which are nothings, avoiding a confrontation with the nothing that is a thing. And here we see clearly the full meaning of his crossing out the "and" in the title. Here we see, in fact, that the scribbling out, the gesture, was part of the title because the content of "*quote,,unquote*" that is Basmajian's is the gestural content: the crossed out lines, scribbled out words, crossed & scribbled out pages. Error, as we said in the beginning, is what we will be dealing with. And error, as we have come to see, is what it's all about. Self as error, as error in the sense of what succeeds in happening despite the strictures set down, the voices nattering at Basmajian, those things that don't fit into the scheme of things. Error is the self, is, in this case, Basmajian, and at the end of "*quote,, unquote*" he has unquoted himself, birthed himself, precisely thru the use of scribbling, crossing out, thru the assertion of what looks like, at first glance, sloppiness, the possibility of the self emerges.

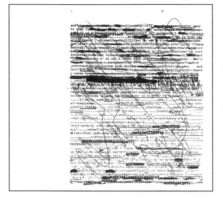 

SHE PUT IT ON

At the end of part two, the end of the book, he returns to the love songs that move through & ended part one. A new sense of the self, a new possibility, has emerged, the sense that it can be acquired, learned, as one acquires any skill, & is, in fact, an accumulation of skills. Basmajian looks out in surprise at the world & at the women/woman he has loved. "She Put It On." Not necessarily in the sense of phony, tho that is alluded to, but rather in the sense that she acquired it thru such & such an experience and then wore it. "she put on a smile." And by extension: if she can, he can. The possibility then, a glimpse of a future happiness, pointed to thru a reclaiming of cliché, a reclaiming of a negative expression as a positive one even as Basmajian has had to work his way thru the negative expressions which flooded him in "*quote,,* un*quote*" to a point where he can say, "I put it on, I put on a smile," & mean it. A point where Basmajian will begin to wear the self.

CONTEXTS THREE

The structure of "Quote Unquote" is a map of a mind in its struggle to define, to believe in, its own existence. Thru minimal gestures, literal physical acts upon the page, Basmajian succeeds in throwing off the "Quotes" that bound him & is "Unquoted," birthed into self into the world.

This reading is particular, is my reading of the texts, but is bodied out for anyone to see. The nuance & content of the texts lie not simply in the words but in the physical acts upon the page, the gestures of the writer, & making obvious the content of the gestures as they occur.

OLD NUN PUBLICATIONS
129 SEATON STREET, TORONTO 2, ONTARIO

A Conversation with Fred Wah and Pauline Butling

1977, 1978

bp: Well why don't we start right off with the Coleridge quote?

Not the qualities merely, but the root of the qualities is transcreated. How else could it be a birth, — a creation?

You use that term "transcreation," as opposed to the term "translation," which is an interesting distinction.

Fred: Yeah, and transliteration.

bp: Right.

Fred: And any other trans that I could ...

Pauline: Substantiation.

Fred: (laughs)

bp: Transsubstantiation — absolutely.

Fred: And the quote, the quote comes after the book was done. Partway through the book I was asked to qualify what it was, what's going on here? Are these translations? Are these representations of the pictures? Are these transcriptions of any kind? That is, are you following some dictionary of signs and symbols that is provided to you somewhere? And they weren't. I think that word "transcreation" came out of a friend who had suggested it or else I was looking through the *OED*.

Pauline: No, I thought you took it right out of Coleridge.

Fred: I forget exactly how it came out but I seem to remember that I went to the *OED* for some trans word, trying to find some word that would click with trans.

bp: Of course there's always that root meaning of translation — carried into heaven without death. That's sort of nice too. In a religious sense, when we say translation, it means translated into heaven, you're carried into heaven without death.

Pauline: Like a direct ...

bp: That's right. You just lift it off the earth. It's still alive.

Fred: Where did you get that?

bp: I think that's in the *OED*.

Fred: (laughs)

bp: God knows we've all overused it in the 20th century, but it's there. You're obviously arguing against the word translation though. I'm wondering what the actual argument is.

Fred: Oh, it isn't an argument against translation.

bp: But it didn't seem appropriate somehow.

Fred: No, translation isn't appropriate for the process that's going on here in my view. In a particular time I had set out to actually translate some Interior Salish texts with the simple idea that surely the natives who lived here, in the 17th, 18th, 19th centuries, would have had some texts, and that Franz Boaz, James Teit, and other anthropologists would have collected these texts. And I fully expected them to be there in the Provincial Museum, or some obscure source, and they weren't. In the meantime I had been looking at John Corner's book, *Pictographs (Indian Rock Paintings) in the Interior of British Columbia*, which he had published on his own. It's a hobby of his. He does it on weekends and holidays. He collects rock paintings, takes pictures of them and does drawings of them, describes the sites ...

Pauline: Very carefully.

Fred: Yeah, very, very carefully.

Pauline: He did the rubbings.

Fred: And I was looking at things like this

— a figure using red, a kind of rust brown ink on white paper, and there was this lovely sense of a very clear graphic, graphicness, going on. So I knew of John's stuff before I knew there weren't any Lake Salish texts. And then I said, "OK! That's all there are." I mean if there aren't any Lake Salish texts, if no one collected them, I can't really translate them, I can't really learn the language or find out what the language is and sit down and do some translations. This is what I have to work with. So then I thought, well, of course, the anthropologists would have collected some transcriptions of the rock paintings. That is to say they would have found out that this meant a certain kind of shaman figure at a certain time of ceremony involving an animal configuration with a kind of performance, that something was going on there that would have been collected by someone at some point. Well no. It turns out that James Teit had collected some very obvious things like bear prints, mountains, river, fish, obvious graphic images. So I didn't have any material there. Yet I was very attracted to these. The first ones were very, very small, like the "turtle canoe baby portage" kind of thing,

where I was simply being attracted to an image, to John Corner's representation of it. When you look at the rock paintings themselves the colours are hazy and it's important to realize I'm not responding to rock paintings, I'm responding to John Corner's drawings from rock paintings, which were these rust-red things.

bp: This line's particularly interesting because it seems to me you've got a visual parallel in the structure you end up with. You've got the pictograph figured.

Fred: In the pictograph itself are two figures in a panel. Now I can't remember if this is a particular panel because I would often find myself in a large panel with lots of figures and I would select, I would find myself focusing in on certain parts of the panel and selecting out of it particular figures. But I think this particular one is, as I recall, one whole panel. So there are two figures. This happens in several other instances where there seems to be an inside and an outside. Two anyway. Syntactically this forced me to set up a turtle canoe, literally, imagistically, and a baby portage. Period. And then get away from that as fast as I could because when I stop to think about it something else is going to happen and I want to stop at that point, i.e. this isn't a meditative process, or a contemplative one, it's very much a time thing.

bp: What comes to you at that moment. It's interesting because in this particular piece I read across — "turtle, baby, canoe, portage" — it allows you that. In fact in the way the final poem works out it allows you a lot of avenues in and out.

Fred: That's intentional. When I read it I read — "turtle, canoe, baby, portage." In the only concrete poem I've ever written,

      nv s ble
    tr ck

which is the hardest poem in the book — took a long time, my daughters helped me — the letters, the phonology, breaks up nearly in the same way the pictograph itself breaks up which was very satisfying image-wise. But it was also satisfying because it satisfied the content. That's been the frustration — every time you write a concrete poem you're satisfying a certain number of levels: content or sound or sight — the play back and forth of those elements.

bp: OK, there you are with a situation where there's literally no language system per se that you can tie into, but what the person, the writer, of the particular text, the particular pictograph, has done is to image right onto the rock. So that means you've got to bring an entirely different writerly process to it. I read it and the term translation is simply not applicable. This seems more like Duncan's "A Poem Beginning with a Line by Pindar" where you have a line, a text, an image from which you proceed. Different obviously but like those series of poems that some writers have done based on paintings. But on the other hand, you seem to have brought a different application to it. Once again there is some translative activity going on.

Fred: Yeah, I allow the pictographs their graphic possibility. I allow that. I want to allow everything present between myself and the pictograph to occur and not necessarily for it all to occur in every instance but that it's all possible — that if I was bound to translation, I would be bound to transcription in this case, and a transcription of pictographs is impossible here because the natives themselves disavowed any knowledge or information other than the fact they said they were here when they got here, which couldn't be true. I mean the paintings would not have lasted that long. These paintings would have had to be done in the last 150 years. So I wanted to pay attention to all possible aspects of the "trans" quality, the "trans" aspect of transcreation, transliteration, transcription, trans anything. That is, I was involved in a process in which something was coming over to me, I was a mediator for it, and the Coleridge quote comes in as an afterthought, or partway through it, as being a reasonable explanation or a qualification like hopefully that it's Coleridge ... how can you argue with Coleridge? And also Doris Cowan in her review, she gets on that, that those are rock paintings done by Indians a long time ago and those are themselves. That is a whole imagistic cultural thing. At the same time, I can acknowledge that I'm there, or I'm here, or John Corner is here, although he himself doesn't enter as a figure in this book, and that is disappointing, as McCaffery pointed out, and rightfully so, bringing that to me. In fact there is more of this book that is coming. There's a lot that's left out.

bp: You've continued to work on the series then?

Fred: Yeah, I continue to come back to the process and the series and other images in it. Like this one:

How does the jazz go?
Autumn moon a bit drunk
in the tree-tops with Wind
(north) & Pacific cloud banks

about 1959 not quite
jamming it but from here
to the coast one big
triple high C and wetter
than a duck's ass just
a sliver of a harvest moon.

bp: Sounds like an improvisation.

Fred: Yeah.

bp: You've got the basic structure in the image and you've improvised around it.

Fred: If you look at the pictograph,

you can see a sliver of a harvest moon, several harvest moons in
fact, but you can't see jazz. But of course you can see autumn. All
of a sudden there's a story being told. So story, i.e. my life, is also
part of what's being transcreated. Or anyone's life. So a certain
segment of my own life comes in as story, as an addendum to
something else said sometime. I mean it's not that I'm not interested in the particulars of that statement …

Pauline: Well, don't you let that become a dynamic thing for you
instead of feeling that you have to … sometimes you do take
them one by one but more often you enter that with a dynamic
situation and come out of it with this. So it's not like this to this.
You've got to enter in there and let something happen before …

bp: Yeah, with this particular text there's an obvious interpenetra-
tion of the two things, it's obviously, as you say, not a sort of one
to one — it's actually a flow back and forth between the two. It
almost goes alternate line for line, almost, not quite, but there's
that feeling of going one to the other in the line structure.

Fred: McCaffery really hit on a very important semiological aspect in this process which is what finally rides over top of it all. Does he call it "semiotic"? I'm not sure.

bp: Yeah.

Fred: But the level of meaning at the moment of writing is the important thing. And wherever it's coming from. One could as easily be throwing the *I Ching*, in a way, or putting your finger on the *Kenkyusha* dictionary and saying this is what's happening right now.

bp: Here, though, clearly you've set up a specific occasion. As you describe the very conscious search for materials — really, it began out of an idea. It's interesting in that particular poem not only are you going really to a preverbal writing state where you have direct imaging going on in the pictographs but you're also talking about pre-*Tish* days. So we get that sort of historical make-up which is interesting. One tripping off the other.

Pauline: I missed that. How did the pre-*Tish* days get in there?

Fred: It's 1959.

Pauline: Oh, in the poem.

bp: In the poem itself.

Pauline: The duck's ass. (laughs)

Fred: Did you ever do that?

bp: Wear my hair like that? No. My brother did. The whole bit.

Fred: I came out of here, out of Nelson, playing in a jazz band, down in Vancouver in 1958, 1959, wearing a duck's ass and drapes and wanting to play trumpet triple high C which was the ultimate.

bp: Maynard Ferguson time. Well, I know personally what's interesting for me about these things is, in essence, the pictographic element of the alphabet. Well, I mean, it's not quite true, but in Book IV of *The Martyrology* what I did do was just start to look at the words and say, "Oh wow, I'm reading things into it, I know I'm reading into it," but when you're doing it you're quite convinced you're taking it out of the thing; at the moment of writing it's just a very pure moment of seeing, "wow," you know.

Fred: Reading into something, do you feel bad about that?

Pauline: No.

bp: Oh no, quite excited.

Fred: Yeah, it's exciting, the process, but at the same time it's something that others are qualifying as "Oh, he's reading into it, he's putting into it something that isn't there," and that's the resistance I had here with these pictographs — was that I didn't want to be the one who was putting into it, into the pictographs, except that I was. Of course! That's part of it! How could it not be? I'm active too. I'm not just simply standing back, as in a travelogue, commenting on these pictographs, rock paintings, "I was there on these rocks." It's not that easy. You can't stand back from it.

Pauline: What about these dramatic ones? The more dramatic ones?

> I walked into a battle
> with the forest
> I tried on the buffalo-horn headdress
> things happened to me
> visions and pictures
> two or three signs
>
> I pushed one way
> and I pushed another way
>
> size gave dance to me
> the deer showed me form
>
> the larval, it
> opens up.

Fred: Oh, that's fun, that just gets to be ...

Pauline: But when you say "I" there, is that a figure in here?

Fred: Yep, that's a figure there in the pictograph, but it's also, the figure becomes me.

Pauline: Or you become the figure.

Fred: It's a drama. I walked into a battle with the forest.

Pauline: Starting here?

Fred: No, starting here (upper left of pictograph) in this one. Now that's interesting too. The direction on a planar level. In this particular one, I don't know why it starts here. "I walked into a battle with the forest," "Oh where's the forest … is this the forest? I think this must be the forest. Maybe that's the forest … those three dots," "I tried on the buffalo-horn headdress, things happened to me, visions and pictures, two or three signs, I pushed one way, I pushed another way," this is the larval, this figure, that's a lovely centipede, somehow that becomes larval, it opens up. It's a selective process so it has to be a trans process. In other words it's not a totally given thing and I think any trans process, it seems to me, is a selective one.

In terms of this, I was interested in what Zukofsky had proposed apropos Catullus and translating Catullus. I was also very interested in Pound's proposition that translation at least could be a translation from any one mode to any other mode. Bunting was very helpful at a point prior to this in explaining possible transes. Trans is something that goes on. A trans to me has become a poetic process. Trans for me has become something that I have now, I can now do. I now feel comfortable going out to something existing between it and the language or having a language happen between I and it that leads to other things. Like calling it transcreation is — that's Coleridge's term ...

bp: A pretty useful term, I think.

Fred: Yeah, it works and I wanted to lead away, I had to lead away from translation. I knew that was going to be a problem in explaining anything to anyone.

bp: Right, particularly the poems about 1959 in Vancouver.

Fred: Yeah, also justifying the fact that I was supposed to be on my sabbatical, supposed to be doing these translations of Interior Salish texts.

Pauline: Some of these are supposed to be puberty rights and 1959 in Vancouver is being close to puberty rights. (laughter)

bp: Well there's also Stein's sense of translation in something like "Before the Flowers of Friendship Faded Friendship Faded." She took George Hugnet's poem, started off to do a translation, but just used it as a poetic departure and hence lost her friendship which is where the title came from.

Pauline: But you're not exactly using these as a point of departure.

bp: Well it's a more contained thing.

Fred: Yeah, they are contained but it is a form of departure.

Pauline: Yeah, but a departure that works within.

bp: That's right, it comes back and finishes within the actual event.

Pauline: Yes.

Fred: Well that jazz, 1959, is the most departed piece in the pieces. It's a real take-off. But some of them are very literal translations; that is I've taken James Teit's interpretations of the pictographs that he published, that John Corner publishes in his book, I literally take those. For example the headdress things in here are straight from Teit. You can look it up. You can say, "Gee I wonder what that is and I wonder if Teit found out what that is." Something like that, you see, that Teit tabulated as a headdress,

it doesn't even get into the poem, I call it "the feathers of my mind," I personalize it, I say I'm there.

> The feathers of my mind increase
> as I reach for the choices
> chance for what else
> other than what I knew (know)
> another talks to me (I think)
> something (things) to see

So it does go all the way from literal translation to literal creation. A lot of drama, Dwight Gardiner pointed out to me, that I hadn't noticed. A lot of direct kind of talk.

Pauline: It's not so much direct talk …

Fred: Well, I mean direct placing.

Pauline: It eliminates you and the pictograph and produces something else. Like there's not a subject and an object.

Fred: But there's more of I, you, he, she, it, in these poems for me than there has ever been.

Pauline: But the I's and you's and he's and she's and it's are part of an event that comes out of it. That's not I as you as subject.

Fred: Yeah, sure it is.

bp: It's a closed world which is literally literature.

Fred: It's dramatic.

222

bp: That's because in essence you get the play. You supply the play, because you as reader are actually going back and forth. You enter into the process and yet one's own reading is obviously still applicable, one's own seeing, so what we're getting is you writing your seeing. What we get is a writing of your seeing, and to a degree there is accurate transmission, and to a degree there is what it trips off in you but it completes itself within the two-page opening format that you use, right?

Fred: Yes, but you must understand this, for example, this one:

Northeast
(from family, a few friends)
I turned
since I had accompanied my father
that far
what was in the world around here
became larger

some part of it
then all of it

Now that enters into the body of writing that I'm working on (*Breathin' My Name with a Sigh* (Coach House Press Manuscript Editions, 1978)). The father, family, the father overlaps and if I had the kind of momentum that you do in your writing I might be able to realize these things coming together.

bp: Well, this seems to me very much a piece with the whole of your work because all of your work seems to grow out of that very strong sense of place; even when you've moved away from here for a long time, it's still lardeau, mountain, it wasn't exactly … you know, "Oh those Buffalo nights! *Freaked Out in Buffalo* by Fred Wah." (laughter) I don't know anyone else who has such a strong sense of place — period. When George Bowering went to Alberta he wrote Alberta poems and you have a whole tradition of Canadian poets who go to places and start to write out of that.

Pauline: Yeah, Purdy went to the Arctic and wrote his Arctic poems.

bp: Now part of that is just the whole thing of being Canadian and going back and forth and back and forth. For you, there's a very deep sense of place, I mean, you notice it throughout your entire work.

Fred: Yeah, I'm stuck with it.

bp: It doesn't strike me as a stuckness, it strikes me as a richness, a particular type of richness. I mean it seems to be what obsesses you and you're stuck with it in that sense. (laughter) It's definitely the centre of your concerns.

Fred: Yes, I could go to the Arctic and …

Pauline: And write poems about Kootenay.

bp: That's right, "Look at the Columbia — I mean MacKenzie." (laughter)

Pauline: "Oh Columbia, where are you?" (laughter)

bp: "How I long for you now." But look, I mean you issued a little magazine like *Scree* and then there was that anthology you edited of poetry from the interior of BC.

Pauline: Sent them overseas.

Fred: Yeah, probably to Czechoslovakia. Canada Council bought them all.

bp: But that's all interior BC stuff.

Fred: I'm interior. I'm really very much here. But that's too easy. I'm very much where you are too. I don't find any difficulty in hearing your language — precisely your language and somebody like Gerry Gilbert's — at all! The language seems very much at home. I don't need a referential language going on.

bp: What I'm saying is it's the content that seems to insist itself.

Fred: Yeah, subject and content.

bp: Yeah, you're taking it as a given and that's what it is.

Fred: Right! No problem with Fred Wah's subject! (laughter) It'll be somewhere! I was very attracted to, I think it was Dorn's book, either *Geography* or *North Atlantic Turbine*, I think it was *North Atlantic Turbine*, where he says on the flyleaf, "I now wish a less geographical address and hope for a more spiritual discipline" kind of thing. And true. At that point I felt "yes Dorn, you've got to get off where you are, on the earth, America, the North Atlantic, Idaho, Gloucester, it's got to be more something else." And I feel that.

Pauline: To get off the place?

Fred: Well, not to get away from it but my poems are very tight. It's not that it takes me a long time. It's not that I spend a lot of time working over and over the language. But what comes is very image-oriented and they're very short, very, ah — it doesn't run on, doesn't develop, doesn't generate other possibilities, and I'm very attracted to generating. The first poetry I wrote was basically a very generative kind of poetry, the kind of poetry you're into bp. Hearing you tonight I was just swooning, caught up again in, for me, that older experience, when you said "tingle your toes," my toes were tingling — of being able to use sounds, use language, use words, use what's happening as something that's flowing on, tidally, a wave, pushing one on. These poems are pretty tight. They don't do that. They don't bring that other sense of writing where it's a thrust or a heave — a kind of breath heave. For the longest time I felt very embarrassed at these pictograph poems because they weren't very writerly. I thought this was cheating. I thought "these are exercises." I was very attracted to Gael Turnbull's *Twenty Words, Twenty Days*, that kind of thing, but also very disappointed that he had had to say that they were exercises. At certain times one feels bereft or bankrupt or short on language, on the activity of it, the dance of it, and you need exercises. Well I hadn't really come into that. These started out partly as exercises, partly as trying to, "Well, gee, what should I do? Like I want to write but what should I do? Should I make it up? Maybe I'll write a story. Why don't I write an epic? Why aren't I writing a novel?" Or, "Let's try this. No. That's not going to work." And then as a kind of afterthought you realize, or I think a lot of writers realize, "Oh, gee I've been writing it for the last couple of months, I've been doing it, I've started, oh gee, I've started! Oh! Isn't that exciting!" And all of a sudden you're in it, you've got that body of being in it already, as you are when you find yourself in something.

Pauline: It takes a while to recognize what's happening.

bp: It's true, it does.

Fred: Like this particular poem right here, in fact, it was one of
the very first …

> Wapiti knows the way, a path
> criss-crossed with events
> within the roots of the flowers of vision
> even inside the mountain of the idea of it
> worn as horns or a headdress outside
> through the trees along the lakeshore
> and all over the mountains' sides
> over the inside and over the outside
> cover of the many, many ways Wapiti knows.

Pauline: That one circles back very deliberately. It makes it a very
closed — were you aware of circling back to close it off? It ends
and begins with the same words. How deliberate is that?

Fred: I didn't even notice that until now. I never noticed that
before.

Pauline: Well you may not have noticed it but I'm sure you were
conscious of it.

Fred: No, I wasn't conscious …

Pauline: Unconscious of it.

Fred: I was totally unconscious.

Pauline: You still did it. It must be an echo for you.

Fred: I honestly, until you pointed it out, didn't know that I'd
come back to it.

Pauline: No, you may not have noticed it but it must have come
through the echo. I'm just wondering why you would do that.

Fred: I don't know.

Pauline: Even unconsciously. Speaking of closed systems or right
systems.

Fred: I think it's rhythmic myself, because to me that's a very
rhythmic piece. When you say "repeating" — I don't think it's
repeating. I was trying to be poetic. But that was an early one.

I remember that one. In fact I think this may very well have been one of the first ones I looked at and was very attracted to as a figure because of many things. It's small. There are three figures, a mountain with trees on it, somebody inside a mountain with a headdress. If you look closely at it, the figure, or at least the way Corner has it, very, very carefully, that's that sunflower hat, and that's small, that's very small. And then there was that early 70s thing for me of being spiritually interested in North American Indian stuff too. So that must have been going on. This is the way, "the many many ways," here this is the way, so I thought, here this is the way, that was going to be a long poem hopefully. In fact, yes, that was, I think, the first poem written and this was the second:

> Here
> this is the way
> strut after strut
> the blue grouse wakens stars for us
> and stroke after stroke
> we pass through night's constellations
>
> that's just what the Osprey sees
> we say
> that's right he says
> we see we see

But you see then there's just what the Osprey seems to be saying, "that's right, he says, we see, we see."

But we have an osprey where we spend our summers, or have had, and the osprey had become a very important personal bird in July and August for me. So I don't know if that's an osprey. I'm not saying that the Indians knew that that's the osprey. I don't feel it matters.

Pauline: What's the voice?

Fred: I was searching for the middle voice. I'm searching for it.

bp: Want to explain that?

Pauline: I was just going to ask you that, if that was the middle voice.

Fred: The middle voice is something that Olson taught when I was a student of his in graduate school. He called it the passive …

Pauline: Not passive …

Fred: No. I'm just trying to think what he did call it. He gave it one of those traditional grammatical names.

Pauline: It occurs in Greek.

Fred: Yes, it occurs in Greek, the middle voice. I don't know what it is.

Pauline: We have passive and active, but we don't have middle, whatever that is. Isn't that the difference? We only have two voices — passive and active.

Fred: Except that Olson saw the middle voice as being the voice of the poet, that that was the voice the poet should seek to …

Pauline: Neither passive nor active.

Fred: Well, to be able to work in passive and active.

bp: The resolution of one type of duality then?

Pauline: Not just that duality but of the subject–object duality. In passive or active it's clear who's the subject and who's the object and the verb's in between. But somehow middle voice eliminates subject and object and it all happens there.

Fred: My sense is, as a linguist, I'm not a linguist but I've tasted linguistics, is that it has to do with tense, it has to do with time, middle voice has to do with time. My sense of searching for a middle voice has been working between a kind of gerundial, participial thing, and a pronoun. Like I could say, "I floating" rather than "I float," which is too direct. A condition …"I floating" … if I could state that. I work towards that. So I was aware of that but I was aware of that in *Earth*.

Pauline: Do you think that has to do with the transcreation process?

Fred: Well, it has to do with my writing but it doesn't have to do with moving from here. I think you apply a tactics of syntax to any picture you look at. I mean you put together a picture, any picture you look at, even a Jackson Pollock, you're going to start somewhere and go somewhere with it.

bp: Yeah, there's a narrative you create in every reading, any active seeing, unless you just stare at a glyph construction and …

Fred: Well, single figure yeah. Glyphs become very interesting to me. I was mentioning to you that book — *The Alphabet and the Ancient Calendar Signs*. It gets into Mayan glyphs. And of course I'm very very curious about the ideogram and pictograph and I don't know enough about them. I want to know more about them. OK, so it's *looking*, and the transcreation I think, for me, has been looking and then language and then the formation of language but always after looking at these things. I do owe every single one of these, although in several instances I tested them out by sending them out as poems, but McCaffery's right, it's really John Corner's book as much as it is mine.

Pauline: Does McCaffery say that or is that what you said after reading McCaffery's review, that it should have been by Fred Wah and John Corner?

bp: He just called to task the use of the term "illustration."

229

Fred: But he's right. The other sense too is that John gets these from the rock paintings and that we're involved in the process of having seen these out there. Or he's seeing them and he's made illustrations of them. He brings them to me and I say, "Wow, I'll do this with them." And by the time they get back to him or somebody who may be familiar with the rock paintings themselves … I don't know.

```
the   sum   of   "my"  knowledge
```

bp: You're not sure what's happening?

Fred: All I know is that the pages with the numbers on them are my pages and that Corner's drawings are very much attached to them, that these in this instance do come from these. The times they have been published individually there's been no problem. People haven't questioned the language as being a foreign language, something they didn't understand.

bp: No, I think it's just that when you do something like that something takes on a different meaning. If you took this as a book of isolated texts you'd find the meanings that people would derive from them would change radically. Here there's a very quick referential thing.

Fred: Like is your interest in this because you have the pictographs alongside them, or?

bp: It's hard to say.

Fred: I mean would you have been as interested in them had they been placed as simply words?

bp: That's a good question. I've never actually sat and looked at them that way. I think so. I would take it much differently though.

Its a place
humpbacked ant
a trap or map
foot/
     the *idea* of foot

a where
  a vegetable
    two lakes and trees
           (pine?)

five 6 seven nine and ten
   its a trap.

I can see a very specific reference here. "5, 6, 7, 9, 10. It's a trap." Take a poem like my "Trans-continental" in *Love: A Book of Remembrances*. That, in many ways, is a take like this except it's all moving by me and I can't fix it. It's both the letters that are running through my head and it's literally things that are coming out of the landscape, letters and numbers on markers beside the tracks.

Fred: It's certainly referential.

bp: Yeah, it's referential but the reference isn't there for anybody to see. I would find a lot of interest in this piece by itself but then there would be a whole blank here. I would not have seen the same thing. Here I see the same thing you see and that makes a big difference.

Fred: See this is the problem. This is a real problem in this trans process.

bp: In what sense?

Fred: Because Steve McCaffery has as much right to ask you for those pictures or literal places to appear as he does of me here. Because I at least give these.

Pauline: Was it in your mind to publish those with the poems at some point as you were writing?

Fred: No. Not until it became possible.

Pauline: When did you make those slides up? When did you decide to read the poems with slides?

Fred: I wanted to have slides made of these things so I could sit back and see them in the dark on a large screen because I wanted to have them blown up. I wanted the sense of a blow up. So I had black and white slides made and when I went back east I read at A Space and Vermont and my sense of it then was that I could blow up these pictures and there would be more going on because they would be bigger. I felt them as very tight. That was before the book came out.

Pauline: That was when you were still writing them because that was when we came back from Berkeley. So when you read down east did you show the slides?

Fred: Yeah. Reading at A Space I showed a series of slides and read these as I went along. That's also a technique of reading because I'm too embarrassed to stand up in front of a crowd and read in front of them so I'll put the slides in front of them and read behind them. (laughs)

bp: "The rock painting speaks!" (laughter) It's always nice having a book in your hand when you're reading for the same reason.

Fred: Then I found out that people liked looking at things. They like to be shown things. But they're really seeing the poems as illustrations of something that they are looking at! If that's true, if they really are seeing, if I show a pictograph up on the screen and then I read the poem that goes with it and they're looking at the one and hearing the other, then the process for them is quite a different process than what happened for me. It has to be if my proposition is true that it's OK for anyone to enter, but as soon as I say the poem I'm stating to them conditions and qualities that are there for them to look at and I don't think they can avoid that.

bp: Well, they can't in this setup but the original question you were asking me was, "Would these have an interest?" I'm saying,

"Yes they'd have an interest," but my referencing on them would be entirely different.

Pauline: You'd simply imagine things from your own experience.

bp: Absolutely.

Pauline: Which is what we do when we read poetry.

bp: Right. You bring your own referential thing. Because I mean there's all sorts of rhythmic things happening here.

Fred: Yeah, language things.

bp: I mean, that's a fairly tight sequence of lines, there: "a where, a vegetable, two lakes and trees, pine, 5, 6, 7, 9 and 10, it's a trap." Very live rhythm. So yes I'd be interested in it But it will be more abstract you see. Here it's not abstract. That's the interesting thing. If you just did it that way it would feel more abstract.

Fred: So when that's with you, that pictograph with that poem, it's less abstract.

bp: Fairly specific.

Fred: And yet that is more abstract than this for you, for any of us.

bp: So that makes your poem, your text, quite definite.

Fred: So, OK, we put one abstract, plus one abstract …

bp: Makes one of them definite if your abstract's based on an abstract.

Fred: It makes one of them concrete.

bp: That's right.

Pauline: Speaking of schizophrenic logic! (laughs)

Fred: Well, it seems to work.

bp: Well, if your abstract's based on an abstract then you've got specific reference — it becomes quite concrete.

Pauline: Oh that's right, two negatives make a positive, two wrongs make a right. (laughter)

bp: So who was wrong here?

some words on *the martyrology*
march 12, 1979

1979

everything is part of something else. somewhere in my 20s i became conscious of certain threads, certain themes & less specific contents that spread thru my work, thru my poetry, its concerns. i began to think of this as one long work divided (roughly) into two sections. *The Books of the Dead* & *The Books of the Living*. i saw *The Books of the Dead* as being comprised of *The Journey* (1962-63 — discarded), *JOURNEYING & the returns* (1963-66 — published CHP 1967), *The Undiscovered Country* (written 66-67 & worked at till 71 or so when i discarded it), *Scraptures* (1965 to 69 — published various sections in magazines & pamphlets) & *The Captain Poetry Poems* (1965 to 1968 — published by Blewointment 1971). the problem was i couldn't make it work. *The Journey* & *The Undiscovered Country* failed because i had not yet grasped the full principle of the *utanniki*, the poetic diary, & as a result i romanticized my experience to a disgusting degree. i temporarily abandoned this notion and began work on *The Martyrology*. along the way two other linked works appeared: *Monotones* (1967-69 — published by Talonbooks 1971) & *The Plunkett Papers* (1969-71 — discarded for the same reasons as *The Journey* et al). still i pushed aside the notion of the larger work, tho i was aware of the links, & continued working on *The Martyrology*.

the text included in this anthology — Book IV of *The Martyrology* — began after a long period of silence (approximately two years chronologically, February 73 to January 75) but much longer subjectively — & hence the Merwin quote at the beginning:

> Looking for it all over the place
> three years
> carrying it all the time like a baby

a period in which i thot *The Martyrology* had perhaps finished itself. then the line "purpose is a porpoise" came & from that strange beginning the poem itself began to unwind.

the echo, of course, was a bissett quote in "a funny name for claimed similur creaturs / one a porpoise / th othur a dolphin," a quote which reverberated for me with the similarities & differences between bill's work & my own. it began (& begins) too with a statement of my poetic goal:

> the precision of openness
> is not a vagueness
> it is an accumulation
> cumulous

thus the "Clouds" section (which follows "The Book of Common Prayer" in Book II) was re-invoked at the same time as a statement of my retroactively recognized formal model (the *utanniki*) was restated — opening the self as wide as possible while struggling for precision thru a meditational process of accumulation. since the "Clouds" section was also the one which outlined the history of the saints' migration to earth, "left the white streets of that higher town / to tumble down the long blue highway to the trees' / tops," i was led back gradually thru a pre-occupation with surface, & the depth implicit in it, to the "A / B / ginning / of the town / the saints came down from." and i was led too to draw back certain veils that had lain across my sense of language (ca. 1967 in "postcard between" — "vague // like the clouds // my language was"), precisely because i was "down at the surface where the depth is," reading words as single sentences in which messages lay. at the same time the pun's strength (auditory, as in "purpose" & "porpoise," or visual, as in "the M / the ME / the s is / a way of starting") was utilized far more than in any previous book. these accumulating energy points thrust me thru Book IV in one year, the poem being written as one long continuous take, a formal evolution from Books I, II & III and leading on into the chains of the forthcoming final book of *The Martyrology*, Book V. *The Martyrology* spans 12 years of my writing (1967 to 1979). with Book V behind me, as far as the journal

writing aspects, i found the notion of *The Books of the Dead &
Living* returning, gaining focus precisely because *The Martyrology*
seemed finished but some larger vision seemed barely begun.

what is a long poem? perhaps it is simply a long life or some
trust in the durational aspect of being alive. it's a tremendous leap
of faith to even start one, to even think "hey i'll be alive long
enough that this form seems the best way to say what i have to
say." certainly some faith in process pushes me on knowing even
as i do so that the question of audience, who precisely the poem
is intended for, is an interesting & unresolved one. as the work
continues i actually feel i may have finally begun *The Books of the
Living*, have written myself far enough to the other side of my
childhood as a writer, as a human being, out of my past, out of
the dead days into at least a present that is life & from which my
perspective, my contents, can change. this was my perception in
the mid–60s, that i would reach a point where my concerns, such
as they were, would undergo a shift, but that the books that came
before (the ones i then had yet to write) were the absolute soil
out of which those (these in this case) would come.

where do those earlier works fit? that is the question that still
troubles me. in a sense they are sub–texts to *The Martyrology*, and
as such do not so much come before it as they do lie under it. i
suppose an ideal reading would be one which begins with *The
Martyrology*, but then dips into *JOURNEYING & the returns,
Scraptures & The Captain Poetry Poems* along the way, much as one
might read earlier history to gain a better appeciation of a particular period. this is a notion only, a tentative map. i have begun a
new work, "A Counting," which continues on from Book V of
The Martyrology. the first Book of the work, "A Book of Hours,"
abandons the talk about language that so informed *The
Martyrology* & moves outward into the concepts, people & places
that have evolved in & around the writing. lines that i wrote in
the unpublished "May Day Book" in the spring of 1976 seem
appropriate to this whole struggle:

dying & being born & dying
& being born & dying & being born

Ken Norris: How did you first come to concrete? Was it your own engagement with the typewriter or were you aware of a tradition?

bp: I would say that when I very first began I came at it from Kenneth Patchen; I came at it from his drawn poems and things like *The Journal of Albion Moonlight.* I was doing, in a sense, poems in the shapes of things; this was very early crude stuff. I didn't do very much of that, but that was there. I liked that element of Patchen but I didn't know how to integrate it. Then in 65, really, I just became aware that it didn't matter what I set down, what mood I was in. I was essentially churning out the same poem, and that I could become very proficient at that poem cause that's what it was, it was a poem and had this minor variation and that variation but had a complete lack of any technical facility. There was a type of arrogance, I thought; that is to say I was coming to the occasion of the poem to force myself upon it. I was being arrogant rather than learning. So I sort of made a conscious choice to play. The very first concrete that I did was a thing called "Popular Song": it was black and red and then red and black. It was a conscious decision to play. The poem goes

WAR *BLED*

WAR BLED

Here I was. I was typing poems but I wasn't paying attention to the page. So I began to do it and I started with these things I called "ideo-pomes." They were very much that, very much based on typewriter things. In the first issue of *Ganglia* I did some pieces that are longer, say two pages, that used a lot of visual repetition as the basis of departure for what I'm talking about, or counting, listening. It's pretty early stuff, fairly *el primitivo*, but it sort of showed me the way in.

KN: At what point did you become aware of the Dadaists and the Surrealists and how important do you think they've been to you?

bp: I became aware of them through a friend of mine, Jim Alexander, probably around 63. I was into Patchen around 61 & 2 and the Dadaists around 63. I'll tell you what struck me about them; there were a number of things, really. There were hardly any examples; I had nothing that I could actually look at. The whole problem with what is known as "avant-garde" literature in the 20th century — I've made this point in a TRG report — is that it's like we're dealing with amnesia; we've got this repressed tradition so that you end up, when you start writing this way, you end up regurgitating a lot of what's already been done because you can't get your hands on the stuff. So you literally have to make your own way. In a way I made my own way, so that when I look at some stuff I can say, as some reviewers have said, "Hey that was done in Berlin in 1921"; I look at it and say "Yeah, well I guess it was done in Berlin in 1921, but this was done in Canada in 1965 without knowing what was done in Berlin in 1921." About Gertrude Stein, they would all talk about her biographically but wouldn't know how to deal with the literature, so as a result included very, very, very few examples, just the merest hint. But I was intrigued by the report of Schwitters' "W" poem, just that that was it and he read it, that blew my mind. Then in 64 I think it was, Michael McClure came up from San Francisco to Vancouver and read his "Ghost Tantras." So I heard those, which a lot of people didn't like but I thought "Hey, that's interesting!" He'd tied it to a specific beast context but I liked the fact that he was letting sound out. And bissett was working a lot with silence at that time; I went and heard him read too. It was more silence than actual chanting and sound at that time. The Dadaists for me were more of a spiritual influence, that is to say, I knew somebody had done something. I wasn't quite sure what exactly they'd done, but the sense was that if some guys could get up there and kick out the jams why shouldn't I do it? That gave me the encouragement. So it's one of those things, you start doing something and then you start to track down all the other writers you've heard rumours about who are doing it. So, in a sense, it gave me support. I didn't really have examples because you couldn't lay your hands on examples. I wasn't going to a university. I didn't have access to rare book rooms that had the material.

1979

KN: Could we start by you talking a bit about what you were trying to do in *Scraptures*?

bp: *Scraptures* was my first attempt to bust out of simply being in one mold, that is simply being a poet who did visual things or being a poet who did sound things, or a poet who did traditional poems, or ideopoems, as I called my more visually oriented poems, or whatever. So *Scraptures* was the first one in which I cross-pollinated, in essence, where I started working between forms. And it proceeded very nicely. The title came from the notion of scriptures, scraps of things, of pictures, of everything together, which became *Scraptures*. The very first one arose out of the opening of the Bible: "In the beginning was the Word and the Word was with God," redesigned on the page visually. So it's a fairly classic and literal approach to visuality, and then I began to bust out of that with the second and the third. I began to get into prose sections and I got into comic strip oriented sections, two of the sections are done as sound poems, though there are visual versions of those two as well so it lends itself to a print text. And out of that emerged the saints, in the fourth sequence I think, the saints came lurching onto the scene. The saints were born *out of* language but language had its base in that initial Christian cross type of visuality, fairly simplistic, George Herbert approach to visuality, which generates its own contents and its own directions.

KN: What was your intention in trying to merge all those different approaches to language?

bp: Because no one system is complete: it doesn't matter what system you create, it's simply one pair of glasses through which you view the world, you view reality. And because I believed that formal solutions released some contents and surpressed *other* contents. I was interested in greater hybrids; I was interested in creating alternative possibilities for myself, so that to a degree in my talking and, at that time, in my working too, I was much more concerned with the issue of form because I believed, and still believe to a degree, that if I could find a new form other contents would be released that I did not have conscious awareness of at that time, that it was an issue of finding doorways. Form was a doorway through which you let certain contents emerge. Traditional form had its powers but alternative forms had different powers and released different contents and released new realities. Through these things you got new glimpses into the nature of things, and that language has its own laws, and I was trying to discover something about those laws in terms of poetic activity.

KN: What contents did you find that the form of comics opened up?

bp: Steve and I talked a lot about this in one of the TRG reports, but partially with comic strips what you have is an alternative form of notation which is already universally accepted, which is the narrative frame in certain sequences, the frame as a narrative structure, certain visual shorthands like the v in the sky which is a bird and a circle which is the sun or the moon, the puffy line which is a cloud. You had a type of vocabulary, you had a way of combining that vocabulary that was visual; and out of my interest in — well I had a prior interest in comic strips, when I began working with concrete poetry and also became aware of what the Brazilians were doing with semiotic poetry, where they were basically using a lexical key — man=triangle, woman=circle — and then creating other combinations, and out of that you could do translations and, once again, create another reality. I realized there was an existing semiotic system which was comic strips to which you did not need a lexical key, which used sound effects, and through this you could present certain notions of reality, certain realities in themselves that you *could not present* purely through words. Later, it was through comic strips and basically in *Love: A Book of Remembrances* that I really came more to terms with what I think of as the runic potential of the alphabet, which is to say that an "a" is the signifier for an "a" which is the signified and it is itself, so that when you mark down an "a" you are not describing the name of something, you are creating something in the world. At that level of the visuality of the single letter you are creating in the very pure sense of the word, you are creating thingness. Whereas with a word, like "door," you are referring back to the world of things. The word "door" also has its thing-ness, which is its "d" its "o" its "o" and its "r" and has that double potentiality. Partly I glimpsed this through drawing circles and beginning to substitute the word "moon" for the circle. In itself, these are very simple things, which at the same time for me became an imagism of the comic strip form, in beginning to — as I felt it anyway — have much more appreciation of a certain type of depth about language, words and the alphabet that I had not been able to get through before. It led me into a lot of things, eventually into Book IV of *The Martyrology* where I'm reading words as sentences that say things about single letters. Similarly, in a different way, I used the character of Captain Poetry as a kind of comic strip type of character, a super-hero. Working on a pure content level, it was the notion of poet as super-hero. Particularly in Canadian poetry, the kind of *courier du bois* image of the poet; you go into a bar, slam your poems on the table and order a few rounds of brews for all the guys, which was an image I was never too attracted to. In *Captain Poetry* there was a lot of working with that kind of imagery and basically ridiculing it.

KN: When you were talking about the runic potential of the alphabet there seemed to be a suggestion there of how visual poetry carries over or bridges over to sound poetry.

bp: Yeah, well once again in sound poetry you're dealing with the thingness — of sound. When sound leaves your lips it enters the world of noise. We're sitting here, there's a jet going by, we can faintly hear the sound of the tires of the cars on the rain-wet pavement out there on Davenport, and out of this melange of things at the same time there are the voices talking, the telephone bell ringing, the faint hiss of the tape recorder and you are simply one element in that world of noise. Obviously a very good use of speech is words and language and what you communicate purely on that verbal level. But then there's the whole area of emotional tone, the feeling that is in your voice. So that in sound poetry you're dealing with the thingness of sound, if you release it from words and start to deal with those other contents, which is the way I've tended to work. At the same time you can work with it purely as sound phenomena in a more musical sense. What I've been more interested in is the language of non-verbal speaking. I've been interested from a language point of view, not a music point of view. I can see why our sound poetry sounds musical and has musical qualities because we bring in rhythm and all that thing, but I think of it as language, I think of it as a writing activity.

KN: Well, it seems to me that you have quite a consistent aesthetic running through your visual and your sound work.

bp: They all seem part to me of the same thing, yeah. And then again there's this desire which *Scraptures* shows, which, in a different way *The Captain Poetry Poems* showed and which *The Martyrology* definitely shows, which is this desire to bring it together again. Once you take it away, you isolate it for a while, then you bring it all back together again with a very heightened sensibility of all these things, and in that sort of explosion that happens when you bring everything back together, new contents are released and new formal possibilities are also released, are remarried if you like. I think the formal possibilities for writing or the range of craft is much more enormous in the 1970s than it's ever been in the history of writing, but the vast majority of writers absolutely ignore it, or feel it's not significant. They don't seriously treat that present possibility that modernism and the 20th century have released for poetry. What we could call the "other tradition," that includes Dada, Futurism, both the Russian and Italian schools and so on, releases whole other sets of formal possibilities. Those, to me, seem all to be part of the range of composition. So I do not denigrate the old forms but I don't think they're the only thing that exists. In pushing forward these other things people *assume* an attitude you must have against rhyme

— I use rhyme like crazy. I use rhyme more than anybody I know except I use it internally, and as a way of linking back in after singing a particularly hot chorus, I get back to the rhyme point.

KN: You and bill bissett are often spoken of almost in the same breath when people talk about sound and visual work and the two of you have been really close over the years. Do you see your work as being tightly linked with what bill does, or do you conceive of the connection as being more of a mutual support system?

bp: I have gotten a lot of inspiration from bill's work. There are similarities, even as there are similarities between mine and Steve's work. We work in the same area of concern, which includes visual poetry and sound poetry and drawn works and so on; so on that level they are linked. There are tremendous differences between how I and bill write, tremendous differences.

KN: Well, in terms of sound poetry, you both seem to share a commitment to voice.

bp: That's right. We do *poésie phonetique* as opposed to *poésie sonore*. bill on a certain level *sings* his more, although I have pieces in which I specifically use song. bill sings his work more and dances his work more than I do. The biggest difference is that he works with an ecstatic base in imagery. With him it's almost ecstatic religious experience that he's dealing with, with obvious bases in sexuality, altered consciousness and so on. I've had trance experiences while doing sound; the basis of it comes out of language orientation towards the release of new contents which, in the case of sound, includes emotional content.

KN: Perhaps what strikes me the most is that I feel that you're both religious writers.

bp: I would say yes, there is obviously religious content and religious concerns in what we're doing. This is something that is obviously there for me as early as *Scraptures*. It's a content that's emerged. It's kind of surprised me because I did not have an intensely religious upbringing, we went to church occasionally. For a long time as a teenager I thought of myself as agnostic; I believed in God but I couldn't tie my brain around any of the organized religions I stumbled into. The closest I came was

Mahayana Buddhism, and when you study it one of the things they teach you is that it's wrong for a Westerner to adopt Eastern ways, that all religions will take you to nirvana. There's obviously a religious content in my work and it's something a lot of people have found disturbing because, interestingly enough, most critics don't know what to do with religion. They either feel like they have to be converted on the spot, or something, but they don't know quite how to deal with it as a content.

KN: But, you know, the way you and bill present it is not polemical or preachy. It's essential to the work and you can't really avoid it and yet it's not really trying to convert the reader, and I think that throws people off balance.

bp: Right. I suppose it's true, I hadn't thought of this before, until we're talking about this and, who knows, my view of this may change when you leave this room. But yes, in a sense I suppose there is a background, that is to say that the landscape through which bill's poetry moves, and through which my poetry moves, is inhabited by some sort of God figure or figures as the case may be, some sort of religious backdrop which comes into and out of focus, which is not presented as something you should convert to but rather is presented as part of a reality in which we are interacting, sometimes to our own stunned surprise. That's more the way I see it. A movie I always liked was *The Good, the Bad, and the Ugly* because in it the Civil War is just this background against which this other, very private drama is going on and yet, on a bigger scale, the Civil War was the drama, but in the movie it's just something that pops in and out. It's a bit that way. And even that sense of *Scraptures* is that there are scraps of scriptures, it comes in and goes out of focus. These are phenomena of reality or of living in the world that one has to come to terms with. I can't dismiss any content as insignificant, I can't dismiss any content that I run up against, I have to deal with it. In the period when I was very language obsessed in my writing I was partially language obsessed because I was trying to find a way to find the right marriage between the inner words and the outer words, to paraphrase Gertrude Stein.

Introduction to *The Arches: Selected Poems of Frank Davey*

1980

I

In any selected writings there are at least two courses open to an editor: 1) take the best from the different periods of an author's work or 2) take the best. Frank Davey's work divides very clearly into three main periods. The first covers the books published between 1963 & 1966. These are: *D-Day & After* (1963), *City of the Gulls & Sea* (1964), *Bridge Force* (1965) & *The Scarred Hull* (1966). The second period covers the books published between 1970 & 1974. These are: *Four Myths for Sam Perry* (1970), *Weeds* (1970), *King of Swords* (1972), *Griffon* (1972), *Arcana* (1973), *The Clallam* (1974) & his previous volume of selected poetry, *L'An Trentiesme* (1972). The third period covers the years 1978 to 1980 & includes the various drafts of *War Poems* (published in the Coach House Press Manuscript Editions series) & the as yet unpublished *Edward & Patricia*. Not included in this listing are the various critical works, published & unpublished, that the author has generated.

Like many other writers in Canada in the 1960s & early 70s, Davey lived his apprenticeship in public. The apprenticeship itself stirred excitement & controversy because of his co-founding & editorship of *Tish* & the poetics it espoused. Indeed, that particular period of his work (a surprisingly short span of time) still forms the basis of most critics' views of his work & of the thinking behind it. This, despite the fact that Davey has moved away from that point & has himself rejected a great deal of it. In his interview with George Bowering (*Open Letter*, 4th Series, No. 3), he stated: "I'm a stranger to a lot of my older work. I haven't read it lately, I haven't paid much attention to it — it's written by somebody else ..." & in his introduction to *Tish 1-19* (Talonbooks, 1975) he listed all the things he found embarrassing upon rereading: "Particularly embarrassing to me are the frivolity of the opening editorial, the pedantry of 'The Problem of Margins' (*T*3), the snobbery of my remarks on John Newlove's *Grave Sirs* (*T*7), and the wordiness of my attacks on Acorn (*T*11) and Layton (*T*12)."

This process of review, rejection, re-incorporation is there as early as *The Scarred Hull* where, in one marvellous line, he rejects the implicit romanticism of his second book, *City of the Gulls & Sea*, labelling Victoria instead, "City of the dull & seedy." It reaches a flowering in the wonderfully complex *Arcana* where manuscript pages from the early 60s are drawn into the work as found texts. However, in those early years, as stimulating as his poetics & his arguments for them were, his application of them fell far short of their potential. Rereading the early books, one clearly encounters a young writer, cocky, obsessed with issues of craft (& still interesting on that level), but without a full grasp of the implications of the philosophy he was moving towards.

In a letter to Peter Miller in 1964, published, in part, on the cover flap of his book *Bridge Force*, Frank Davey stated, "... I tell only what I know, and speculate, never. Only with the validity of fact, and the form of the natural object, can a poem hope to survive in a world that admits only the real." It is, if you like, a statement of the despair underlying Modernist poetic theory. The world "admits only the real" & therefore all else is doomed to destruction by the world. But if what the poet knows is slight, if the life experience is still thin (& here i take "experience" to include the realms of the emotional, intellectual, physical, spiritual, aesthetic, etc.), then the poems themselves can only be slight. As knowledge increases, the poems gain depth & resonance, which is precisely what happens in Frank Davey's work from 1970 on.

By 1979, reflecting on a note included in Michael Ondaatje's *The Long Poem Anthology* (Coach House Press, 1979) on *King of Swords,* a poem he had written in 1972, Davey stated, "This is a major insistence of the poem: that all its elements whether Arthurian, American, or personal are happening on the day of the poem's writing. None of these elements to me were allusional, historical, or even archetypal — they are intrinsic to the phenomenological now." This is a much different theory of knowledge. A more simplistic reformulation of Williams' "no ideas but in things" has been rejected & in its place stands a sense of the human being as a construct of what he or she knows at a given point in time. And that knowledge is part of the *now*, the absolute present of the writing & the reading, reshaping itself as the writer moves thru time, accumulating a history of a writing, & a history as a reader of that writing. The "real" has shifted. The subjectivity of knowledge is acknowledged. The writer is free to move between contradictory & shifting modes of thot because the nature of thot itself is a construct.

This is the second volume of selected poetry that Frank Davey has had published. The first, *L'An Trentiesme*, was edited by the author & was subtitled "selected poems/1961-70." This one could be subtitled "selected poems/1970-80," because in editing it i have chosen to exclude all the books published before 1970. The earlier material exists, can be consulted, & is important for historical reasons. But the published work from 1970 on is vastly superior & gives a much clearer picture of the author's intent & power. In any case, my suggested subtitle is illusory since the compositional dates of the work included in this collection span the years 1964 to 1980. As always, we are dealing with that illusion of publication versus the reality of composition.

II

I mean I'm not a literary writer, I'm not writing about literary topics. I'm writing about my life and my experience with it, and there's all kinds of material there and it's a struggle just for me to cope with that. So I go to literary sources or mythological sources or anthropological sources because I know, I have a hunch, that the knowledge I need to articulate whatever I have to articulate is going to be there. That's my only motivation.
— Frank Davey, *Open Letter*, 4th Series, No. 3: 179

The thrust of Frank Davey's work is remarkably consistent. He is concerned always with relationships, of man to woman, woman to man, captain to passengers, notions of responsibility & duty within a context of trust, & of how that trust is realized or betrayed. Sometimes the thrust is political or historical, sometimes entirely personal, but the issue is always there.

> Can't you see
> where it all leads? Arthur
> driving his spear thru Mordred's body
> the son, thrusting himself up on the shaft
> to axe
> his father. Both
> playing it straight. A faithful
> re-enactment of the son's incarnation, & still
> continuing — women like you, Margawze,
> lusting to be duped, beaten
> taken; suckers
> like me.
>   — *King of Swords*, xxx

Or, in the angry & chilling *The Clallam*:

> The cocksucker. Screams
> all around him & yet he makes
> no move to rescue even one
> from those first two boats.

Or later:

> Of all the shit. With the *Holyoke*
> alongside & offering to take off
> the last 11 passengers, Capt. Roberts
> keeps them aboard to bail.
> Thinking not of the boards tearing
> but only of his uninsured ship, his own
> agglutinating capital.

Implicitly, then, an issue of power & of how power is used. Not in the sense, necessarily, of power struggle, but in the sense of that power we give to one another in relationships, in opening up to each other, allowing ourselves to become vulnerable. The power & trust we give over to those who, like Capt. Roberts, we assume to be trustworthy because of the situation. As love itself is a situation in which we make assumptions. This notion of human trust & how it is treated carries thru to the *War Poems* in which the small boy's trust in his parents is implicit, his view of the world governed by the "truths" they give him, the sense of "the real" they impart to him. As in "The Drunks," where a man & a woman in a car crash into the tram the narrator & his mother are riding in:

> My mother
> says they are drunk, but they do not look drunk
> they are crying
> & that is not the same & the car
> I am sure was going only
> twenty miles an hour.

And later, in "The Shopping List," the small boy reflects on the responsibility of the parent towards him, the child, when he is sent to carry back some groceries that are much too heavy for him:

> One of the things I thought about
> was that a big person would know easily
> how much groceries like mine
> would weigh, & that my mother might figure it out
> at any moment, & come to rescue
> both the groceries & me.

But when he finally meets her, he also confronts his fear:

> … what really began to worry me
> was that perhaps she'd known the weight
> all along, & had been planning to meet me
> here, laughing, just below the hilltop.

249

The thrust of this content i am pointing to then is realized in three ways. To begin with (& dominantly), in first person narratives of relationships in which the central figure of the poet as unselfconfident human being struggling for personal articulation amidst literary stereotypes is powerfully presented.

> A poem. A helpless accumulation of conceit.
> A blend, boysong thirty percent, dacron seventy,
> masking the veins, the blackness of my wrists.
> — from "A Letter," *Weeds*, xviii

> Let me not read poems. Let me not learn
> poetics. Let me detest
> images of my words in journals,
> anthologies, in all those places
> where habit is habit, let me not love
> competence, heroism, idealism, I am not
> competent, not heroic, not idealistic,
> I cannot change a goddam tap washer, or cry
> upon a photod corpse —
> I am only
> a writer, struggling to hear his own
> words, speaking.
> — from "The Mirror" 9, *Arcana* 72

This is not the figure of the prophet, at least not as we have come to expect it. Davey argues for the writer's place in humanity precisely because of what he or she can articulate of the human condition. He is explicitly not beyond human experience.

> None of this is magic.
> My fear of not being loved
> is not magic. My fear of being loved
> so that dying in some aircraft's splintered tumbling
> I lose love, is also not magic.
> — from "The Mirror" 14, *Arcana* 77

He invites the reader to be critical of his stances.

> I write this fucking pretentious poem.
> — from "The Tower," *Arcana* 30

> Dying the death of Arthur, emblazoning
> my initials on books, on manuscripts
> of poems, telephone
> memos. Swaggering
> to your door with chocolates,
> flowers. Playing the classroom
> like theatre, the teacher on horseback.
> Writing jokes, for poems.
> Writing poems, for love. & you.
> Thinking to have married a king.
> — *King of Swords*, xviii

And he stands before us, ultimately, stripped of power, conscious the mystery resides in the world, not in the role of the writer.

> The only process
> is moving now onward. Causing breath
> to follow breathing. I walk naked
> within my clothes, within
> this hostile air. I write these words
> that someone, will remember me,
> or at least finding me here
> poisoned, burnd, loved, unloved, will see words
> moving.
> — from "The Mirror" 14, *Arcana* 77

A record then of trust, of trust misplaced, of trust betrayed, of folly & of the fool's role in folly. For the narrator of Davey's poems is both king & fool. It is this quality which makes Douglas Barbour remark in his essay, "Frank Davey: Finding your voice: to say what must be said: the recent poetry" (included in Jack David's *Brave New Wave*, Black Moss Press, 1978):

> Though the poem is in no sense *actively* feminist, it cer-
> tainly supports a feminist vision … Davey clearly shows
> how invalid the great images of Romance are to our
> survival, both psychic & physical, today; or, at least, he
> shows how carefully, and with what subtle understand-
> ing, they must be invoked … viscerally apprehended
> connections form the core of the poem's argument con-
> cerning our divided, violent, sexist cultural heritage.

So too, the captain of the *Clallam* is both king & fool. He has
assumed the mantle of power, taken on responsibility for others,
but can think only of himself.

> Capt. Roberts later is found
> to mistrust psychiatrists, insurance salesmen,
> marriage counsellors, tow-truck drivers,
> detest paying bills want to keep religion
> all in the family …
> > Determined
> to avoid paying salvage to any
> "of them opportunistic bastards."

He has the power of kings in his hands, but is, in sum, too much
the fool, too governed by petty considerations.

Although Davey rules himself out as subjective in the beginning of the poem —

> This is not a documentary of the *Clallam's*
> sinking. There are documents
> but no objective witnesses
> of the *Clallam's* sinking. The survivors
> were not objective. I
> am not objective.

— he gives us only that one nod towards objectivity. For the rest
of the poem, his rage at this type of callous neglect is obvious. It
echoes too the anger of the narrator in *King of Swords* at too easily gotten notions of heroism, etc., as a form of responsibility.

The "flower of chivalry" —
fuck the women, murder the babes.
— *King of Swords*, xvii

Davey would be rid of all such easily assumed "traditions." He constantly draws us back to the present fact of the world we live in. And as much as the beauty of his language moves us, as much as the predicament of the narrator of the situation described stirs us, he constantly reminds us that we live in this present world, with all our strengths & weaknesses.

I do not know who sits here. Whose trousers
of sliding amber, whose shoes, flashing back my
questions. It is naked I should sit. Only the
singleness of the unflesht bone, the blackheads
upon the protruding knee, the round belly sag-
ging, over the red hairs. Like this poem. Sags on
your goodwill.
— from "A Letter," *Weeds*, xviii

```
i've "read of" this. i've "heard of" that.
i've "studied" this. i've "glanced at" that. i
"think" this. i "know" that. i "believe" this.
i'm "aware of" that. i "feel" this. i'm
"convinced of" that. i "feel" this. i'm
"convinced of" that. i "have a sense of,"
"an intuition of," "a feeling for," "a sure
knowledge of" this. i "conclude" that.
```

He will not allow the literature to become an escape for us, a place in which we can assume masks of mastery. Instead, he confronts us with images of both his weaknesses & ours, of the orders & disorders of our daily lives.

> Today it is late afternoon. The puzzle
> is still incomplete. I have not shaved.
> There is a light bulb burnd out in the hall.
> In the kitchen sink dishes have fallen,
> broken.
> — from "Luna," *Arcana* 53

And images too of what happens to people who blindly put their trust in captains, to readers who blindly put their trust in narrators:

> The lifeboat drowns,
> Your wife,
> holding your child & waving,
> drowns. Your child
> calling your name,
> drowns. You
> stand splay–legged at the rail
> watching your first
> Hollywood movie.
> — *The Clallam*

The juxtaposition of life & art, of how both the reader's & the writer's actions in this activity of literature are indexes to their daily lives, is implicit in most of his poetry &, as we shall see, explicit in virtually all of his criticism.

> For Capt. George Roberts
> even goddamn Ned Pratt would have put away
> the Scots metaphor —
> — *The Clallam*

All the way thru this essay I am using "narrator" strictly in the sense of "one who tells." And the act of telling tells us at least as much about the narrator as anything else. Nowhere is this more apparent than in the third way in which the thrust of Davey's content is realized.

In *War Poems*, the narrator is alternately third person & first person. Indeed, in various drafts (as published in Coach House Press' Manuscript Editions), individual poems shift from first·to third person or vice-versa. In all of these poems, despite the often horrifying details of what is happening within the poem, we are most aware of the young boy, the audience for, the recipient of, the parental actions in the poem. He is sometimes the first person narrator of the poems & sometimes is described by (we assume) the adult Davey. But in every situation, we are aware of the effect of the parents' actions upon the boy, how this situation of trust is being handled &/or abused.

> ... "Well when is
> Bob going to play?"
> one of them asks. My dad says,
> "Come on, boy, they'd like you
> to play for them," & clears
> a plate of cake
> from the piano bench. I walk between
> the knees & sit down
> where the cake was, switch on
> the fluorescent light
> above the music. Right at the first notes
> the conversation returns to long tales
> of weddings, relatives bombed out again
> in England, someone's mongoloid
> baby. & there I am at the piano.
> With no one listening or even
> going to listen
> unless I hit sour notes, or stumble
> to a false ending.
> — from "The Piano," *War Poems*

So this content, this theme, in the reading i am giving here to his work, emerges for me as the dominant one at this point in Frank Davey's writing career. But it is by no means the only thing happening.

III

The sea is also a garden.
— William Carlos Williams

Certain images run thru the length of Frank Davey's work: the garden, the mountain, the sea, the sinking (or sunken) ship, images from the tarot (the four elements, the King of Pentacles, of Swords, etc.), &, conglomeratively, images of daily living, of the life together of men & women. There are a number of ways of approaching these reappearances.

First, we could view them as symbolism. Certainly, proceeding from the Williams quote above, one could draw out the parallels between the sea & the garden, between the weeds & the sinking, or sunken ships. One could build, too, upon the religious history of the garden (Eden, Gethsemane, etc.) & what happened in them (their relationship to the power/responsibility theme i have outlined earlier in this essay). One could argue, on this level, the similarity between Davey's images & those of D.G. Jones in *Under the Thunder the Flowers Light Up the Earth*, a poet whose criticism (but not his poetry) Davey has specifically rejected in his essay, "Surviving the Paraphrase."

Secondly, we could view them in terms of their autobiographical content. This is explicit & one could certainly build on this at some length.

Thirdly, we could approach them as instances of rime. And it is this notion of rime, of riming images & themes, that i wish to take up here, because as seductive as the other paths i have outlined are, they lead us off into the subjectivity of the critic/reader. As much as the bulk of our critics seem to use explicit or implicit psychoanalytical criticism — i.e. deducing what a poem "means" thru its symbolism &/or illuminating the present poem thru the writer's past life — they have too little understood the phenomenon of counter-transference that Freud, and others since (including, and perhaps best of all on this subject, Frieda Fromm-Reichman), warned against. If they had read & grasped the importance of these mechanisms they would know that symbols not only reflect on the unconscious life of their source, but also draw from the unconscious life of those who gaze upon them. Only very recently, in essays written by John Bentley Mays & Eli Mandel, have English Canadian critics begun to look at what the symbols they are gazing upon have stirred in them & how that influences their reading of another's writing. No reader can stand aloof from the writing. The writing draws us in.

There are, however, formal qualities that can be pointed to & it is this notion of riming themes & riming images, as outlined by Davey years ago in his essay "Rime: A Scholarly Piece," that interests us here:

> Rimes of image work best at the level of association, providing that sense of recall — again resemblance and/or contrast — that so often strikes us in our daily living. The best rimes of image are those that *occur* to the poet, and not ones that he has searched for. These guide the poem by a natural law, as it were, of incidence or coincidence. Rimes of theme are more thoroughly in the hands of the poet. Stretching over series/sequences /years of poems, these only reveal themselves if the poet has a unifying vision of his world and his relation to it. Rime is structure; reflects order. Only so much as the poet's vision is ordered by his own sense of occurrence & recurrence, by a sensitivity to the rhythms/rimes of the natural world, will he be able to give rimes of theme.
> — included in C.H. Gervais' *The Writing Life* (Black Moss Press, 1976)

Obviously, then, a measure of Davey's growth as an artist lies, at least partially, in how, in the books from 1970 on, the power of his imagery, his themes, build & the skill with which he rimes them. The work which is pivotal, &, strangely enough, largely ignored, is *Griffon*. Here, the theme & image riming builds to a first crescendo. The French explorer La Salle's ship, which sails on top of the water, intermediary between water & air, is itself named for the mythological griffon, part lion (earth) & eagle (air). The griffon figures prominently in the Rider–Waite tarot in

The World & The Wheel of Fortune cards of the major arcana. It is one of the four beings that surround the wheel, the wheel being composed of the juxtaposition of two wands. The World card rimes these images, the woman in the middle holding the two wands, & in each corner the face of the same being, in the same placement, as on The Wheel of Fortune card. In *Griffon*, the ship "swims / the St. Clair River." The beast, the image, is transformed:

> You have disguised your wings.
> "Missing in Action" the families
> were told. Now
> not missed anywhere. Your claws
> tread the bottom. Prowling wrecks,
> chewing on carrion. Kept alive
> by dreams of shining swords,
> formica washrooms.
> — *Griffon*, 10

The domestic/tarot setting of *King of Swords* is evoked in the last two lines, while the earth/air composite is also made over into a thing of water, is referred to later as "rooting / his dreams in our waters," tying the notion of the sinking to plant images of ships rooting themselves in the earth beneath the waves. As earlier the deck of the ship is evoked as a kind of garden setting:

> The bulwarks
> are hung with wild turkey, bear.
> The seamen lean over the sunlit taffrail
> chewing joints of venison, drinking
> wild grape wine.
> — *Griffon*, 3

Fire is evoked in the "smoking wings" (tied to air) &, later, when the poem states "the muskrat / were burning" (earth/water animal rimed to the earth/air/water Griffon as ship & as beast). The domestic/tarot images & themes of *King of Swords* echoed earlier are touched upon again at the very end of the poem in the lines, previously quoted, "gathering / mythology & real estate for another people." That phrase "for another people," & the earlier "rooting / his dreams in our waters," rimes again the theme of power, its abuses & uses, its sources in our own history.

So quickly
the imperial flag streams
at the lake bottom.
— *Griffon*, 4

And the Griffon (here rimed to the British lion & the American eagle) emerges as a theme rime:

Lion & eagle.
Profit & empire?
— *Griffon*, 11

In this very process of theme & image riming, Davey evokes the actual fabric of the unconscious, a more simplistic level of symbolism being eschewed in favour of a layering of images & concrete details which rime durationally, i.e. in the history of Davey's work (the evoking of images & themes previously utilized &/or touched upon but here combined in new ways in a new setting), & in the history of "History" (La Salle's naming of the ship (the ironic future rime of the American eagle which separates from the British lion (griffon then in La Salle's time?))) & in tarot image rimes. This layering invites a similar riming activity as a response in the reader's mind. As in a good piece of music, one sees/hears fresh images & grasps new nuances & tones on each rereading/hearing.

I referred to the *Griffon* as the first crescendo. In *War Poems*, a second crescendo occurs with all the images outlined above recurring in new combinations among new details. The theme of power/responsibility is evoked & explored (as outlined earlier in this essay) & other major themes in Davey's work such as the whole phenomenon of loss, etc., are interwoven. But since we have only excerpted from that book in these selected poems, I will not dwell on it in this introduction, but simply point you towards it.

IV

> I have been concerned with how literature is read, how interpretations occur, how impressions are formed, tones apprehended. By implication I would also know how words, images, and structures operate to cause interpretations and impressions. Literature differs from non-literary language in being interesting for how it is said long after its denotative content has been absorbed and understood. In fact, how it is said is the locus of literary content, and denotation the least reliable of its many signifiers.
> — Frank Davey (unpublished forward to an unpublished essay-collection titled, "Surviving the Paraphrase")

Although his criticism is not included in this selection, it is important to point out that in it Davey has consistently argued for the same thing he has talked about so passionately in his poetry. His notion of the fool/king as embodied in Capt. Roberts of the *Clallam*, is of the person who talks responsibility but does not live it. It is the Captain's actions that reveal him for the person he is &, as the cliché goes, "actions speak louder than words."

This old saw could be reworked to read, "the form of the thing (what a person does & how they do it) speaks louder than its content (what a person may be writing &/or talking about)." The well-known phenomenon of great content being there in even the most trivial of art points to the reality of a work's formal qualities as what determines the effectiveness, power &, ultimately, the truth of what a person is saying.

In his essay, "Surviving the Paraphrase," Davey, addressing the whole problem of a purely thematically oriented criticism, remarks:

> The movement here is towards paraphrase — paraphrase of the culture and paraphrase of the literature. The critic

extracts for his deliberations the paraphrasable content and throws away the form ... My objection here is based on a principle formulated by Frye: "the literary structure is always ironic because 'what it says' is always different from 'what it means'." Thematic critics in Canada have been interested in what literary works "say," especially what they "say" about Canada and Canadians. They have largely overlooked what literary works "mean" — for the attempt to establish meaning would take them outside thematic criticism.

— from "Surviving the Paraphrase," *Canadian Literature* 70 (Autumn 1976): 10

Throughout this essay (largely a discussion of D.G. Jones' *Butterfly on Rock*, but, in the process, a discussion of the whole notion of thematic criticism as it is practised in Canada), Davey views this insistence on themes to the exclusion of other considerations as irresponsible, defensive &, at worst, destructive to the work & the culture. The critic concerned with his theme loses sight of the primacy of the work he is drawing from, is, in essence, dominated by self-centred concerns, even as Capt. Roberts lost sight of his greater responsibility towards his passengers because of his selfish concern for his capital investment.

But I talk of this here only to show you how the same concerns inform both his poetry & his criticism & how they embody a singular consciousness arguing for a greater awareness, greater responsibility, on all our parts.

V

This has been, as its title states, an introduction. In writing of Frank Davey's work, one could take many directions. All of them could & would have their validity. Hopefully, as readers, you will engage the poems on many more levels than the few i have sketched here. As simple an act as the books you choose to read before & after this one will affect what you bring to this reading experience, & will allow you glimpses, rimes & associations not even the author was aware of. Hopefully, too, you will be led back to some of the earlier work from your reading here, and on to the complete *Arcana & War Poems*. My one regret is that i was forced to excerpt from those two works. The book unit is integral to Frank Davey's work as a writer & is his significant unit of composition (as should be clear from even this selection).

To end this essay, then, a small note on riming images in the title of both this book & the poem from which it was drawn. It is, of course, thru the arches that one enters the garden. The arch evokes both the mountain, in terms of its solid form, & the opening or entrance way. The song the father in the poem sings, "Underneath her arches," located the arch in its sexual context as well, thus shifting the garden towards its sexual rime, & the top of the arches as the Mount of Venus. The particular arch in the poem is built out of old hydro-poles, evoking ships' masts (carriers of fire (electricity)) transformed into carriers of earth (plant/honeysuckle (& again here the sexual image as in Lena Horne's marvellous version of "Honeysuckle Rose" which she pronounces, lingeringly, "Honey, suck a rose")), the pole itself evoking the association of transformer (electrical, but here punned to create a further rime on the process of the writing). It is tied in the poem, too, to death, as the ships are tied to death, to sinking, to loss. The final arch in the poem is "a sculptured arch / of laurel," in a graveyard. But it is also where, at the end of the poem, the small boy sits waiting for his father to arrive "whistling & humming," for, in this case, a song (the poem) to begin.

```
i want to alternate with narrative i.e. switch
places with the story.
```

Some Sentences, Paragraphs & Punctuations on Sentences, Paragraphs & Punctuation

1982

The following paragraphs from various writers are models(?)/ examples(?) of certain standard structurings in prose, what information they convey, & what it is in their structure that conveys that information. They are by no means the only structures but in focusing on them we gain some notion of how words move & what they move in us when they move that way. In short, by looking at prose at this level we learn *how* the story gets told.

⌘

Old Mother West Wind came down from the Purple
Hills in the golden light of the early morning. Over her
shoulders was slung a bag — a great big bag — and in
the bag were all Old Mother West Wind's children, the
Merry Little Breezes.
Old Mother West Wind came down from the Purple
Hills to the Green Meadows and as she walked she
crooned a song.

Simple sentences in a children's story-book tone. The tone is established by the repetition of key words, which function then as rhymes between sentences & parts of sentences. The second paragraph opens in exactly the same manner as the first but switches from a description of the setting of the journey to a description of where the journey took her, a shift from "in" to "to." Thus the journey itself is imitated in the movement of the paragraphs. We feel ourselves progress.

⌘

There was a baby born named Ida. Its mother held it with her hands to keep Ida from being born but when the time came Ida came. And as Ida came, with her came her twin, so there she was Ida-Ida.

The mother was sweet and gentle and so was the father. The whole family was sweet and gentle except the great-aunt. She was the only exception.

An old woman who was no relation and who had known the great-aunt when she was young was always telling that the great-aunt had had something happen to her oh many years ago, it was a soldier, and then the great-aunt had had little twins born to her and then she had quietly, the twins were dead then, born so, she had buried them under a pear tree and nobody knew.

Nobody believed the old woman perhaps it was true but nobody believed it, but all the family always looked at every pear tree and had a funny feeling.

This example again uses simple sentences &, by the same device as described above, establishes a children's story-book tone. There is an implied "once upon a time" in front of the opening. We are placed into the language of story-book to tell a non-story-book story. A distance is established between the content & the language of the telling. The pacing of the third paragraph, one long sentence, with the absolute minimum of commas for intelligibility, adds an urgent, almost confessional, feeling to its unfolding. The author retains the tonal device but switches to a much more complex sentence to reveal the complexity below the simple surfaces we are reading. The use & non-use of commas seems to shift. In the third paragraph they are used to notate the beginning & end of explanatory asides, but asides in which the most highly charged and revelatory emotional content is placed. They are not asides as we usually think of them but mirror, thru Stein's own sensitive study of psychology, her sense of how the most pertinent information is often buried in them. Similarly she does not use a comma or dash at the end of the first paragraph to separate off

"Ida-Ida," tho we expect her to, precisely because not to do so allows her, thru the ambiguous stress on "there," to convey extra psychological content, i.e. "so there" (which is to say in the world outside her mother's womb (& causally then, because of what had happened)) "she was Ida-Ida" (not simply Ida). We see then that this use & non-use of punctuation is a way of signalling additional information. It continues in the fourth paragraph where what could be two sentences separated by a period are instead linked with a comma in order to show the causal & continuing link between the two statements. It is a way of, in this case, underlining. This complexity co-exists with the simple child-like surface of the piece.

ᛁᛁ

Imagination dead imagine. A place, that again. Never another question. A place, then someone in it, that again. Crawl out of the frowsy deathbed and drag it to a place to die in. Out of the door and down the road in the old hat and coat like after the war, no, not that again. Five foot square, six high, no way in, none out, try for him there. Stool, bare walls when the light comes on, women's faces on the walls when the light comes on. In a corner when the light comes on tattered syntaxes of Jolly and Draeger Praeger Draeger, all right. Light off and let him be, on the stool, talking to himself in the last person, murmuring, no sound, Now where is he, no, Now he is here. Sitting, standing, walking, kneeling, crawling, lying, creeping, in the dark and in the light, try all. Imagine light. Imagine light. No visible source, glare at full, spread all over, no shadow, all six planes shining the same, slow on, ten seconds on earth to full, same off, try that.

In this example commas are used to group together as brief breath pauses what could have been handled as discrete sentences. Thus a way of thinking is conveyed, not merely thru the short, very simple sentences, but, thru the use of commas, the way the

thots enter the mind in a rush, piling up one against the other, &
then are punctuated by full stops. This allows the author tremendous control over the rhythm of the piece by virtue of his ability
to choose which moments occur as commas & which as periods.
Capitals within sentences are used to notate vocalized statements
& differentiate them from the narrator's interior voice. Thus no
need for quotation marks. Tho the story-book tone device is
used, the comma/period technique allows the author to modu-
late the tone's effect.

[·]

An overcast sky. The bay windows shut.
From where he is in the dining room he can't see out-
side.
But she can. She is looking out. Her table touches the
windowsill.
The light makes her screw up her eyes. They move to
and fro. Some of the other guests are watching the tennis
matches too. But he can't see.
He hasn't asked to be moved to another table, though.
She doesn't know she is being watched.
It rained this morning about five.
Today the air the balls thud through is close and heavy.
She is wearing a summer dress.
The book is in front of her. Begun since he arrived? or
before?
Beside the book are two bottles of white pills. She takes
some at every meal. Sometimes she opens the book. Then
shuts it again almost at once. And looks at the tennis
matches.

Again simple sentences but minus the story-book tonal device.
Here the grouping into paragraphs creates the overall rhythm of
the piece. The first paragraph presents the overall scene. The second describes "him." The third "her." The fourth "him," "her" &
"them" together in the setting. Then back to "him." Then over to
"her." Then move to the overall scene. Not just the content but

the way in which it is presented, the way in which the reader is moved thru the situation, places the reader & characters in a relationship removed from one another. There is no attempt to engage the reader but rather an attempt to distance us in order to convey the distance that exists between the characters. We "feel" as they do. Indeed, as the succeeding paragraphs show, there is nothing "special" about the characters. They participate in the same reality as the other characters. The circular movement of the paragraphs, taking us from distant (the scene) to close (him &/or her) back to distant again, emphasizes this content. The feeling of disengagement is increased by the flattening of tone achieved thru a combination of short sentences & simple noun/verb structures. The final three sentences, which could in fact have been written as one long sentence, presented in this fashion emphasize the feeling of fractioning & disjointedness in the character.

ㅂ

    I first heard Personville called Poisonville by a red-haired mucker named Hickey Dewey in the Big Ship in Butte. He also called his shirt a shoit. I didn't think anything of what he had done to the city's name. Later I heard men who could manage their r's give it the same pronunciation. I still didn't see anything in it but the meaningless sort of humor that used to make richardsnary the thieves' word for dictionary. A few years later I went to Personville and learned better.

The complexity of the sentences has not increased but the introduction of slang changes the tone & hence the feeling of the piece. It is not child-like. The fact that the content focuses on the "sound" of the word, coupled with the simplicity of the sentences, evokes a story-telling mood. By beginning every other sentence with "I," the author clearly establishes the narrator's voice, that he is, once again, telling a story, & sets up the final laconic understatement for the punchline it is. All of this has the effect of hooking the reader, pulling him or her into the narrative. The complexity of the sound, as opposed to the simplicity of the sentences, is increased by full & half alliteration and by the use of full and part rhyme. The "er" in "Personville" & the "oi" in "Poisonville" are picked up by the "ir" & "oi" in "shirt" & "shoit." The character from whom the narrator heard the word, Hickey Dewey, has a rhyming name. The "B" in "Butte" & "Big" sets up an alliterative pattern & emphasizes & complements the alliterative "p" sequence "Personville," "Poisonville" & "Ship" with the "sh" of "ship" being echoed subsequently in "shirt" & "shoit." He rhymes "name" with the "same" in "the same pronunciation," underlining the point. And finally rounds it off with the "richard-snary" "dictionary" rhyme which is the source of his mis-direction.

ᴴ

> Once I was young and had so much more orientation
> and could talk with nervous intelligence about every-
> thing and with clarity and without as much literary pre-
> ambling as this; in other words this is the story of an
> unself-confident man, at the same time of an
> egomaniac, naturally, facetious won't do — just to start
> at the beginning and let the truth seep out, that's what
> I'll do — . It began on a warm summernight — ah, she
> was sitting on a fender with Julien Alexander who is …
> let me begin with the history of the subterraneans of
> San Francisco …

The long opening rush leading up to the first semi-colon mirrors the content of the sentence. We are shown the "nervous intelli-gence" at work. The "this" before the semi-colon points us back into the part of the sentence we have just read & forward into the rest of it. And now, thru the extensive use of commas & dashes, the halting, preambling voice emerges. The final sentence mirrors the "orientation" comment as the author searches for & establish-es a beginning point. The first "…" notates the classic pause of an interrupting thot & the subsequent switch of direction. The sec-ond "…" notates the beginning of a flashback. These are the two most effective uses of the "…" notation. The dash after "do" delays the period with an aside, a crucial one in which the author takes a mental breath & outlines how he will really begin, & thus the very correct final dash to bring us back to the period we have been anticipating & the real beginning of the story.

◻

Moon & Sun are passing figures of countless generations, and years coming or going wanderers too. Drifting life away on a boat or meeting age leading a horse by the mouth, each day is a journey and the journey itself home. Amongst those of old were many that perished upon the journey. So when was it I, drawn like blown cloud, couldn't stop dreaming of roaming, roving the coast up and down, back at the hut last fall by the river side, sweeping cobwebs off, a year gone and misty skies of spring returning, yearning to go over the Shirakawa Barrier, possessed by the wanderlust, at wits' end, beckoned by Dōsojin, hardly able to keep my hand to any thing, mending a rip in my *momohiki*, replacing the cords in my *kasa*, shins no sooner burnt with moxa than the moon at Matsushima rose to mind and how, my former dwelling passed on to someone else on moving to Sampu's summer house,

the grass door too
turning into
a dolls' house

(from the eight *omote*) set on a post of the hut.

In this text the two balanced sentences, whose halves are separated by commas, begin a building of intensity. The second sentence, by beginning with an "or" structure that dispenses with the comma that could've been inserted before it, sets us up for the explosion of comma'd phrases that punctuate the long, rushing, fourth sentence. The breath is delayed, is held. The third sentence, a simple story-telling sentence, by its placement increases the feeling of the held breath. The opening of the fourth sentence, with its two single word phrases, interrupted by the aside (notated with the two dashes), means that when the four word phrase "drawn like blown cloud" is reached, we are literally drawn out, even tho the phrase is, in fact, very short. This leads us into & thru the beautifully constructed "here & there" catalogue of the process of yearning the writer has gone thru, mirroring his own agitated, distracted mood. The insertion of the poem as we near the end allows the elision of a verb whose action is mirrored in the very placement of the poem in the text —

> "land how, …"
>   *this* (poem) *was*
> "… set on a post of the hut."

— and brings us out of the past of the writer's reminiscences and reflections into the present of the reading.

〔H〕

   As for the enjoyment which is derived by a really discerning mind and a truly living heart from a thought beautifully expressed in the writings of a great writer, this is no doubt an entirely wholesome enjoyment, but, precious though the men may be who are truly capable of enjoying this pleasure — and how many of them are there in a generation? — they are nevertheless in the very process reduced to being no more than the full consciousness of another. If, for instance, a man of this type has done everything in his power to make himself loved by a woman who could only have made him unhappy, but has not even succeeded, in spite of efforts redoubled over the years, in persuading her to meet him in private, instead of seeking to express his sufferings and the danger from which he has escaped, he reads over and over again, appending to it "a million words" and the most moving memories of his own life, this observation of La Bruyère: "Men often want to love where they cannot hope to succeed; they seek their own undoing without being able to compass it, and, if I may put it thus, they are forced against their will to remain free."Whether or no this is the meaning that the aphorism had for the man who wrote it (to give it this meaning, which would make it finer, he should have said "to be loved" instead of "to love"), there is no doubt that, with this meaning, the sensitive lover of literature reanimates it and swells it with meaning until it is ready to burst, he cannot repeat it to himself without over-flowing with joy, so true and beautiful does he find it — but in spite of all this he has added to it nothing, it remains merely an observation of La Bruyère.

Generally speaking, as the complexity of a sentence increases what is actually happening is that the author is digressing more & more within the body of the sentence. He is building up related asides, substituting full phrases for adjectives & adverbs, etc., etc. In this example which consists, despite its length, of only three sentences, each sentence is a model of this activity. The third sentence uses a bracketed aside to argue the content of the quote in the previous sentence, while the main body of the sentence advances & deals with the idea advanced in the main body of the second sentence. This type of sentence is constructed on the model of the tree, growing branches as it reaches out & yet retaining a clear beginning & end in terms of the central content. But what we are most aware of thruout is the phenomenon of the branching & this is what gives such sentences their distinctive tone. The use of dashes around the aside in the first sentence signals a larger, declamatory, & more public statement than the bracketed aside in the third sentence (the brackets there signalling a *soto voce*, private aside).

❡

Most of these paragraphs are taken from the beginning of books & stories. I have done this because the sounds are often struck most clearly at the beginning of the prose work & the author depends on the clarity of those rung notes to carry you thru less obviously rhythmical sections. The observations here are relevant to the pieces under discussion but are not exhaustive in terms of other qualities that can be evoked using such techniques. The repetition of key words mentioned in the first & second examples can also be used to chart obsession, etc. But if you begin to understand exactly what the punctuation & hence rhythm of your sentences is conveying & what the overall sound of your sentences are conveying, you can begin to manipulate them more skillfully to obtain the effects you want.

The following is a list, in order, of the source of the texts used in these notes:

Old Mother West Wind by Thornton W. Burgess (Little Brown, 1934)

Ida by Gertrude Stein (Random House, 1941)

"All Strange Away" by Samuel Beckett included in *Rockaby and Other Short Pieces* (Grove Press, 1981)

Destroy, She Said by Marguerite Duras, translated by Barbara Bray (Grove Press, 1970)

Red Harvest by Dashiell Hammett (Alfred A. Knopf, 1965)

The Subterraneans by Jack Kerouac (Avon, 1958)

Back Roads to Far Towns by Bashō, translated by Cid Corman & Kamaike Susumu (Grossman, 1968)

Remembrances of Things Past by Marcel Proust, translated by Andreas Mayor & Terence Kilmartin (Random House, 1981)

"Syntax Equals the Body Structure": bpNichol, in Conversation, with Daphne Marlatt and George Bowering

1982, 1985

Roy Miki: After talking to bp, we thought we would begin this afternoon session by asking him a very simple, but perhaps profound question: how does such a long poem as *The Martyrology* begin, and why a title that refers to "martyrs," an old term for figures that one would think had been largely laid to rest in the 20th century? George Bowering is here to talk about his writing in *Autobiology,* though of course he won't confine himself to this one text. Similarly, Daphne Marlatt has agreed to talk about her writing, and in particular about the composition of *Steveston.* Along the way, we'll also talk about variations on the extended form, the "long poem" as it's termed.

bpNichol: To begin with, I don't think anybody sets out to write a 15 year poem. I think I would have stopped if I thought it would take 15 years, because at the time I wouldn't have been able to encompass it. I was working on a series called *Scraptures.* The title was a sort of layered pun, obviously on "scraps of things," "scriptures," and "raptures." I started that little series with a concretization, a visual re-working of the opening line, "In the beginning was the Word and the Word was with God," which James Reaney published in *Alphabet* magazine, a long long time ago. About the third or fourth of the series, David Aylward and I discovered these saints' names in "st" words in the English language. We were looking for a title for a poem by David about killing an asp — he was doing this series of "Asp" poems. He had taken the word "grasp" and had written it "asp arg," so we had this image of someone choking a snake. This is the way it is in the heady world of avant-garde poetics! Anyway, we both had this image as we were both looking at the word "stranglehold," and we both simultaneously saw "st. ranglehold," and thought that it was a marvelous discovery. That was about 1965 or 66, and that's sort of where it ended for David, but I began to see these "st" words as saints. Then I found that I began to address them — and I literally mean I found, I was not expecting this. I began to address these pretty rabid rhetorical pieces to the saints in *Scraptures*. I realized that these saints had, for me, taken on a meaning and a life; that is to say, they were more than merely puns.

When I started *The Martyrology* in the late fall of 67, I didn't know what I was starting. Really, the opening lines of the poem were, "december 67 / the undated poem is / found and forgotten," because I'd stumbled across this poem in a drawer that I could not remember writing, which is an experience you often have, you know: did I write that? I began out of that sense of trying, in that initial moment, of dealing with one's own history of a writing, that there are things you remember and things you don't. For me, the most problematic book is Book One. Originally *Monotones* was part of it, but I removed it and made it a kind of an unstated prologue. But I was dealing with the fact that I was writing the thing, and there was obviously a secret book in my mind that I had neither the technical control nor the life experience to get to. That was the idea behind those quotes (in Book One), you know, the sort of little background things. Their main purpose was to point to the fact that there was a larger thing going on that even I couldn't apprehend at that point, and to suggest a larger history that I hoped would make itself clear as I went along. So I just began, as I so often do in my writing. On the whole I find I am led by my ear, which is very similar to being led by your nose when you come right down to it; I mean you just track the thing and see where it takes you. I had no overall plan, other than that the structure was something that would evolve as I went along. In fact, that's been the way it's been.

RM: What about the title, *The Martyrology*?

bp: A friend, Julia Keeler, who used to be a nun, was doing her PhD thesis (I got to know her at the U of Toronto library) on minor religious poets of the 1590s, and the minor religious poets were truly minor in the 1590s! One marvelous poem she and I both churtled over was called "The Martyrology of the Female Saints," which had some of the worst lines ever written in English language poetry, including the truly epic: "They cut off both her paps and thus ended her mishaps." (Laughter) It was a pretty heavy understatement given the circumstances! Anyway, through Julia I was introduced to that concept of a martyrology, simply the notion that it was a book in which you wrote out a history of the saints. And since, in a curious way, the saints were language, or were my encounter with language, the possibility of the journal form or the *utanniki* form also opened up — I was writing my history of the saints, my history of my encounter with language and so on. At times I thought it was a little too downbeat, as a title, so you get tempted to change it, but it still seems accurate.

RM: Could you explain *utanniki* as a form related to *The Martyrology*?

bp: The *utanniki* is a classical Japanese form of which Bashō was really the first practitioner, with his *Records of a Weather-Exposed Skeleton* and other great titles. And probably the most famous example is Bashō's *Narrow Road to the Deep North* and Issa's *The Year of My Life*. Essentially, what you get in the *utanniki* is a mixture of prose interrupted by poetry, interrupted by prose, interrupted by poetry, interrupted by prose, and that linkage goes on. Though that is obviously not precisely what happens in *The Martyrology,* what does happen is a constant formal interruption; that is to say, I'm dealing with form this way, then I'm dealing with form that way. I try to get very articulate when I'm revising, so I know what I'm doing when I revise, but in the moment of writing it's a much more subjective experience and my big check is: is the form evolving? If it isn't, I get worried and a bit suspicious that I've simply started to plug in, and that I've found a convenient form I can shove anything into, which is something I've tried to avoid doing.

George Bowering: Poe says that's the form of all long poems, like *Paradise Lost.* They're all prose interrupted by poetry.

bp: Great!

GB: There must be an essay in there somewhere.

bp: Yes, I sense it, at least worth an MA thesis!

GB: *Paradise Lost* and *The Martyrology*: A Comparative Study.

⌗

Jack Miller: bp, in the interview in *Outposts*, you mention that "syntax equals the body structure." Could you explain that statement, and George, could you expand on this by talking about *Autobiology*?

bp: I discovered — and this is what that statement comes out of — that emotionally and psychologically speaking we learn that we often armour the body, the easiest illustration of which is: if I live in a house with a low doorway, I'm probably going to end up walking like this a lot. (Hunching) I've seen tall people do this when they've lived in situations where the ceiling is low. You get an armouring of the body. I discovered that the order in which I wrote my poems allows certain contents in and keeps other contents out, i.e. the syntax I choose, the way I tend to structure a piece, form per se, permits some contents and excludes others. So what I was trying to find, because that is part of a larger thing I've been working towards, is a way to increase my own formal range (something I'm still trying to do), and therefore not merely be stuck, shall we say, by the physical limitation of my body at that point, i.e. just because I'm walking around with my shoulders up like this, if I can learn to relax I can see the world in a slightly different way and so on. If I can keep moving the structure of the poem around, hopefully I can encompass different realities and different ways of looking at things. In that sense, I've always seen a connection between the breathing I do and what comes out of me, the words I do, so syntax/body structure, sequence/body structure, but also the body of the poem. I don't know if that makes it clear or muddy, what I've just said. Muddy, eh? George, explicate that! (Laughter)

GB: *What bp was trying to say* — !! It's interesting, because I just stumbled across a piece I used in my class this year, that explained T.S. Eliot and certain of the Imagists as people who replaced regular syntax with the syntax of the image. And you've replaced syntax of the image with syntax of the body.

bp: Something like that. In a way, it's an over-condensed statement; it's a conversational statement. I mean, were I to sit down and write that out, I'd probably take about 5 pages — and here I am, yet again, in conversation trying to explain it!

GB: Are synapses a part of the body, or are synapses something that happens between parts of the body? Your poems are built on synapse, right? They live or die on synapse. I don't know, is synapse a thing or the name of an action?

bp: It happens between ganglias!

GB: *Ganglia* hasn't come out for a long time!

bp: *Ganglia* stopped publication in 1966.

GB: Well, it's easy to figure out what body and *Autobiology* have to do with one another. Again, in terms of anecdote, it was when I started writing with a pen instead of the typewriter — I've written with a pen ever since — and that happened because the first piece was written in a kitchen in an Irish working class portion of London, England where I didn't have a typewriter. I wrote the first chapter of it there, then didn't write any more until I came back home to Montreal and for some reason, I can't remember, took up the poem. There was a happy coincidence between the manner of composition with a pen — it was also written in prose — and the subject matter. Both came together and became the definition of the other, or the extension of the other one.

bp: The only other thing I'd say about that too — when I initially wrote, I was trying to notate my voice as it happened, which is the same, get the syntax down to notate the body, breathing. But then I reached the point where I was able to take the notation and challenge myself with it, as when I do ve–ry or vo-cab-u-lary. Of course, if I walked around talking like that, I'd sound like an idiot. But I can get it to create a very particular sound effect. I can then start to use syntax and, by extension, notation, to push and challenge me in my reading, and to extend the range of the sound that's possible in a piece too. So partly that statement comes out of ruminating about all of that.

JM: Does punctuation fit into this somehow? I was thinking specifically of some of the poems in George's *Autobiology*. Some are punctuated fairly carefully and some have an absence of punctuation.

277

GB: I think they're all badly punctuated in terms of the logical realist punctuation that you pick up in grade 6!

JM: But why in some and not in others?

GB: The same reason why a lot of things happened with barrie, I was reading Gertrude Stein at the time, but it was probably also related to the fact that I was away from the typewriter for the first time and the involvement with actually seeing words spilling out of a pen — see, the typewriter reifies what the linguists tell us: that every piece of punctuation is absolutely equal to every other little piece of information, i.e. there's a key for it, so when you're typing on a typewriter, it's normal to keep punctuation clear. It's just as much work to make a dash as it is to make a comma, and to make an "n," but when you write with a pen, you can't get the words down as fast, so that information which doesn't go clack when you touch the key just disappears. That's part of it. The other part is that it's true that a lot of punctuation is spoken by the body; I mean, you can hear commas and so forth, but the body was a given in that instance, that's to say, this was really happening, so with that as a given, then the other one wants to float. That's not a logical answer, but it's the answer. Whereas with a typewriter, I think it's really true, what Olson was hinting at, that you can almost bypass the body when you're composing on the typewriter, that it's the brain just using part of the body to get out onto the page — or the mind does perhaps, and that's communal, rather than singular.

Daphne Marlatt: I always compose on a typewriter, and I don't feel that the body isn't there. In fact, I find that there's a kind of rush possible on the typewriter — because you can type that fast — that equates very definitely with certain body states.

GB: My mind's faster than my body.

DM: Well … yes, but I'm thinking of *Steveston*, and I'm thinking that what I was working with in *Steveston* was very much an orgasmic feeling of trying to gather up everything and move it out — right out to the mouth of the river. I mean, the syntax and body and landscape become totally interwoven. And *Steveston* was all composed on the typewriter. I took handwritten notes while I was down there, but when I came to actually compose, it was on the typewriter.

GB: But *Steveston* partakes of your habit of trying not to get it said — well, filling the poem with parentheses, second thoughts, and the thought that breaks to qualify and so forth.

DM: Well, I wasn't trying not to get it said. I was trying not to arrive at the period. It was trying not to arrive at the end!

GB: It's a backwater coming into the language.

DM: The end of the poem is both what is desired and what you don't want to have happen. barrie talks about that all the time.

RM: Was the composition of *Steveston* fairly all-consuming for you when you were doing it? Was there any kind of composition-al rhythm, as the sequences formed?

DM: There was a rhythm in terms of the trips. I'd go down to Steveston about once or twice a week and I'd take notes in a little notebook. It was very much of a collaboration, because I would often go down with Robert Minden, who was doing the photographs, and we would talk on the way back about what each of us had experienced. And I would avoid sitting at the typewriter that day. I would wait till the next morning, because morning is always the best time for me, and roll in a blank piece of paper and see what came up! That was the immediate compositional rhythm.

RM: Did you have any sense of closure as it was being written? The first poem is definitely a beginning ("Imagine a town"), and the last has a strong emphasis on circles, cycles, completion, beginnings and ends.

GB: But the pieces are not published in the order you wrote them.

DM: No, they're not, and moreover, I didn't think I was writing a long poem. I just thought I was writing a sequence of poems about this place Steveston, and I was rather shocked when Michael Ondaatje suggested that *Steveston* is a long poem.

RM: What's the difference between a sequence and a long poem? At what point do sequences become "long," which seems to be an over-riding term? Certain things are discrete units, and as you begin talking about a transformation in which all these discrete particles become part of a larger frame, or larger space, there's suddenly a leap to "long."

DM: Well, yes, you see, I think a long poem builds on itself, and I didn't have any sense that *Steveston* was building on itself. It was more like something was there that each poem was a stab at, was an attempt to verbalize, or articulate.

bp: You thought of it more as a book than as a long poem.

DM: Yes, I thought of it as a book, as a single experience really.

bp: At this point, in a way we don't have the terminology or the terms to talk about the differences between different types of longer structures.

RM: Robin Blaser's sense of serial poem, as I understand it, is the sense of going into a dark room. The lights go on in a single poem of the series, and then go off at the end. There seems to be a de-emphasis upon memory. Every piece in the sequence does not pick up the memory of the previous ones. The poet goes into the dark room for each one, and the narrative evolves out of that movement. But bp's sense of accumulation in his compositional method suggests a process analogous to that of cell-division where nothing is finally ever lost and where memory is impor-tant. All of the past is always coming into the present not to determine but to condition the way the present will go in the composition. The poem, then, begins to accumulate a history, which is that point I think that *The Martyrology* can be seen as a long poem. I'm thinking of history in that really literal sense of quantifying time. Of course, a serial poem can be a long poem too, so there are variations of what we call the "long poem" and these require more attention.

DM: You're speaking of the history of itself?

bp: Yes, of the writing. In that sense, there's obviously a big differ-ence between *Steveston* and Michael Ondaatje's *Billy the Kid*, which you can see as vaguely similar types of structures, and *Allophanes* which has a "long" structure.

RM: George, do you think of *Autobiology* and *Allophanes* as sequences, as serials, or how would you describe them?

GB: I tend to think of those two, especially *Allophanes*, as something like a serial poem. *Allophanes* is filled with self-forgetting when it comes time for composing the poems — that you self-forget in order to hear the voice, or in that case voices, that are speaking the poems. And each one clearly has its own integrity, and you don't consciously say: Okay, there are 3 lines of development going on in this poem, and now I have to work each of them to an independent and then a dependent climax, or something like that, what you would get in one of Frost's dramatic, extended poems. The rule that I held for a lot of my poems starting with *Autobiology* was that when I became aware of what the poem was repeating, or what it was concerned with — in that case the intelligence of the body — as soon as I thought of a case or an example that would fit, I would discard that idea entirely. (Laughs) The same thing worked with Part Two, *Curious*, the poem about the poets. There were some poets I wanted to be in there, and some poets I didn't want are in there and some of the ones I wanted are not in there, because I already said, "Oh, I know, I'll stick so-and-so in there." The act of composition was an urge, but there was nothing outlined for it, and as soon as something became outlined for it I just chucked it out.

DM: Did you have any sense of connection or none between one individual piece and the next?

GB: Well, I would remember lines. The longer the poem gets — my novels are written the same way — the voice that's speaking to you has various sources and eventually one of the sources will be the poem because it's got so much body to it. So in *Autobiology* I begin to hear the poem which I have not looked at, and certain lines come up over and over again, I guess images too, but more lines or sequences of written words.

Barry Maxwell: The order the pieces were published in *Autobiology*, is that the order you wrote them in?

GB: Absolutely, and the typesetting goes exactly according to what happened on the page, although they're written in prose. When it was first typeset, not in the Vancouver Community Press version but in the McClelland and Stewart version, they typeset it to make its lines end where the typewritten Vancouver

Community Press lines ended, so that it was really skinny and all wrong, and when they sent out sheets to be reviewed, everybody thought it was verse. Somebody reviewed it in *Books in Canada* and said it was really terrible verse. After I complained, it was changed for the final publication. But no, the order was exactly as written, so much so that I didn't even know that there's two chapters called "The Breaks" about broken bones. When I wrote the second one I guess I had totally forgotten that I had written another one about broken bones. When I came later to read the poems several months after the first draft was made, I was really surprised to find that I had two chapters with the same name. Since that time, I've never varied from that method.

RM: George, how important was the writing of *Autobiology* for you?

GB: It was really important … well, it's not important at all in the world, but in my experience it was important, because it got me back to writing with the hand, it got me writing prose, and it got me out of the lyric.

bp: Well, you absorbed your Stein influence at that point.

GB: Yes, in terms of how it caused other writings of mine to happen, it's probably the most important book.

RM: And the breakdown of the division between reading and writing that occurs really makes reading a foregrounded experience in that book.

GB: Funny, the writing should be reading that's difficult to follow, because of the punctuation, but it's apparently easy to follow, because of the punctuation. Strange.

DM: The voice is so strong in it, I don't think the punctuation matters.

GB: Very self-reflexive, is what it is.

bp: Wyndham Lewis would have called it the naive voice.

GB: I tend to think of it as the demotic voice. (Laughs)

[H]

Juliet McLaren: Daphne, you said *Steveston* was rearranged. How? What did that do to it?

DM: I wrote it ten years ago, so I'm trying to remember. It seemed to me that the form I was interested in wasn't linear but cyclical. I guess an example would be something like what you do with a kaleidoscope when you turn it and the bits make this ring. Well, that's due to the reflection of the mirrors, but it makes a circular form. And that thing in the middle, which is the unspoken, which is what each of the pieces is working towards, still exists in the centre as that unspoken. So what I tried to do was arrange the poems in a way that would respect that. Now, it had an obvious beginning piece because that entrance piece is very initiatory, and then it had an obvious conclusion. But the conclusion — and I wrote it as a conclusive piece — was really an attempt to recreate the cycle all over again. I don't remember how I ordered the pieces in the middle. I don't remember what the principle was for ordering.

GB: What about the other *Steveston* poems; were they written at a different time?

DM: There were three others, written at the same time. One was published in *Sound Heritage* (V. 4, No. 21), a piece I felt really belonged to the whole *Steveston* experience, but I couldn't get it right until after the book was put together, so it never appeared as part of the book. The others were sketchier.

GB: But you could have stuck it in when Michael Ondaatje did the *Long Poem Anthology*.

DM: Yes, I know, but then I would have had the problem of trying to figure out where it fitted, its proper place.

GB: So you were saying, no, it doesn't go in there after all.

DM: I still think of it as belonging, but in some more tangible way. And the first *Steveston* series, which appeared in the women's issue of *I's*, was another sequence all of its own, not really about Steveston. I started it about Steveston, but it turned out to be about Vancouver's skid row.

〔H〕

Irene Niechoda: bp, I have a question about space in *The Martyrology*. In Books One and Two, almost consistently, you've got a page that's silent, and then there's talking. Then, all of a sudden Book Four just talks! In the Coach House book, that's sliced away, and they've left out the illustrations and everything's just put on the page and it doesn't work as well —

bp: That's just so I'll see how they'll anthologize it after I'm dead!!

IN: I want to know how the silence works with the talking and the illustrations, and the clouds. I also want to know the difference between your use of the clouds in there and your use of the rectangular illustrations on the right hand side of the page?

bp: Right, you don't want to know much, do you? (Laughs) Okay, let me get something out of my mind first, so I can answer your question. I'm still thinking of this syntax thing, which I'd forgotten I'd said. I don't know that I agree with it anymore, the more I think about it. I mean, I agree with the notion I was dealing with, that breathing's an extension of your body structure, and when you're trying to notate your breath, what you're going to get is the syntax of your body. That's what I was saying. But subsequent to that interview, I would say I focused more on learning how to move the line around differently and using notation. In short, it's not an absolute. It was kind of a stab of thought at that time.

When I talked about the formal evolution of the work, that's partly what I'm talking about. Book One deals with, really, each poem occupying its own page. In Book Two the first two sections — "The Book of Common Prayer" and "Clouds" — are that way, but then I began to run the poems over the pages. In terms of the work, that meant the lines were coming at you much more quickly. I take spatial notation as being significant, so those page pauses (in Books One and Two) are full pauses between poems. Whereas when I'm doing them one after the other — like, there's this poem, a little cloud, then this poem — the cloud was just in lieu of using the typographic bullet or the little empty box, or the squig of a man holding a fish in his hand, or whatever you're going to use to separate poems. I thought, why not use clouds, since that was the saints' home. Those were all hand-drawn by Libby at Coach House.

So in Book Three I was dealing with information coming at me much more rapidly. And also, of course, in Book One and in Book Two you're dealing with titled sections, "Friends as Footnotes," "Sons and Divinations." In Book Three I moved away from the title, i.e. implying that what I began to do then was to say, these are becoming less and less discrete sections and more and more they're moving toward being one unit; except that there are a few named sections — the interludes are named. By Book Four, I threw out the idea of section titles entirely. Book Four is really one long poem. It's very interesting how, when you're writing the long poem, the fact that it's happening for you in discrete sections is very nice. It means that even though you're writing the open-ended long poem, you've got this experience of closure, so you can take a deep breath. But in Book Four there was really no room for the deep breath, so that even though it took me a year to write Book Four, it's like being in a constant state of agitation, in a curious way. That was part of the formal evolution.

What happens in Book Five — which is coming out, quick plug, "this fall," he said — is that I begin to deal with chains of thought. I try and track a phenomenon that happens to me, not that frequently, but sometimes you're writing along and suddenly two lines occur to you. This line could go here, or it could go this way; in Book Five I start to write both of them. That became the chains — the writing would branch and this gave you a choice of reading paths. Then what happened as a result of that was, in a way, I'd be writing in a notebook and thinking, what was the last part, well here, okay, continue on from there … so it's like Book Four in that it's continuous, except that the narrative thread is all over the place. So I began to try and deal with the decentralized narrative. That is, can you have narrative and at the same time decentralize it? Can you "tell the story" and not be sequential? From my experience with Book Five, I think the answer is yes! What you have are twelve different chains. You begin at one point, but really it means that any reader is going to have a different experience of that book. No two readers are necessarily going to have exactly the same experience with that book — which is true anyway, because every reader comes to a text from a completely different associational base, so what they're bringing to the experience is so radically different from what another reader brings. The chains highlight that reality of the reading act.

Now what's happening in Book Six — I didn't even recognize Book Six when it started, and this has been constantly true for me in *The Martyrology*, which is why you frequently read published statements by me saying *The Martyrology* is now finished. I think it's over and then I realize it's still going on. Fred Wah says I should just shut up and keep writing. A nice combination of thoughts! In Book Six, the writing began to break apart into discrete books, which are really an extension of the chains, the one I branched into twelve chains. In a way there's an implication that any one of those can go in different directions. And that's kind of what happens in Book Six with what I was reading today, the four books that have emerged so far, two of which are finished and two of which aren't.

So that's a kind of a take on the formal evolution of *The Martyrology* that I was talking about. What's always an utter surprise for me is where the form ends up going. Partly it grows obviously out of my own creative dissatisfaction — for example, the middle of Book Three, I got really fed up because it seemed that its structure was like 19th century classical music. It was borrowing from symphonic structure. I don't even like 19th century classical music, so where was I getting this from? Well, I was getting it through Pound and some of the long poems I'd read, which were using classical musical structures. What I wanted was a sound that was more, to my point of view, contemporary. I wanted, you know, the Art Ensemble of Chicago, I wanted Ornette Coleman, I wanted M. Kagel, that sort of thing. That's really what pushed me to try to get away from the long, sonorous line I was using in Book Three which kind of reaches a real crescendo there, and then in Book Four it just breaks apart completely.

IN: Yes, it's great. Book Four has got more energy than the other books.

bp: Well, it doesn't feel as ponderous, for sure.

IN: And I guess you're playing with the change in the page colouration and the disappearance of the frames?

bp: Absolutely, that's because my final step of composition is the page. Once I've written the whole thing, which is just written long hand and then typed up and so on and so on, then I get the page proofs. That's when I have to deal with the reality of, here's the form I've chosen, and this is part of the form I've chosen, this machine, so I have to deal with this frame. And even though it's a long poem, you're dealing with this unit. One of the things that's never really been decided in open verse notation is what happens at the bottom of a page. Does it break in the middle of the stanza,

```
i find myself continually writing about the
writing, but then, of course, the reader is
continually reading about the reading.
```

as in prose? Do you just ignore it? Well, I can't ignore it — that's my problem. To me it's a significant break. If the poem breaks there, I have to deal with it. I have to shuffle the poem around to get it to work. Now, because I'm dealing at such length with the poem, in a way I have more choice than the person who's written one tight little poem where every word is precise. I have a lot of compositional choices, just because of the length of the structure I'm working with. In that way I have more freedom to move.

IN: What about the top of the page, though? Even in Book Four sometimes you start this far down, sometimes you start farther down, and I still take that as a pause — I read that as a pause in sound, but then some of them change. Is that a difference in actual time?

bp: No, that's sloppiness in layout. They should all start on the same line. That's a typographic invention really. That would have been the advange of using a bullet. They just didn't know how big or small those clouds were going to be. It's just like in real life, the weather's unpredictable.

RM: The book as a form then becomes a limit that has to be taken into account in the compositional process?

bp: You don't in music, but then you've got the stave within the page, which I don't have — or in essence the page is a single stave that I have to deal with, when I'm composing. I've become really conscious of this with Book Five, literally, my final stage of rewrite is when I get the page proofs.

RM: What would McClelland and Stewart do?

bp: I wouldn't publish with them! They think they're really going the distance if they give you a choice of two typefaces! They've really busted their hump for you as an author — "Hey, this stuff's not going to sell anyway!"

RM: Daphne, are you conscious of the book in the sense that bp's talking about, that a page is only so big and people literally have to turn the page so that there's always something hidden now?

DM: It's interesting, I am when I'm writing in short lines. I tend not to write poems that go beyond a page. Sometimes they're a lot shorter than a page. It's always a huge leap to put in a new piece of paper. But I don't feel that way when I'm using a long line, as in *Steveston*, or when I'm writing prose. And that has something to do with the momentum — the momentum just runs right over the edge of the page.

bp: Of course, there are clearer typographic conventions in prose. In prose, we have learned to ignore the page. The ideal prose notation will be the long, continuous line — ladadadadada — they're reading bytes of information, but there is actually no convention around it in poetry. It's a problem we haven't solved yet notationally.

Shelley Wong: I want to ask Daphne specifically about this matter of space. I asked you once before and you said that in the Talonbooks edition, in terms of starting in the middle of the page, the decision was arrived at by you and the designer Dwight Gardiner.

DM: Yes, and that was because here you actually do have a non-standard, non-8 1/2 by 11 piece of paper which is bound with a bunch of other pieces of paper, so all of a sudden that gives you more possibilities, but like barrie I didn't compose thinking that I would begin halfway down the page. It's a decision that gets made after the thing's written and you suddenly have a design editor who's willing to play around.

SW: How did you arrive at that decision to start halfway down the page?

DM: Because of the space. I really wanted a lot of white space around the print.

SW: What was the white space doing?

DM: It was for the language to resonate in, and it had something to do with the photographs also. It was a way of giving non-verbal background to the language which was not contained, or containable, in a page as the photos were.

[H]

bp: It's very interesting, when Phyllis Webb's book *Naked Poems* was published originally, I remember there was an outrage in lots of reviews at how much white space she left on the page. People were saying, what a waste of paper! And they didn't mean that the poem was bad; they were really outraged that she wouldn't squeeze it up.

GB: They were complaining how much you had to pay per word to buy the book!

bp: But I think it's precisely with that white space — that's how you suddenly read silence at that point. You know, the word space suddenly magnifies. You're really aware of that white space all the time, but you never foreground it. But when you suddenly leave a lot of white space, you foreground it and it always affects readers, whether they register it consciously or just as a kind of subliminal hit. Their eyes turn the page, and they're looking for type at the top and it's not there. Drop. Which is why, Daphne, you're saying that you read that as significant space. It is significant space. That's why you've got to be careful that your designers do it right.

DM: It was also part of the contradictions of that book, because there's a lot of stillness in Robert's photographs. They're very still photos, and there's a lot of movement in my language. The white space had something to do with mediating that difference, I think.

The business about white space is interesting for another reason. The photos are framed by the white space surrounding them, and I think this also happens with single-page shortline poems — it's very visual, the arrangement on the page, as barrie was saying — but I think something else is at work with the longline poems, something that has more to do with "background" (to use a visual metaphor) or silence (an acoustic one) to intervene between the verbal rushes the poems are. A river, in flood, keeps on rushing, no pauses, no breaks, but I suppose I felt the poems couldn't do that because, besides exhausting a listener, that would suggest something that didn't happen in the composition. They came in discrete rushes, not as one prolonged flood.

⊡

Carol Lane: About voice in your writing, Daphne, I was interested when you said that you composed on the typewriter, because I have a sense of both this incredible rush, and also of a breathlessness, like these breathing pauses. Does the typewriter help that, because it can keep up?

DM: Yes, the breathing pauses punctuate the rush, and so prolong it. And the typewriter invites you to go out to the very end of the possible margin. That had a lot to do with it, because I was coming from very short line poems. The poems in *Leaf/leafs* are very short, sometimes just one syllable, and words are dropping over the line break, in half. It was a high to suddenly say, the line's going to be as long as the page is wide. So there's what I think of as a really prose urge to push always to the end and yet to forestall arriving at it. That fascination with syntax, where you don't think about it but it arrives; you find yourself in situations, and then you respond in the moment, but the situations are syntactic situations: how do I get out of this one? I'm not ready for a period yet.

ᴴ

RM: What about the use of the first, second and third person voice in writing?

GB: I write in the third person for the reader, who is me. I guess it's complicated but it's simple in one sense — so that you can't express yourself, and so you can have that experience you have as a reader. If it's written in the third person, you and the composer are looking perhaps at the same angle at the thing, with a little parallax; whereas, if it's written in the first person —

bp: Don't look at me, I write in the first person!

GB: — the reader is made into a second person who is being spoken to, and therefore distanced. That's part of it, and the other part of it probably has to do with puritanism. But you see what I mean. If you're reading, "He did this and he did that …," you and the writer can maybe even fill the same space.

bp: I write in the first person partly because one of the goals I set for myself when I was 18 or 20 was to find a way to write about completely emotionally loaded material without sentimentalizing it, without "romanticizing" it, and without melodramatizing it. And when I say "romanticizing," I probably mean melodramatizing. Which is harder to do in the first person. I also like the "I." I think you need it in terms of the "we," to articulate that. I'm not a reader who necessarily feels distanced by the "I," either. I find that as the "I" goes on, I start to identify with the "I" if it's speaking in ways I feel some kinship with. To me, that's not necessarily my reading experience, so that could be a subjective reading experience on George's part.

GB: It's not subjective!

bp: Pardon me, on his part; it's not logical, but it's definitely psycho-logical. You get a different effect with the third person, but that's partly the fashion of the times, you know. For instance, Stein's notion of the continuous present, the i-n-g verb, still tends to be unfashionable. We prefer the still photo, the "ed" ending, we prefer it framed. "I shot the picture," as opposed to "I am shooting the picture," frames it, finishes it off, and you move on discretely; whereas in that continuous present, there is no closure. I've heard people in writing classes say, "Never use 'ing' verbs." What a weird statement. What they really mean is they don't like the sound; they don't like that feeling of non-closure. Or they'll say, "no confessional poetry to magazines." Now Sylvia Plath has got to be one of the big hits of the century, right? Would we call this confessional poetry, or would we call this confessional poetry?

GB: Yes, I was going to say a little while ago that you use the "I" because *The Martyrology* is a kind of confessional autobiography.

bp: Yes, but it's also dealing with the notion of journal. All I'm saying is that you get fashions of the moment that don't necessarily relate to the problems of dealing with the word "I" or the word "he." I mean, it's a different problem to write in the "he"; it can be very difficult to write in the third person impersonal. It can be as tricky for a person to do it as when he writes in the first person. In fact, for some people, when you can tell they can't control the "I" — if you can't control the "I" in your writing, the trick is to write in the "he" or the "she." Then you'll get control of the "I." That's the way you get it.

Rob Dunham: George, what would have happened if you had sat down and started to write "Old Standards" (in *Particular Accidents*) in the first person?

GB: I think I wouldn't trust it. Actually, it's really funny, because I'm writing (as I keep saying I'm not) the beginning of a long poem now, and yesterday I wrote five lines to it, and I'd been trying to write it in the third person. That had worked before, because before that I was writing in the third person in order not to write at the second person. Now, I said, okay I'm going to write in the first person plural to try to write in the first person, and it wouldn't work at all, so I slipped into first person singular, but I made a mental note to come back to that stanza and change it, I don't know how but I'm going to change it — because, immediately I find myself saying, oh! I'm writing in the first person, that means I get to say whatever I want.

bp: So for George, "I" means the license to kill!

GB: When you write "I," I reach for my gun!

RD: When you write "I," you're going to be writing for the next fifteen years.

GB: Ah, but look how the "I" has changed. You've got a totally different "I" now, writing "A Phoenix Too Frequent" Six rather than One. It's a different "I."

bp: That was Steve McCaffery's nickname for *The Martyrology*. When I kept saying it was over, he called it "A Phoenix Too Frequent" Six.

GB: Your first person has almost become for you a third person now.

DM: No, I think that's an important thing, what both of you are touching on. Because the "I" fundamentally has no limits. It can eat up the whole world. And the "he" or the "she" is out there in the landscape. That's part of the difference. It's a limitation.

bp: All of the tons of George's literary essays are in the "I," right? "I, George Bowering was down at the Cubs game eating a bunch of peanuts and drinking beer, when I found myself thinking of Hesiod" … a typical opening line.

GB: Right, right.

DM: So what is this? Some kind of weird inversion happening?

bp: Most of us would write our essays in the third person. George just likes to flip things around.

RD: The "West Window" poem (in *The Catch*) is in the first person, isn't it? What happened there? (Laughter)

GB: But it's not about my observations. It's about other

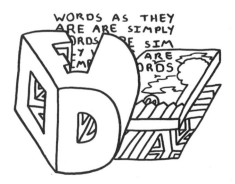

things that happened, plus it's an imitation of Wordsworth and Keats and other poets, so it's not my "I" exactly.

bp: He's got it tightly rationalized!

GB: No, I just realized — one just realized that! My conversation is in the third person.

DM: That's interesting, because what you've said, George, is that for you, the "I" is a persona whereas for most people the "he" or the "she" is the persona.

bp: And in fact, Daphne, as you were saying earlier, the trick, when writing in the "I," is to find out what the limits are. Getting control of the "I" in your writing is to realize you can't devour the world. You can start here, and you might get as far as there, before you've died of botulism, or something. You just can't do it. That's part of getting control of it, because if it simply becomes an exercise in megalomania, it's bad writing.

꒪

IN: I have a question for bp. Talking about first and third person, what happens when you use the first person "I" followed by a third person verb?

bp: As in?

IN: I have one example here — I know there are more — "I is inside."

bp: Well, often when I'm talking about "I," I'm talking about the "I," that is to to say, your I, his I, her I, my I, so on.

IN: As opposed to the "we"?

bp: Or as opposed to the "he." I'm trying to deal with that. See, to me, pronouns are more universal, that's why I like them. I think it's harder for a general reader to identify with an "I," I would agree, but I think that we get into to that eventually. He, she, we — it's looser, it isn't named. Naming, though on the one hand it claims, often distances. So in trying to deal with the reality of how we perceive and so on, I often prefer to use pronouns. In those cases, that shift to the third person verb is to indicate that type of usage of the word "I." "I" is an interiorized concept — in short, "I" is inside.

RD: George, I was just thinking about what happens with your third person. Though you say you don't trust the first person because it allows too much subjectivity, there's something very affective about your third person. It has an elegiac quality.

GB: Yes, I'd say that's true. My novel (*Burning Water*) is probably the best way to talk about that because there's an understood "I" who's another George, in other words, Bowering in that text writing the whole thing about "he" or "him." Any time you write, there's an understood "I." So if you're talking in the first person presumably either those two I's collapse or there are two distinct I's, one ironically beholding the other one, I guess. You might be right to say elegiac, because there's probably the feeling I'm generally after when it comes to writing. Unlike barrie, I tend to write about something that did happen rather than something that's happening right now. That's a difference between you and me, and might easily be why I go for the "he." You cannot be elegiac with the first person, can you? The other person will say, "Go cry on someone else's shoulder," or, "You may feel a sense of world smear about this, but I don't." In a sense, I'm trying to seduce the reader who says, "Oh well, if you're saying that about him rather than about yourself, then it must be more true."

᛬

Valerie Rodd: bp, I was wondering whether you have the same sense Daphne does about pulling things with you through *The Martyrology*, and possibly not wanting to end the poem as well.

bp: Yes, there's a real ambiguity about it. I mean, on the one hand, I love and embrace the fact that it doesn't end. On the other hand, I do keep issuing these statements saying it's over. As a totally subjective experience, I find writing to be a tension between the sheer delight of writing and kind of an almost unbearable agony about the fact that it's still going on. Both things are true at the same time, you know.

VR: Can you relate that to this whole problem with the I, and the use of the first, second and third person? I think there's something you're going to confront at the end of the poem —

bp: In a way, it's also one of the things I've written about, and I'm consciously trying to fight. It's what I call the immortality game. It was a great experience working at the U of T Library. As you'd go through the poetry sections, there would be literally hundreds and thousands of volumes of stuff that you'll never get around to reading. It teaches you a certain amount of humility. How many of us have really heard of Bertha M.C. Shaw, author of one of my favourite inadvertantly bad titles, "Just Kneel Down on the Good Ground and Kiss It for Me: Request Made to a Soldier on Leave," same wonderful author of "Ode to a Green Strawberry" and other classics.

GB: Published by Fiddlehead Books!

bp: Now, now! In a sense, then, it seemed to me that in a lot of classical structure what you get is a flight from mortality. You build the structure that will live beyond you. Obviously, you die and your works go on beyond you to some degree, assuming there's not some major catastrophe, but on the other hand, you take something like Ur (which is why I got into the whole Dilmun thing), we didn't even know about Dilmun until the tablets at Ur were discovered. I mean, that was literally a lost city. There was no other reference to it until they discovered the tablets containing the Gilgamesh legends, and that's in the 1880s. I had that line in the poem I was reading today, "finally all reference vanishes." So there's a notion of high art that I find impossible to believe in. It doesn't make sense to me. It seems to me that existence is more temporal than that. On the other hand, you're also writing this thing which could exist beyond you — hence that other line, this poem continues — "I die years before this poem can possibly end." When I say, the closure you're talking about is death, I'm not being facetious. In that act of the thing, you're writing towards its end and its non-end.

GB: You shouldn't say that, barrie, because that means you're going to keep writing that poem till you die, and there'll be some critic in Ontario who'll find the obvious solution.

bp: I thought of that, George. I think I wrote about it some-where. (Laughs)

ꔷ

RM: bp, how does technique relate to your sense of contempo-rary poetics? What's the larger meaning of the concern with the writing act, the placement of words on the page, and how a poem gets composed?

bp: I always liked what Philip Whalen wrote years ago in *The New American Poetry*, that his work was a "graph of his mind mov-ing." Well, when I'm talking about this thing of facility, of craft in the old sense, it seems to me you're talking about a connected-ness, say a cultural connectedness. Then there's the history of our own writing, the history of the writers we have learned from, and the wider, broader history of writing. And there's that nice theo-retical concept, all literature, which is something none of us could ever read.

Once you begin to realize all that, nonetheless, here you are in your writing, and writing, I think it's fair to say for all three of us, is the most meaningful activity. So in a way you have this bizarre relationship to the world — a rather solitary activity is your most meaningful way of relating to the world. To me, therefore, it seems a responsibility. A personal moral stance I then take on is to expand my technical range, my range of what is possible in my craft, to know that I don't write a certain way because I choose not to, not because I can't. It's very easy to dismiss a certain way of writing, but the fact is, you couldn't write that way to save your soul. I mean, if God promised you wouldn't go to Hell if, you couldn't do it. So it seems to me that you're engaged in the very human activity of trying, in the vocation you have chosen, to relate to existence — to try to do that in the best way that is absolutely possible.

GB: Or as Gertrude Stein said, If you can do it, why do it?

The Medium Was the Message

1982, 1989

This will be an idiosyncratic essay, concerned subjectively with memory, a memoir of a kind and yet lacking that essential centre of most memoirs, the meeting with the particular person, McLuhan in this case, tho we did in fact meet, but lacking that story since it is not the point or gist of what I wish to get to. What I wish to get to is the notion of influence, and confluence, and certainly congruence, all of which is, as McLuhan understood, more than mere word play, but rather a very serious word play, and, as the Bard said years ago, "the play's the thing," and we were all playing on the same mere after all.

No one punned more seriously than McLuhan. When he took his own aphorism "the medium is the message" and punned it into a second volume entitled *The Medium Is the Massage* he was opening another door into another range of thots. You could of course say that McLuhan was echoing in this device one of his favourite writers — James Joyce. But Joyce was interested in encoding and McLuhan in decoding and that is a decisive difference. It was McLuhan who showed some of us how the pun could be used again, seriously, in the 20th century. Joyce was the first writer to take the pun seriously since the 17th century. And *Finnegans Wake* takes his advancement of a particular application of pun just about as far as you can. So McLuhan reversed the process. He used pun to open up where Joyce had used it to layer. There is a lightness of touch to McLuhan's writing, an airiness, that has often been mistaken for a lack of depth. But the wonderful thing in reading McLuhan is precisely that he was using language to take off, using it to soar free of an artificial notion of what constitutes profound thinking, utilizing instead the mind's ability to leap, to follow fictional highways to real destinations, to mix its metaphors until they match. This was the essence of his "thot probes," and his use of pun was part of that general strategy.

McLuhan's advantage here was that he started as a literary critic and thus was grounded in the notion of decoding. Symbolism wasn't something you put into a piece of writing but rather a stored potential you needed to find a way to release. This notion of release (not description (i.e. getting it down *in* (or into) the writing)) governs McLuhan's thinking. He is not trying to fix "a" or "the" reality — he wants to open realities. This is a writer's perspective, closer to poetic thinking than old critical notions of thematic analysis. It is also, from my point of view, a particularly Canadian stance, that ironic relationship to "thot" that sees you can catch ideas (and hence their thinkers) with their pants down. It informs a lot of contemporary Canadian writing and it certainly informs McLuhan's work. And he was too much the "Pataphysician, tho he himself would probably never have used the term, too much the punster to get caught in the trap of thinking there just was one code to crack. The sand is quick in time, and the real question is always "how far can that thot carry you?"

There's an old notion in science-fiction that's useful here which is the notion of hyper-space, a region not governed by known space-time laws into which ships move in order to cover vast distances more quickly than ordinary space-time would allow. The "thot probes," and what I'm calling "Pataphysical thinking, are like that. You suspend the "normal" demands that logic or sequential thinking impose on you, shift into a mental hyper-space, and are whisked vast distances to a destination back inside normal space-time. McLuhan, to the rage of his critics, did this constantly. And make no mistake, the destinations he arrived at were real, the statements and ideas he came up with had the ring of truth, which is why they impacted the way they did. But they were also disposable vehicles, and this is important to remember. McLuhan was not attached to his thots in a possessive sense. They were vehicles he used to get him places. If I get possessive about the plane that takes me from Toronto to Vancouver I'm forgetting its utilitarian function and the fact that it's only one of many possible planes and many possible ways to make the trip. And once I reach *that* destination well it's only one destination. There's really no point in building a career around landing in

Vancouver, around one thot, one idea. McLuhan understood he was working with "theories" and that the danger with "theories" is we come to think of them as "truths."

Pun then, pun as part of a larger strategy but specifically pun for its musicality, the ability it gives a writer to strike many notes at the same time. The pun we began with, where "message" becomes "massage," throws the second term, "medium," into high relief, making us conscious of the many meanings of that word. And it's interesting too that that was the accusation levelled at McLuhan, that he was a kind of intellectual spiritualist, pulling ideas out of mid-air. McLuhan was the medium then, and the medium was the message. Lots of people went to the medium too, reached out thru his works to contact the spirit world, the world of muse, of hyper-space, of 'Pataphysics and divine fictions. The influence then was modal, a style or way of thinking which if it did not go directly one-to-one (i.e. "he" took his ideas from "her") gave a justification for, or a framework for or, thru example, a permission for work that emerged from various writers. It was something to react to or follow from or move in tandem with. And many writers, including myself, did and continue to. In standard critical terminology we could say that McLuhan "anticipated" the literary-based philosophical models of Barthes, Derrida, etc. He was not a critic, tho he wrote criticism; he was a literary thinker who refused to be limited by accepted notions of what profundity is. But he was profound and he was ambiguous and he was witty and his actual method of thot, the serial leaps of his mind, influenced many of us. He understood that writing was not simply what is written but rather, in the very way you approached it, the very terms you set for yourself, became and becomes a strategy for living, a model for how to deal with the "reality" of the world. He showed how the medium became the message and how the most profound thot becomes cliché, becomes archetype. He showed us, too, a way to re-energize the language, the word world.

The Prosody of Open Verse

WITH FRANK DAVEY

1982

Our intent in this essay is to describe the notation that we take
for granted in both our writing and reading of contemporary
open form poetry. This is not to say that all contemporary poets
use this notation, but most of them use some element of it, along
with more traditional ideas of notation. All the notational ideas
we will be discussing presuppose a familiarity in both writer and
reader with certain fundamental linguistic concepts, specifically
with *stress, pitch, terminal, phonological phrase,* and *sign.* There is
nothing particularly esoteric about these concepts; they became
current in linguistics several decades ago and could probably be
inferred by any perceptive reader who took the time to figure out
how certain writers have structured the language of their poems.
Indeed, these concepts have become, at this point in time, the
invisible underpinnings of open form verse notation. However,
neither the role of these linguistic concepts in shaping the
notational system nor the system itself have been thoroughly
described.

1. Some Definitions

STRESS. Linguists call this feature of language the prominence
given to a syllable by its being pronounced more loudly or
vigourously than other syllables in its environment. All syllables
receive stress — contrary to the old system of "stress-unstress"
scansion of poetry many of us were subjected to in grade school
— and can receive it in infinitely variable amounts. Four degrees
of stress, however, usually suffice to describe a single clause or
phrase: in descending order *primary, secondary, tertiary,* and *weak.*
The stress we most need to attend to in poetry is not too surprisingly the primary; it is here that many of the other important
features of the poem will occur.

PITCH. All musical sounds have pitch; the human voice is such a sound, being produced through the vibration of a column of air by the vocal cords. In music pitch is an absolute value but in speech, and hence in the notating of poems, it is relative. Normal pitch contours use four relative levels: extra high, high, normal, and low. There may be slight variances in each level but not enough to become confusing to the hearer.

TERMINALS. At the separations between words pauses can occur — sometimes a mere slowing of tempo, sometimes a clear pause accompanied by a pitch change in the preceding syllable. The former is normally unpunctuated when it occurs in prose. For instance, in the sentence, "I'll do it when I have time," there is a terminal between "it" and "when." Linguists call this a "level terminal," to distinguish it from the second group of terminals, "rising" terminals that occur at the end of questions, and the third group, the "falling" terminals that occur at the ends of affirmations.

PHONOLOGICAL PHRASE. Also called a phonemic clause, this cluster of syllables is the smallest phonological construction that can appear as a complete element in speech. It consists of one or more syllables, bounded by terminals, and marked by a single primary stress. Examples would include both "I'll do it" and "when I have time" in the sentence above, single units such as "Wow" or "Damn" or longer ones such as "In the cool cool cool of the evening." Primary stress in these examples falls on the syllables "do," "time," "wow," "damn," and "eve."

SIGN. Although all phonological features of speech are also "signs," here we mean by "sign" the various visual elements that constitute the written language. These include not only the letters of the alphabet which imperfectly act as signs for speech phonemes, and the various conventions of punctuation and capitalization, but also such spatial devices as paragraph, stanza, isolation of phrases, words, and letters, variations in typographical size, and the length of a verse line.

2. The Line and the Line-break

The line in contemporary open verse consists of one or more phonological phrases, and ends on a terminal. There are no enjambed lines; unlike in traditional or "closed" notation (sonnets, blank verse, etc.) every line-end signals a pause or terminal. The contemporary line is not necessarily a simple graphing of the poet's speech pattern but can be a deliberate enforcing of primary stresses to create a particular content and/or rhythmic effect. That is, the sentence, "I'll do it when I have time," in poetry might occur in the following ways:

> I'll do it
> when I have time.

This would be a graphing of normal speech pattern.

> I'll do it when
> I have time.

This relocation of the terminal shifts the primary stress in the first line from "do" to "when," creating a subtle shift of content.

> I'll do it when I
> have time

Here the stress shifts to "I," the content becomes more emphatic, personal, and consequently more dramatic.

> I'll do it when I have
> time.

Here the stress' shift to "have" increases the dramatic content and suggests more passion.

> I'll
> do it
> when I
> have time.

The increase to four primary stresses creates less distinction between syllables, a quieter, more personal tone and slows down the rhythm.

I'll do it when I have time.

In open verse such a line asks the reader to observe no terminals within the line and to observe the single primary stress on "time." Because of the rapidity with which this line would have to be spoken to avoid an additional terminal, this would be an energetic line, possibly an angry one (although a reader might well "read in" one or more terminals unindicated by the writer, particularly if generalizing from traditional verse forms in which the line often contained unmarked terminals). If indeed the writer had wished this line to contain a terminal other than the concluding one, he has not signalled so to the reader.

The convention here is that all terminals (with the exception of "optional" terminals many poets create to enrich a line with deliberate ambiguity) must be indicated by some form of punctuation, either traditional or spatial.[1] Within the above line a terminal could be indicated as follows:

I'll do it   when I have time
(Earle Birney commonly uses this notation.)
          or
I'll do it, when I have time.
          or
I'll do it — when I have time.
          or
I'll do 'it' when I have time.

in which the specifying of *it* by single quotation marks both locates the primary stress and signals a terminal immediately after. (Fred Wah uses this notation.) I'll do *it* when I have time. Italics can serve the same function as the specifying quotation marks (in typewriter notation this is achieved by underlining).

I'll do it
                    when I have time.
(George Bowering commonly uses this notation.)

This sixth punctuation differs from the first five in signalling not only a level terminal but also a distinct drop in pitch — a lowering of voice. In the first version "I'll" and "when" have essentially the same pitch, but a longer pause is notated between the two phonological phrases than in version two, even longer than if the line were divided into two separate lines beginning on the same margin. The spatial punctuation of the first and sixth versions allow considerable flexibility in that the space between the phrases can be varied in visually measurable units in order to signal pauses of varying durations. Both Birney and Marlatt use such a notation, usually increasing or decreasing the space geometrically — e.g. from 6 typewriter-spaces to 9 or 3. Although each reader will experience these pauses differently, the notation still allows the writer to indicate relative lengths of pause, and thereby to have more control over the rhythm and pacing of the poem than would be possible through conventional punctuation.

It is precisely by delaying the terminals, or increasing their frequency that the number and location of primary stresses is determined and complexity in rhythm is achieved.[2] Long lines can alternate with short ones and rhythmic patterns can be established.

Each relocation of a terminal relocates a primary stress; each introduction of an additional terminal creates an additional primary stress. The primary stress communicates meaning through emphasis, so that differently stressed but identically worded units can "mean" quite different things. By accurate locations of terminals, a writer can enforce a specific meaning by enforcing a specific location of primary stress.

Thus Keats' famous line in this notation,

When I have fears that I
may cease to be

because of the primary stress on the second "I," signals much more self-concern than

> When I have fears
> that I may cease to be

with its primary stresses on "fears" and "be." (In Keats' own notational system, of course, such considerations of stress, pitch, and terminal were indicated only by occasional punctuation marks, and usually left to semantic interpretation.)

One last fact about the line in this notation is that long lines composed of only one or two phonological phrases indicate a very rapidly paced poem; short lines indicate a relatively slow pace. This phenomenon is related to George Trager and Henry Lee Smith's discovery that the primary stresses in English speech tend to be "isochronous," to occur at regular intervals of time, and that phonological phrases, no matter how many syllables they contain, in a given passage of speech all occupy roughly the same amount of time. A long phonological phrase — "I'll do it I'll do it I'll do it I'll do it I'll do it" — (properly read with no internal terminals and a primary stress on the final "do") could leave the unsilent reader quite breathless.

3. Between the Lines

Space in such notation represents time, as when a line break indicates a terminal or when varying amounts of space within a line indicate terminals of varying duration. Consequently the increasing of blank space between lines — double spacing, triple spacing — is used by writers to indicate even larger amounts of time without words. Some will re-inforce the largest units of such time with printer's devices or asterisks that insist on a complete stop in the rhythm of the poem. Sometimes, for a yet more insistent pause, the writer will direct his text from an unfilled page to a new page (as in the original edition of Dudek's *En Mexico*), or for an even greater degree of temporal separation between the lines allow a blank page or pages to intervene (Phyllis Webb approaches this in *Naked Poems*).

4. Pages

The one weakness of the above spatial conventions is the "enjambed" page break that occurs where the page cannot contain the sheer number of lines in a poem. How can a writer signify that no stanza break, no extended terminal, is intended by the shift to the new page, that this shift is merely an accident of book design? "(no stanza break)" types the writer at the end of each page of his typescript, before sending it off for publication. Clearly any instruction such as this interferes with smooth transition rather than facilitating it. It seems to us that what the notation requires here is a typographic convention. Perhaps there could be an agreement to treat the page break as in prose — i.e. ignore it; printers would then have to avoid the coinciding of page breaks with significant space between lines or stanzas. This is probably the best approach since it fits the reader's preconceptions of the reading act. However, it can lead to an awkward arrangement of lines near the page break. An alternative would be to create an agreed-upon typographic signal that would indicate the presence or absence of a stanza-break at the page juncture. Since open verse notation is still evolving, it is possible that some solution to this problem will eventually emerge.

5. Multiple Margins

The left margin (or "base margin") of the poem and each consecutive line that returns to that margin begins on the same pitch — i.e. if the first three lines of the poem are all aligned on the left, then what you have is a continuous pitch-rime running through that margin. This pitch does not change unless the writer relocates the margin. The most common way of changing pitch[3] is the drop-line, which we described earlier.

> I'll do it
> > when I have time.

This drop denotes a drop in pitch, but does not signal how far, or to what point the pitch falls, merely that it does fall. When one returns to the base margin from the end of the drop-line, one does not necessarily return to the opening pitch of the poem but merely to a higher pitch than that which began the drop-line.

A common way of signalling a definite change of pitch in the base margin is the insertion of several blank lines, or even printer's ornaments, between stanzas. Here the opening pitch of the second stanza can be higher, the same, or lower than that of the first, since the passage of time insisted upon by the spacing allows the new stanza to occur as a fresh beginning. Some writers use, instead of radical spacing, italicized stanzas to indicate this kind of pitch change. Others will create alternate margins for lines or entire stanzas, margins that indicate returns to pitch-levels different from that of the base margin. Robert Kroetsch does this in *The Ledger* and *Seed Catalogue*. A poet can also allow the base margin to float from line to line, or stanza to stanza, in order to suggest a wider range of pitches than is normally used in daily speech. This is what George Bowering does to the margin in *Allophanes*.

The multiple margin is unfortunately one of the most mis-understood features of open verse, often used to denote nothing more than a desire for 'variety' in the visual effect of the page.

6. Spelling

Some writers, in their desire to have the printed form of the poem signal as accurately as possible the poem's spoken form, will alter the spelling of words to enforce specific pronunciations. Robert Duncan and George Bowering both spell the unvoiced final consonant of the past participal as "t" rather than "ed" — "reacht" rather than "reached," "lookt" rather than "looked." Bowering also deletes the apostrophe in contractions such as "don't" or "can't" because it has no phonological significance. Paradoxically, he retains the apostrophe of the possessive case, although it also has no phonological value and no ambiguity would be created by its deletion. bpNichol removes the silent letters from words like "thought" ("thot") or "through" ("thru"). The effect of such variant spellings is to emphasize the poet's concern for the oral dimension of the poem, and to a lesser extent to argue for spelling reform. Nevertheless, the fact that such spelling changes are applied inconsistently suggests that they are above all a matter of individual preference and controlled by subjective factors. They have not become a standard signal of open verse notation.

The one writer whom we know of who attempts to apply a system of phonetic or "aural" spelling consistently is bill bissett. In his case, these spelling changes are one of several indicators of bissett's disdain for arbitrary convention and his preference for the "natural." In bissett "the" is rendered "th," "come" is rendered "cum," "you" is rendered "yu." Here the oral form takes total precedence over the print form and the grammatical and orthographic conventions that have grown around it. Once again, although bissett has influenced one or two writers to change the spelling of selected words, he has not altered the general practice of open verse notation.

7. Embedding Other Notational Systems

Special effects are often achieved in open verse poems by including within them passages written in other notational systems. Such alternate systems include "concrete" or visual notation, paragraphs of prose, the written form of the play, any of the traditional closed verse forms, various found elements, the interview format, or that of the personal or business letter. Examples of these abound in contemporary Canadian poems: Kroetsch's use of found materials in *The Ledger* and *Seed Catalogue*. Ondaatje's use of the interview in *The Collected Works of Billy the Kid*. Nichol's use of the prose paragraph and the play format in *The Martyrology*. Webb's use of "concrete" notation at the beginning of *Naked Poems*. Stuart McKinnon's use of the personal letter in *The Intervals*. In all these examples, since the majority of other notations signal their own structures clearly, their introduction allows the writer to take advantage of both the historical connotations and special sound qualities they possess. Each thereby becomes yet another element in open verse notation.

8. Other Punctuation

Certain particular uses of common punctuation signs are found in a great deal of contemporary open form poetry.

A. THE OBLIQUE (/)

This is commonly used to denote a pause shorter than a comma but longer than the normal pause between words in a continuous flow of speech or, in linguistic terms, the shortest possible level terminal. To many readers' ears, this pause will not register but it does exist. A second use of the oblique is to set up two words or concepts side by side that the writer wishes to occur almost simultaneously in the reader's mind — e.g. "his/her," "she walks/he holds" (both examples taken from Fred Wah's poetry).

B. THE UNCLOSED PARENTHESIS (
This is commonly used to indicate an interpolated comment that becomes the main text.

C. *ITALICS*
As well as their use to indicate a change in pitch (see section 5 above), or their standard use for emphasis, italics are often used by poets like Gwendolyn MacEwen to indicate direct quotation or dialogue. Since in such cases a change of pitch also occurs, the italics serve as a double signal.

D. THE PERIOD.
There is a particular use of the period that one sometimes encounters in open verse notation — e.g.:

      the star   .   our bodies

Here the writer (Victor Coleman) signals a longer than normal pause followed by a full stop followed by another longer than normal pause. Whereas the pitch normally falls at the end of a sentence, here the delay of the period allows the pitch of "star" to be level, and the fall in pitch at the period to be unvoiced.

E. CAPITALIZATION
One of the most distinctive features of open form poetry for most readers is the lack of capital letters, particularly at the beginnings of lines. Most writers of open form poetry have chosen to work within the logic of the sentence, and therefore only capitalize at the beginning of complete sentences. Some — bill bissett for one — have taken this further, and reserve the use of capitals for emphasis, usually of loudly voiced utterances. The

lack of capitalization, particularly of the pronoun i, sometimes signals certain underlying political and religious beliefs. Such use would normally be identifiable through the presence of related thematic statement.

We have tried in this essay to describe the current practice in open form poetry, to be descriptive as opposed to prescriptive. Open verse notation is still evolving; problems, some of which we have tried to indicate, remain to be solved. Throughout we have avoided the term "free verse," believing it to be both denotatively misleading and weighted with unfortunate historical connotations.

Notes

1. Writers sometimes, at their discretion, do not notate every terminal in a line, precisely because they want the terminal to "float," to occur at the reader's "option." This is not mere sloppiness, but a deliberate notational choice to create a rhythmic ambiguity that will allow part of the line to be formed in the reader's imagination. In fact, this choice demands that the writer control the rhythm of the immediately adjacent lines in such a way that they can accommodate any reading of the ambiguous line.

2. The other factor here is, of course, rime. Skillful use of both end rime and rime within the lines of a poem allows particular primary stresses to be grouped together to create counter rhythms on top of both other groups of rimes and the basic rhythms of the poem. It should be noted that rimes are most audible in syllables which receive primary stress, and inaudible in syllables which receive weak stress.

3. At the level of content, a change of pitch is normally experienced as a change in voice — e.g. from didactic to reflective, from public to private, from confident to unconfident, etc.

Notating Sound Poetry — An Introduction to *The Prose Tattoo: Selected Performance Scores of The Four Horsemen*

for Karl Young

1983

One of the first problems confronting the group when we formed, after having gone thru the orgastic preliminaries of screaming our guts out in free-form improvisation, was an issue of notation (& hence structure). We wanted to find a way to write down certain more complex pieces we had ideas for where, tho elements are improvised, other elements were fixed. In acoustic sound poetry there is no fixed tradition of notation. Vive la liberté but vive la certain limitations. We were moving into the whole area out of poetry, not out of music or theater, tho some of us had experience in these forms, and we wanted "readable" texts as an element in performance. Not exclusively but we wanted them there.

Hence the birth of the grid. We no longer remember who came up with it. Like many things in the group it probably began with one person but has been worked with & adapted so that it now belongs to the group. Going thru the earliest texts (ones we performed at our first public reading) the idea is there in everybody's handwriting. "Coffee Break," "Poem No. 1," "Seasons," & the not included "A Motive for Metaphor," different graphings by different hands, all use the grid. The early graphing of "Seasons" shows some of the problems we were up against.

It looks more like a flow chart & was very hard to follow. But does that mean that "Seasons" was first? Probably not. But I think that's the version of the story I like best, because "Seasons" was the first group composition. Everybody wrote for it & the recorded version of the piece remains one of the most interesting pieces we've done. And it makes sense, this origin story, because the complexity of the piece means we would have had to come up with a workable notation system to even compose it. So let's say that's the "official" version & go on from there.

The grid has not been our sole method of notation. Like most acoustic sound poets we have used Raoul Hausmann's notion of optophoneticism — sound reading/interpretation of spatially organized text. Hence compositions like "Sixteen Part Suite" & "The Room (A Valentine) Winter's Day." But does this make the scores "visual poems"? In the strict sense no. They are meant to be read aloud &, indeed, in some cases we have deliberately worked against the "pictorial" sense of page in order to foreground the texts' compositional basis as a fixed element in an interactive dialogue with the speakers. We have often taken optophonetic mini-texts & used the grid as a way of organizing them as in "The Dreams Remain." And, of course, we have used variations on the basic grid in order to achieve different effects, remembering always that both "page" & "grid" are simply conventions.

```
one   of   the   things   the   Concrete   Poetry   movement
taught  us  as  writers  was  to  reclaim  the  small
gesture.  some  texts  need  to  exist  separate  from
our  desire  to  "collect"  them.  once  we  become
sensitized  to  what  is  happening  tonally,
imagistically,  rhythmically,  etc.  within  the
smaller  gestural  works  we  are  then  in  a
position  to  introduce  notes  with  exactly  those
qualities  into  a  larger  composition.
```

This raises another point. The movement from page to page, & the movement from rectangle to rectangle in the grid, are used to the same ends — to notate transition points.[1] The grid does not, indeed cannot, dictate pitch, rhythm, duration or any colouration the performer may put on the text. What it does do is define who's doing what when, with whom, & what elements they have to work with. Thus a combination of optophonetic and grid notation systems, old-fashioned memory work, & extensive improvisation (in terms of both abstract sound & dialogue) have been the basic elements in all our performances. This in itself tells you what is missing from this selection, i.e. many of what we think of as our major pieces — "Mischievous Eve," "Stage Lost," "In the Middle of a Blue Balloon," "Theme," "Tetralogue," "Mixed Metaphors," & "Paul Dutton's Dream." They are not included for the simple reason that they are not notated. Their notation exists only in our minds & in isolated text elements. And this highlights the compositional reality of the group, which is that the four of us have composed the major pieces. These are the real flowering of our twelve year project in collaboration. The texts offered in this collection (with the exception of "Seasons" & "Schedule for Another Piece") are the ground, individually or collectively offered, from which the major work grew. Obviously then they are central to our work but they are not the centre. The centre is an ongoing compositional workshop in which the four of us take anywhere from days to years to compose as a group and to which we bring fragmentary lines, half-formed ideas, dreams, works in progress, et cetera et cetera, and out of which, thru a kind of bricollage, the compositions take shape. For example, "In the Middle of a Blue Balloon" began as a solo piece by Rafael, grew into an expanded exploration of psychosis performed by the group, was then recorded & the recording has now been worked in as an element in the most recent version with Rafael, its originator, standing silently (almost invisibly) in the background as bp & Paul fight in the foreground & Steve appears to be attempting to watch the original piece on a television whose back is toward the audience. The solo version of "Blue Balloon" shows up again as an element in "Final Repetitions" (included in this collection under its earlier title,

"Strongarm for Louis"). These short descriptions do not do the performed pieces justice but give you some idea of what can happen to a single text.

I repeat that the group compositions are the major compositions. Obviously they are formed by four individual voices but it is that moment of group identity that we have striven for. In an historical sense then this collection runs the risk of falsifying our history, but then print is an inadequate medium for our ultimate goal. Even phonograph recordings and tapes run this risk, as they remove the living performers from the audience's presence, and freeze what should be an ongoing process. This is part of why we insist that the texts are simply scores, simply the tracking of an oral intention, not, in their intention or most basic form, visual poems. The individual group members as improvisors are what bring the pieces alive, much more so than any "composer" we could identify. Composer is an inadequate term for sound poetry. What you do is set up an intentional framework, a scheme of opportunities. And that is why, tho we have listed the authors of particular pieces in the index, this list should not be taken as measure of any one person's contribution to the group. No one is more or less important. We have been and remain four idiosyncratic presences and only the four of us make up The Four Horsemen. Our strength as individual writers can be measured by our individual writing, but our strength as a group is only measurable by what has happened when we have effectively joined our intentions compositionally, &, ultimately, in the final stage of composition — in performance.

If these scores, then, are simply scores for the use of a single performance group, why publish them? Three of the pieces, "Seasons," "Schedule for Another Piece," & "Headspace," are texts which we have developed into performance pieces. Although the performance pieces only exist in performance, the texts remain interesting & readable. A great deal of contemporary concrete poetry has been created primarily for the eye, but readers have found ways to vocalize it, converting into sound what was originally intended as image. Many of our grids & optophonetic scores can be read as secondary visual poems, visual poems that are by-products of group performance, much in the same way that many visual poems, originally intended for the eye, have generated secondary oral readings. Much of the reader's experience with visual poetry can be brought to these scores; in addition, the reading of scores as visual poems can extend the reader's sense of the possibilities of visual poetry in general: imaged sound can fertilize visual poetry in much the same way as visual conventions have stimulated recent performance art. We will be pleased if we have opened doors to further developments in visual poetry thru our performance work. Readers primarily interested or involved in performance art may find many uses for this book. We hope that they include many we have not thought of ourselves. As I said above, our aim has been to set up a scheme of possibilities. Of course, any performance artists wishing to use these scores in their own work must obtain permission from The Four Horsemen. Inquiries should be sent to bpNichol at 98 Admiral Rd., Toronto, Ontario, Canada M54 2L6, or to the Horsemen via the publisher.

Note

1. The difference is that the grid fixes the sequence of choices whereas the page-to-page pieces allow the text (and hence the sequence) to be shuffled.

When the Time Came

I

An Entrance Monologue

My original ambition was to take the first chapter of *Ida* & go thru it with you step by step, showing how the construction of Stein's sentences & paragraphs is twinned to what it is she is saying; how, in short, her saying says. I'd thot "first chapter" because in an earlier essay ("Some Sentences, Paragraphs & Punctuations on Sentences, Paragraphs & Punctuation") I'd gone into the first page of *Ida* fairly thoroughly, albeit from a different point of view, & the sheer symmetry of moving from the first page to the first chapter definitely appealed to me. The reality of what I'm going to do today has turned out differently from its intended reality largely because of the approach I elected to take, which is to say the approach I elected to *try* (& I'll put the emphasis there — I'm going to *try*) — to deal thoroughly with the first five pages of *Ida*. I want to deal with Stein's writing in its real context which is the flux & flow of her actual texts. I *don't* want to extract her meaning so much as slow your reading of the text down thru the use of that ancient & beneficent device, the extensive commentary, forcing you to linger over the deliberateness of her craft & show you how, tho she was whimsical & had a highly developed sense of play, the whimsy & the play were part of an overall & continuous strategy of engagement with some of the central issues of any writer's writing: the role of the I; the relationship of the role of the I to the function of narrative time; the whole issue of narrative time in general. I confined myself to five pages because I decided finally that what I was interested in was developing a general strategy for reading Stein, trying to convey to you the excitement I feel when I read her & why I feel it, & given that, that I was more interested in doing a few pages carefully, at a pace we *all* could absorb them, than doing a whole bunch of pages hastily. I'd also like to emphasize that I include my own I in there when I say *all*, because my guide was the feeling in me after five pages that that was a hell of a lot to absorb, & why didn't I leave the next few pages for another lecture, or another critic even, but leave off at a point where the I & the we could both see clearly what was happening.

When I was much younger than I am now, chronologically speaking, but about the same age mentally, tho without the experience I've accumulated since then, I started writing a book on Gertrude Stein's theories of personality as revealed in her early opus *The Making of Americans*. The general scheme was to go thru & extract the many & very clear things she'd said about personality types & demonstrate both the consistency & accuracy of her particular classification system. This is easy to do; it would just take a gross amount of time — say two years or so if you were working at it full tilt. I finished two chapters of the work, sketched out an additional four, even published the initial two, & then abandoned the project. It took me awhile to see why I'd abandoned it, but the why is very important to what I'm going to talk about today, so it's worth taking a moment or two to talk specifically to that point. Now you'll have noticed I said "talk" when here I am rather obviously reading to you from some prepared notes, prepared sentences in this case, so right away you're grasping the principle of a real-time fiction. The writer is finally a writer. She/he is not a talker. Even tho this is only the third time I've presented these words to an audience, I am *presenting* them — virtually the same ones as in the other times — I am not talking/creating in any spontaneous sense. Tho it's clearly this I addressing you, this I is using words the I managed to write down in its hotel room at English Bay one late November afternoon (tho of course right now, in the time of the writing, it's today at English Bay & I'm imagining a you which is tomorrow & other days in the future & me saying, or you reading, these words). Therefore I say, & I just said (whether in an oral or a print sense), this whole talk is a kind of fiction. And it's precisely this borderline between the real life of the I & the I's existence in narrative time, any narrative's time, that was one of Stein's central concerns. She was exploring the continuous present & she wanted writing to occupy a continuous present. She very specifically asked us all in her *Geographical History of America*: "Oblige me by not beginning. Also by not ending" (157). I.e. — continue. Continue continuously. Give the text the reality of its existence as an object & let that object be continuously present to you — timeless in that sense. So how could I continue extracting? I was violating Stein's text when I did that, the very spirit of her text, & I was, of course, proving the validity of Heisenberg's Principle of Uncertainty as it applied to literature. By extracting I was bringing the text to a dead halt & we were no longer observing it as it was & therefore our observations ceased to have any validity. We're in danger of that even in what we're going to do today but at least in this case I'm going to encourage you to, if you feel like it, read on ahead of me & just let what I'm saying drift in & out of your own relationship to the text. Don't let me stop the particularity of that relationship. Just let me help if the help's helpful. That was one of the things that struck me in Grade 8 when Miss Nethercut, our English teacher, would be reading from Charles Dickens' *Oliver Twist* & we weren't supposed to read on ahead, we were supposed to stay with her, & she'd stop every few minutes & say "Barrie" or "June" she'd say "where am I?" & you'd have to have your finger on the correct spot. Don't keep your finger on the spot. It doesn't matter if you miss what I'm saying because it's what Stein's saying that's important. I'm going to be insisting the same information in different ways because that's what Stein did & you'll get the real flux of the definite particles if you simply read away. Okay. Here we go. This is a reading of the first five pages of *Ida* entitled "When the Time Came."

II
The Definite Particles

Resist the temptation to jump too far ahead in terms of knowledge. i.e. Let the net of information arise mainly from the text at hand. **Read** the book you're **reading.**

This is the announcement of what Stein proposes to deal with, that the self, the Id(e)a of I, + tIme, are inseparable, but that the I exists beyond notions of sIngularity.

THERE was a baby born named Ida. Its mother held it with her hands to keep Ida from being born but when the time came Ida came. And as Ida came, with her came her twin, so there she was Ida-Ida.

The mother was sweet and gentle and so was the father. The whole family was sweet and gentle except the great-aunt. She was the only exception.

But the exception becomes the rule. Stein allows us some foreshadowing here by implication.

This whole opening is very rich + dense. What is being dealt with is the notion of "self-consciousness" + the idea that the "self" also births the "not-self", that those who never confront the I/I remain sweet + gentle, that only the great-aunt, who bore twins + buried them under the pair tree, the one who faced the **issue** of a doubleness, is different, + makes others feel funny.

This is the reannouncement of the "two", picking up from the opening page's Ida-Ida twins theme + echoing the pun on pair as where the two's been buried. These types of punning, underlinings + recapitulations are underlined in the grandfather's statement about trees— "tree" is always the same (repeats itself) but then "In a little while" you come to see how each "tree" is unique (insists itself) + "a cherry tree does not look like a pear tree". Stein is drawing on a natural model to once again insist her distinction between repetition + insistence.

This figure of the old woman becomes oracular precisely because she is old + has, therefore, knowledge of what <u>both</u> young + old mean.

The cherry tree can be taken as a pun on "cheery" + hence "sweet + gentle" + hence, too, "innocence" in all its senses which loops back to "cherry".

An <u>old woman</u> who was no relation and who had known the great-aunt when she was young was always telling that the great-aunt had had something happen to her oh many years ago, it was a soldier, and then the great-aunt had had little twins born to her and then she had quietly, the twins were dead then, born so, she had buried them under a pear tree and nobody knew.

Nobody believed the old woman perhaps it was true but nobody believed it, but all the family always looked at every pear tree and had a funny feeling.

The grandfather was sweet and gentle too. He liked to say that in a little while <u>a cherry tree</u> does not look like a pear tree.

It was a nice family but they did easily lose each other.

So Ida was born and a very little while after her parents went off on a trip and never came back. That was the first funny thing that happened to Ida.

The days were long and there was nothing <u>to</u> do.

Here we expect the word "trees" to occupy the fourth position but instead we find it buried in the word "streets". "trees" become "streets" even as a "cherry tree" does not become a "pear tree". In each insistence of a thing some transformation must take place. Otherwise it is simply a repetition.

She saw the moon and she saw the sun and she saw the grass and she saw the streets.

The first time she saw anything it frightened her. She saw a little boy and when he waved to her she would not look his way.

She liked to talk and to sing songs and she liked to change places. Wherever she was she always liked to change places. Otherwise there was nothing to do all day. Of course she went to bed early but even so she always could say, what shall I do now, now what shall I do.

Here is part of Stein's theory of narrative + her theory of personality. The I(da) is always changing places. And indeed in this story each time an Ida is mentioned you are never sure which Ida. Each recurrence is not a repetition but a fresh insistence + hence a fresh revelation.

Once you realize + accept that Stein is dealing with **insistence**, not repetition, then its clear that two different "now"s are being pointed to — two different time periods. The comma between them is used to mark the time shift, to underline the time shifts any narrative contains.

And thus arises this entire paragraph, a commentary on time.

Thus also the following paragraph's insistence that <u>Ida</u> is not <u>idle</u> but is as a day is — "always the same day". Yet it is important to remember that Ida <u>is</u> Ida, & that the <u>now, now</u> structure parallels the <u>day, day</u> & <u>Ida, Ida</u> samenesses & differences. Each is a discrete unit of time & being, tho they have the same name. <u>Ida</u> is not <u>idle</u> but she is <u>Ida</u> & these are not exactly the same.

Some one told her to say no matter what the day is it always ends the same day, no matter what happens in the year the year always ends one day.

Ida was not <u>idle</u> but the days were always long even in winter and there was nothing to do.

Ida lived with her great-aunt not in the city but just outside.

Ida was not idle, &, in fact, as the earlier sentence made clear, "always could say, what shall I do now, now what shall I do." Which of course is a graphing of the I in motion, the I insisting Itself.

Here we see how the exception becomes the rule, becomes the ruler of Ida's life, as the great-aunt, who is linked to Ida-Ida thru the pair tree, becomes the one who raises Ida & Ida, the one by whom her days are ruled.

Stein makes use of the doubleness of this little logic loop. Everything here is _not_ Two, yet _is_ Two + yet, too, is one. Really, of course, it is 1 plus 1. But it is not Two.

Indeed here is a third 1 who restates the theme of I + I's desire to dIalogue with self. I talks to I. Thus for any of us there is an experience within self of "I?" "da?". Q + A.

> One day it was not Tuesday, two people came to see her great-aunt. They came in very carefully. They did not come in together. First one came and then the other one. One of them had some orange blossoms in her hand. That made Ida feel funny. Who were they? She did not know and she did not like to follow them in. A third one came along, this one was a man and he had orange blossoms in his hat brim. He took off his hat and he said to himself here I am, I wish to speak to myself. Here I am. Then he went on into the house.
>
> Ida remembered that an old woman had once told her that she Ida would come to be so much older that not anybody could be older, although, said the old woman, there was one who was older.

Orange blossoms were + are associated with marriage (my mother's wedding ring had them clustered on it) + thus a third fruit/tree/sexual +/or romantic word is added (i refer here to its _associational_ net + _not_ some private symbolism of Stein's). The "or" of "orange" (part of the "either/or" _two_ term formulation) is also important.

This reiterates a point Stein made in THE MAKING OF AMERICANS, that we are never to ourselves as anything other than young men + women in our consciousness of self. That the Idea of "older" is something only the "old" can convey to us. This is underlined later in the text by Ida's growing older leading to her being sixteen. It is those for whom time is almost over that the concept "old" is fully revealed to.

Everything is **transformed**. Things become like other things. Each thing/episode/experience has its separate existence & is transformed within it. This is the notion "insistence in narrative", that as you move forward & encounter the same words/ideas in new constructions & configurations they are different & have a new existence. It is this very difference in each moment that must be conveyed if one is to have a complete description.

She was very young and as she had nothing to do she walked as if she was tall as tall as any one. Once she was lost that is to say a man followed her and that frightened her so that she was crying just as if she had been lost. In a little while that is some time after it was a comfort to her that this had happened to her.

She did not have anything to do and so she had time to think about each day as it came. She was very careful about Tuesday. She always just had to have Tuesday. Tuesday was Tuesday to her.

They always had plenty to eat. Ida always hesitated before eating. That was Ida.

She has time to contemplate the natural insistence — each day as it comes. And these days, as we have seen, are I days, the discrete units of the I's existence. They are also Ideas.

to do.
Tuesday, which is, of course,
Two's day or Ida, Iday which is also the "They" that opens the next pairagraph (& each is the graphing of that pair Ida/Ida). "Tuesday was Tuesday to her"; the same & different each time she encountered it.

325

Ida began to wonder if that was what was now happening to her. She wondered if she ought to go into the house to see whether there was really any one with her great-aunt, and then she thought she would act as if she was not living there but was somebody just coming to visit and so she went up to the door and she asked herself is any one at home and <u>when they that is she herself</u> said to herself no there is nobody at home she decided not to go in.

That was just as well because orange blossoms were funny things to her great-aunt just as pear trees were funny things to Ida.

Here the theyness of the she is drawn out as is indeed the whole question of whether anyONE is in the house with the great-aunt. The I's continual strategy of creating a not-I, another self which comes to visit the house in which the I lives, & then abiding by its judgements, is sketched.

And only a few paragraphs earlier we'd heard how the orange blossoms in the one person's hand "made Ida feel funny". Since they are funny things to both Ida & her great-aunt we are pointed back to that sense of how the <u>one</u> has the potential to become more than one. One pair-agraph about pair trees +/or ange blossoms, the potential for more than one in one. Particularly when we remember it is <u>one</u> of the <u>two</u> who come in <u>one-by-one</u> (one bi one (& hence <u>two</u>) that has the orange blossoms, & the man who wishes to speak to himself.

The other point here is that "orange blossoms" are not "orange blossoms" when they mean "marriage", i.e. "When is a door not a door? When its ajar." This is a transformation that happens thru the <u>insistence</u> of multiple meanings (i.e. <u>NOT</u> symbolism).

326

The one-bi-one pun leads us into
this whole statement about, specifically,
sexual choice +, more generally, the
notion of what constitutes choice (as in
the earlier choosing to be Ida Ida, or
I/not-I). Love is blind, + blind to the
issue him or her. Determinist + absolu-
tist psychologies do not allow for that.
Love is born blind. Age has nothing to do
with it. (It is also worth remembering
Stein's aphorism: "I am I because my
little dog knows me". There is the
notion that in the twinning, the recognition of the other, the not-I, is what
brings the I into its true existence. And
what is Love but that recognition, that
blind sighting.)

And so Ida went on growing older and then she was almost
sixteen and a great many funny things happened to her. Her great-
aunt went away so she lost her great-aunt who never really felt
content since the orange blossoms had come to visit her. And now
Ida lived with her grandfather. She had a dog, he was almost blind
not from age but from having been born so and Ida called him
Love, she liked to call him naturally she and he liked to come even
without her calling him.

It was dark in the morning any morning but since her dog Love
was blind it did not make any difference to him.

It is true he was born blind nice dogs often are. Though he was
blind naturally she could always talk to him.

This is Stein's statement of pronom-
inal choice (a continuation of the one-
bi-one), that some she's quite naturally want to call him she, that Love,
that dog, is blind to the categories
people would place on it... "it did
not make any difference to him."

(I'll pause briefly simply to point out that this line is also an injunction to the reader + as such reinforces the approach we are taking to the text here.)

→ One day she said. Listen Love, but listen to everything and listen while I tell you something.

Yes Love she said to him, you have always had me and now you are going to have two, I am going to have a twin yes I am Love, I am tired of being just one and when I am a twin one of us can go

out and one of us can stay in, yes Love yes I am yes I am going to have a twin. You know Love I am like that when I have to have it I have to have it. And I have to have a twin, yes Love.

The house that Ida lived in was a little on top of a hill, it was not a very pretty house but it was quite a nice one and there was a big field next to it and trees at either end of the field and a path at one side of it and not very many flowers ever because the trees and the grass took up so very much room but there was a good deal of space to fill with Ida and her dog Love and anybody could understand that she really did have to have a twin.

She began to sing about her twin and this is the way she sang.

On a "One" day she says to him "now you are going to have two."

Here there is the double notion that the self has selves (six I's in three IIves) + that in love we are twinned ("yes Love yes I am yes I am"), that the beloved is a twin I (en-twin-ed). Love is the twin ("I have to have a twin, yes Love.")

There both is + there isn't space. It is a question of point-of-view. Point-of-view is itself a means of transformation, the "given" in translation.

Stein is also playing here with the whole notion of description + its inaccuracy on the level of language. Even as she moves out to describe the house her description keeps contradicting itself... "the trees and the grass took up so very much room but there was a good deal of space" to fill..."

This is the opening theme restated, that time enters with the I, & here the additional complexity or notion that it enters with the death of the not-I. The possibility of the not-I is born with the I & inside time is not-I whereas tIme is I.

Following on the heels of the earlier "I have to have a twin" (the anticipation), we have the birth & the contemplated death of Ida Ida.

Oh dear oh dear Love, that was her dog, if I had a twin well nobody would know which one I was and which one she was and so if anything happened nobody could tell anything and lots of things are going to happen and oh Love I felt it yes I know it I have a twin.

And then she said Love later on they will call me a suicide blonde because my twin will have dyed her hair. And then they will call me a murderess because there will come the time when I will have killed my twin which I first made come. If you make her can you kill her. Tell me Love my dog tell me and tell her.

This is a rather complicated play on "love me, love my dog" but the dog _is_ love + in love the I is twinned & the instruction is to both I's + to the I that is other, that love must flow both ways, that tho she made her she didn't make her. The I must love the other I

But there is also a warning not to take this as autobiography ("tell me and tell her") because in fiction (+ IDA _is_ a novel) you create all kinds of not-I's. A little later on in the novel she says: "Little by little she knew how to read and write and really she said and she was right it was not necessary for her to know anything else." Everything she or you or I could want to know is there in the writing. The writing is, in that sense, self-contained.

329

Thru all the punning + word play we are constantly reminded that there is nothing funny about Ida but that funny things do happen to her, + certain things give her, + other people funny feelings. This constant emphasis on the meanings of the word "funny" points to the doubleness of all the play. Stein knows the doubleness of her entendres but she is not trying to be funny ("There was [is] nothing funny about Ida [the novel, in this case] but funny things did happen to her." Serious punning.

This is ryme, a reassertion of the issue of sexual choice, + a play on the classic palindrome "a man, a plan, a canal — panama".

Like everybody Ida had lived not everywhere but she had lived in quite a number of houses and in a good many hotels. It was always natural to live anywhere she lived and she soon forgot the other addresses. Anybody does. There was nothing funny about Ida but funny things did happen to her.

Ida had never really met a man but she did have a plan.

That was while she was still living with her great-aunt. It was not near the water that is unless you call a little stream water or quite a way off a little lake water, and hills beyond it water. If you do not call all these things water then there where Ida was living was not at all near water but it was near a church.

It was March and very cold. Not in the church that was warm.

By this point in the narrative Stein is playing with the **language** of description. Each assertion is followed by its flaw if considered as a logical statement + the useless generality + hence uselessness of most description (precisely because it is inaccurate on the level of language) is pointed to.

Similarly in her discussion of where Ida lived, Stein asserts that in the flow of life (+ there is an equation here to the flow of reading) one quite simply forgets one's former address. You are moving on + "it was always natural to live anywhere she lived." So in reading, as you move on you are forgetting things addressed to you as reader +, unless you are going to extract plot, this is natural.

III

An Exit Monologue (& some acknowledgements)

> what i started to do was write down everything
> i had thought about the issue of the
> "journal" as a formal model for the long poem
> & realized what i was really talking about was
> the "notebook" as a formal model for the long
> poem and that what i had done in my own
> writing was to write down notes in order to
> build a larger composition.

There is no conclusion to all this which is exactly as it should be since what we have been dealing with here is a beginning. Indeed I have found that each time I do this with a group of people additional meanings emerge. In a recent presentation Marlene Goldman pointed out how, when Stein says (or has Ida say), "I am going to have a twin yes I am Love, I am tired of being just one and when I am a twin one of us can go out and one of us can stay in …," she is also addressing her own shift away from the autobiographical works & back towards fiction. She is precisely interested in the interface between the authorial I & the fiction's I (the I of Ida &, as a contracted statement, "I'd'a done it if I had time" shows us how the I of the character is the I of "I would have," the I of the conditional phrase, the phrase in which we express the fictional possibility). Kris Nakamura also pointed out how the Ida in the first Random House edition is decoratively glyphed at the top of each page as follows:

I^DA

In this way both the I & the A achieve their singularity & the D is brought into question. She proposed it as the first letter of a two letter configuration viz:

$I^D{}_A{}^L$

where D is Death (& one condition of the not–I) & L is Love (another condition of the not–I). These exist at this moment simply as thots stirred by that most recent talk. There are more. Obviously I do not agree with critics like Marianne Hauser who said in her review of *Ida* at the time of its first appearance: "To look for an underlying idea … seems as futile as to look for apples in an orange tree." Once you accept that everything in Stein is deliberate gesture, forms part of a consistent & evolving whole, Stein makes sense, an almost perfect sense.

As a final note I would add my thanks to the people at Simon Fraser I first delivered this lecture to, & particularly to Juliet McLaren & Barry Maxwell who helped me clarify the business of the orange blossoms.

Talking About the Sacred in Writing

1983, 1988

... As everyone has said, the topic is a gigantic one and, in fact, I feel it's the area I probably feel the most hesitant to talk *about*, because my notion of my relationship to the sacred, to some sense of godness, of the beyond, otherness in that sense, has all the elements of "pataphysics — which is to say, the way I tend to think of "pataphysics is that very often you climb a fictional staircase that you know is fictional; you walk up every imaginary stair, you get to your imaginary window and you open your imaginary window, and there is the real world. You see it from an angle you would not otherwise see it from. So there's a sense for me in which I will start to follow a line of thought that I think of as fictional, or that at least I consciously know is fictional, and yet I find myself in a mental space — in a belief space — where what is happening in the moment of the writing takes on a kind of absolute reality at that point in time. It has the effect of a kind of flickering — that is to say, it's always flickering, I'm there, I see it, I absolutely believe it. When I move away from it and I'm no longer in that state, I find it hard to imagine the state of mind I was in when I wrote that thing. This has forced me to redefine, for myself, a notion of what faith is — that is to say, in some way I suppose I have the faith to follow the fiction far enough for it to get me to some kind of real perspective. I have to have some consciousness, then, of what I am doing and of where it seems to be imaginary, but nonetheless I get to a space which seems to give me a real perspective. This also makes it tremendously difficult to step aside from that process and talk about it. The best talking I've done about it, in a way, is in the poems I've written — but will that shut me up?! No!

Having said that — what I've been trying to deal with for years personally in *The Martyrology* (and hopefully by talking this way it can perhaps be useful, I don't know, you'll have to be the judges of that) — when I stumbled across the saints with David

Aylward in the ST words in language, and for David that's all it was, it was puns — but for me, I suddenly found myself writing a series called *Scraptures*, in which I was addressing and talking to these saints — long, very argumentative, shrill poems full of extreme rhetoric and, you know, lots of talk about the language revolution and so on was going down. I realized that for some reason these figures which had arisen out of language had a meaning to me that I would not have imagined, that I only got to through the pun, which is why I've tended to follow the pun ever since. But when I began to do that, I began to become more conscious that I had a belief, in essence, in the sacredness of the activity of language — not in the particular language necessarily. My own particular limitation is that I am a speaker of English, and it's the tongue I work in, and it's the tongue I am familiar with. But I think it's the activity of language itself, which is different in each language space you enter. I have a profound belief in *that* as a sacred activity — that is to say, *something* goes on. Now, you can use it to crack cheap jokes, you can use it to make profound statements, you can use it to deal with the political necessities of the world, and you can use it to write love poetry. You can use it for all sorts of things, but the activity itself has a tremendous power that has to be, within itself, respected. Now, it seems to me — what I've learned for myself — is that once I respect that activity of the language, then through the language I am literally led to things that I would not arrive at otherwise. Therefore, in a real sense I give up, on the one hand, some sense of the self as guiding the poem, though on the other hand I put a tremendous emphasis on getting my technical chops together so that when I am in the midst of the poem there's nothing standing between me and following it wherever it wants to go. If the poem has an urge to suddenly go off in this direction and write long, Proustian-style sentences, then I'm not going to stop because I'm hung up on the semi-colon and don't know how to push it around. I have to somehow have the ability to follow where the thing itself leads me.

The other thing making this difficult to talk about is obviously there's a unity in that act and the only way I can talk about it is to divide it into sections. There's me and there's the moment of the writing and there's the language that's leading me — but in some real sense when it's all working, it's one activity. I'm not dividing it up, I'm not stopping and thinking, where does the poem want to go, or whose turn is it to lead in the dance. I'm just doing it, and I'm writing the thing. And that activity has come to seem to me the essence of what I was reaching for as a kid in my religious experience. On a personal level, I was raised a Presbyterian, with lots of time in the United Church because there weren't that many Presbyterian churches around — and because my parents both loved to golf on Sundays and therefore did not really have a strong case for pushing me to church, though they felt guilty. This meant that I was in a real sense free to develop my own relationship to the concept of church. Sometimes I went, sometimes I didn't; if I liked the minister I stayed, if I hated the minister I didn't stay. But I always admired my father's relationship to God, which was: he was totally scared shitless of Him. The one time we got Dad into a church after 25 years, for my sister's wedding, he was white the whole time he was walking down the aisle. It just literally had to do with being inside a church. He had an old-style sense — I mean it's a little too extreme, I don't think it's necessarily useful to be scared out of your mind — but I see in a real sense that there was some sense of awe operative in my father. He didn't just take the thing for granted, and on the whole he'd rather avoid the whole issue in one way, but it was because it meant a tremendous amount to him.

In pursuing that line myself as a kid and going through all the kinds of, if you like, distortion imagery that any kind of organized church throws at you — like Ellie, whom I'm married to and who was a nun at one time, was telling me the wonderful thing that Catholics have: the pure milk bottle, which was purity, and the spotted milk bottle, which meant you were into the majors at that point. That was the kind of illustration she grew up with. I grew up with Sunday school comics in which great, sweating Corinthians battled I can't remember who, but it was all done like Superhero comics, and heaven was a place of clouds and of people in funny white robes. Those types of images had a tremendous influence on me and, of course, are there in *The*

Martyrology in terms of Cloudtown and so on, which is obviously a heaven as I was taught as a Presbyterian. But in moving through those types of images, the issue also became then, well, did I believe in God as I had been taught Him? Did I believe in some concept of a god-energy? What did I believe exactly? And though I moved away from that for a long period of time, I was never able to move completely away from some sense that there is a political reality to the world, an emotional reality to the world, and it seemed to me there was also a sacred reality to the world. The big temptation, of course, was to simplify it in some way. The issue still seems to me fantastically complex, and I don't fully understand my relationship to it at all, and I probably won't.

For myself, I've been trying to work out a no-gimmees relationship to the godhead, which is to say, I don't want anything for my belief. This is a very difficult concept to work out. Do I still then believe? I don't know why I'm going after this. You know how you set yourself these goals — like I decided when I was 18 that I believed in process in writing, and then about a year and a half ago I woke up one night in the middle of the night, and I woke up Ellie and said "Why process?" You know, after something like 20 years. So you get these little underpinnings you're working from, and I've been trying to work out a concept of — because a) somewhere that's what I believe, b) I'm very tempted by the notion constantly that I get something for believing. You know, that it means it makes it easier, it means I go somewhere when I die, it means that I'm finally going to have a permanent address — that would be nice, I moved a lot as a kid — or it means that I will get something back for it. All these seem to me very limited notions of what belief is, or what the sacred is, and of my relationship to that phenomenon in living. So, as far as I can articulate it at this time, that's what I'm aiming towards, a no-gimmees relationship to that idea. I don't necessarily get anything for the belief; it's merely an attempt to contact, if you like, another level of the reality that we live in.

At the same time, the other that's happening to me, which grows out of the same pursuit, is an attempt to deconstruct the I. And where that's leading me at this point is towards a further examination of the concept of family. It's nice the way the word

"i" is located in the middle of the word "family," because almost
everyone I knew who was a writer was also often in some flight
from or argument with their family on some level, and more and
more it seems to me that family is the closest touch we have with
something like a tribal structure that's still going on within the
confines of the existing societies — in the case of my own family
(and I was just at a family reunion this past weekend, I should've
worn my family reunion hat), but it also tends to cross historically
all sorts of political boundaries, which becomes more and more
interesting to me — the different systems of belief my family has
moved through in time, and so on. I see that as related to the
other quest, though I can't necessarily, completely tell you the
relationship.

Slightly garbled, but as good as I can do it.

Multiplex letraset a language event:
Review of (Untitled), by Peggy Lefler

1983

Canada has been particularly fortunate in its practitioners of alternative poetics in the emergence of a number of accomplished manipulators of new materials & technologies. Among those new materials, tho we tend to forget that it is such, is letraset. Hart Broudy, arguably the best visual poet in the world when it comes to utilizing letraset, staked out new turf when he moved from the dependence on whole words or letters, or the utilization of letraset as an element of collage (viz. bissett, McAuley, etc.), into extreme fragmentation of letter parts on both a micro (6 pt. typefaces in tiny 2" x 2" squares) & macro (wall-sized constructions) level. But Broudy has long since turned his attention to the photo-typesetter (see *Soundings & Serpentine*) & the whole area of letraset poem has lain relatively fallow.

The preceding is not to suggest that Peggy Lefler is derived from Broudy (I don't know if she's seen much of his work) but to suggest & underline a context for why I feel so enthusiastic about her work in general &, more specifically, about her recent Coma Goats Press publication. The single untitled text is printed on cardstock & comes in a brown manilla envelope on which Lefler's name has been stamped. Your first clue to the text is right there. It's by someone (i.e. there's no title to point you anywhere, be it towards some specific political &/or emotional context or some specific series in the author's working). For that reason we have to approach the only clear word in the text — "proud" — as first & foremost a pure language event. After all, she could've called the work *PROUD* or "*proud*" — and chose not to. In one reading of the piece then, the word "proud" can be viewed simply as source & indeed we find u's, fragments of p's, d's & r's, are the basic building blocks & at least part of what they build (if we take the word "proud" as a page orientation clue) is an upside down R, a P, a d & a p back to back, & hints as well of a 3-dimensional r.

But one of the strongest things about this text is the way it hovers between picture & poem. The word "proud" invites us to read in meaning. The breakdown of pride, the I of it, mirrored in the conversion to the open O of prOud, the way the tiny squares beneath that word (the dots from i's in a Futura typeface? (double punning on periods freed from their function of closure)) fall away, & the fractured line (macro stem of a lower case i) on the left hand side of the page at each of whose junctures a letter A (as beginning, language source, etc.) is placed as marker. At the same time the fine lines to the right suggest pages, frames, the edges of un-named books (this in a pictorial perspective reading) emphasizing both multiplicity (the nature of publishing after all) & singleness (page as text as book). At the same time, however, it is also simply itself, a construction of lines on a surface, & we can reference it as single glyph, a macro-alphabetic gesture built out of the micro (& isn't that finally what any language text, any book, is?). And that o in "proud" (& the constant flipping she does of the u) becomes a clue to turn the page, to keep turning & changing our relationship to the work, to both read in & read out.

I like what Peggy Lefler's doing here. She's very much her own person & what's refreshing is to see someone doing so much with the plasticity that letraset allows & taking it into new regions, too. She's inviting us as readers to include the semantic & the non-semantic, to broaden our awareness of what the language net can catch. She knows knowledge & proud have no i but pride & ignorance do. The trick, as I said, is to ride the i in but ride the o out (which is how you get inside & outside the language too).

Interview: Stuart Ross

bpNichol Talks about Consumer Resistance

1983

Stuart Ross: Why did you decide to write a 3-day novel?

bpNichol: Basically, I'd always admired Georges Simenon, who wrote the Inspector Maigret novels. He had this way of writing his 120-140 page novels in something like nine to eleven days. He'd lock himself away in a hotel room. And he wrote a tremendous amount — something like 285 of them in his lifetime, and the thing about it was that the quality of the writing was very good. That was the first thing. The second thing was that around 1978 my sense of how inspiration worked changed radically. Up until then I kind of had an uncomfortable relationship with the notion of the Muse. You know — I didn't quite believe it, but would sort of use it when I talked about it. And it suddenly occurred to me that really writing was a state of mind and that the trick was to be able to contact the state of mind. There were things in your life that made that impossible, but basically you should be able to write whenever you wanted to.

A problem if you're a writer who believes in process, which I tend to be, is that your thinking doesn't necessarily move on unless you leave a certain amount of time, because you tend to be thinking about the same things within a certain sphere of time. So it means that you don't, in fact, write every time you feel like it, but you can certainly write when your thinking has moved on, because that way you can contact the state of mind.

So, putting all those together, I really wanted to enter the contest ever since I'd heard about it, and last year was the first year I had the opportunity.

SR: Were you surprised at all by what you came up with?

bp: I don't know. I just sort of went into it. I had an idea of what I wanted to write. There were certainly things that I didn't expect that I would get in touch with — there were points in the writing that I actually got fairly upset in the sense of what I was writing about. That was a surprise to me. It didn't stop me. I kept rolling.

What was also a nice surprise was to realize that, in fact, I could write in that sustained a fashion, because I've tended to be a writer who'll work on something for a period if time, put it aside, come back to it later, and hence I tend to be working on a lot of things at the same time. I remember one year I totalled it all up and I was working on 40 series and projects of things, some of which take 10 15 years to come to fruition and some of which happen very fast. So it was interesting and a treat to realize that if I really put my mind to it I could actually work something straight through that way.

SR: Do you look at *Still* with any regret now?

bp: No, I'm quite pleased with it. It does exactly what I wanted it to do. If it hadn't, I would never have bothered to hand it in. I've been writing long enough that I don't get that six-month flash-back.

I remember when I was 18 and writing, I'd write THE GREAT POEM and a week later I'd think it was shit. That gradually lengthened to six months and then a year, two years. Then that all disappeared as I got more control over the writing, a better idea of what I was reaching for.

SR: How do you perceive, in *Still*, the relationship between the descriptive passages and the dialogues?

bp: In writing, I always want to do two things: there's what I'm going to write about, from the content point of view, and then there are problems, or questions I have, and the only way to answer the questions is to write something that addresses those questions formally. In *Still*, I was very interested in completely separating dialogue from description, and seeing what happened to the reading experience. So, suppose there was no one-for-one connection between these two things. Well, what I found in talking to people who've read it is that, as a reading experience, in their minds they tend to combine the two things.

This is often indeed true of the traditional novel. That a lot of description, and the way the reader perceives the description, is as something that stands between them and the meat of the story. So they want to get through the description on the way to the plot — i.e. description is never part of plot. So, I just did that thing that readers do, which is, I took a readerly role and completely separated description from dialogue.

SR: Between the sound poetry, which tends to be quite abstract in terms of content, and stuff like *Journal* and *Still*, which seem very personal, do you see some kind of cross-over happening?

bp: Well, yeah, I've been accused of almost everything. I've been accused of being too personalist. I've been accused of being too impersonal. The fact is what interests me is the range — of what's possible in writing. I just decided a long, long time ago that I was not going to accept someone else's definition of what constituted "high art" and what constituted "mature voice" … or *any* of that stuff. I had to give myself the freedom to move where it interested me.

One thing you don't realize when you're 18, but you realize sometime later, of course, is that the longer you write, the more you accumulate a history of your writing. So that what you begin to have behind you is, as it were from your own point of view, a body of thought — whether or not it's that from anybody else's point of view. (Laughter) They might not think it's too thoughtful at all. But, in a certain sense, there're questions you're beginning to pursue, and answers you're looking for, and that's *part* of what constitutes this notion of "mature voice." But a lot of it seems to be just a person narrowing down what they're attempting. Now, for some people that works very well and they get better and better, while for some people it marks a dying off. They become less interesting, I think.

So, on the one hand, I was very interested in the actual life of language — what happens in just pure intonation, pure expressiveness. I've also been very interested, though, in taking that information and synthesizing it in some way, to do something with what I learned. Both the description in *Still* and the kind of insistent tempos of *Journal* obviously are led by the ear — they come out of an interest in sound. And that usually was the governing factor in the writing of each of them.

I just see it all as part of an ongoing kind of search to broaden my formal base. I just think the issue of form is enormous, the possibilities at this point in time are enormous, and it seems to me, all the while, most writers don't even scratch the surface of what's possible. They stumble across three or four techniques and they think that that's the galaxy. Well, it's not.

SR: In your work, you've got all these major things — *The Martyrology* books, and *Still* now — and then you've got the stuff you've been doing since the beginning. You're still doing leaflets and xeroxed work, grOnks and so forth …

bp: Yeah, I still gasp them out from time to time.

SR: What importance do you attach to your self-published things?

bp: I think the notion of importance comes out of the notion of what a book is. So, if a book is supposed to be a mature summing up of your best thoughts on x and y, then some of what I've done certainly violates that notion.

When I began publishing, which was in the mid-60s, basically what I was working out of was — though I hesitate to use the word — the "tradition" of concrete poetry at that point in time, in which what you tried to do was to find the right form to put the work out in. So that it wasn't so much an issue of writing x number of poems, and then you do a "mature culling" of that, and you hone it down into the collection, and you hand out the collection — which is a tradition I certainly like — but in the concrete tradition, each thing has its own form, so you have poems which literally should just come out as cards, you give each thing its own setting, its own life, its own place. Maybe later you collect them.

So, I was working out of that. Also, it has always seemed to me there's really no excuse for not seeing your work be in print. It may be a little harder for prose writers, but as a poet you can always find a way to publish in some manner. That's what so impressed me when I met John Curry, because here he is and he's doing the most exquisite rubber-stamp things. I'd never seen anybody do so much of it, and such great rubber-stamp work.

And when Nelson Ball and Barbara Caruso were running Weedflower, they did the cleanest mimeo of all time. Or the reverse effect: bill bissett, and, say, d.a. levy, when he was very active, before he killed himself, with their really intense and very quick things. d.a. levy would do them and bind them in wallpaper and so on.

So I was very interested in the quick thing: mimeo as a quick, fast form at that time. I was very interested in those types of things, because it seemed to me that was part of the — that sort of flew in the face of the notion that "Gee, it's really hard to get your work out there." Well, if you wanted to get out and argue for your work, you want to fight for it, then you have the means and you can put it out. You can do it quite easily.

What it means, though, is you won't necessarily get the big presses publishing you, you won't necessarily get the big magazines publishing you, but then that becomes the issue: is what you're interested in doing getting your work published and seen, or is it getting an imprimatur from certain people? I think where you go crazy is when, unless you get so-and-so's approval, you feel you're doomed.

If, indeed, you're doing new writing, which other people don't like, then you've got to bypass them, and let other people get access to it. It's that old thing Gertrude Stein said: Anything that is really new is going to be ugly to us, because it won't fit any of our existing definitions of beauty or aesthetics.

That's why, at a certain time, I was much more active in that kind of publishing. Gradually, that way of publishing made people aware of my work, and gradually they began to understand some of what I was trying to do.

At first, I remember when I published *Scraptures Second Sequence*, standing in The Book Cellar watching people go through it. They'd pick it up, and they'd see there are three words to a page, and kind of flip, flip, flip, and they'd be through it in 30 seconds and say, "*What the fuck was that?*" and slam it down on the shelf. So I knew I was up against, as they say in the trade, consumer resistance. (Laughter)

There's so much attached to a "book": the formalness of a book, and the fact that the book is bound, and the fact that it's typeset — those are part of the real content of what a collection of poems say way before you ever get to reading the poems. What it says to the reader is "Take it seriously." But you can assault that, which bill bissett did for years.

SR: What kinds of things are interesting you as a reader these days?

bp: One of the things I realized about my reading for the last three years is that the bulk of my literary reading is stuff in manuscript — partly because of teaching creative writing now, but also because of the amount of editing I was doing for Coach House, occasionally grOnk things, Underwhich, *Open Letter*, and *Poetry Toronto*. So almost all my literary reading was unpublished work. But I needed a break from that, and so I've been cutting back in my editing.

SR: What were you reading when you were 18, or whenever it was that you began?

bp: 1962, eh? Lemme think ... a lot of Kenneth Patchen, a lot of Chinese poetry in translation, a friend had introduced me to the Dadaists. I was reading about Kurt Schwitters, and then it was bill bissett who introduced me to Gertrude Stein. And at about the same time was when I read Sheila Watson's *The Double Hook*, which was quite a revelation. The situation is much different now, but at that time, other than your contemporaries and three or four other writers, there really wasn't that much that was news, that one could stumble across in Canadian writing. At that time, it was almost a necessity for stimulation to look across the borders, towards Europe, or towards the States, and then so *much* activity began here that keeping up with what's happening *here* occupies my time. What's been happening here has been *wildly* interesting in the last 20 years.

Notes for "Journal" Conference Paper

1984

I've been composing this piece out of fragments of journal jottings as it were, combining various thots that occurred to me at different points, aiming to present some sort of cohesive — if not "argument" — at least "discussion" of a particular alternative to narrative per se, which is to say the form of the journal. Obviously I'm taking "narrative" to mean "story" in some sense & right away that's open to argument but then the whole term is open to argument so I'm just taking a giant step to one side & declaring that really what I want to talk about is the "journal" as a model for the long poem because, for me, it's been an alternative to writing a poem based on someone else's life or a poem based on my life, which is to say it's been an alternative to biography or autobiography as a model for the long poem. And just before we leave this point let me linger over that term "alternative" too, because nothing supplants something else. I'm just running along beside things & I'm way in the back of the pack as far as the history of literature as a whole goes, but the fact that I'm up & still running after all these years at least gives me some right to open my mouth & make a few observations. So let me start autobiographically.

Somewhere in the early months of 1982 I woke up with a very clear question ringing in my head: "Why process?" I mean I woke up, somewhere in what we tend to think of as the middle of our lives, wondering what I had meant when I'd said to myself, quite consciously, at approximately the age of 18, "what I'm interested in exploring in my poetry is process." And then March 2, 1984, right here on this campus, after a reading I'd done with Frank Davey & Judith Fitzgerald, I found the closing lines of Book VI of *The Martyrology*, lines which I'd just read for the first time in public that night, echoing in my head — "this business of process / nothing more than / the moment's grace" — & realized

I'd finally come to an answer to that question. But the question is worth going into to make the answer here clear, & both the answer & the question are inextricably tied up with *The Martyrology* & its formal model, the *utanniki* or poetic journal (&, by extension, the journal as journal (poetic or otherwise)), which is why I'm bothering with this preface; I'm trying to get from *there* to *here*.

Let me start, then, with an assertion: the journal is almost always present as an element in the continuous poem. Its partialness, incompleteness, serialness &, yes, processualness, make it a logical model upon which to build formally. Certainly, in my own work, its use of intimate detail, of private reference & temporally tied specificity, has worked as a formal framework for *The Martyrology* and for part of what *The Martyrology* attempts — the building of a life work in which the building of a life is also reflected. Is it then autobiographical? Certainly it borrows from autobiography but as a form the journal never attempts to tell the whole story, the whole life, but rather to write down the moment as it occurs, to track that perception in the instance of its perceiving. Thus tho its surface is autobiographical its intent is, from the point of view of scale, radically different. Nor does it concern itself with internal consistency, that false patina of logic that autobiography (or indeed biography) gives to life, but rather to notate & note the things that, in the words of Paul Newman in *Cool Hand Luke*, "seemed like a good idea at the time."

Most of the writers writing continuous poems in Canada use some element of the journal in their structure. This is a logical &, as I said earlier, an almost inevitable thing, since inherent in the notion of the continuous poem is the idea of process & the journal is the premier formal model for process. (Work in some stuff re *Field Notes* and what Daphne did with *What Matters* (she went back to journals *not* to writing autobiography). Don't forget Earl Miner's useful book too (an occasion to quote from & acknowledge that debt).)

But not autobiography I said. The journal is not about summing up. Autobiography is. Journals are not concerned with truth per se, or fairness in that sense, but rather in recording the perception of the moment. The perception of the moment is dross for the autobiographer except as it contributes to the already perceived larger pattern. The journal is not about pattern at all. It is about disconnection & dailiness; life, one could argue, as it is actually lived. Naturally the temptation to turn journal into auto-biography is almost irresistible & frequently given into.

The great trap in all this is, of course, the question of authenticity. The neophyte processual writer hesitates to change a syllable because, after all, that's the way it happened. But again, once you realize that the journal is not really about the way it actually happened so much as it is about an occurrence in language you begin to realize why Bashō et al felt totally free to revise their poetic journals until they got them right — right in an art sense since what they were concerned with was transforming the moment into literature. The concern to preserve the moment as it "actually" happened is, once again, the concern of autobiography. The concern to transform the moment into writing is the concern of journal-writing.

One may argue, of course, that the journal doesn't even have to be about "I" tho of course one is always aware of the "I" in any journal, i.e. the particularness of the intelligence. Exactly! I'd agree, and thus one is free to use quotations from anywhere, lists, receipts, etc. — all those marvelous things that form part of a journal — accounts of conversations with friends, things ripped out of context, found in virtually every sense; anything that the eye falls upon can finally be included.

Very early on in my own writing, in both the *Scraptures* sequence & *The Captain Poetry Poems*, I was trying to find a formal model that allowed for length but was not haunted by that old bugaboo of consistent tone & voice. I wanted the disjointedness I found in my own life & that of my friends, something closer to what Stein had talked about in terms of things as they actually are. I wanted a container but one that would allow things their own shape & texture. I found it when I began to write as if I were writing in my journal & then retrospectively realized part of what Bashō et al had been up to in their *utannikis*. Because the other thing it allows you is a different relationship to the I. You can't finally negate the I. It's there in the most automatic of writing if only as the guiding intelligence that set up the framework, so I also wanted something that acknowledged the I but did so in a different way. I was avoiding autobiography but I wasn't avoiding the I. What the journal allows is all of the framing I, the subjective I &, most wonderfully of all, the totally inconsistent momentary experience of jumbled continuity that most of us experience as I, i.e. (& isn't it nice that the "i" is there in "i.e." — so what's the "e" eh?) roughly 16 hours on & 8 hours off per day.

Note Book a composition on composition

Things I Don't Really Understand About Myself

1) Why I write at all.
2) Why I write the way I write.
3) Why I chose to start *The Martyrology* in the first place.
4) The so-called "real" relationship of any of this to my general theories of writing.

⌐⌐

The reasons I'm aware of for starting *The Martyrology* are entirely subjective and essentially irrational. At that point in my writing life my individual poems all seemed such poor little orphans that I was constantly looking for a home for them, a context, and it was out of that feeling that *The Martyrology* emerged. Naturally such feelings don't really fit into reasoned arguments of "beginnings" or "origins." They fit, rather, into the general category of things that, like Paul Newman said in *Cool Hand Luke*, "seemed like a good idea at the time."

⌐⌐

"He spun a tale." Me, I prefer to pun the tales. Donkey tricks. That notion of the muse can be a mule, makes jackasses of us all. And that is poetry.

⌐⌐

What tends to happen in criticism is that the critic establishes a continuous criticism, a body of work which uses the books it looks at to build theories or systems of thot. The longer the critic goes on writing the less the critic needs the literature. Certainly contemporary criticism no longer depends on particular works of literature to make its point. And, one assumes, the reverse is also true.

⊠

For me the fact of my writing always precedes my theorizing about it, i.e. when I'm writing theory I'm writing an account of "why" I have chosen in the moment of composition to write in a certain way. It has never worked for me to invent a theory of writing & then to try & write on the basis of that theory.

⊠

The assumption seems to be that "if" you're writing a long poem you're making a bid for immortality, somehow seeking to encompass your age, something the way your parents used to say "c'mon, act your age." Of course that's got nothing to do with anything. One simply writes the way one writes and readers are free to read the way they read and whether anybody's still reading you a few years down the line is in a lot of other hands, not your own, and depends on a lot of political / social / economic factors. Thus what one is often / mostly wrestling with in writing is the present tense, trying to find alternatives to the larger narratives within which writing seems to exist, the political / national / historical / psychological (& so on) frames within which it is (will be?) read.

⊠

With the shuffle text readers are freer to insert their own formulations into the mix precisely because the structure is more porous, lacks the obvious narrative links. Indeed, given that readers could get over regarding the text as sacred, one could imagine this piece having so many other reader comments written in (thus transforming the role of the reader of course) that what you are hearing today would become simply a sub-text, a footnote in a much different sequence of notes, and my role would be changed from writer to reader. This is analogous to how criticism can affect writers and is why, in one's writing life, depending on your stance or your sense of how these things influence &/or shape you, it can be useful if the body of your writing is a few good jumps ahead of the body of criticism about your writing.

〔‖〕

the hardest thing about using autobiographical detail in the long poem is to get the reader to accept it as what it is: words in a book revealing exactly the amount of information necessary for that moment of the composition. autobiographical information seems to raise the desire for more such information, as if knowing it would somehow increase one's appreciation of the text when, in fact, the exact opposite happens; the additional information changes our reading of the text & thus distorts it.

〔‖〕

reading is not just one kind of experience. we use it in different ways to fulfill different purposes & desires. why not texts then of such synaesthesia that they touch as many desires in the reader, fulfill as many purposes for the reader, as possible?

〔‖〕

if the composition is still in progress then the form is still in progress & i can't talk about the over-all form. if the form is finished then the composition is complete but needs to be fitted in. in completeness an incompleteness 'n in incompleteness a completeness.

To readers: the remaining sections of this essay are distributed throughout this book on pages 31, 40, 62, 80, 114, 142, 156, 230, 253, 262, 287, 313, 331, 371, 389, 400, 416, 424, 452 and 471.

The "Pata of Letter Feet, or, the English Written Character as a Medium for Poetry

1984, 1985

I. MOUNTING THE ANALOGY

i'm going to start with a quote that i first came across in my reading 23 or 24 years ago.

> 'Pataphysics is the science of the realm beyond meta-physics ...
> (Roger Shattuck rephrasing Alfred Jarry's definition in Shattuck's "Superliminal Note" (in *Evergreen Review* Volume 4 Number 13, May-June 1960))

Now since metaphysics has to do with inquiry into first things, ontology, how seriously are we to take something which alleges to deal with that which comes before, is itself beyond or surrounds (in some sense) the ground of being? The answer, of course, is very seriously and not very seriously at all. And anyone who has looked into the literature of 'pataphysics, the works of such writers as Alfred Jarry (the artist who invented the term) and say, René Daumal (whose *Mount Analogue* remains, for me, a central text), will recognize that what is at work is wit — serious wit.

> 'Pataphysics will examine the laws which govern excep-tions, and will explain the universe supplementary to this one; or, less ambitiously, will describe a universe which can be — and perhaps should be — envisaged in the place of the traditional one ... (Alfred Jarry in "Exploits and Opinions of Doctor Faustroll, Pataphysician," translated by Simon Watson Taylor)

Having called this talk "The "Pata of Letter Feet," the pun there, considering i just read you the quotes i've read you, should be obvious. It is, of course, a serious pun, because poetry has its physical reality, its metaphysical reality and its "pataphysical reality and, in my experience as a writer, it's at the interface between the eye, the ear and the mouth, that we suddenly see/hear the real "pata of poetic feet. Now the term for that interface is "notation," not just "writing" (tho it obviously is written and the results are writing) but "notation," the conscious act of noting things down for the voice. And in that noting down you are instructing the eye on the movement of the tongue for the pleasure of the ear. Good poetry gets the writer's tongue in your ear, breathes into it, & makes the whole body squirm with the pleasure of it. i read to pipe the reed of poetry. Obviously then how i read influences how the reed gets piped and there's a whole range of notes i can't even notate unless i change what my focus falls on in the reading. i need to make the familiar unfamiliar and the unfamiliar familiar. But that's the craft of writing and in that very word "notation" i can begin to show you the "pataphysical dimension i'm referring to. There *is* notation. There is *no* tation. The word erases itself. No it doesn't. Well yes it does but only if i read it that way. And that's not real. Except, of course, that it is real. i can literally point to it — no tation. So i'm pointing to something which is erasing itself even as i point to it. And that's important too because that phenomenon is one of the identifying features of the "pataphysical, that even as you say it exists you know it doesn't exist and even as you know it doesn't exist you see that it exists and so on. Thus one is led thru chains of "pataphysical logic where each step coheres only for the length of the transition and then disintegrates, disappears behind you even as a new, unexpected step appears in front of you. And, of course, if you linger too long trying to decide whether or not to take that next step it too disappears & you never make it.

This is where i've chosen to start talking about the interface between the eye, the ear and the tongue (or mouth) and in doing so i'm putting you at an advantage because it's only in the last ten years or so that i've realized how much Jarry's notion of 'pataphysics (particularly as i found it embodied in the work of René Daumal, his poems and his unfinished novel *Mount Analogue*) influenced me in my thinking. What i thot i was doing for the first 13 years was simply struggling with the question of how to notate my poems.

II. "The Optophonetic Dawn"

Something which i assume most *visual* artists, i.e. painters, etc., acknowledge or recognise to some degree is the surface upon which they make their marks — be that surface canvas, paper, whatever — its textures and dimensions and what relationship that surface ends up taking in regard to the finished work or, for that matter, works. For most writers that surface is, unfortunately, so utilitarian, so taken for granted that it is, for all intents & purposes, a non-issue. Oh sure they know *that's* what they have to write things down on, and they know they've only got so much physical room in which to move but ... so what? For them there is *no* tation, precisely because that surface or, to fix it in its writerly terminology (and thereby outline part of the problem), page is not so much a thing upon which to make marks with a pen or pencil or lead-type, as it is a perceived set of social values — i.e. if it's blank, white and 8 1/2 by 11 it's basically telling you you better get busy and fill it up if you ever want to get a book published, whereas if it's 5 1/4 by 7 1/2 and filled with justified type, *your* justified type, you know you've made it. Now i'm saying all this, i've just said it, and the point may appear arcane or trivial, but it's worth pointing out that studies have been done (one of which, at least, was reported on in the journal *Visible Language*) suggesting that were books printed on grey paper far fewer students would have difficulty learning to read. These societal givens do have impact and more than implication. Now since something as obvious as the writing surface is not perceived as remarkable it should then come as no surprise when i say that the component parts of words are not seen as remarkable either. Since the main focus is on stringing words into meaningful phrases the letters too are viewed in a purely utilitarian fashion: they get the job done. Unless of course the writer makes a spelling mistake in which case the writer is suddenly very aware of the letters. After all the letters are meant to be seen but not heard. Aren't they? Except we do hear the letters, at least as parts of words. Don't we? But, putting all that to one side, the point that i wish to make (or anyways *one* point that i wish to make, and we'll make it *the* point for now) is that the surface chosen in that initial moment presents the same situation to both the painter and the writer: a place on which to make a first mark, a place to begin. And both artists are relying on light, its physics, and the ability of marking to, in essence, manipulate light, in order to communicate to their potential perceivers.[1]

At this level of things both the painter & the writer have access to a similar experience, which is to say an objective experience of creation. If i take that brush and make a broad red stroke across the canvas i am bringing that particular gesture into being. It has not existed before in the world. Similarly when i take my pen and make that first mark, that mark that is not yet even a letter, i add something potentially significant and in its own small way unique to the larger body of created things. But there is a very real sense in which i also experience that creating activity when i write a first *letter* on the surface i have chosen because when i do so i am creating that *particular* letter. This is a very important distinction to make. Normally in writing writers think of themselves as naming things: i write the word "dog" and i anticipate that you will, to some degree, envisage a dog, i.e. all four legs, a tail and lots of bow-wow-wow. But when i write a letter i am not naming in the same way. i am creating a brand new A or B or whatever letter i choose to bring into being. The letter does not stand for something else in the way that, once again, the word "tree," say, stands for a tree. A letter is itself. Using the old Sausserian distinction between the signifier and the signified we could show that relationship this way:

signifier	tree	A
signified	🌲	A

where, in each case, the top terms are always in the same relationship to the bottom terms. When i make an A i need no adjectives or any other descriptive devices to get across the concept of A. Each A partakes fully of A-ness and is in itself unique. We could look at this another way and say that what we are seeing here, in our alphabet, is the trace memory of the Norse rune. Since i must have an image of A in order to write A obviously then when i do write an A i invoke it, bring it into being in an analogous way to that in which when the rune for tree was inscribed the ancient Norse saw themselves not as naming but rather as invoking the thing itself.[2] It is, of course, true & not true what i am saying; it is, itself, a "pataphysical observation. When i write an A i am, am i not, naming a sound. Well, not really, because the sound & its names are inseparable. The problem gets even more complex when we realize that the signifier and the signified are indeed A and A but that the referent is, in this case, the vocal construct A. So A (the signifier) together with A (the mental concept and therefore the signified) constitute a sign that we agree will trigger the sound A. But that takes us back to the "pataphysical observation that it is difficult to separate the trigger from the gun. This notion of something triggering something else (in this case the eye triggering the tongue & ear, translating an impulse from a visual medium into a sound medium) is, after all, a pretty fair definition of exactly what the power of invocation is supposed to be (a point which i'm going to return to).

To go back to what i was saying earlier, obviously when i write the word "dog" i am, on one level, combining three uniquely created letters to make a fourth thing: a shape, a word which *also* has extra referential value. Now clearly that extra referential value is crucial to human communication but what i want to focus on is that it is precisely at this point, the point when the word forms, that most writers come into consciousness. The phase before that that we've just been talking about tends to remain outside of their consciousness and yet, obviously, they all pass thru it on the way to consciousness; they just don't think it has significance.

Let's take another little "pataphysical step to one side and look at that last word — "significance." If i really read that word (i.e. if i actually *look* at it) i can see that it says "sign if i can" & then adds "ce." That final "ce" has its interest too because i pronounce it as an "s" sound as when i sound the word "see" or the word "say." The fact that it's not fully sounded here seems mimetic in terms of the meaning pointed to, i.e. sign (but only) *if* i can s ... (what? see? say?). Significance itself partakes of that conditional state.

This business of seeing what's in front of you, of actually dealing with the reality of that surface and of the marks you place on it, is central to any notion of notation; i *see* it so i can *say* it. And the notion of speaking the vision (and the wonderfully compact word to describe that phenomenon — "seer") is at the emotional and historical root of poetry. Now notice how there are two terms even here tho, which is to say there is "speaking" and there is "vision," there is the oral (and therefore the aural) and there is the visual. Language, of course, partakes of both dimensions, travels at the speed of sound and at the speed of light, in spoken time and mental time. It is this very doubleness which tends to confound writers and readers. And there are huge debates and differing schools of thot, differing schools of writing, which have as their central proposition the primacy of either the visual or the oral aspect of language. But in the reality of writing you are always envisioning the speech in order to speak the vision. The act of writing is the act of notation.

When the Dadaist Raoul Hausmann wrote his seminal essay on notation in sound poetry and called it "The Optophonetic Dawn," he pointed in that titling to the conceptual breakthru inherent in the notion of notation: i am making the invisible visible; i am bringing into light what has been in darkness; i am seeing sound. Writing is, as i implied earlier, invocation. In Hausmann's notational system he declared the page to be a visual equivalent of acoustic space with placement on the page denoting pitch, type size denoting volume, type overlays denoting multiple voicing, etc. Kurt Schwitters took that notion a step further when he performed his "W" poem, a single giant letter W painted on a card which was held up in front of the audience & then "read" for however long it took Schwitters to complete that particular day's reading, implying in the very act that W in its various manifestations lived at innumerable levels of pitch, volume & duration, that in his case the single W stood for all such manifestations. His approach was to bring into being what his single W named, to decode, an almost archaeological activity. It is easy to see then why, in the 1950s, the English painter Bob Cobbing was able to begin reading his abstract paintings, performing them, because for him that visual field suddenly became the outward gesture of, the physical manifestation of, an inaudible acoustic space he now desired to make audible. Similarly Paula Claire's readings of leaves and stones because she had now begun to use "reading" as a way of seeing the world. (Steve McCaffery has pointed out that what Claire has done is to bring the referent (the real world thing) into the sign to occupy the position of the signifier. This observation points to how Claire's "reading" both raises the issue of and challenges what is signified, opening up a potential metaphysic on the question of the deliberateness of her chosen test, its writerliness.) The real revolution in poèsie phonetique (to use Henri Chopin's distinction between that poetry which is acoustically based (poèsie phonetique) and that which is electronically manipulated (poèsie sonore)) is not in the sounds generated per se (i doubt that anyone's come up with any new ones) but rather in how it has changed the notion of notation and, as a result, the very act of reading. Charles Olson did a similar service for open form verse when he pointed out that the typewriter allowed a writer to notate, to some degree, *how* the poem should be read. What i want to do in the next part of this talk is to take you thru a few poems of my own and show you how everything i have just been talking about came together for me.

III. MY MI ME

i should begin this section by saying that i am, in this talk today, skipping over certain bridging steps crucial to how my sense of notation developed, but i'm doing that in order to simplify the progression and get as quickly as possible to the heart of this "pataphysical dimension of language i'm talking about.

Popular Song

this first plate was
my first published
concrete poem

I'm using song as metaphor and
then breaking down the verb
to yield the literal content

WARBLED
WARBLED

this technique continues into the present

Blues
↑
a purely visual
poem that depends
on a sound reference

here I'm paraphrasing an old
blues —"love, oh love, oh careless
love" — to slant the reading
of "evol" towards "evil" and
support the visually derived
blues moan

Cycle No. 22

all the
CYCLE texts
were modeled
on the notion
of wallpaper
i.e. patterns
that looped
visually and
could be
repeated in
visual patches.

4 —4 —5 —

DRUM ANDA WHEEL
ANDA DRUM ANDAW
HEEL ANDA DRUMA
NDAW HEEL ANDAD
RUMA NDAW HEELA
NDAD RUMA NDAWH
EELA NDAD RUMAN
DAWH EELA NDADR
UMAN DAWH EELAN
DADR UMAN DAWHE
ELAN DADR UMAND
AWHE ELAN DADRU
MAND AWHE ELAND
ADRU MAND AWHEE
LAND ADRU MANDA
WHEE LAND ADRUM
ANDA WHEE LANDA
DRUM ANDA WHEEL

the visual insistence
of typewriter
spacing creates
a very sound
poem. which is
to say that
PERformed it
has a clearly
mimetic effect

equating the
particularity of
the typing event
with performance.

VERSION EXECUTED MAY 6/80
ORATOR TYPEFACE ON IBM SELECTRIC

so here a purely visual idea led me
into sound — from the eye to the ear.

the movement from drawings with letters in them to ———————→

the breakdown of the figure is really the breakdown or reorganization of the sign.

the notion of imminence

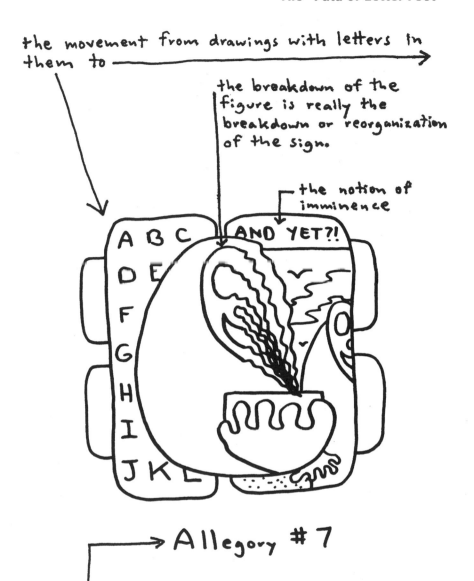

A B C
D E
F
G
H
I
J K L

AND YET?!

Allegory #7

the title addresses how the collecting of meaningful objects or signs into an aesthetic whole sets up <u>the promise of</u>, <u>the implication of</u>, meaning. this turned out to be a "Pataphysical principle.

replacing the drawn images with words about them +/or simply with words +/or letters

a line of type if viewed as landscape becomes a horizon

the reader / the writer

there is a sun setting

here there is a horizon

someone thinks

the frame here (even as in ALLEGORIES) the notion of aesthetic grouping per se. the images are replaced by their description viz. Curnoe. it also retains the syntax of the comic strip.

Frame 6

a section from INTERRUPTED NAP,
a text for performance

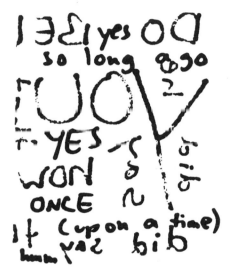

utilizes bleed through and spatial
relationships — a variation on optophonetic variation — to suggest vocal
interpratation.

DRAFT OF AN EPILOGUE TO "INCHOATE WORLD"

(from *The Martyrology* Book VI Books)

35,000 feet above Saskatchewan
less than a foot between me &
all that air, these airs err
insubstantial as comparison
spots to which we come, position ourselves
heirs to the veaucabulairies
terrer that fires us
all gollems finally
someone marks our fourheads
four elements there
                    we lurch forward
enact tradition
                monstrously
familiair
        familheir
tri bull
        labyrinthinemine
a tour of
gnossos
logos
osos
        (o that s.o.s. of
consciousgnoss)
or that old question
"who's the boss?" (b.s. os)

the notion of process

*here (and in what follows)
a Joycean-style punning
but over here*

minos most of our memory
we function out of loss
amigos

        unless i've got a pun
i can't write it down

ink think ←——— simply the drawing out of what is already there in the language.

"is that what you mean by procoss?"
[harbor lights
th'arbor of masts &
sails off the edge of your world   a view
venue   STREEts
lower&upper
middle voice/tongue/world]
i mean the earthyear the puns get the more the pen can pin it down to

Pan plays the world 'pon his flute

old bullfoot amazes us
pipes bright as language
                sleepy giants
who will wake you
mourn your death &
dance your resurrection
                                and from this point on an evocation of what is happening in the "Pataphysical moment.
                dreaming world
[the rivers branch like
trees
        someone's always leaving

[catch in the voice the
ship

        water water water you
        doing?

[meme eau: i'm just looking at the sea 'n world
                [eauver & eauver]]]
something fishy when the tongue slips

[glimmering surface
invisible depths
across which the boats skip]

"I'll write you a letter
[A to A]]

giant talk

the long waged war
the fight or struggle for
the mind
       boarders in these rooms words open

i said that be

you said that be

             FORE

we said that be

they said that be

warned

      letting the future know
we're playing thru
gulf the gulls & mist rise out of
stretches between "me" & "you"

August 23 to October 25, 1983

IV. conCLUEsion

What i have tried to do in this talk is to suggest a way of seeing, a way of reading, one which my own poetry increasingly draws me into. i spent a fair amount of time sketching the framework in which my thinking has been moving, a framework thru which i am able to get a particular view of the world. i am not going to try to tie this off, since i have not in any sense tied off this area of my actual practice as a writer, but there are a few conCLUEding REmarks, concrete clues that set the bell ringing for me each time i remark or make my mark re these surfaces (faces that stare back at me).

In trying to demonstrate the way in which my own atten- tion moved from issues of notation to, finally, me noting what i was notating with (i.e. the letters, parts of words, etc. that i was combining to make my spells), i found myself drawn to give this essay its alternative title: "The English Written Character As a Medium for Poetry." On one level that's almost a nonsense title; what else do we write poems with in English but the English written character? Well really the alphabet is Phoenician eh? And of course the same one is used in French and Spanish and Portuguese and and and. So at a certain point when i bring my poems down to the level of the letter i also begin to move freely between languages, or between certain languages, or at least in a space where the particularity of my language is over-ridden by the particle clarity. That was one of the strengths of the Concrete Poetry movement — its ability to be international because it did not require the usual kind of translative activity. It is also true that at this level of things you are very in touch with the essential arbitrariness of signs. One of my favourite mental exercises is still the one that Wittgenstein proposed in either the *Blue* or *Brown Book* where he said: "Look at a door, say a sound, and mean by that sound the concept 'door'." This is also the essence of any fic- tion, the imbuing of the created thing with meaning, i.e. an "intentional" focus. Earlier, in his *Yellow Book* lectures, Wittgenstein remarked:

> To say that the use of a word, e.g. "cube," follows from
> its meaning is to treat the word as if it were the visible

face of a hidden body, its meaning, whose rules of combination with other hidden bodies are given by the laws
of geometry.[3]

As it happens we do tend to treat words exactly as Wittgenstein
describes, no matter how inaccurate that may be. But what "pataphysics does is to treat the word as if it were the visible face of a
visible body and then go on to talk about what can be seen of
that body. This is the move into talking about words as sentences,
into reading, as deliberate gestures, the chance collisions of word
particles. It is obviously not the only way of seeing the world but
it is a way of seeing the world and it allows us a particularly
unusual angle on the passing parade, the pass of knowledge.
Wittgenstein hinted at such an approach when he said:

> In general the sentences we are tempted to utter occur
> in practical situations. But then there is a different way
> we are tempted to utter sentences. This is when we look
> at language, consciously direct our attention on it. And
> then we make up sentences of which we say that they
> also ought to make sense. A sentence of this sort might
> not have any particular use, but because it sounds
> English we consider it sensible. Thus, for example, we
> talk of the flow of time and consider it sensible to talk
> of its flow, after the analogy of river ... Discussion of
> "the flow of time" shows how philosophical problems
> arise. Philosophical troubles are caused by not using lan-
> guage practically but by extending it on looking at it.
> We form sentences and then wonder what they can
> mean.

And later, in this same lecture (from his Cambridge Lectures,
1932 to 35) he stated quite clearly what philosophers and writers
like himself are up to: "We are pulling ordinary grammar to bits."

As i remarked at the beginning i have had to simplify in
order to get all this information in. There were other steps &
concepts in my own development of a coherent notion of
notation, including the concept of "hinging" (beginning the new

line with the last word in the previous line)[4] and, out of that, what i called "schizophrenic logic," i.e. where i let the new line absolutely change the direction of the meaning of the last word in the previous line. Much, tho not all of what i have talked about, is, i suppose, glosses on the notion of the pun, milking that concept for all it's worth. And if we palindromize that idea we get:

lait pun : nuptial

When we pun we make merry, wed letter to letter to spell anew. When we mean our making we make a meaning. And with the pun we have in language the closest effect in poetry to both chording and/or playing clusters in music.

What i have tried to show then is what my idea is — literally, my point of view — how an attention to words & letters, an

```
every  kind  of  writing  has  its  own  texture,  its
own  overtones,  its  "sound."  if  i  want  access
to  the  full  range  of  what  is  possible  in
composition  then  i  cannot  exclude  any  of  those
sounds  from  my  compositional  field.
```

attention to the surface details of writing, opens a "pataphysical dimension. It is a dimension filled with short-lived phenomena, phenomena which we tend to think of as "merely" ephemeral and/or "on the surface," the dimension of the coincident, a "universe supplementary to this one." Nowhere would i assert that this is the only valid approach to writing. It isn't. But i have tried to give you an experience of what that dimension offers and why it draws so many writers — Kroetsch, Marlatt, Bowering, Brossard, McCaffery, Tostevin, Barbour, etc. — in thru its constantly relocating door.[5]

Notes

1. This is, admittedly, an arcane point, but points to one reason why (i believe) writers and painters share such an affinity.

2. It is interesting to realize that what disappears in the notion of the Norse rune is any idea of a signified or a referent. i have a mental image of the signifier but the act of writing it down does away with its referential value since i am in the act invoking the thing itself, i.e. literally bringing it forth into the moment of the writing.

3. Wittgenstein goes on to say: "Geometry is not a physics of geometrical straight lines and cubes. It constitutes the meaning of the words 'line' and 'cube'. The role the cube plays in its geometry is the role of a 'symbol', not that of a solid with which inaccurate real cubes are comparable."

4. As a development of hinging note the following poem from *The Frog Variations* (which also extends a notion of rhyming and is only accessible once you start looking at words in a different way):

> splash
>
> splayed beneath the bending ash
> fragile children of the great bog
> frog
>
> pond
>
> poised under the autumn frond
> more singers of the dark water croon
> moon

5. i should point out, as a final note, that i don't know that *any* of the writers i mention here would use the term "pataphysical to describe this element of their work. Nor am i at all sure that my definition of the "pataphysical matches that of current 'pataphysicians.

Sketching

1984

> The action of the verb "sketch"; to draw the outline or
> prominent features of (a picture, figure, etc.), especially
> as preliminary or preparatory to further development; to
> make a sketch or rough draft of (something); to draw or
> paint in this matter.

Everything that follows is preceded by a conversation i had with
Margaret Avison circa 1965 when i worked at the U of T Library
shelving books and she was working on a thesis project (compar-
ing, as i recall, translations of Homer (Pound's etc.)) during which
time in one of many conversations that we had she made the
remark that she wished, as a writer, to have the kind of freedom
to sketch that painters had, i.e. to not always have to make a
"complete" composition. There was an implication here too that
not everything that was a sketch necessarily became a larger composition; and, as i have pointed out elsewhere, it was Margaret
who gave me the title for an early sound poem of mine — "Not
What the Siren Sang But What the Frag Meant" — one of those
beautiful, witty and eventually highly influential asides she used
to make to me. Now i put those last two thots together into one
sentence in order to make the point that what she was dealing
with in part was a theory of knowing, that knowledge is in itself
fragmentary, that we are lured onto the rocks not by what the
siren sang but by what the frag meant, the few scraps that come
down to us — Homering pigeons. We can take this further into
our relation to the divine, what we know of the metaphysics of it
all. And that, of course, is exactly what happens in her work, in
the move from *Winter Sun* thru *The Dumbfounding* into *sunblue*.

i want to focus mainly on the pieces in *sunblue* which
include the word "SKETCH" in the title (12 in all) but it's worth
stopping first to look at that movement in Avison's titling because
it does relate to what we're talking about. Considered purely as

themselves (i.e. without reference to what they reference or encompass in terms of groups of poems), we see that movement from a white cold light (light but no heat and hence wintery, minus the green and growing world) thru the moment of recognition (the dumbfounding and hence founding but in an absence of words (dumb)) into that lovely pairing "sunblue" (all lowercase (as opposed to the all caps titling of the words "SKETCH" and "OR" (and i want to make a point of that because she is making a point of that — the definite title is presented less definitely than those two words of indefiniteness "SKETCH" and "OR"))), evoking the child's drawing of the yellow sun in the blue sky (in which, when i used to draw as a kid, there was always an overlap between the sky and the sun creating a green nimbus, a "sunblue"), a return to a changed notion of the light. In the titling we see an imaging of the spiritual rebirth pointed to in many of the poems. And the term that stays and is changed is "sun."

Xsun / y / sunZ[1]

The sun no longer closes, it opens, is changed in language, moves from iSOLation to being part of a larger cosmos/wordworld/field. And this includes a dumb founding, a rebeginning in not knowing,[2] a changed notion, therefore, of what knowledge is. We can see this clearly in the two poems that end *sunblue*, one titled "SKETCH: Child in Subway" and the other titled "The Bereaved"[3]: the first, a quick image of a child hurrying down the subway stairs, hands clutched in his/her parents', rushing towards and into a waiting train, the poem's concluding couplet —

wherever his day's lifetime may
go in its faithful unpredictability.

— celebrating the child's differing sense of time ("day's lifetime") but indexing as well the faithfulness of flux, the way in which knowing is undercut by the very unpredictability of the world and that that changeableness is always with us; the second in which the children's "red and blue and green" voices are described both as the Ur tongue and

... a barbarous tongue,　　lost on
that unmirroring, immured,
that thumping thing,
　　　　the heavy adult heart.

The children's voices in that second poem are, in fact, as she
goes on to say, "the immemorial chorus." We can see here that
whole notion that knowledge is always beginning anew, that we
exist not in a state of knowing but in a state of not knowing, that
we are constantly being born again into the world not knowing
(the child in "From Age to Age: Found Poem" is described as
speaking "as in the morning day / when Adam names the animals." And the title here, again, points to knowledge as "found,"
not possessed, as part of the world of chance occurrences, the
"faithful unpredictability") Thus the "SKETCH" poems move
from a noting of detail (as we expect in a sketch) — the lush
description of "SKETCH: Thaws" with its image of imminent
revelation ("everything waits for the / lilacs, heaped tumbling —
and their warm / licorice perfume"); the precision of "SKETCH:
Weekend"; the invocational power of "SKETCH: Overcast
Monday"; the imagistically evoked parallelism of "SKETCH: A
work gang on Sherbourne and Queen, across from a free hostel
for men" (the piece functions structurally like an extended haiku)
— to the sudden change of perception in "SKETCH: Cement
worker on a hot day" where the yellow hydrant which has been
just a "knob / shape" is transformed by the workman, and the
poet exclaims:

Yes　yes　a hydrant
was always there but now
it's his,　and flows.

The transformation is an interesting one precisely because something which was once perceived as solid and essentially
immutable is now perceived as being in a state of flow, a source
of, in that sense, flux. It is also important that the worker's activity
is seen as a claiming activity ("it's his") yet not the usual kind of
claiming activity, i.e. he does not "possess" it, it "flows." This

notion, that the activity of claiming is not an activity which fixes, is repeated in "SKETCH: CNR London to Toronto (I)" where the described brushheap's eventual destruction is imagined and included in the sketch. Or similarly in "SKETCH: CNR London to Toronto (II)" and "SKETCH: From train window (Leamington to Windsor) in March" where what is sketched also includes the notion of what is not sketched, "*invisibility*" and "the hidden culvert."

In both titling and the assumptions and direct statements of the texts, a notion of knowing is constantly put forward, that all this (i.e. poetry and what we *knowte* down) is partial knowledge, rests on a dumb foundation that we cannot, finally, articulate (as noted in the titling of "SKETCH: End of a day: OR, I as a blurry" (it's important to focus on that title since the first line of the poem makes "I as a blurry" part of a longer descriptive phrase, thus very deliberately altering its meaning, and the too hasty reader might judge the title phrase to be merely a partial quotation, which it is not — "I" is a concept not in focus, or perhaps composed of multiple elements that together blur it, or create a blur in their flickering back and forth, and "day" too is never a casually used word given the obvious meanings that "sun" has in Margaret Avison's work)). It is the very partialness of knowledge that is emphasized by the use of caps on "SKETCH." "SKETCHING" is foregrounded and writing is backgrounded. The writer cannot *know* (and therefore present a *complete* composition); the writer can only sketch and leave the larger composition in other hands.

a sketch ketchs
amo meant

Notes

1. i've chosen "Y" deliberately here because of its religious and algebraic connotations.

2. If i am "sunblue" i am green, i.e. innocent, in a state of not knowing.

3. There is, of course, another set of references pointed to, but i'm being selective. And what i'm saying isn't negated by them.

frog	fro?	fr?g	?rog
f?og	?r?g	??og	f?o?
?ro?	fr??	f??g	???g
f???	??o?	?r??	????

The Book as a Unit of Composition

WITH FRANK DAVEY

1985

To compose books of poetry rather than individual poems which may later be gathered into book shape is to accept from the beginning of the writing not only a large-scale and long-term task but also the partial directing of one's writing by the book that one has undertaken. Understandably, poets who see inspiration as occasional and unpredictable, and who in fact seek to augment the spontaneity of each writing occasion, may see the prospect of composing a "book" as a restriction on their creativity. They prefer to write the poems that occur from day to day and arrange these into books later. Poets who compose in terms of "book," on the other hand, appear to assume that inspiration is partly of the writer's own creation — that one can write when one wants to write, that one's creativity is a process one can initiate or invite, that writing can be a partnership with a large and growing set of texts of one's own accumulation. For such writers the shaping of the book is an element that enters into the writing of each of its texts; the book shares the attention of the writer equally with the text at hand.

Arranging into Books Later

Poets who do not compose in book-length units will typically arrange their poems into books (or have an editor arrange them) when a sufficient number of pages have accumulated. When badly done, this process is more a packaging activity than a composing one, but certain compositional principles do enter into each arranging, and for many poets the process serves as a kind of apprenticeship into book composition. The book that is created here is, no matter how little care is taken in its creation, a new composition. Each poem which was previously an independent text becomes a structural unit in this new composition. If the new composition seems to be without shape or purpose, editors of publishing houses — who are involved after all in the publishing of books rather than poems — will frequently ask themselves why these poems are being proposed for publication as a book.

Such collections can be given book shape in a number of ways. They can be structured by sequence of composition, a sequence which will often reveal hidden patterns of language, thematic repetitions or an evolution of style. They can be grouped by themes (as Earle Birney's 1967 *Selected Poems*) — although this is a somewhat risky method because two poems that when separate seemed mutually reinforcing will often appear redundant when juxtaposed. (Grouping by theme, in fact, can be a useful preliminary way of locating and discarding relatively weaker pieces.) Highly contrasting poems can be grouped together so that their intrinsic qualities are emphasized by the juxtaposition (as in most of Irving Layton's books). Complementary poems — ones in similar language but on different subjects, ones from similar perspectives but in different voices, ones on similar subjects but in contrasting tones — can be grouped so that the groups propose a complexity beyond that offered by the separate poems (as in most of Raymond Souster's collections). Poems can also be grouped on formal grounds (as in bpNichol's *As Elected*). These "packaging" methods can be interwoven; for example a book could be divided into two time periods but the poems within these periods be grouped according to language, theme, point of view, etc.

Composing Texts Toward a Book

To conceive of a poem as a book is to create numerous structural possibilities. The various texts within the book have the potential to inter-relate much the way stanzas inter-relate within a poem. The various standard components of a book — its title page, half-title page, colophon, its typeface, columns, margins, gutters, signatures, paper — have the potential to participate as signs within the writing. The individual texts may borrow a book-structure from outside the book (as James Reaney's *A Suit of Nettles*), generate one from their own materials (Louis Dudek's *Atlantis*) or interact with a pre-existent structure to create a new shape (Robert Kroetsch's *Seed Catalogue*).

The Book As a Closed Structure

One of the first decisions a poet makes when undertaking a book is whether it will be open or closed in its external form. To adopt a received literary form — like that of Spenser's *The Shepherd's Calendar* adopted by Reaney or Rilke's *Duino Elegies* adopted by Bowering in *Kerrisdale Elegies* — is to adopt not only a structure but foreknown beginning and ending points for the book. Nevertheless, the inner space of such a book remains open. While Bowering knows there will be 10 Kerrisdale elegies, or 38 poems in *Genève*, he does not foreknow how any one of these will develop or how it may interact with its fellows.

The intertextual advantages of such adopted structures are considerable. The new text can constitute a criticism of the original as in Bowering, an ironic application of it as in Reaney, or a re-writing of it as in Margaret Atwood's *The Journals of Susanna Moodie*; questions of material content and point of view can be resolved early in composition. The attention of the poet can turn away from the "what" of writing and focus on the "how" of the writing process itself. The borrowed text often lends to the new text from the beginning a given body of information which the borrower need not build but merely be worthy of; the presence of this information frees the borrower from the creation of the field of background reference necessary for any extended text (the equivalent of setting in the short story or exposition in the theatre).

A similar "closed" effect can be achieved by structuring one's book around a well-known story, as E.J. Pratt's *The Titanic*, and accepting the parameters of narrative that story has come to have. Again, the focus of the writing falls on how the story will be told rather than on what the story will be. The received material can be not only an historical event but an individual life (as Florence McNeil's *Emily* or Judith Fitzgerald's *Beneath the Skin of Paradise: The Piaf Poems*) or a personal experience such as giving birth (Daphne Marlatt's *Rings*).

Finite structure can also be borrowed from sets of "magic numbers," themselves a kind of story. George Bowering's *Baseball*, with its celebration of nine innings, nine players, nine muses, seems almost inevitably a nine-part poem. There are many such numbers and poems: seven wonders of the world, seven sins, seven years' bad luck, twelve months, twelve labors of Hercules, twelve books to the Renaissance epic, *Twelve Letters to a Small Town*, four lunar quarters, four football quarters, *Four Quartets*, three fates, three wise men, three wishes, three musketeers, three strikes an' yer out, *Three Fate Tales*, ten little indians, ten commandments, *Ten Elephants on Yonge Street*, two kinds of people in the world, two paths diverging in a yellow wood, two solitudes, "The Two Fires," *Two-Headed Poems*. Some numbers have commonplace stories — *two*, the stories of marrying or choosing, of yoking or tearing, the both / and of Atwood's "Marrying the Hangman" or the either / or and and / but of Kroetsch's *The Sad Phoenician*. Some are overwhelmingly magical; *three* is not only three wishes and three fates but three little pigs, three bears, three blind mice, three graces, three billy goats gruff; *seven* is not only seven wonders and sins but seven dwarves, seven seals, seven sleepers, seven liberal arts, seven seas, seven against Thebes, seven pillars of wisdom, seven-year itch, seven hills of Rome. As in choosing a story, choosing a set of numbers both closes the outer boundaries of the book and opens its inner space. It gives the writer an overstructure for the book (or in the case of Kroetsch's *The Sad Phoenician* an organizing syntax) but provides only a given number of starting points for the texts themselves.

My Heart Is an Open Book

It is surprisingly easy to avoid or subvert the sense of closure upon which the front and back covers of a book seem to insist. Subtitle a book "volume 2" and the front cover becomes transparent and the back cover resonates with ambiguity. Refuse the accepted ending of an historical story, as George Bowering refuses that of George Vancouver's voyages or Margaret Atwood that of Susanna Moodie's life, refuse a received characterization, as Atwood refuses the traditional characterization of Circe in her "Circe / Mud Poems," and space opens around the expected limits of the writing. Similarly a "baker's dozen effect" can be created in any sequence built around "magic" numbers. A 13 book epic, four little pigs, sending the poem into the open possibilities of (as Ray Souster called them) extra innings. As Robert

Kroetsch in *Seed Catalogue* both uses and misuses the received text. The act of borrowing any set of material automatically provides the possibility of interrogating or violating that material. So that what begins as a closed form is always potentially open; one can start by structuring one's poem around the days of a Lenten calendar (as Susanne Collins at York University once did) but later break one's fast — write two or three texts for a single day, or write past the day when the poem was scheduled to conclude itself.

The Book As a Field

Open or closed at front and back, between its covers the book is always potentially a field of dynamic relationships. While it is conventional to view the standard mechanical parts of a book as external to its processes, to regard them as merely part of the container in which the text is placed, even these can be invited to participate in the activities of the text. The cover can be made literally a box, as in bpNichol's anthology *The Concrete Chef* or his books *Still Water*, *Unit of Four*, *Aleph Unit*, and *bp*. The pages can become loose pages of paper, as in most of the above, or become tear-out sheets for constructing a poster, as in Steve McCaffery's *Carnival*. Violate this book. The usual roles of the cover, half-title and title pages can be subverted placing upon them information that enriches the text, as occurs in Christopher Dewdney's *A Palaeozoic Geology of London, Ontario* in which the cover and title page emulate those of Canadian government publications. On the interior pages the text can spill from the expected blocks of type into the margins and gutters (as bill bissett said in his introduction to *We Sleep Inside Each Other All* — "whats this margen doin here eh"), or onto adjacent pages. McLuhan insisted both these things would happen once writers stopped viewing the book as a sequential medium (see his *The Medium Is The Massage*). Individual pages can grow into fold-out sheets or be printed on idiosyncratic paper stock, as in the multi-coloured pages of early books from bill bissett's Blew Ointment Press. A book like the above, or like Gerry Gilbert's *Lease* (printed in three contrapun-tually bound signatures)[1] argue that the conceiving of a book as a physical object can be every bit as much a part of its composition as the actual writing.

Even more important, the body of a book can be regarded as a field of interacting texts rather than as a sequential line of words moving from the top of the first page to the end of the last. The goal here is to create neither a uniform text (that implies a single perspective or a single value system) nor an assortment of unrelated texts. It is rather to create a community of texts that relate, interrelate, contradict, inform, confirm, reiterate, expand, symbolize. This is the kind of multi-voiced text that Robert Kroetsch achieves in *Seed Catalogue* where he mixes found text, verse, dialogue, prose, anecdote, and at times Dadaist ("do die do die do die do die do die do die") chant. Or that Dewdney achieves with his mixture of prose, verse, visual poems, and collages in *Palaeozoic Geology*. Such writing liberates the book from the limits of genre, in ways similar to those used in fiction by Dave Godfrey in *Dark Must Yield* or Jack Hodgins in *The Invention of the World*.[2] It questions the authority of any written text, proposing that it is the sum of texts that can have authority, not the single voice or single perspective. The potential "poetry" of such writing lies in the unarticulated material between the texts, created by the tensions between them — much the way the "impact" of a Shakespearean tragedy lies in the unarticulated vision of human life that has been created by the sum of its words and events. Such a piece of writing is Lionel Kearns' recent poem *Convergences* in which documentary fragments from Captain James Cook's 1767 voyage to Nootka Sound, Kearns' meditations upon these fragments, his reflections on his mediations, and 18th century engravings of drawings made by Cook's crew are all juxtaposed to create a whole which provides no definitive answers but a clear vision of human difficulties.

The Collected or Selected Poems

The two most important requirements in the collected or selected poems is to preserve the integrity of the earlier publications and to reveal the shape of the accumulated work. If the poet has been composing and publishing book units, the collected should preserve their shape (as does Margaret Atwood's 1976 *Selected Poems* and Robin Blaser's edition *The Collected Books of Jack*

Spicer). If individual books constitute a larger work, its shape should be realized, as in Robert Kroetsch's *Field Notes*.

Such retrospective collections have a tendency, despite a certain celebratory quality, to be reductive in nature. They contain disparate work between two covers; they winnow down the work and make it more graspable. A special effort needs to be made to preserve the heterogeneity of the work of poets whose individual books have been idiosyncratic and which have made particular use of the typographic and design potential of the book form. The arresting use of blank space in Louis Dudek's *En Mexico* was lost in his *Collected Poems* while a similar use of space in Phyllis Webb's *Naked Poems* was preserved in her selected poems *The Vision Tree*.

Probably the best way to organize this kind of collection is to recapitulate the original writing or publication chronology. If the poet has not composed in terms of book units, the chronology should be that of separate poems, and the poems should be dated.

Transcending the Book

Many writers eventually discover the book itself to be every bit as much a limitation on their writing as the short poem. Even the book that achieves an open and unpredictable structure implies closure where it ends, and in particular closes off its own material from that of other of the writer's books. As mentioned earlier, unbinding the book can be one way of dealing with this problem (as English novelist B.S. Johnson did with his *The Unfortunates*). The possibility of pages becoming lost, of each edition of the book being collated in a slightly different fashion (some elements left in and some left out — as in certain issues of bill bissett's magazine *Blew Ointment*) defeats the very notion of binding, and the book becomes a permeable object. Such an approach also alters the writer's compositional process, i.e. if you know the book is going to be unbound you no longer have to concern yourself with the usual connectives between the book's various parts (such connectives in fact tend to destroy the effect of the unbinding because they allow the reader to reconstruct one of the author's private reading sequences and construe it as the definitive secret order of the book).

This notion of the permeable book is also present in the open-ended or continuous poem — viz. Louis Dudek's *Continuations* or Robert Kroetsch's *Field Notes*. Since only a starting point is presented, the notion of a book is subverted from the outset, i.e. the work in being continuous cannot be gathered or completed in any way until the author's death. In popular culture even the author's death does not necessarily bring closure to the work (see, for instance, the various authors who have continued and extended the works of Ian Fleming and Arthur Conan Doyle).

In the continuous poem there is no concept of an end point, thus the concept of "book" crumbles. Instead there is a work which may or may not, finally, be encompassable within a single set of covers. Even the starting point need not stay fixed. R. Murray Schafer in his major composition *Patria* wrote and interpolated a Part O years after the first appearance of Part I. In such works the poet is seeking to encompass his world in a single heterogeneous structure rather than to articulate it in brief and discrete utterances. Typically the writer begins writing the short discrete poem, moves on to the book-length composition, and moves finally to the continuing all-encompassing work — as Pound moves from the lyrics of *Lustra* to *The Cantos* or Dudek from the lyrics of *East of the City* through *Atlantis* to *Continuation* or Olson moves from discrete books like *O'Ryan* to *The Maximus Poems*. Robert Duncan makes this change by incorporating the short poem and the discrete book into his continuing work, moving from the separate poems of *Heavenly City, Earthly City* and *Caesar's Gate*, and from the unified sequences of *Letters* and *A Book of Resemblances* to a concept of book in which discrete poems and various continuing poems are interwoven in the volumes of a continuing series of volumes; this presentation argues that all Duncan's poems, whether brief or long multiple-sectioned poems serially composed over a number of years (like "The Structure of Rime" or "Passages") are merely roots and branches of the writer's total body of writing. Implicit in all these writers is a dissatisfaction with the shorter work, a dissatisfaction which would appear to be concerned with its separating of incident from incident, its buffering of contradictory elements, its implying of a definiteness of closure one rarely experiences outside of poem or book. In each case the final work is inclusive, incorporates contrasts and contraries, varieties of text, offers neither discrete fragment nor unity, but rather a Whitmanesque embrace of multitude. Daphne Marlatt's work, which has been from almost the beginning composed in book units, offers in *What Matters* an intriguing variant of this movement to increasingly incorporative structures. In *What Matters* she gathers discrete poems, poem sequences, and a book-unit, *Rings*, together with previously unpublished material such as journal entries, into a new heterogeneous composition. The implication is clear: *What Matters* could in turn become part of an even larger composition — which might grow not only from either end but from points within the work as well. Similarly Gerry Gilbert's *From Next Spring* takes a number of previous books, pamphlets and poems and works and reworks them to create the new composition; his immense unpublished *Moby Jane* brings together most of his work to date and reveals how the individual books constitute parts of a single "whale of a tale" continuing writing.

Various "ephemeral" media, such as posters, mini-pamphs, broadsides, cards, etc., can all function as alternatives to the set of cultural meanings that the "book" carries if they are in fact composed as the unit of composition. Like the work of Pound, Dudek, Olson, Duncan, Gilbert and Marlatt, such media suggest the cultural arbitrariness of the book-unit, and invite the consideration of alternatives. But where "book" is used as part of a book-challenging composition (both *The Cantos* and *What Matters* are, after all, published as books), then the play with the very notion of book, and the rejection of book as the final container, can become part of the richness of the text.

Notes

1. In *Lease* Gerry Gilbert takes the reader thru the "book" three times, forcing one to shift the book itself in order to read it, and changing the relative size of text and page at each reading. In an earlier radical deconstruction of his own work he took all of a previously published book of poems (*White Lunch*) and cut it up and arranged it in a double-page spread for inclusion in *The Cosmic Chef: An Evening of Concrete.*

2. Godfrey conjoins film script, essay, parable, newspaper story, interview and the stream-of-consciousness narrative; Hodgins composes his novel in sections of heroic narrative, oral history, mock-epic, a scrapbook of newspaper clippings, and first-person narrative.

Poet Tics

FOR CHARLES BERNSTEIN

1985

I think I'm leaving the essay form behind. This is all I want to do
anymore. Write down my thots a note at a time. Give up that
false surface which insists unity and let the unity find its own
point of cohesion.

Or not.

⋈

So there I was in San Francisco. I'd thrown my back out, badly,
and was limping around the bookstores — first downtown and
then later out in Berkeley — looking for books by Charles
Bernstein. I went to five bookstores in a row. Literary ones. They
didn't have any of his books in the first four. But in the fifth one,
Cody's, I found a copy of an early one called *Shade*. And I thot as
I was buying it well maybe this is how you can tell the really new
poetry. It never seems to make it into the bookstores.

⋈

At some point I began to realize that I wasn't going to make it to
the colloquium on the new poetics because after all there was
Ellie & Sarah to think of and I'd been out of town a lot and my
back still wasn't better after five months and really I had to stay
home and take it easy. And that seemed right. Sometimes there
just isn't time for poetry. You get the tic, but nothing happens.
You're in idle, turning things over in your mind, your mind
turning over, marking time, marking, time.

⋈

Having realized I wasn't going to make it (to the colloquium that is) I thot well really I should write a statement about what I'm up to. But I've spent the last five years trying to be very articulate about that and periodically Steve tells me I'm just making a fool of myself and I say "well that's what I believe" and he just laughs or looks exasperated. I think I know what I'm doing. I think. I know. What I'm doing.

〔ㄐ〕

I keep saying I don't know why I write. And I mean by that that beyond all the talk I've already done about it there's something in me that simply loves to write. And it's that something I don't know the why of. Something that happens outside of any notion of wish or desire. Like a tic. Did I say that? Yes, like a tic.

〔ㄐ〕

It's true. I've begun to think writing's just a kind of tic, a reflex as it were. And then on top of that one comes up with explanations about why one's particular tic is a little farther out than one's neighbour's. Future is tic.

```
to alter is native to some of us, the desire
to create the alter native tongue. but maybe
the clue is to alter natives to narratives.
that's what steve keeps saying. steve mccaffery
keeps saying, "the real crisis is with the
readers." we can't assume we're speaking their
native tongue.
```

⌗

The first trick was to give up the illusion of mastery. It's like the old zen teaching lesson. I used to think you achieved mastery (with any luck) somewhere in your 40s. Now I know that what it's all about is apprenticeship. Masters are an illusion. The term "apprentice" is also an illusion, but useful in a transitional way while part of me still clings to notions of mastery. Like the way I feel when I meet a writer I really respect. Just another tic I guess. Just another genuflect from the autonomic poetic system.

⌗

I wanted to write about all that stuff which underlies craft. Autonomic's a good metaphor for it. Or tics. Like when I first got the right to vote I voted liberal and when I really looked at it I realized it was because my dad had always been a liberal. Psychological residue which translates into social residue. I don't think writers are any more useful than gardeners but part of me wants to feel special. That's another tic to understand, another rictus. An aesthete tic.

⌗

Writing's my way of making sense of things, of staying sane, gives me some inner feeling of balance that makes it possible to live in the world, in time. Tic talk.

⌗

What I'm mostly aware of are the contradictions. I keep meeting writers who love junk culture but keep it out of their "serious" writing. And I've always wanted to find ways to get that all in, everything under one roof. Because on the one hand I've been interested in control (& hence "notation" and all my work with open form poetics) and on the other hand I've been interested in all those things you can't control but only, perhaps, contain. So

I've tried to set up poetic environments in which those uncontrollable effects can tic away alongside, or even inside, the controlled ones. And there I was in Amsterdam and the sign across the road said "Artis" and what it meant was "zoo."

Artis a zoo.

Poetry for sure too.

Narrative in Language: The Long Poem

1986, 1988

1

At a certain point you decide to start with what's in front of you. There's no point despairing of a subject, or carrying on some misguided search for a "great" theme when all you have to do is start with what's in front of you: the blue lines, the ink, the pen, the letters the pen shapes, the words the letters make, the table, the window, those leafless trees, these leaves in this notebook in front of me, you — the stuff of poetry.

2

Ordinary language is the hardest to write. Ordinary life is the hardest to live. The minute you write or say the word "ordinary" you draw too much attention to it & it ceases to be; ordinary that is. Extraordinary when you point to it.

3

The extra has to do with singling it out. So that what is extraordinary in language is how what is ordinary is ordinarily transparent or invisible to us. Which includes its narratives too, or possible narratives, stories you see & find there if you choose to.

4

Of course the alphabet is a narrative — that movement thru your ABC. And any word you write is a displacement of that primary narrative. So that all writing always deconstructs some given even as it notes another given down. Or let's say that what's given is that the given shifts depending on how you choose to look at it, has more than one face, more than one aspect. Or to write is to continually reshape the given, watch it flicker in & out of different focii before your, or just after your, very eyes.

5

What's interesting then is not simply to tell
the story but rather to find the story that's out
there in the midst of all that flickering, let it
reveal itself. You already know the story you set
out to tell, there's no hurry with that one, so really
why not start by listening? This sounds paradoxical
but isn't. When I set out to tell a story I begin by listening. When
I set out to write one I begin by reading. You're always waiting
for the ordinary to shift & reveal yet another face. And to glimpse
the face of the ordinary is, in fact, to be given something. To grasp
the given we have to stand still long enough to receive it. You just
never grab at the first thing that's held out to you. That was a lesson my maw taught me when I was five and I tried to grab all the
presents off my friends as they came thru the door to my birthday
party. "Don't grab at the present," said Maw, "wait till it's given to
you."

6

Once you realize that the given is constantly reshaping itself, that
its new orders, the words in this sentence say, are essentially arbitrary, a useful set of conventions, then the notion of narrative
becomes one more element that shifts in the telling. I always liked
the way my great aunts & uncles, my grandmothers, told their
stories. The stories were always funny, even the saddest ones, and
they were constantly jumping forward & backward in time on a
purely associative basis. When you were with them, listening, you
went with them, gave yourself up to the pleasure of the story. And
that's how you get the given. You give in.

7

7 given things that totally influenced me and that I thot of as part
of everyone's ordinary experience but that people now tell me
are part of what makes my long poem, *The Martyrology*, difficult
& inaccessible:

1) the habit of mentioning personal names in telling a story
even when the people don't know the person. As in:

"I was going on this trip with Fred, an old friend of mine, when suddenly …"

2) the scene in Disney's *Alice in Wonderland* where the caterpillar makes letters out of smoke which float thru the air as he sings the vowels in the alphabet.

3) sitting in a movie theatre with my friends watching the horror movie about kids sitting in a movie theatre with their friends watching a horror movie when The Blob rolls in thru the projection booth and everyone in our movie theatre & everyone in their movie theatre turning around & looking up at the projection booth.

4) singing "I Got a Gal in Kalamazoo" with my sister, especially the part that went:

A B C D E F G H
I got a gal in
Kalamazoo

and then later

Hi there Mr. Jackson
Everything's O
K A L A M A Z O
O what a gal!
A real piparoo!

Those connections & shifts. Which we sang over & over again.

5) watching *Duck Amuck* starring Daffy Duck, where everything that's usually given in the cartoon world, background, foreground, figure, soundtrack, keeps shifting & disappearing on Daffy.

6) the fact that in Wildwood Park in Winnipeg the different

streets &/or sections were named after the letters of the alphabet so that when I was first learning the alphabet I was also learning my way home.

7) hearing the crows sing "When I See an Elephant Fly" in Disney's *Dumbo*, & memorizing all the lyrics because the puns in it were such a revelation to me:

> I saw a peanut stand
> Heard a rubber band
> Saw a polka dot railroad tie

Etc. The ordinary made extra-ordinary again.

8

When we write as we write we are always telling a story. When I write as I write I am telling the story of how I see the world, how it's been given to me, what I take from it. In the long poem I have the time to tell you that in all its faces or, at least, in as many faces as I've seen so far. Even when I'm not telling a specific story, I'm telling you *that* story. A narrative in language. The long poem. How I see the world.

Interview: Geoff Hancock

THE FORM OF THE THING: AN INTERVIEW WITH bpNICHOL ON GANGLIA AND grONK

1986, 2001

Geoff Hancock begins the interview by asking bpNichol about his views on chapbooks.

bp: From a publishing point of view, it's almost as expensive to publish a chapbook as it is a book. Typesetting is a bit cheaper. But the setup time, and working with the manuscript, is as complex. A chapbook is as hard to market, if not harder, because it is slimmer. The difference in cost between making a book and a chapbook is not that big, nor can it be sold for that much less. Perhaps two-thirds the cost. But it can only be priced at a certain amount or it looks ridiculous. Unless it's clearly a limited edition, or an alternative press that exists to "get the thing on the record."

GH: Is that how you saw grOnk?

bp: grOnk is an on-the-record press. It's not a little press, and it's not a press that's attempting to reach a big audience. It's a press that argues for certain people's work, though there's not a big audience for this stuff now. Maybe there is for the writer, but maybe not this part of the writer's work. So let's have a permanent record of it some place. grOnk is also a more news-oriented press than blewointment was. bill (bissett) ran it almost as a community statement, to show what writers are doing.

GH: Sounds like you have a big argument with that notion of immortality.

bp: I'm not trying to create a permanent record of greatness. I'm trying to get the news out right now for other writers. Hopefully through that, I argue for a wider based readership.

GH: What's the difference between a "little" and a "little-little" press?

bp: A little press is a different kind of publishing. "Here's a writer who deserves a book! This writer is neglected, or wants to publish with whomever." A little press publishes books. It may do chapbooks for political reasons, but it is not dedicated to the notion of the chapbook as a tool for argument. The publisher thinks there is enough material here that deserves a book. For most people, if you take the UNESCO definition, that's a bit on the small side. For most people, a book starts at around 64 pages, four or five signatures. The Canada Council adopted the UNESCO definition of a book in 1977. The consequences were enormous for Canadian small press publishing. The decision meant the end of chapbooks, posters, broadsides, ephemera, printed objects, everything printed except standard sized books.

GH: Tell me about Ganglia Press, out of which *grOnk* magazine began.

bp: The press began as a little magazine, *Ganglia*. Within a year or two, some books began. The two ideas of book and magazine were there together. *Ganglia* magazine also published two "book /issues" of the six issues of the magazine.

(...) At first, *Ganglia*, in its structure, if not its content, was a traditional little magazine. People mailed in poems, you take some, send some back. The paperwork started to mount up. It was also a traditional little press on the level of accounting. Suddenly we had to keep track of all these accounts. Both David and I got really irritated by the sheer work we had to do. Writers began treating us like a big concern and got pissed off if we didn't answer right away. So much bullshit went down! So quickly, we found a lot of poems we liked. But within five issues, we began to refocus. "Are we really interested in publishing a general poetry magazine?" In terms of that initial impulse, of publishing west coast writers in Ontario, that was no longer a problem. *Island* magazine and others began publishing those people. In the meantime, I was more caught up in visual and sound poetry. Though I was writing in the more traditional field, looking out there, it seemed to me that no magazine, with the exception of occasional pieces in *Alphabet*, was publishing sound and visual work. The impulse began to change the shape of the magazine. *Ganglia* was becoming burdensome. I wanted something that was quicker, and I wanted something that involved no accounting. Since you lose money anyway with a small press, why not do it for free? Do it for free as a news-sheet. Part of the reason for this was *Tish* which I read in Vancouver. It was lively. Though I took argument with its tone rather than its poetics. By tone, I meant *Tish* was adamant that theirs was the only path to follow. Though if you look at the writers who came out of *Tish*, it wasn't true in their lives. We were young then! I've always been more of an inclusivist than an exclusivist. To me, the range is interesting. Looking around, I saw lots of generalist little magazines and little presses. The idea of doing that seemed like a total snooze to me. Why not focus on where my real excitement was? That became my guiding principle in all the subsequent years. Why not publish the stuff that excites me for political reasons, for poetical reasons, or political/poetical reasons? So we let *Ganglia* drift into oblivion. *Ganglia* was thought up by David Aylward. A ganglion is a connection in the brain, a synaptic connector. In fact, a small magazine, which sprang off from *grOnk*, was *Synapsis*. We liked the notion of brain activity. That seemed relevant to the idea of poetry and perception.

GH: *Ganglia* was very much a poetry oriented press and magazine. Were you that much more interested in editing poetry than in editing prose?

bp: I write prose, I read prose, I'm interested in editing prose, but my heart beats faster around poetry! The traditional poem excites me more than the traditional short story does, which is an interesting drawing line.

GH: (interviewer's note) *grOnk* magazine began as a free mailout. Quickly, the number eight became symbolic for the publication. bp, David W. Harris (aka David UU), David Aylward, and Rob

Smith were the four principals who put money into it. The two active editors in the first eight issues were bp and David UU.

bp: Once again, it's safe to say it was my idea. David UU was in there for sure, and the others were in for friendship reasons, but it wasn't a driving force for them. We ran them off ourselves, mailed them out ourselves, put the money in ourselves. The benefits were fantastic. We were able to send news from Canada to other writers we admired.

GH: (interviewer's note) Other writers, like Andy Suknaski, were able to see their work published in an international context. With the second series, which began after David UU moved to Vancouver, bp began to push it into single author issues. Everything in a way became "books" or little pamphlets, or little gestures. bp also began the mini-mimeo series.

bp: Little wee foldouts that we published and sold for five cents — the Five Cents Mini-Mimeo Series. Bookstores wouldn't stock them because they were too easy to steal, and then they'd owe me a nickel. The name "grOnk," of course, was the sound made by the dinosaur in the BC comic strip. That's why the giant O. grOnk! A dinosaur's open mouth! We liked the abstract sound, plus it was an announcement of difference. You couldn't pin down its existence in the real world, though it had its real world existence.

GH: (interviewer's note) The focus of *grOnk* was entirely experimental or visual poetry with a sound bias. From a publishing point of view, Nichol was interested in getting for Canadian writers a broader base on an international scene. His own first successes, in fact, were abroad. Presses in Europe were accepting of his work. In North America, Canadian writers were not seen as a serious issue. In that sense, Nichol says, all writing is regional. American writers tended to be influenced by American writers because they find their concerns less alien to them.

bp: They might be influenced by the style of Julio Cortazar or Borges. But as far as their content goes, their socio-politico-emotional issues tend to come out of their peer group. The great argument in English language Canadian writing is between England and America. For the Australians or New Zealanders or

Latin Americans to get a leg into the argument is almost impossible. It helped for a while if your background was a white-centred "ethnic," but even that has ceased to be an edge as far as English language Canada is concerned. That was a big concern for me. I have strong feelings about it. On the other hand, that has to do with large states of mind. On the immediate level of publishing and being published, you're interested in news, and what's going down, and you find the news where you can find the news. As for me at that time, the news was in Europe and South America and those were the writers I corresponded with, sending magazines out, and getting magazines back. That was the form most correspondence took; you sent out magazines and got magazines back more often than letters. That's what *grOnk* was, a letter-in-progress. For a long time, I did a *grOnk* News Notes. I'd publish anything that came across my table. I'd write it up and

```
we put everything in our notebooks: lists,
drafts, fragments of prose, of poetry, of
music & plays, essays, journal jottings, quotes,
personal notes, etc. some notebooks you keep
chronologically. some you don't. to those of us
who use notebooks, the notebook is the
structure within which our writing exists but
not necessarily the structure we retain when we
publish our work. but it is a structure & it
could be a model on which, from which, to
build a poem.
```

send it out with *grOnk*. But postage kept going up out of sight. The whole notion of a freebie became more and more expensive to do. In a funny kind of way, the printing got easier and cheaper because of quickie printing and plastic plates. But stamps made it trickier and trickier. It got harder to get a third class mailing permit. In the 60s it was easy; you just walked into a post office and said, "I'm a press."

GH: Did you have somewhat the same sense of Dudek and Souster that a writer-controlled press could affect the direction of literature?

bp: The impulse was there before I formulated it. For some writers, like Steve McCaffery, the formulation of his thinking, and his practice are very close together. They occur at the same point in time. For me, there's a three to six month lag. It used to be longer. It seemed natural to me to say if nobody was going to publish me, then I would publish myself. What took me longer to utter as a basic formulation was that it is easy for writers to seize the means of production and do it themselves. I look at someone like Norman Chadwick, of Toronto's Martin Garth Press which publishes *The Shit*. He published a novel in variant editions. It's no different for prose writers. You can do what Crad Kilodney or Stuart Ross do; sell it on the street. Now, if you're writing a Proustian epic, then you need a big publisher. But if you're writing a Proustian epic, you're probably going to have trouble getting a big publisher! Writers can seize the means of production. But they can't necessarily get a big audience that way. When writers are talking about their publisher problems, they are talking about the problems of getting a big audience. If what you want is to get the work out there, on the record, available to the immediate circle of writers you know, who are your lifeblood and keep you rolling, and to have something to give away at bookstores or readings, it's possible for any writer to get published to some degree. That formulation was there for me and it made a big difference to me. I'm a strong believer in writer-run presses, particularly with poetry. To me it's almost a moral/ethical thing. If, as writers, we aren't going to get out there to publish the writing we believe in, writers whose work pushes in a positive direction, then who else is going to? That's what Dennis Lee and Dave Godfrey felt around Anansi. Their concern was around prose. They are the ones who got the prose thing going in Canada. They got it going with the Spiderline Series, a group of cheap novels gang-printed on the same day. Jack McClelland had done Sheila Watson's *The Double Hook* — my favourite novel of all time — in that cheap paperback format. But they hadn't done much with it. Cheap commercial novels were done in paperback.

But they weren't necessarily a gesture towards building a Canadian intellectual tradition through prose. The Spiderline Series was exciting at the time. Here were people who felt the same energy in prose. Let's just get a whole bunch of novels pumped out. We didn't just have to have three Canadian novels a year. That idea took hold in people's brains.

GH: (interviewer's note) With the flurry of magazine and small press activity, it was no longer possible for one magazine to dominate, as *The Tamarack Review* had for so many years. That magazine began to slide from importance, interest, and influence in the late 1960s, bpNichol claims. People also lost interest in *Tamarack* when it rejected Victor Coleman's poem, "Cunnilingus."

bp: It was gutsy of them to accept it, and gutless of them to reject it, especially when it was already typeset. That was happening, and then the Canada Council came in with the money. When the Canada Council came along, there were a lot of presses in place looking for ways to find money. These organizations were ready to take the money if it was handed out! We never saw ourselves as the Hogarth Press. In fact, if you look at the back of the mini-mimeo series, you'll see a notice, "instant garbage for the nation's waste baskets." Several things influenced *grOnk*. The monthly publication (schedule) was borrowed directly from *Tish*, though the magazine had a different audience entirely. *Tish* was an inspiration for one notion — you didn't have to have subscribers. It could just be something you sent out if you thought the writing was interesting to people. If they write back, or send back stuff, it was interesting. Another model in terms of the variations in formats was the whole impulse behind international concrete poetry. The varying shapes of Ian Hamilton Finlay poems were published with his presses and other concrete people. The person I was most in touch with was the late d.a. levy of Cleveland. We had the Cleveland-Toronto-Niagara axis going for awhile. d.R. Wagner was in Niagara on the US side. Then bill and myself. We were all out of the "dirty mimeo" school of thought. *Ganglia* was probably the cleanest of the bunch. Get it done and get it out; it's news. bill was using collage as an internal principle. He had the most regular magazine look of any of them, more so than d.a. and d.R. I had given up on the regular magazine thing and was more interested in the news I found interesting. It was also a way to respond quickly to the work. *Ganglia* was more like a newspaper in my thinking about it. A lot of my editing was news edited. "I like this line — the rest of it is just okay," and "what's happening in this line is goddamn exciting, let's develop it and get it out right away!" Occasionally, I got a superb piece, but … I was not looking to preserve immortal works in magazine form.

GH: Sounds like 1960s drug-induced thought.

bp: The drug culture did not play any part in my press because I never took drugs. At the period in my life when I might have taken drugs, you were *persona non grata* if you lost smoke at pot parties and I did, the first couple I went to. I was no good that way. I used to go through stages of mind without the benefit of drugs like LSD and mushrooms and found them freaky enough. I was trying to get out of that headspace. I was not attracted to the idea of drugs. People talked about mind altering, and that's the way my mind went without drugs. I was trying to get out of that space so I could do some work. A lot of people assumed drugs were involved because the work was so far out. They assumed I was on really heavy shit! They'd come up to Toronto from the states and ask, "hey man, who's your connection?" I said, "hey man, I don't have one!"

GH: Who helped out?

bp: Basically, John Riddell or Steve McCaffery helped with various aspects of the press. I got some hands on involvement from people who helped collate and so on. But I never sat down and discussed the press abstractly. I did it. The press was designed to be responsive. So a publishing program was not worked out in advance. The points at which I had too much stuff backlogged were the points it went dead for a time. It ceased in a way to be in/out. I wanted a system that was in/out. *Ganglia's* sense of an audience was very specific. I had a mailing list. Since I was not going for newsstand sales, except locally if someone would stock it, I would just mail the thing out. I had a very specific idea of who its 250 readers were. The publications all became book/ issues in the end because I could make a slightly chunkier thing. I could give the authors more copies so they could sell them at readings. At that point, I would have an element of the audience who was unknown to me, but at least were potential readers for this person's work. I re-read some issues of *Alphabet* not so long ago and they are still interesting. There's still some stuff I can pick up on. I saw myself, in the phrase I used, as "the language revolution." A lot of shit-kicking rhetoric went down. I was interested in work that pushed against the boundaries, that dealt in some way with the reality of the text on the page or the reality of the text as it existed in sound. These were the issues that interested me as a writer. I knew I appealed to a minority audience. That's why the idea of a newsletter made sense.

GH: Was this an exciting time to be involved?

bp: Toronto was not an exciting place to be in the early part of the 1960s, say 1963 to 1966. Having a correspondence with Cavan McCarthy in Leeds and other writers like Bob Cobbing was a tremendous encouragement. bissett was a great encouragement, though he was in Vancouver. Not a lot of people were interested in what I was interested in. There was a feeling I was just crazy, and the feeling I was pursuing an absolute dead end assailed me in those days. Fortunately, I have a pleasant stubborn streak. I will follow a thing as long as it interests me, though I can't see the reason for it. Those were harder years. Around 1966, David UU came down from Collingwood. He was excited, up about the stuff. We yakked a lot. I had a lot to do with Dave until he moved to the west coast in the fall of 67. After he left town, there weren't many people here. Then, Steve McCaffery moved here from England. That made a huge difference in my life. Here was someone who was concerned with the same issues, and covered the same ground from his own angle for his own reasons. Steve and I are very dissimilar writers. But we share a lot of concerns. I always concerned myself with design, typeface, and papers on the press though you wouldn't necessarily know it by looking. I was working with two or three concerns. One was I would experiment with the actual physical size, whether it was

folded or stapled, whether it had a drawing. In the later period of
grOnk, and the last few years, when all the principles had changed,
I experimented with ready-made formats. I'd just walk into an
office supply store and see what kinds of things they had, plastic
covers, and other weirdness. These things are often expensive, cost
heavy on the format side. But they lead to interesting solutions.
This is almost the opposite approach to traditional publishing. The
first is, you have a piece, and you wonder what shape it should be
in. With this, you have a shape, and you wonder what will fit it.
grOnk went through distinctive periods. The first was the monthly
series, like a monthly magazine. That was the old series. The
second part of the old series, each in eight issues, began to move
quickly to single author issues. Then I began to issue them out of
order. It drove librarians wild.

GH: It was your equivalent of Ed Sander's *Fuck you; a Magazine of
the Arts*.

bp: Only I was more insidious. I would have Series Eight, Number Five, followed by Series Eight, Number One. I used to work
in a library. *Blewointment* did the same thing, only their numbering was false. Mine was consistent, which was worse. The old
series was a mail away, which went to 64 issues. One still hasn't
properly appeared. But they are all basically done. Some were
double issues of *grOnk* which doubled as *Ganglia* publications.
They varied from 250 to 500 copies. Then, I began the middle
series, of 24 issues, a multiple of eight. That was a subscription
series. Once again, subscription proved truly boring. But, I
managed to get all 24 issues out. I let most people's subscriptions
lapse after 12 or 13 issues and kept putting it out. Then I did the
grOnk, *Zap*, and *Flash* series of 50 copies each. I gave them to the
authors to give away. I've been working on the final series, of
about 100 copies each. Now I give 60 to 75 copies to the author
to distribute as they see fit. I keep 25 for my immediate give-
aways. There's also the *grOnk* Random Series. That's anywhere
from 50 to 500 copies. It's hard to collect a complete set.

GH: (interviewer's note) Throughout Nichol's life, *grOnk* also
existed as a press. Some of the publications were issued as cassettes
through Underwhich Editions. Copies were given to the authors,

and Nichol kept the rest. He saw his publications as "support documentation."

GH: Did you learn the technical aspects of publishing through trial and error?

bp: We wanted to start a magazine. How? What was the cheapest? What seemed cheapest at the beginning was a mimeo machine that I bought. It eventually rusted out in Steve McCaffery's basement through neglect. We hand-cranked lots of it. That's the way we printed most of *Ganglia* magazine. Issues five and seven were offset. Issue six never appeared. Issue eight was printed at Weed/Flower press by Nelson Ball on a tiny machine. *grOnk* was printed at Speedy Printers. Plus the occasional mimeo, and the run of the Five Cent Mini-Mimeo Series. A few were offset. After number 39 or 40, they were offset. The Speedy Printshops were a late 60s early 70s thing. That was a case of technology giving me access to a way of quick printing. As a kid, I had always made up books of my poems. In my mid-teens, I made up copies of books of poems and gave them to my friends. I was always playing with the form of the book. I was a voracious reader. I think if you read, and unless you are totally oblivious, you are always aware of "page." When we began to work on *Ganglia* and *grOnk*, one of our first organizing principles was that we did not want somebody's poem facing somebody else's poem. As early as 1964, we said everybody should have their own space. So that leads logically to concrete poetry. Everything should have its own space. Sometimes a really good piece looked not as good placed against another poem. They were not always complementary pairs. Even strong poems might not look so good side by side. That's not something you'd do with your own manuscript. We would put a drawn piece on the other page, something entirely different.

GH: How did you get involved with Coach House Press?

bp: About 1964 or 1965, I met Stan Bevington of Coach House, and began to get a lot of hands-on experience with type and typography and a fantastic basic training. I was already open to it. I did not see a press as something someone did for me, labour for hire. I wanted to get in there, down and dirty and involved. The chance to do some hand typesetting was fantastic. I was interested in "collectibles," as I was a collector. But that was not my motivation. I was just thinking of the Tonto Or, a *Ganglia* press series. They were all done on offsets, back in the days when you had lots of paper samples to choose from. Stan had lots sitting on shelves, and Coach House was easy access. I could use a proof press, which is an easy-to-use flat-bed press. I was setting up the type. Stan was encouraging of that kind of involvement. I learned a lot from Stan about books and book design. Stan was a good person to learn from because he was always arguing within and against. He was a traditional hand-set typist who got interested in linotype, and then computers. He was my first introduction to computers in the early 1970s.

A *grOnk* "first edition" doesn't have the same "power" as, say, a Hogarth Press first edition. The context of the time is as important as the text. Because the texts were "news," there's some that date, and some that don't. I was not involved in that kind of editorial process which would say, "These are the ones that last for all time." I'd simply say, "Here's what's new." Someone else can collect them, if they want, on a "timeless basis." I was interested in the half-life of the poem, the decay, and the fact that things faded away. The model for me was Keats, dead at 26. All that bullshit about "make it wait, make it a considered thing," was not for me. I could be dead. I thought I would die at 18. So it was all gravy for me in the years since then. 23 years of gravy — that's nice! It was an *idée fixe* I got when I was young. My impulse had nothing to do with preserving in that sense. To get it on the record, yes. But even that was a later thought. Earlier on, the thought was to get the news out. I published tons and tons. Lots of Europeans, bill bissett, Dave Phillips, Andy Suknaski, Martina Clinton, Beth Jankola, Pat Lowther, lots of Steve McCaffery, lots of David UU, some Mike Ondaatje. I worked closely with the authors if they were close. Generally, I published someone because I liked their work, and wanted to get their text out. Sometimes, it was just one text of a writer whose work I didn't usually like. It was good to defeat my own thinking. I never went after grants. I did it when I had money. That got a little more random at times. That's the impulse with Underwhich Editions. However, we did a little press catalogue that included Ganglia, Anansi, Talon — the Busy Beaver catalogue was an attempt to include everybody's little books. That was a late 60s impulse. That was an interesting time. There was

Ganglia Press, Island Press which remained "little-little" and alternative. Then there was Anansi and Talon who began to operate on a different scale. But there was enough affinity that we could do a joint catalogue. *Ganglia* and *grOnk* had some influence, though it's hard to say what, after looking over the sea of mundane writing. I think of Victor Coleman and Dennis Lee as discerning editors who worked with the text. They worked with the author more than I would. I tend to take the text as it is, make my suggestions, and they take it or leave it. I take the text as it is because it already interests me. Behind *Ganglia* and *grOnk* was a strong idea: to focus on certain work, to argue for that work, and to put enough of the work forward so that readers could get a feeling for the sheer quantity of people who approached the text this way. Then, they could get used to that kind of text, and develop reading habits around it. It's not saying too much to say that in its own small way, and despite its own small readership, that this effect is inherent in the idea of a small press. If you start with a small gesture, the ripple effect spreads out. You don't have to worry about the audience size for your work to have impact. Once you get hung up on the numbers game, you can get really depressed. *Ganglia* and *grOnk* had an impact on the international scene by giving some presence to some writers from Canada who were working on the visual thing while it was happening. They (*Ganglia* and *grOnk*) had an impact on the national scene by making people aware poets were doing this in Canada and in other countries as well. That was an authentication of it. In Canada, there's no better authentication than the fact it is being done elsewhere. It's like buying a car. Am I the only one buying this car? Does that mean parts will be hard to get? People feel the same about their reading. *Ganglia* and *grOnk* widened the notion of what was possible for the Canadian reader. Perhaps the texts weren't the most original in their areas. But I wasn't interested in that. I was interested in the reality of literature as something you do while you are alive. You write while you are alive, you live somewhere while you are alive, you want readers while you are alive. It's fine and dandy to say, "well, they'll read it while I'm gone." Horseshit! You don't know that. If you want those, then you have to go out and argue for the audience. That's what I did. As for the 1980s, kids of 18 don't seem to read widely. In poetry, there's a lot of good writing, but very little that is exciting. Even stuff that is stylistically competent or advanced doesn't give fresh insights into the human condition if I'm just seeing another exegesis on a human relationship that I got from the Greeks (and more powerfully because of the philosophy behind it). But the umpteenth poem on me and mom, the home scene, or me and my relationship to the lyric impulse, which is the bulk of Canadian poetry, doesn't give me any news. So I'm not getting anything fresh from what they are talking about.

GH: How about on the level of language?

bp: No.

GH: How about on the level of metaphor?

bp: No.

GH: So what's going on?

bp: It's okay poetry, well written, competent, but not very exciting. Partly it's reader's taste. But how many poems can I read about two people fighting in a darkened room? I've heard that beat. I've been criticized for my formalism. You can see the bones of my pieces. When I look at the traditional poem or story, that's an exoskeletal structure. I can see the beats of the poem, the pegs they hang their narrative on. I can see the whole thing laid out, like an X-ray. I'm looking for something that acknowledges that, and then does something with it. In the mid-60s, the most common male poem was from the *courier de bois* tradition. The poet comes in from the woods, slams his axe on the table, and declaims a poem about his sex life. That has its own boredom. With different beats, that's been the popular male voice in Canadian poetry for years. It's there in a different way in Pat Lane. Al Purdy does it brilliantly. Early Leonard Cohen does it. Pat does the other big Canadian thing with the poem — go to another country and write about it. What has been really good, has been the growth of regional presses. But most of those presses are still regional. Stan Bevington joked at a recent Coach House Press editorial meeting that we were the last press still to publish west coast writers. He was worried about becoming a regional press like everyone else. But it's not regional if it's from Toronto; it's centralist!

The Dart, Its Arkness: David McFadden's *The Art of Darkness*

1986

The title of this essay is a little overly contrived perhaps but to the point. David McFadden never just throws straight at "the truth," as though only a bull's-eye will do, he keeps hitting at it from various sides and angles. And along the way the arcs of his imaginative flights illuminate whole arks for the soul, places you can enter, come in out of the rain, the storms, and claim as your own.

A case in point is his absolutely marvellous *The Art of Darkness*, a book which I've kept by the side of my bed, taken with me on buses, subways, trains, planes flights, etc., constantly since it first came out, a good two years ago. And here I am only now taking the time to sit down and tell you about it. It's full of so many wonderful moments, wonderful hours, that I've barely known where to begin writing about it. I'm a fan. I've fallen in love with it. I've lost my heart to the way the mind is led through and into new areas of the imagination, and that's because it's a book for the mind and the heart. There's a lot of stuff passes for poetry in Canada these days, and very little of it is for the intelligent heart or the feeling mind. But *The Art of Darkness* is.

There are, of course, as we've come to expect almost as our right, what we might call the "usual" McFadden poems, those marvellously witty juxtapositions of ordinary events with profound insights. Take, for example, "Country Hotel in the Niagara Peninsula," which begins with an incident in a pool hall and ends with a precise definition of the act of writing. There are funny poems which talk of deeper things, like "Velma's Giant Cinamon Buns," poems which remind me of the time that McFadden said to me, after a particularly successful reading in the late 60s, "I can make them them laugh, now if I could only make them cry." And then, as if addressing that very statement I have just quoted, there are poems of such incredible frankness, such openness, like "Letter to My Father," that we wince to read them. Or poems full of the contradictions of being, like "Kitsilano Beach on a May Evening," poems that call into question the too simple images we throw onto the screen of the word "poet."

But having said all that is only to begin to suggest the richness that is available to any reader in this wonderful book. And having said it, I want to focus on the two long poems within which the rest of the book is contained, the poems that open and close the book, "Night of Endless Radiance" and "Country of the Open Heart" — because in these poems in particular something very special is happening. I want to try to articulate my sense of it, leaving open, of course, the question of whether my sense is the author's sense.

There are a few lines in McFadden's introduction that set up what I want to explore, the essence of these two poems and, I think, the book as a whole:

> Anything but total absorption in the insanities of the surface seems cowardly ...

And a little later:

> Love isn't all but it must take precedence over all, no matter how difficult, fraught with indignities, embarrassing and unfashionable it may be. Now as never before it's our civic duty as citizens of the world to subject ourselves to ecstasy, to go beyond and discover the new oceans of ecstasy that lie waiting for the pure pilgrims of love, and to return and talk about it indiscriminately, passionately, like a fundamentalist door-knocker.

Passion is the key note in this whole book. McFadden's voice has often been misheard as being laconic or whimsical, but here he wears his beating heart on his sleeve and the reader can't miss it. There's a tone of high moral outrage fuelling the writing. Not that it comes through in terms of some shrillness or scolding that informs the voice-voices in these texts. Far from it. But what I mean is there's a sense of high purpose, a sense of not settling for the safe line, the too-pat perception, or the recycled psychological insight. McFadden's going for the jugular in every line, and if your jugular can take it it's exhilarating.

Particularly in the two long poems, where something amazing is happening. Each is concerned with the heart, as metaphor for the emotions, as beating organ, as central point, as a word among the quest for true spirituality and a coming to terms with both these terms in the lived life. But as the line quoted earlier suggested, a lot of where that's happening is right on the surface of the poem. I said he was wearing his heart on his sleeve and I meant it literally. So does McFadden. It's the country of the open heart after all. Oh!

I need to quote a long chunck of "Night of Endless Radiance" to illustrate what I'm talking about. From part IX:

> The night is afloat in the mind of the dreamer
> and the one-eyed light of an approaching train
> becomes an illuminating flower from heaven
> and the world is a station where such glorious light
> shines through occasional chinks to illuminate
> the halls of hell. The radiant flower was warm,
> with a passion that plunged forth courageously
> into further dimensions of awe (the sound
> the heart makes as it opens a little further).
> Every day you age two days
> and every night you become one day younger
> for time stops when the sun goes down
> and the dreamer's life falls apart
> for there are too many patterns to smash
> and the one pattern she wants can never be found
> and the quiet path through the quiet woods
> keeps branching and before the branches
> reconverge her life will be all but over,
> and as soon as one path is chosen it too branches
> until she becomes trapped in her own originality,
> lost in a grain of sand inexhaustible as a star.
> For the mind works better when completely naked,
> solemnly flashing in the middle of the night

like a beacon of incredible flesh, a wild blossom
blinking music into deepest space.

And the dreamer is afloat in the radiant night.
Even her phone is off the hook …

If we track the surface of this excerpt from the text we can see very clearly what's happening in both these poems. In the first place night is afloat in the mind of the dreamer. But at the beginning of the next stanza the dreamer is afloat in the radiant night. Again, at the beginning of the stanza night is afloat in the mind of the dreamer and through this night the light of an approaching train is seen. This transforms into an illuminating flower from heaven. But then, even though night is inside the mind of the dreamer, the world (presumably the one in which the dreamer sleeps) is a station (and therefore, presumably, the destination of the train) where such light shines through the chinks in the walls and illuminates the halls of hell, which are in the world which is in the mind of the dreamer. Even earlier, in part I of the poem, the writer has described images as being:

like rays of light from stars viewed
by people on a train heading into the northern night

And this is literally true of course. Images arc passed onto us through light, are part of that branch of physics, and are, at the same time, a physik for the soul. But the point is, there's that train and there's that light. And going back to that earlier notion of the station there's the statement in part V that

… no one listens
not even the whispering crowds of time travellers
masquerading as rosy velvet puffs of consciousness
in the middle of Service Station Nightmare.

And we know the Time Traveller could be the dreamer for whom time has stopped, "for time stops when the sun goes down." Everything is part of something else. "Country of the

Open Heart" first occurs as a phrase in "Night of Endless Radiance." And then the poem begins with the line: "When the phone rings in the middle of the night." Naturally there's a sleeper dreaming there whose dream it enters. Because at this end of the book, as the poem says:

> … the human race has awakened and now
> must reverse itself and fall asleep again —

But even though "Country of the Open Heart" grows out of "Night of Endless Radiance," "Night of Endless Radiance" is embedded within it. That earlier poem is changed by our reading of this later poem and vice-versa.

It is this very porousness, the way in which images shift and transform, that allows the light in McFadden's poems to shine through. The chinks are created and through them illumination pours into the halls of hell. And McFadden is dealing with illumination, spiritual and physical, and he breaks new ground in talking of it, rhyming metaphors with a casual bravura and punning in high seriousness. When he talks of light-hearted dreams, we know what he's talking about. And when he talks of thought as "the thin king … thinking," we see and hear the play of intelligence. McFadden doesn't just talk about his visions, he presents visions to us. We are not just readers then, in some old sense, but rather seers, witness to the miracles played out in front of us.

The way that phrases keep returning, as images, as new similes, is also the way in which McFadden keeps us most on our toes and teaches us to teach ourselves. The world is transforming around us daily. It's all happening there right on the surface. Don't retreat from it. Deal with it. Or deal with whatever it is right now because tomorrow it may be different again. No such thing then as final answers. Or no easy way to blame anyone else. As McFadden points out in the fourth part of "Country of the Open Heart":

> … thus in the sea, when tides are strongest,
> the surface often shows its calmest face
> and the agony of cruel crucifixion

lies behind the saint's beatific smile
as your writing, when it appears to be
pretending to reflect spiritual truth,
is merely moving through the nature of itself
like a snake awakening on a mild spring morning.

Let's take one other example, an example which illustrates why
I'm hesitant to take this review much further. In his introduction
to the book, McFadden says, "Analysis of these poems is strictly
forbidden." And in truth I've tried not to analyze the poems but
rather to deal with my responses to them, what it is in them that
keeps me excitedly rereading the book. But McFadden himself
does suggest a strategy for reading. At the end of the first part of
"Night of Endless Radiance" the poet writes:

And there is only one test for true minds:
if they were to jump in the sea en masse
would dolphins save them
and with them on their Quasimodo shoulders
disappear in the moonless night
bound for Ancient Isles of Splendour?

And in the very next part says:

Miscellaneous crowds of apes swarm
in and out of the night like schools of dolphins
crossing imaginary equators …

I don't think there's any doubt who the apes are, but let's press
on. Subsequently the poem says of the mind:

… It has an ability
to disappear, a love of appearing and disappearing
here and there …

Now I'm drawing these lines out just to suggest how the mind
must operate to read these poems. The true mind needs to take
the leap and see if it's carried, dolphin-like, plunging into the

depths, above the surface, through it, crossing imaginary equators or, as stated later, "sobbing with uncontrollable sorrow." I don't think it's reading into the text to suggest that what McFadden's trying for is that interplay between surface and what lies below the surface while at the same time avoiding the locating of the term "depth" in any naive geographical or physiological location. The very way the location of the mind shifts in these poems suggests that.

It's human passion this work is full of. McFadden doesn't want the poem to be just one thing, he wants it to be all things full of feelings, good and bad, of wit, wisdom, spiritual revelation, of detestable emotions you'd rather hide under the nearest rock. He knows you need to admit them all if you want to break through into the country of the open heart.

"You need another line here. That'll do."

```
by  now  we  all  realize  you  can't  really  get
away  from  narrative.  you  can  make  it  difficult
to  detect  the  pattern  of  your  intention,  down-
play  it  as  it  were,  but  there  is  always  at
least  the  secret  narrative  of  your  compositional
process.  so  what  are  we  saying  when  we  say
we  are  seeking  alternatives  to  narrative?  we
are  saying  we  are  trying  to  get  away  from
always  telling,  from  that  kind  of  a  need  to
know.
```

Introduction to *The Last Blew Ointment Anthology Volume 2*

1986

The first time i heard bill bissett read was in a classroom at UBC in late 1963 or early 64. In my mind it has always been linked with a reading that Michael McClure gave around that same time (before or after? i can't remember) on that same campus, in a very similar if not identical classroom, from his then just recently published *Ghost Tantras*. In his reading McClure growled and howled in his beast language, and in his bill used some abstract sound elements and a lot of silence (bill was working with silence as an analogue to visual space at that time). i'd been reading about sound poetry in 62, 63 because a friend of mind, Jim Alexander, one of the editors of the long forgotten magazine *Adder*, had convinced me to buy a copy of Motherwell's *The Dada Painters and Poets*, for which insistence on his part i remain eternally grateful. Jim thought i should read the Dada book because i was so interested in Kenneth Patchen's painted books and the typographic elements Patchen used in his prose. Jim was right of course and along the way i was reading about sound poetry, the writing and performances of Hugo Ball, Tristan Tzara and Kurt Schwitters. Now the key word here is "reading," and this is where this long preamble ties into what i'm trying to introduce you to, *The Last Blew Ointment Anthology Volume 2*, because it was the appearance of the first issue of *Blew Ointment* that drew me to bill's reading in the first place. i had been "reading" about sound poetry but i'd never had a chance to hear any and when *Blew Ointment* appeared with bill's marvellously innovative texts, texts that violated everything i had been told was a "rule" of poetry, i figured that his reading of these texts had to be something to hear, had to be pretty close to what i was "reading" about in the Motherwell book, and i went along to hear it. i wasn't disappointed.

When that first issue of *Blew Ointment* hit the Vancouver bookstores, October 1963, Dave Phillips, Jim Alexander and I all bought it and read it. After all it was the new poetry mag in our town, an alternative to *Tish*, which had a very heavy "this is the *right* writing" stance, and flat out experimental in its orientation. That first issue included the single poem by bill that probably opened my head up more than any other — "now they found th wagon cat in human body." i heard a possibility in that poem i had heard nowhere else, one i couldn't have articulated at the time but which i now recognize as the possibility that the language could speak for itself, had its own qualities separate from whatever the meaning i might wish to will into it. Years later bill kindly dedicated that poem to me, i guess because i've slavered and drooled about it so much in my enthusiasm over the years. There're two other things to realize here. One is that as far as i could see at that time (and indeed at this time) what bill was doing had no antecedents. He was himself, going in his own direction and, along with Martina Clinton and Lance Farrell, breaking brand new ground in the process. The second thing to realize is that this was a Canadian i was excited about. i didn't have to go gazing south of the border or across the sea to find that hit of adrenalin that really new writing gives you. It was happening right there in that first issue. Believe me when i say that that was a rare experience in those days. Dave and Jim and i had a lot of talks, a lot of arguments, a lot of differences of opinion about that first issue. i remained excited by it, by the sense of possibility it represented to me. And when i saw that bill was giving a reading i went along to it. As i've already said i wasn't disappointed. Where McClure's work seemed too tied to a biological model, bissett's pointed beyond it to the page, back to the voice and outward to the whole world of operating signs, to a region between poetry, painting and music.

i moved from Vancouver shortly after that, at the end of April 1964. i hadn't met bill at that point but i sure had met his magazine. And one of the first things i did upon reaching Toronto was to write to him and send him money for a subscription. Then when i finally had a few poems i felt worth publishing one of the first magazines i sent stuff to was *Blew Ointment*. It was the first one that published me too, a poem called "Translating Apollinaire" in Volume 2, #3, August 1964, and of course i was very excited by that. bill and i exchanged a lot of letters, wrote and talked about a lot of stuff. David Aylward and i began *Ganglia* magazine and in the first issue published, among others, bill bissett. We also started talking to bill about doing an issue devoted entirely to his writing. When he came thru Toronto in 1965 he stayed at my place. We talked about Stein, about writing in general, pushing the boundaries, all those things, and finalized *We Sleep Inside Each Other All*, the bissett book, bill's first, published as the fourth issue of *Ganglia*.

Blew Ointment remains, for me, a model of what a magazine should be, eclectic, far reaching, more interested in the "news" than in preserving "great" literature, a map of the mind of its editor, his interests. That's what always made it interesting. It's also what made *Tish*, *Island*, *Alphabet* and *Imago* interesting. They were all magazines in which what you were tracking was the passionate interests and stance of the editor(s). Whether you agreed or not, their takes were so much their own that you were educated by them one way or another. *Blew Ointment* reached its full flowering in the still incredible summer 1966 issue (Volume 4, #1). In it bill combined an astounding number of printing and binding techniques — rubber stamping, mimeograph (ordinary printing and running pieces straight off the screen), xeroxing, off-set lithography, found elements ripped from the pages of other magazines and interleaved randomly (thus making each issue unique), letraset collages, typesetting, the utilization of different sized "pages" within the same set of covers. It was wonderful. It still is. i visited bill in the summer of 66 while he was putting the issue together. He was cranking stuff out on an old 1903 ABDick mimeo the day i arrived. i looked at the pieces he was running off — some of David Aylward's asp texts — on random sized bits of paper he'd culled from the garbage behind some print shop. The texts were blurred and bordering on the unreadable. i said, "bill, you can't read these!" and bill said, "yeah, but they're in print" and the relativity of that phrase struck me. the way in which bill was always trying to undercut the arbitrariness of the authorities we grant including the "authorization" that being published gives to our work.

Blew Ointment published anyone that interested bill. That was what made it interesting. And since bill's own concerns roamed widely it published a pretty vast range of stuff. i was reading Eva Tihanyi's slam of Volume 1 of *The Last Blew Ointment Anthology* in *Poetry Canada Review* (Volume 8, #1) the other day and thinking of how readers have in some way changed, or at least how the readers i knew when *Blew Ointment* began weren't, as Tihanyi says in her review, simply "looking for a handful of good poems." i think she's probably right in her assumption that many readers in the 80s tend to read books looking for the "good poems" in them, in the same way that so many opera listeners have come to bide their time in the opera waiting for the "great" arias, or play-goers to await the "great" speeches. Nobody reads books anymore, they read poems. Nobody reads magazines anymore, they read individual entries. In that same issue of *PCR*, Rosemary Aubert makes the incredible statement that these days "poets seem to be taking more care than ever to arrange their collections in the most advantageous way. Most often," she says, "this means grouping poems around a strong theme, an important event, or even a character." Has it come to this? Is it really NEWS that writers write *books*? That magazine editors are editing the entire *issue* of a magazine? Both the way poetry is taught and the authority that anthologization of individual poems gives to a writer's writing have certainly helped to create this bizarre state of affairs. The rise of the generalist magazine has helped reinforce such a sensibility, the magazines that don't particularly stand for anything because they are trying to be all things to all people. But *Blew Ointment* always stood for something. Love it or hate it, it was clearly bill's magazine and represented his point of view, his current passions, his heart worn on his printed sleeve. So all this is to make the point that you hold in your hands Volume 2 of *The Last Blew Ointment Anthology*, the final final manifestation of bill's sensibility as a magazine editor. Read it as such. Don't read it looking for "good poems," read it as the map of a mind looking back over 20 odd years of publishing, important publishing, and saying "this was interesting, and this" and then throwing in a few treats along the way because he knows this is the last go round for this particular beast. You'll stumble across some good poems i'm sure, probably even some great poems, but they're not the point and they never were. Me, i'm going to miss *Blew Ointment.* It made the scene richer, more unexpected, more varied. It was the kind of contribution from a little magazine we needed then, that we still need and always will.

Primary Days: Housed with the Coach at the Press, 1965 to 1987

1987

I was looking at an ad for *Parachute* magazine the other day which announced itself as dealing with all that was current in contemporary art — and the list was, indeed, impressive: dance, video, performance, film, painting and sculpture. There was, of course, a noticeable absence — writing. Does that mean writing is not a "contemporary" art? It doesn't seem to have struck the editors of *Parachute* as particularly problematic, even though what they're putting out is a magazine full of, presumably, writing. But it struck me, admittedly for the 534th time or so, how the visual arts have co-opted the word "art," and how even tho most "contemporary" artists (we'll use *Parachute*'s definition here) are overly obsessed with thematic criticism (an approach that most cutting-edge literature has done away with), or borrowings from various contemporary schools of philosophy and literary criticism, they would seldom, if ever, bother to cover what's current in writing in their magazines. "Even tho," i said. There's a further "even tho."

Writing, precisely because it is *written*, is, at least in part, a visual art. It's also a sound art (a very sound art, says David UU, but that's a pun for another day). It lies, therefore, at the juncture between painting & music, taking something from each but remaining itself. Because it is built up out of words *and* ideas, it can also be seen as lying at the juncture between painting & philosophy and between music & philosophy — a three-part relationship which is much less funnel-oriented than it sounds — and between those juncture points is the area which Dom Sylvester Houedard referred to as "borderblur," the area where the distinctions break down and become useless. There are other things which can or should encompass the juncture points of which i speak here, a super-, or supra-, relationship: the misnamed (because of the "visual arts" connotation) performance art; theatre; film &/or videotape.[1] R. Murray Schafer's idea of a

Theatre of Confluence is one of the most striking examples of what i am pointing to. But it's also a macro concept as opposed to what i take to be the more micro notion of borderblur.[2] For a writer all this should become brilliantly clear the moment that writer gets involved in the hands-on business of publishing.

This is really an article about the Coach House Press as it was in the 60s and early 70s, with a few additional notes to bring it up to now. It's not, hopefully, a nostalgia piece, nor does it say anything about what the press is today, but it is, as an article, an attempt to use the form of the memoir to write a subjective account of both what happened and (in, & because of, that process) what anyone should know, including writers, about the activity of publishing (subjective because i'm going to write it from the point of view of how i came to know what i know — a little presumptuous perhaps, but the only way i can find to voice this). i started with those first two paragraphs just to make clear that the book is a visual event, a sculptural multiple, a machine in which the reader is the only moving part. And this article wants to be about where words meet what we more traditionally think of as the "visual" arts, which just happens to be, in one of its manifestations, exactly what made Coach House Press so interesting and so important. This is not about writing per se then — tho it is written and, in that very fact, says something about writing — but it is about one of writing's major destinations: print.

This sense of writing as a visual art is not, of course, nor should it be seen as, new. Certainly many writers and many painters in many countries have realized it. Taking some specifically Canadian examples: look at Greg Curnoe's large-scale canvases composed entirely of words, as well as those incorporating language as part of the composition; or Steve McCaffery's multi-panel typewriter text *Carnival*; or Rosalind Goz's use of words in her drawings; or Sean O'Huigin's visual poems; or Barbara Caruso's *Van Doesburg's Alphabet*, a pen-and-ink series now in the Art Gallery of Ontario collection; or Robert Fones' use of language in his more recent shows at the Carmen Lamanna Gallery. Nor is the use of off-set lithography to create art objects new. Look at Kim Ondaatje's Factory print series. Or Michael Hayden's direct working with the medium in his prints

423

(i.e. no intermediate state of a "painting" or "watercolour" being reproduced). Etc. Etc. And, as you've probably already noticed, look how all the visual artists referred to above have all worked with, or thru, Coach House Press over the years. That list could go on and would include Jack Chambers, Michael Sowdon, John Boyle, David Bolduc, Roy Kiyooka, photographers David Hlynsky, Rick Simon, Jim Laing, Marilyn Westlake, etc. etc. As I said, this sense of the visualness of writing is not new; unfortunately it still seems to be news to some people. So let's look a bit at the history of this, of how these connections have sprung up and where they've gone, the areas they've reached into in the process.

I first visited Coach House Press in the early winter of 1965. I'd met Stan Bevington and Wayne Clifford at a New Year's Eve party, December 31, 1964, a party that Josephine Hindley-Smith, who was still active on the folk-singing scene in those days, and who had lived at the Press briefly before heading off to England, had thrown during a return visit to Toronto. Both Wayne and Stan invited me around to visit the press so, being a curious young writer, i went. Coach House Press at that time was housed

```
what  i  noticed,  as  i  was  getting  ready  to
read  this  piece  to  the  conference,  was  that
steve  was  sitting  there  in  the  front  row
rubbing  his  eyes  and  i  wondered  what  he  was
seeing  that  i  wasn't.
```

in an old coach house near the corner of Dundas and Bathurst where, in fact, the Scadding Court Community Centre now sits. Stan had an open-door policy in those days. He was a fine printer at that time, still contemplating the purchase of his first Linotype machine. He had a nice old proof press, as well as the large

Challenge Gordon that remains the Coach House logo. He had a lot of offcuts (paper remnants from other jobs) and anyone who wanted to get their hands dirty was welcome to use them, and his seemingly inexhaustible job cases full of type and his proof press, to print up small cards or even books. Wayne tended to hang around too. And various other writers, sculptors, painters, photographers, etc., including Dennis Reid, Kog Reid, Joe Rosenblatt, Bob Daigneault, Judith Cowan, Doris Cowan, etc. Stan was interested in your interest, and would spend hours giving you instruction in the fine art of typesetting. For me this had a fundamental effect on my view of literature. i was already heading this way anyway, which is to say towards an increasing awareness of just how visual literature was, because of my interest in visual poetry, etc., but there's no doubt about it, the effect of setting my own texts, letter by letter, word by word, line by line, was to create in me a whole new awareness of all the components that go into any literature.[3]

i know it affected me. Shortly after first meeting Stan and Wayne, we began work on what became known as my purple package, a slipcase that included a long poem, a flip poem, a record of sound poems, and an envelope full of visual poems and poem/sculptures. Everybody contributed ideas to the project — we were soliciting them from anyone who walked thru the front door — but in particular: Wayne did the typography on, for instance, the "drumm" poem; Victor Coleman (more on him in a minute) helped me edit the long poem; Stan did the overall design as well as contributed money to pay for the record; a cast of thousands came down to the press and helped with the collating. Here was a case in point; we experimented with everything including varying page sizes, different coloured inks — printing light-blue text on grey pages (a failure — you could just make it out if you held the book up in a strong light) and cream text on white card (a success — the poem, a permutational insistence of the word "milk," became "homogenized" in the process; you had to look hard to realize it wasn't simply a drawing of a milk bottle) — and different coloured papers, bound and unbound texts, etc. All this was, as mentioned, collated by hand and held together inside a specially constructed slipcase.[4] We brought it out in the late winter of 1967 and sold it for the incredibly cheap price of $2.50. We couldn't figure out at first why it was selling so well till we realized the paper in the thing alone was probably worth $2.50. We gambled and raised the price to $3.50. It still sold. We were amazed.

In the fall of 1966, Wayne Clifford, who up till then had been the unofficial editor of the press, moved to Iowa to further his studies and Victor Coleman got involved as the new unofficial /official editor. Victor's been a tireless force on the Toronto scene for years, involved in one way or another in just about everything of significance that's happened. Besides editing the magazines *Island & Is* and assisting Ray Souster in the editing of *New Wave Canada*, he was involved from its beginning with *A Space*, founded *Only Paper Today* and, subsequently, co-founded *Music Works*, was involved with all the correspondence art activity of the 70s, co-wrote and performed in various alternative radio projects as well as a number of stage musicals, is involved with programming at the Music Gallery & on CKLN, etc. etc. I'm mentioning this diversity because Victor, as much as anyone, helped bring a lot of interested visual arts people into and through the press. Coach House Press was, quite simply, one of the places where things were happening and people wanted to drop in and hang around and, maybe, get involved. Both Victor & Stan encouraged this. And one of the off-shoots of hanging out was that ideas were exchanged, projects were born, collaborations happened.

Two of the most visible manifestations of this were the Coach House posters and the Coach House postcards; art for the streets. Anyone and everyone had access to the postcard series. The cards could be printed along with covers, thus saving set-up costs, so anyone who wandered thru with an interesting photo or collage, or who came up with one while sitting around the table, had the chance of seeing that idea turned into an instantly available multiple. Posters were somewhat different, arising, as they did, most often, out of book design. But the number of people who contributed ideas and/or designs to book covers (&, indeed, books themselves) is long and interesting. One of the best examples, and still a personal favourite of mine, was the Greg Curnoe /David McFadden collaboration on *The Great Canadian Sonnet*, a big little book originally published in two volumes but later combined into one small fat beautiful book which alternated a page of David's text with a page of Greg's drawing. The drawings were later exhibited at the National Gallery. Greg and David reunited in the 80s[5] to do *Animal Spirits*, a deluxe limited edition hardcover collection of short stories. In the late 70s David Bolduc designed and illustrated Wayne Clifford's *An Ache in the Ear*. And a very recent project with a similar strength to the Curnoe/ McFadden collaborations is Dennis Tourbin's *Port Dalhousie Stories* for which John Boyle did a whole series of stunning drawings.

But we were talking of how writing itself is visual, and that takes us into typography and the whole crew of wonderful book designers and typographers that've worked at the press including besides, of course, Stan Bevington — Nelson Adams, Glenn Goluska, Glenna Munro, Rick Simon, Robert Macdonald, Jerry Ofo, Janet Zweig, Paul Collins, Libby Oughton and Gord Robertson. And that's not to mention the writers like Wayne Clifford, Michael Ondaatje, Frank Davey, Christopher Dewdney, Robert Fones and Victor Coleman who also contributed ideas and designs of their own. There are the obvious things that any good book designer does — the cover and the title page — but a good one, and Coach House has had some of the best, designs the whole book with, as much as possible in Coach House's case, the collaboration of the author. When we were putting Daphne Marlatt's *What Matters* thru the press, Nelson Adams and i spent hours working out a way to translate Daphne's particular use of internal spacing in the typewritten drafts of her poems into typographic terms. The result was a text that was faithful to the author's original. On the other hand when we were putting my *Two Novels* thru the press in 1968, i came in with the idea of doing it like an old Ace Double-Book but it was Victor who suggested to me making the reader read it as if it were written in Japanese (i.e. from right to left). That added a whole dimension to the original edition i hadn't thot of. Design is that interplay between intent and ideas that the text itself suggests.

Obviously Coach House is not the only place where things like this were happening (Michael Snow's brilliant *Cover to Cover* springs instantly to mind, and bill bissett's unique work with his own Blew Ointment Press) but Coach House is an interesting case in point. Forms like "artist's books," usually done in editions of one, tho obviously interesting and informed by their own validity, remain art gallery based. In all the exhibitions i have ever seen of such projects (both here and in Europe) access to the object as book remains closed off from the reader. Her function is therefore relegated to that of viewer, a traditional gallery/visitor relationship. i have seen only two or three artist's books that actually allowed the viewer to begin to take up the expanded role that "reader" implies. As Michael Sowdon remarked in Ron Mann's movie about Coach House (and i'm paraphrasing here): "What working at the press allowed was the chance to have a visual idea, print it (in the form of a poster, a postcard or a book) and see your work out on the streets within a matter of days, where all kinds of people who'd never walk into an art gallery were exposed to it." In fact a problem for Coach House was that people liked the posters we did so much that they were always taking them down and taking them home. We'd end up papering the same spot ten times just to keep the information the poster was dealing with in front of the public for the necessary time. But the point is that you had something which had all the qualities of a precious object — well-crafted, etc. — but which was cheaply available to anyone who wanted to own one. "Artist's books," as a concept, work off the notion of "Holy Book" and are linked, therefore, to the idea of knowledge as being the purview of a chosen few. The "book," from the invention of movable type on, carries with it the notion of the dissemination of its information, both its intellectual and its art values, to as large an audience as wants it. George Bowering's *Baseball*, an early Coach House book printed in the form of a baseball pennant, complete with a green fuzz cover, was both a precious object, plainly sculptural in its design (tho the design grew logically out of the text), and instantly accessible and available to anyone who wanted it. The McFadden/Curnoe Big Little Books, working off of and within the idea of a pre-existing popular culture format, were the same.

The separation of "illustration" (which is how we now categorize drawings printed in books) from the notion of high art only began in the late 19th century. At Coach House it was reclaimed, largely because nobody was ever just illustrating; they were working collaboratively to create works of art that could be sold cheaply in multiple copies. As the technology developed and changed new possibilities opened up, and anyone wishing to track the shift in Coach House from hand-set type through linotype to the various computer systems that the press has used is welcome to do so. Definite changes accompanied each stage. But here, in this article, i've tried to suggest both the nature of the marriage between the visual arts and the written ones, to underline the notion that writing is, in any case, visual and can be categorized as such, and to show how the book has, for years, provided one of the major interfaces. We live in the midst of language, surrounded by books, and, as a result, the nature of both has become transparent to us. We look thru the books to the content inside them. We learn to speed read so that the words too can be strip-mined for their information. Thus are we made more ignorant. And painting, sculpture, dance, photography, etc., *all* the so-called Fine Arts, suffer, because we look but we don't see. Once the surface of the world, of its objects, inhabitants, etc., becomes transparent to us, it quickly becomes unimportant to us as well, and things that should register — political, social, ecological — don't.

Anything but total absorption in the insanities of the surface seems cowardly ... (David McFadden, *The Art of Darkness*)

Look at these words. Look around you. What do you see?

Notes

1. A case can be made for including videotext in this list, or any of the other emerging computer-based arts that use the sound chip and the graphics as well as the text capabilities of the computer. Malcolm McLaren made the interesting point in an interview that the fashion show, when well done, combined at least two of them — music and visual presentation.

2. I'm using "macro" to denote large-scale structures &/or formal choices that include all the concepts/disciplines/arts discussed, and "micro" to denote the individual concepts/disciplines/arts within those larger fields, i.e. themselves as themselves. Thus borderblur is a micro concept that deals with the point where the individual art begins to blur at its "boundaries" and take on characteristics of what we think of as another, separate art. The Theatre of Confluence begins by including all other arts within itself, a macro concept, with room, therefore, for the notion of borderblur as part of what it's doing.

3. a) The letters — look at the choices available to you in terms of faces, in terms of point size, in terms of upper and lower case, etc.; and look at the way, say a "g" shifts its configuration depending on the face it's set in and the difference in visual meaning between the differently shaped faces.
   b) The words — look how the spacing between words absolutely affects your ability to read them, the speed with which you can or can't take in a text; the distance between words beyond which they begin to set up new relationships.
   c) The lines — how justification affects word-spacing and/or is affected by uses of certain kinds of visual notation, be it in prose or poetry.
   d) The ink — the colour, the density.
   e) The paper — the colour, the density, the presence or absence of water marks, decals, etc., how the concept "page" is a subset of the notion "sheet" & depends on both the press size and the choice of, and hence the capabilities inherent in, the binding method.

   And over and beyond all of the above, what happens if you add illustration? If you look at words as "illustrating"? The questions keep multiplying. And look what's happening; you're looking! And all the answers to all the above, and quite a few other questions, affect how you look and, therefore, how you read.

4. We actually designed the whole thing to fit together in the form of a simple puzzle which very few people ever seemed to try to solve. That's why so many copies you see are damaged; people jammed the parts back into the slipcase any old way they could, never seeming to remember that it had all fit together quite neatly when they first purchased it.

5. I like the rock & roll media sound of this phrase.

ALL
THAT
SIGNIFIES
CAN BE
SOLD

Interview: Steve McCaffery

IN TEN$\frac{T}{S}$ION: DIALOGUING WITH BP

1987, 1988

Steve McCaffery: Most impressive about *The Martyrology* is the binding of the writing to an incontrovertibly written space; the impossibility to be anywhere (as a reader) but in the writing. There seems a preference, on your part as a writer, to stay within the materiality of the writing and to repudiate the traditional notion of instrumental language as an ideal transit. I've felt this most strongly in your visual poetries — especially in your use of comic strip conventions ("panelogical semiotics" i think we humorously termed it): the frame, the speech and thought balloons — it is less a resort to pictoriality (which was the root of Eugen Gomringer's objections to your work), than a powerful and challenging extension of your concern for mass semiotic systems and the enduring presence of a stubborn, counter-ideological materiality of the written in popular culture. Would you agree? Would you say that your dominant poetic is a materialist one?

bpNichol: Tho I have a fondness for the idea of the ideal transit (the pleasure of reading as a child & so on), language, and in my case specifically the English language, seems so clearly an arbitrary construct whose rules we're still in the process of deducing (viz. Chomsky's attempt with the notion of deep structure, etc.) that it's simply not interesting for me as a writer to work any other way than with language's materiality. The "rules" of grammar are a later superimposition (as bissett never tires of pointing out) and don't necessarily reflect the total potential or even the actual daily functioning of language. They're an attempt to tame something very wild and very woolly. I'm for the unsheared word. The rest too often leads to baaad writing & thinking.

SM: I've come to see the predicament of the reader in your work as that of a figure trapped within an historically specific rhetoric of transaction. (I'm proposing this notion of a rhetoric to avoid a structural partitioning of the reader-writer relation into a binary opposition and to place it inside the larger socio-cultural issues of contractual agreements, mechanistic, formal and structural necessities.) The issues of intention, production, regulation of meaning and control inhere as subtle sub-formations in *The Martyrology* and raise the issue of empowerment. Your use of proper names (especially first names) might be cited as one instance of a textual power in operation. These proper names, that weave through *The Martyrology*, seem to function as agents of exclusion, denying the reader a truly active engagement with the text. They create a semiotic impasse, a cul de sac within the rhetoric of the transaction between writer and reader. Often the work is extraordinarily generous to a reader, offering multiple possibilities for semantic production and play inside a textual space that does not beckon to an authorial origin beyond the work. But at other times the poem effects exclusion, tending to force a reader into a passive reception of privileged, or even closed, content:

> & two days later
> driving out of Fort Smith
> 30 miles to little buffalo falls
> ruth rees, ellie & me
> watched the water drop
> > 60 feet into the basin
> (Book 4)

 Your work constantly employs this alternation (often very complex) between systolic and dyastolic movements in the economy of the meaning; between expansions into intractable and vertiginous anagrammatic territories (where the reader is free to engage the text as an undetermined and unfore-closed site for semantic play) and contractions into fixed functions, minimal threats to the semantic

433

order and a retrenchment of the orthodox notions of reader and writer as the passive/active polarities of a linear message. Would it be fair to say that in *The Martyrology* this juxtaposition of different linguistic orders is never situated within a theatre of open confrontation and that as a consequence you shun the momentum of a potential dialectic and settle with presenting an oscillation of contrasting, but never opposing, forces in the language? Or perhaps, further, that you abnegate a responsibility to carry through the work's full textual aspects?

bp: First, I would tend to agree that readers take proper names in a very fixed way: which is to say that proper names excite voyeurism. Readers tend to feel they have to know more about the person named before they can go on. Otherwise they feel as tho the writer is holding something back on them, is deliberately excluding them from an intimate circle of knowledge the writer has access to. As I've said elsewhere, I think this is a totally false notion, one that has been fed by magazines like *People*, *Rolling Stone*, and the general craze for personality profiles and banal biographies. I've outlined in a number of different places my justification for doing what I'm doing with proper names but I don't mind rehearsing my reasoning again and, hopefully, even expanding on it a bit.

a) In daily living we meet all sorts of people — at parties, in restaurants, through friends we bump into in the street, at shopping malls, etc. — about whom we learn nothing more than their name and the fact that they're friends of so-and-so. We gain a certain impression from these encounters, impressions that are definitely our own, and that suffice. If we meet these persons a second time our knowledge of them expands and so on. This is one of my intents in naming, on a first name basis, people encountered in the course of the text, i.e. to recreate that ordinary experience, to have that kind of parallel emotional experience operating in *The Martyrology*, not analogically but actually as part of the reading experience.

b) Because of the predominant usage of first names[1]"characters" are built up simply through the deletion of information, i.e. "David" is never just one David but a variety of Davids encountered during the writing of the text. The cumulative effect is to create a "David" who borrows from the lives of all the Davids I have known and know.

c) My Grandma Workman (Leigh), and, indeed, almost all my great aunts and uncles on her side of the family, told stories where they would mention proper names just as part of the gesture of story-telling. You never stopped them to ask who these people were because it was irrelevant to the story at hand. What the names did was locate the narrative in a moment of reality. That was their entire function.

So I am doing more than one thing here. On the one hand, the reader is always free to do exactly what she or he chooses. They can tear the book to pieces if they want. They can treat it as a supply text for their own writing. They can choose to not read it. I'm aware of that freedom the reader has. At the same time I'm often trying to work with things that happen to the reader in the reading experience, with what I guess we'd have to call the psychology of the reading experience, and attempting to skew it slightly to see what happens. The use of proper names is, therefore, a deliberate confrontational device, an attack, if you like, on naive notions of biographical and psychological criticism, since "David" is many Davids and the "i" is more than a biographical gesture. I would say that it is an open confrontation but that it is not, on the whole, recognized as such. It is done in a fashion different from your own tho I think, having done that recent interview with you

for *Musicworks*, you too have come to feel that an oscillating economy of apparently opposing forces is a useful way to keep the dialectic alive.

Obviously then, I don't see this movement back & forth as expansion & contraction. I see it, as my various answers up to now should have made clear, as a way of working with the psychology of the reading experience, with the way in which readers advance and retreat. The separation of description & dialogue in my novel *Still* is another good example of this way of working. I'm also, obviously, questioning whether these forces are "opposing" or simply "contrasting." These days I tend towards the latter. I used to think the former. That's one of the things my way of working in *The Martyrology* has led me to. So, finally, I don't think I've abnegated my responsibilities, but it's certainly true there are implications in what I'm doing that are not yet dealt with. If there weren't the work would be over.

SM: In your playful destruction and reassemblage of words, the subject and its relation to meaning become a prime issue. If a reader can get beyond a distanced appreciation of (or irritation at) the display of wit in these pun productions, then a radically different subject emerges and one not predicated upon the orthodox logic of the sign. A subject deprived of unity and circulating as a textual effect among the verbal fission and the shattered syntax of the language.

bp: I've always been fascinated by the subject. To begin with, it had to do with pronouns. In the years before *The Martyrology* I spent a certain amount of time throwing the "I" out of my texts. I even went through a two year period of refusing myself the permission to use it at all. At the end of that time I felt I had a better grasp of it and began to explore it again without worrying about its taking over the work in the way I once feared it would, i.e. the lyric voice and its excesses. Of course I am interested in excess but I'm interested in doing something with it, in including it in my thinking. My novels, as you know, are mostly an exploration of pronouns, of what emotional baggage they carry or can be made to carry and of how they carry it. The i of *The Martyrology* is a multiple i, an amalgam of the traditional lyric voice and a series of complex fictional and near-fictional i's. It is also an historical i, which is to say an i which partakes of history & is not the same in Book 6 as it was in Book 1 precisely because it has moved on in time, knows both more and less, has been changed by being in the world and by being in the book. Since it is a word, I can say (as I have said) that its meaning changes. For me it is one of the richest words in the English language precisely because in its being in the world it is word, letter, vowel and a psychological construct that is absolutely relativized by its user. As should be obvious, too, I distinguish between the "I" of these responses to your questions and the "i" of *The Martyrology*.

But it's not just the pronoun. The fluidity of nouns fascinated me. I worked for a time in the mid-60s with a concept I called "schizophrenic logic" (I'm not arguing for the accuracy of the term here but simply noting the name it went under in my own mind at the time). Basically it consisted of making image jumps on the basis of different meanings nouns could have, so an image of fingers hovering over keys jump/cuts on the basis of the word "keys" to become part of Florida's coastal geography. But not just one of those; repeating such jump/cuts until the poem ended miles away from where it began. I had a confirmation of this in 67 or so when reading one of the early Lacan translations in *Yale French Studies* where, in a footnote, he remarked how in the speech of psychotics the signified slid below the signifier. That fluidity of nouns & pronouns, of naming and the range of what we think of as the subject, the exploration of that, remains, for me, perennially fascinating and perennially rewarding.

SM: Could you speak of the political (or perhaps the absence of it) in your work. For many contemporary writers the analogy between linguistic and political forms is paramount to their investigations, e.g. the tacit acceptance of commodity fetishism in certain habitual reading tendencies; the ideological contamination by representation or reference. Neither of these concerns emerges as a major issue in your work, but rather the orchestration of discursive differences and a presentation of plurality in a polygraphic space. Would this be a correct assessment? And if so, what political implications do you see in your work?

bp: I've partially dealt with this question already. But to

go on. Had I started writing at a different point in time under a different set of influences then obviously the work would be much different than it is. That's one of the historical facts *The Martyrology* partakes of. Since one of the major tasks of the work has to do with an examination of the notion of "history" (that "memory of an amnesiac" I've referred to elsewhere), "history" in every sense I can see of it, I don't think of the work as apolitical. I think of it as addressing very real political issues but definitely addressing them in its own way. I would agree that certain bells are not rung and therefore we are deprived of the chance to salivate to them. But then, as you know, I'm constantly amazed that a lot of the same writers who are dealing with the analogy between political and linguistic forms don't seem to deal at all with the political fact of the book as part of their project. Or with, say, small time entrepreneurial capitalism in the starting and funding of their magazines, little presses and distribution systems, etc. But then that would be to superimpose my agenda on their own (tho such a superimposition is a frequent readerly tactic).

SM: At a time when many writers are moving towards temporality as the dominant experience of writing (the "time of the signs") you seem to be opting for a spatiality as dominant. What's most impressive in the later books is not what is said, or demonstrated, but the manner of its disposition. There's something at work other than syntax and sequentiality. This leads me to consider *The Martyrology* less from a psycho-temporal aspect (the notion of the poetic journal, for instance, that seems to cling to obsolete senses of time and subjectivity) and more as an organization of powers, and spaces, much in the way Paul Virilio speaks of Pure War and logistics, or Michel de Certeau speaks of "practices of space." *The Martyrology* suggests writing as a spatial practice. For example, the multiple choices of Book 5's chains promise perambulatory gestures, walks, digressions (sidesteps), etc. This dominance of spatiality seems guaranteed by the presence of fragments rather than wholes. Juxtapositions, collisions, slips, spaces, twists, gaps … these seem the figures of a rhetoric of space which determines *The Martyrology* as a literary object. The work's refusal to assume a panoptic stance and the deliberate eschewal of totality and closure also suggest its consideration as a major text of space rather than a poetic journal of lived time.

bp: I'd agree with this. In fact at this point in time it's the intrusion of certain kinds of temporal structures (e.g. the numbering of the books) that trouble me most and that I'm seeking solutions to, compositionally. I would agree that my applying the term *utanniki* to my work was a misnaming and, in fact, you were the one who pointed that out to me when I was working on an early draft of my "Note Book" piece[2] and I used the occasion of that text to say so. But as with any provisional struggle towards articulating, the term did inform the composition of *The Martyrology* for a number of years, i.e. it helped me to think about it, even tho, in the final analysis, what I was doing was not writing a poetic journal. The work does have a journal aspect as one of its considerations of the nature of discourses about history. The journal also plays into the idea of autobiography and allows me to explore the autobiographical voice as a literary construct.

SM: A slight digression re style. Let me offer Greimas' definition of linguistic style as "a linguistic structure that can manifest on the symbolic level ... one man's basic way of existing in the world." Style, for myself, is fundamentally political; it asserts singularity (the "one man's way" of Greimas) — singularity of the group, the individual, the nation, the class. In a way I see you as avoiding style in *The Martyrology* by multiple usage. The French critic A. Medam speaks of "inhabitant rhetoric" and this sense of rhetoric is intensely apropos of your own practice. *The Martyrology* as I'm proposing it would be understood as the polygraphic seizure of various sites of discourse, rendering the practice of writing utterly and uncompromisingly nomadic.

Moving on, however. Very often you manipulate the fundamental elements of a lexical order. In your wordplay you speak of truth and of truths beyond. Can these be related to a certain erotics of knowledge that is constantly threatening to manifest in *The Martyrology*?

bp: I suppose it could. I don't know that I would formulate it that way myself. But what I have done is formulate it as an experience of *ekstasis*, which is to say that I am not reporting to readers my vision, but rather presenting to them a way of seeing, giving them the actual experience that I had so that they can experience it for themselves, have their own vision, their own experience of *ekstasis*. To any play there is an element of eroticization, of libidinal discharge, and thus your implied argument for an erotics of knowledge makes sense to me.

SM: *The Martyrology* as a sign system frequently creates losses and the inversion of an intentionalized production into an expenditure. This marks the site of the paragram. In addition, the work seems dominated by *tactics* that cash in upon the opportunities to subvert standard meaning and its syntactic supports. This results in a tremendously unsettled work, a contradictory text whose logical aporias significantly prohibit a panoptic reading of the work.

I see the development, movement and growth of *The Martyrology* as bearing an analogy to city growth and urban spread. You present a polygraphic arrangement of a space that's remarkably similar to the arrangement of a complex city. From towering, monolithic, "corporate meanings," to sub-cultural graffiti, and the individual utterance of "letters" that distribute themselves like footsteps through corridors and passages of meanings, frequently taking detours, diverting the text away from purposive accumulation.

Your wordplay frequently suggests itself as a motor function of an individual and locally assertive letter or sound. You present the word as a critical site, often juxtaposed with "illegal" spatial "shapes" such as comic strip frames and hand-drawn figures. All of this reminds me of the subversion of a dominant commercial discourse by graffiti. On the New York subway, for instance, gestures in ink or spray paint often delete a prior writing, but also proliferate to become atmospheric, and the meaning of their movements and eruptive occurrences can't be fixed or explained. This is very similar to the implications of the eruptive wordplay in *The Martyrology*. But this wordplay too established a rhetoric of "walking." Let me quote a short phrase of Michel de Certeau: "To walk is to lack a site." The site/non-site opposition in your work links it to some of the work of Robert Smithson. (This connection becomes extremely apparent if we insist on treating *The Martyrology* as a spatial, not a semantic, practice.) A system and profusion of sites, not senses.

The writing consists of manipulations of a number of fundamental elements that divert and move meaning into "other" areas. Within this writing (as a spatial practice) word and letter relate as site to non-site and the transphenomenality of the paragrams relate homologously to the social, everyday "practice" of walking. The letters walk and "to walk is to lack a site," hence the letter emerges as a non-site within the site of the word or phrase. This involves a radically different view of the letter, as something other and more than a simple combinatory component in a hierarchical integration. The word, considered this way, becomes a perambulatory site, a localized meaning to which the deviations of the letter-sound elements can be referred. Emerging from this is a concept of the word as the scene of surprise, of self-seduction and semantic meandering. Meaning as a "walking" takes the following form of progression. There is a relationship between a site from which meaning issues and a non-site that it creates. This is exactly the transphenomenality of the paragram. It illustrates too how the solidity of the poem's textual fabric is dependent upon these innumerable gaps, displacements and exitings; letters leaving the words they formed; chains of language suddenly ending in a fork and discontinuity. This is very much the same as the practice of human space within the site of the city.

You unleash two kinds of spatial movement: the one exterior (the letters walk outside of their words); this is a movement of counter-metonymic departure that results in deviance and lacuna. The other is an interior movement and manages the more "traditional" sections of the work where the mobility occurs on the level of a narrative development carried out inside the structural stability of the signifier. Your writing in places makes meaning "habitable" as a scene (another urban value); it allows play within a system. You present ways of leaving but also present methods of re-entry. You enact its sacrificial expenditure but also demonstrate its recovery and reinvestment.

If *The Martyrology* is the structural homology of spatial practices within the city, then the pun which follows will be wittily on the ball:

sieve — civic — sievic

The Martyrology as a sieve is a model that appeals to me. Its sifting of meanings through its practice of spaces is a marvellous alternative to a fixed critical or panoptic analysis. As a reader, one inhabits *The Martyrology* rather than reads it. Space — as the practice of difference — also petitions the origin. If writing occurs as a spatial practice, then writing is always the practice of moving to something else. The primordial spatial practice might be the child's differentiation of itself from its mother's body, that initiates the fort/da, the here/there and the site/non-site distinction. *The Martyrology* as such would relate to the child, i.e. a similar infant site that is there without the other but in a necessary relationship with the thing-now-absent. So we are back to writing as footsteps, or fossils, as the marks of that which has disappeared, a situated non-site and a present absence.

bp: Given the paradoxical problem that denotation and intention are rife in the essays and papers dealing with the problems of denotation and intention, you can, I'm sure, appreciate my interest in having various kinds of discourse together in one text. As I have frequently asserted, I am much more interested in inclusiveness than exclusiveness. I like the mix partially because in any consideration of history it is difficult to speak of one thing as being "ahead of its time" and another "beyond the times" when both are occurring contemporaneously. Similarly, with the notion of "obsolescence" referred to earlier, if a significant portion of the population still uses a particular mode then obsolescence is relative to that awareness. I would oppose what I'm saying here to people who seek to place themselves alongside, or buoy themselves up through an identification with, a tradition, as though it were an immutable body of undisputed fact rooted in time. Such people are the same ones who would've rejected the sonnet as being too Italian when the sonnet was first being introduced into English poetry (there is some justice in that argument given that the rhythm of the sonnet is, for an Italian speaker, very close to a natural speech rhythm, but is an artificial construct for an English speaker). In short, I reject both the idea that today's idea instantly rids us of yesterday's and the idea that yesterday's idea is necessarily better because it has stood the test of time (whatever that test is — duration? then there shouldn't be the struggle there is to get people to accept visual poetry seriously. Look at all the work Yars Bollin has done on visual elements in Ukrainian poetics books of the 17th century, etc. (I'm still irked by Gary Geddes' comment in his revised edition of *20th Century Poetry and Poetics* that concrete poetry has not stood the famous test referred to)).

I can see and appreciate the analogy between city structure and *The Martyrology*'s structure. Certainly both are constructed, both tend to be open-ended, bounded only by things external to their internal agenda. In both cases disparate, if not polar opposite, elements can exist side by side. But it's also important to point out that the text is not a city and that the weakness of analogy is that it's analogy and takes us away from the thingness of the thing we're considering (in this case, the text). "There is an order to be discovered, not imposed." (I'm indulging in that disgusting habit of quoting myself here.) On the other hand I use exactly the same analogy in Book 4 of *The Martyrology* when, in discussing the nature of Cloud Town, how its streets and houses shifted constantly, dissolving, forming and reforming, I say that only language retained that multiplicity the saints were used to. (There's even an earlier sense of this in a poem I wrote for Margaret Avison in 1965 or 66 where the line "vague / like the clouds my language was" occurs, tho obviously I don't get to the city analogy.)

Forgetting the city tho, I have, for years, been working in my writing with the concept of space, space as something the reader encounters in the reading, working to understand that and to see what kinds of meanings it carries and what kinds of meanings I could get it to carry. In an introductory essay to a work in progress called "Unsigned," I've been detailing the various kinds of meanings I've discovered and/or been able to get it to encompass. Certainly *The Martyrology* is another place in my work where that investigation has gone on.

When you remark on my presenting "ways of leaving but also of re-entering meaning" I am reminded again of my 1966 "statement" where I talk of that very desire, to present in writing as many exits and entrances as possible. There I was talking about it in terms of a still inarticulate sense of the "other," which at that time I think I saw simply as another human being. Even with the recognition of the larger question of "otherness," that still seems to me something that I desire for this text: "as many exits and entrances as possible."

I think that given the length of the work, *The Martyrology* ceases to be a reading experience, at least in the way we have come to think of it. Its very duration means that you must, as you say, inhabit it in some sense. Particularly since there is no "plot" to hang on to, only ideas, and the ideas relate to the terms used in the text and the very way the text is functioning. My thinking about it is still evolving. In that sense I probably treat the text more as a reader than a writer, i.e. when the text closes it continues to evolve in the mind of the reader tho it is over for the writer. This text has not closed. I continue to read it and write it and it continues to revolve & evolve.

Notes

1. There are exceptions where the first and last names of certain people are noted. These have more to do with the "i" of the poem, bolstering the seemingly biographical portion of that exploration. But they do serve the double function of throwing a biographical light back on the first names we are discussing here.

2. See "Long-liners Conference Issue," *Open Letter* 6th Series. 2-3 (Summer-Fall 1985). The essay, "Things I Don't Really Understand About Myself," is scattered throughout the book, usually in its own frame.

R-Toys-Us?

1987

I have never been one to get lathered at commercialization aimed at children, or at least, the marketing of characters created to appeal to children. One look at Buster Brown shoes reminds us that the ghost of F. R. Oucault is still with us, though they haven't been publishing his comic strip since early on in this century. My only test is the thinking inside the fantasy world, the social setting in which the characters being marketed live. The Carebears, for instance, are an awful lot like the angels I used to read about in my United Church Sunday School funnies. And who can really object to a bunch of little ponies who run around being nice to each other? Isn't that what the Bobsey Twins did for years? I do start to worry, however, when the fantasy world includes, as Rainbow Brite's does, a race of happy beings who love working down in the mines bringing up the special sparkle stuff that allows the kids to put colour into their world. At that point I start waiting for the new character called Botha to start appearing in your neighbourhood toy store. If Toys-R-Us, then what are those toys saying about us?

We live in a time when still-developing social awareness definitely still lead to excesses. Obvious examples of this are the kinds of reverse clichés that go on. In a laudatory attempt to banish sexual stereotyping, female characters (be they bears, ponies, dogs, whatever) are never allowed to be pink, and male characters are never allowed to be blue. This is not necessarily because of advanced social awareness on the part of the people making the creative decisions but because they don't want to be accused of sexual stereotyping. But precisely because the focus is on what are finally the end products — the surface symptomology of deeper rooted problems — it's usually only the surface details that get changed. Rainbow Brite's world has an obvious debt to the world of Snow White with its dwarves mining diamonds, but the big difference is that the dwarves owned what their labour got them and Snow White became another worker in that world. It was her showing that she could pitch in and work alongside them that endeared her to the dwarves. In Rainbow Brite's world the dwarf/sprites do all the work, provide the comic relief and, though they do their bit when the going gets tough, it's usually Rainbow or one of the colour kids who pulls the fat out of the fire. Now you can be sure that there're no pink girl characters (though there is a Buddy Blue, a wonderful gay liberation name) and that characters who are of different colour all live together in harmony, but they do so in a world built on one race doing the labour while the other has the fun. Contrast this to the world of Strawberry Shortcake where the kids' job was to gather the berries from the garden. They had no one, or no thing, helping them. They did all the work themselves and they reaped the reward. And evil in that world was the Purple Pieman's attempt to gather fruit for his pies without doing the labour himself. Somehow that sounds more like it to me. It even had some wonderful twists. Somewhere along the road, Plum Pudding, who began life as a boy, turned into a girl. And nobody blinked an eye. That's definitely more like it.

Now having said all that, let me go on to say that part of the problem for a parent is that it's necessary to get into the fantasy world with the kid and muck about a bit. I don't know how many parents want to put in the time that that involves. Since children's play appears highly repetitive (though it's more "insistent," in the way Gertrude Stein used the term), adults tend to get easily bored. But getting in there with your kids is the only way you'll find out what's really going down. You have to dialogue with both your kid and the characters your kid is turned on to. I was in a toy store once watching the following scene go down: A boy, about seven, wanted his mom to buy him some of the Transformers — high-powered robots that shoot it out with evil in the world of the future. This mom, clearly opposed to violence and, therefore, to violent toys, wouldn't, no matter how much the kid whined, screamed and pleaded. She was trying to buy him off with a Cabbage Patch Doll and indeed, when they walked away, the kid was carrying the doll while casting longing glances back toward the Transformers. I'll lay odds that when they got home the boy ripped the head off his Cabbage Patch Doll in a kind of orgy of violence the world has seldom seen. Because the problem is that Mom was doing her own kind of violence: she was getting between the kid and his chosen fantasy. I've never seen the approach that that parent took work. I'd be more inclined to get the boy the Transformer or the Rambo doll and then spend time in play changing the meaning of the whole thing, helping Rambo to behave in a more human fashion. Let him take up landscape painting or something that the kid is interested in. It's more fun and you find out things about what the doll or toy actually means to the kid, how it's incorporated into their world. Because every kid's incorporation of their play toy is unique. Once again, violence as a solution is, among other things, a symptomology. Attempting to eradicate the symptom is its own kind of violence. The first trick is not to leap to conclusions but rather to get into what's happening and find out what the toy's meanings are from your kid's point of view, how he or she views and uses the character. Along the way you'll get an entire education. Sure there are high-powered moguls taking high-powered lunches to figure out high-powered strategies to get your kid to buy their toy. But once the toy is in the home you're in a position to work with its meaning because from then on it's out of their control. R-Toys-Us? I don't think so. Toys-R-Ours once they come home, but we have to work with them to make them our own.

Interview: Clint Burnham

BP ON *BOOK 6 BOOKS*

1987

Clint Burnham: What influence has Gertrude Stein had on your work?

bpNichol: Her writing was a tremendous instance for me, an example of a different imagination around writing. It was part of a general thing I was getting into. Besides looking at the meaning of words, the emotional content they carry forth in our daily lives, I wanted to be able to look at words as things, to be able to look at their life as things. They have this existence on the page, they have this existence in sound (which are really two different existences, almost, although obviously related). She was a tremendous instance for me of taking that in an entirely different direction. I had been into it from a visual point of view, the concrete and sound poetry, really through the Dadaists and some of the work of Kenneth Patchen, the American poet. But when I started reading Stein, with things like *Tender Buttons*, I saw someone literally putting pieces together by assembling words side by side and building them that way — because of her whole interest in doing in writing what the Cubists had been able to do in painting. The kind of imagination she brought to writing fired my imagination. The fact that she questioned everything; she questioned the use of the comma, she examined the use of the comma. In *Ida* she found ways to actually reverse the use of the comma; usually you have unimportant information put in between commas as an aside. She managed to nest the important information in the sentence that way, and put the more peripheral information around it as bookends. There was a lot that she looked at in terms of syntactical arrangements of words. And for me there was the possibility that someone did that at that time. I stumbled onto her work through bill bissett. At that time there certainly wasn't access to a lot of writing; the Dada stuff that was available in the early 60s was pretty slim. I could actually dig her work out of the U of T library stacks, and I could look at the stuff and I could get into it and I could read it, and it opened up a lot of possibilities.

CB: Does *The Martyrology: Book 6 Books* continue *The Martyrology*? It seems as though the reader doesn't have to have read the other five books to enjoy this one.

bp: Thank heavens — that'll save readers a lot of exhausting reading. No, you don't have to have read the previous five books, but Book 6 is a continuation of all the concerns and themes that are there — it's just not really a work where there's a strong narrative impulse. The length of *The Martyrology* doesn't have any-thing to do with having a long story to tell, it has to do with having a range of topics that you're talking about; you're allowing a general body of theory to develop out of the very processual act of writing. So I don't think that anyone should necessarily feel as though one has to sit down and read *The Martyrology* from the beginning, in that sense. It's not finally a work that depends on that kind of sequentiality, although there certainly are things in *The Martyrology: Book 6 Books* that you couldn't get in their fullness without having read the previous five books.

The fact that there are six books in Book 6 grew out of the chains of Book 5. Book 5 evolved into twelve interconnected chains which grew out of this phenomenon I've experienced in writing; every once in a while you go to write one line, and you actually have choices: two different lines occur to you and you tend to choose one over the other. What I started to do in Book 5 was to write both lines down and to track them both. This meant that I had different ideas that sort of ended themselves as the chains in the book ended, and therefore I had ceased to deal with those ideas. But the different chains ended at different times and I still had more things to say about the ideas in them in dif-ferent ways; I had to move on to new levels of dealing with them, and that began to spawn the books of Book 6. So the twelve chains branched out into six books. And curiously enough, at the moment I'm working on, altogether, the next six books of *The Martyrology*. I have the ideas there and I've actually begun four of them, and I pretty well know what the other two are going to be.

So Book 6's six little sub-books have actually spawned six distinct books.

CB: In "Book I" of Book 6, "Imperfection: A Prophecy," you write about Buamundus, the giant who was small for his size, who may have spread Christianity to Britain, and is probably now sleeping near Thunder Bay. Is this more of the idea of writing origins, especially the more bizarre ones?

bp: The title of that comes from Corinthians, where Paul says "for even our prophesies are imperfect." That's one of those notions that totally fascinates me and informs a lot of *The Martyrology*, the notion of imperfection, which is part of why it is an open-ended poem. It's over and opposed to the old high modernist goal of perfection and immortality, trying to build the lasting monument that will somehow survive the ravages of time. Buamundus is a real figure to whom there is only one reference in medieval English literature and you can read about him in *The Lost Literature of Medieval England*, a terrific book. The two disciples of Christ are also real figures, to whom there is only one reference in all of the gospels. I've always been interested in these real things of which we've lost all knowledge. In this case the only trace we have are the names of the two disciples and the names of the giant. So what I did was to combine all that with sort of alternative histories. There is a whole history fairly well documented of an earlier Christianity getting to Britain; there are legends of Joseph of Arimathea, in whose tomb Christ was buried. Joseph fled with the holy grail to England; that's where the Holy Grail legend comes from.

So I was taking a bunch of mythological and quasi-historical information and bringing it all together, which also allowed me to deal with these notions of faith, history, spirituality, and how belief, information, and knowledge are dispersed. And at the same time, on a more formal level, I could deal with the narrative poem, because that's also a classic narrative poem; it has its beginning here and its ending there and is literally a story of these people and their journey. These were some of the things I was dealing with in the first book. I was also using the formal techniques of concrete poetry to do a lot of the talking in it.

CB: In "Continental Trance" you re-trace all the train rides you've taken from Vancouver to Toronto. Were you trying to re-live your life along that long line? Your father worked for the railroad when you were growing up?

bp: Yes, he travelled a lot by train, and we had passes and went back and forth by train. It is a trip that I took a lot as a kid, but I think it is kind of the quintessential Canadian experience in a way. We live in this country that is 4500 miles wide, which is pretty amazing; you and I are still inside the same country. It's partly a way of dealing with this, a continental trance, a vision of the country's width. It's an imagination of that; it's also an imagination of how life is lived and how a story gets told, in the sense that one foot follows another, one mile comes after another. To a degree, just moving on in time creates a narrative, a narrative moment, a sequence of events. Along the way I'm allowed the chance to talk about issues that have been on my mind.

There is a whole thing about train trips that runs all the way through *The Martyrology* and is picked up on again and again. My first long poem predating *The Martyrology* is *JOURNEYING & the returns*. There's that whole notion of journeying out again which is also a classic poetic moment in the history of epic poetry. That's part of what I am dealing with in "Imperfection: A Prophecy," that whole notion of journeying out from home, the return to home. In this case I deal with the fact that I'm journeying from what was my home to what is my home. I'm dealing with time changes, the whole notion of travelling, of what arises from it. And also in the history of my family, there are various roots of my family; they've never stayed in one place for more than 85 or 100 years. So there is a kind of rootlessness at the historical root of my family. This is true of certain kinds of social groupings and classes. This is why I then get on, in "In the Plunkett Hotel," to that whole notion of the tribe. The family is the closest thing that I as a western white man have to the notion of the tribe.

CB: In "After Bird" there is the image from bill bissett of letting the bird go and also letting your writing go. Is that how you see the process as you write something — you let go, also releasing yourself?

bp: What I really like about that quote of bill's is that the image is of the bird trapped in the hand, and if you release it, the bird is free to be itself, but you also see how the hand takes up the space. He takes the focus entirely off the bird and puts it onto what is possible for the hand when it ceases trying to capture things. Therefore writing is not an act which is trying to capture the living; writing is the act of occupying the space that's there, with the tools at your means, the pen, the hand, the brain. That little quote of bill's always struck me as a pretty good summary of my own goals in writing. I was not trying to capture the bird and nail its corpse to the page in some sort of paean to an imagined-realism, because I don't think that's real. It's just a dead bird on the page.

```
the word has tended to operate as the given
in poetry, & poetic activity has happened upon
the ground of the word. thus the logical place
to start again, having once experienced the
desire to start again, is with the word. once
you alter the word, be it thru pun, spelling,
atomization, discard, whatever, then all the
other structures have to alter too.
```

CB: When you began *The Martyrology* in the late 60s you played with puns on saints' names and Cloudtown, where the saints come from. What has happened to these early elements? Do you feel you have to return to them?

bp: No I don't. That's what I mean when I say it's not a story, a narrative in that sense. If I'm telling you a joke and I don't deliver the punch-line, that's a fundamental flaw, assuming it's a punch-line type joke and not a one-liner. In this particular work, what I'm dealing with has to do with the notion of process. I am developing certain ideas through time, because many of the ideas focus on the effects of time, not just on the body, but also on the mind, how it changes. Meanings change, the way you focus changes. I'm trying to encompass that in this work, as opposed to a lot of long works where what you get is the person attempting to build this kind of fiction that they have a consistent body of thought from when they start at the age of 20 to when they die at the age of 80. I just don't think that's (here comes that word again) "realistic." In my experience you move on, your thinking changes and develops.

I wanted a writing that would relate that in some way, a writing that would not pretend to an omniscience or to an authority that it didn't have and could, therefore, partake of the real world. It wouldn't pretend itself to be aloof from it or separate from it. That's my notion of what I'm trying to get at, a writing which partakes of the human condition in the sense that we're all vulnerable, we could die at any moment. I wanted the writing to somehow come to grips with that, not to stand above it, as though that were not the human condition, and pretend to pass on solutions that are nonexistent. That's really the project I'm working on. The saints that began the whole thing I finally, in Book 3, saw as unnecessary middlemen, some notion of a god that you don't really need. You finally don't need a whole framework in order to address the spiritual aspect; you don't need priests, ministers, and popes, people who are somehow active agents for the divine. So the saints kind of died off. But it's also the attempt to deal with the individual and what the individual is capable of, and to use certain instances of various people's lives, including my own at times.

Interview: Fred Gaysek, Editor, *Artviews*

1987

Fred Gaysek: How do you view your creative work in relation to your critical work?

bpNichol: I think of myself as a writer who writes about the act of writing. Though I have written what you would call criticism, on the whole in that work I've always tried to foreground the fact that I am a writer writing about other writers.

Critical writing is not necessarily read to get an "objective" critical view of an artist or writer. There are general myths around the notion of objective criticism. These are a little better established in art criticism in Canada, because we have some "objective" art critics, whereas we don't seem to have very many foregrounded, "objective" literary critics. We have a few like Ken Adachi and William French, but if you look across the country, how many literary critics do we have who have the same kind of position as, say, John Bentley Mays or Christopher Hume or as some who write for magazines like *Vanguard*. There is, obviously, lots of literary criticism in Canada, but because literature in general doesn't occupy the kind of marketplace niche that painting does, it doesn't receive the same kind of media attention. You're talking big bucks when you talk about painting and sculpture, although not necessarily for the artist. You're interacting with the commodity market much more so than you do when you publish poetry, which is what I am generally known for.

Putting all that to one side, when I set out to write a piece of criticism, as it were, I usually seize upon it as an opportunity to talk about certain things, such as a theory of writing or certain formal capacities. Usually if I am writing criticism it's because I'm interested in some formal element of the person's writing, and I'm interested in it quite subjectively from my own point of view. It doesn't mean that

I will choose to write that way, but as a writer who reads, I'm interested in that element in the work of other writers.

FG: Do you write any criticism about other art forms?

bp: I've written or overlapped into music. At least I did a review of a book on choral composition of the 20th century, which was quite interesting to do. But that's because I've written pieces for choir, librettos, as it were, for those kinds of things. I haven't approached painting. I find it difficult to apply the terms of literary criticism to criticisms of painting and sculpture. Although I notice most art critics don't seem to have that problem at all. In fact, I find it quite strange the way many tend to read content into paintings which are obviously not content oriented, that seem to be working with the materiality of the canvas, the paint and so on. So the reason I would not tend to write criticism of art, especially of this kind, is that I don't know enough about that materiality, I don't have enough of a close-up feel for it.

There does seem to be a large body of criticism which deals with painting in terms of the social issues that it raises. Certainly there are painters who have that level of work in their canvas. If I wrote about it I would feel a bit like someone who is deaf and writing about music — that I was reading the score or something, but was only appreciating one element of it. To me that seems a very limited way to write about something.

FG: Is there not a role that subjective criticism plays or can play?

bp: The only problem there really is for subjective criticism is the reader that docs not know what's going down, and that believes the myth of objectivity. The problem is very often with the reader. Steve McCaffery said that a long time ago, that the real crisis was with the reader and I happen to firmly believe that.

FG: What sort of crisis are you referring to?

bp: There are many ways in which writers are addressing, as it were, the contemporary condition of human kind, but are there readers who care to read it? There is not a very large audience for serious writing that attempts to come at issues of contemporary life in something other than the ways we are used to. There tends not to be a sense of adventure around writing. There's more of a sense of adventure around the eyes, in terms of painting and so on. People will actually, I think, lay their peepers on something, at least look at it. Whether they look at it closely or not is another whole issue, whether they really engage what the visual artist is dealing with.

A more serious problem, perhaps, is where you get generations of writers or generations of artists who are raised reading criticism by people who have never been practitioners, and who therefore aren't engaging the very way in which the art is made. As a result, we produce people who are trying to create from an intellectual position removed from the working reality of the situation. It's kind of like learning to be a farmer — you can certainly get out in the field and muck around, but suppose the only texts you were reading about farming were idealized tracts by urban hippies from the 60s. You'd reinvent the wheel a lot. There are things you could learn from actually talking to an experienced farmer that would take you a lot further than reading idealized notions of utopian agriculture would. So that's kind of the position, I think, an awful lot of writers and artists are in. They tend not to be reading the source material. They tend to be reading second-and third-hand studies.

FG: What should be the role of critical writing and why or how should it be read?

bp: I think many critics have a lot to say that is interesting and valuable. The record of any reading has value. But it is important that the reader brings an active intelligence to it, and reads it as this person's take, as opposed to reading it as authoritative. The danger is when you get the reviewer cum critic cum whatever who really believes absolutely what he or she is saying, who believes in the myth of mastery, who believes in a set of absolutes. In the whole measuring of things against a kind of spurious notion of mastery, you get, if you like, a blind spot in the critic/reviewer talking to a blind spot in the reader. Thus you have the double blindness. Not a good eye in the house.

FG: In talking to critical writers like Bruce Grenville and Jeanne Randolph, one of the things I've found very interesting is that they state they are writing from a subjective stance. They make it clear that they are looking at a certain artwork and are applying a certain critical theory to that work, be it a psychoanalytical one, be it an art historical one or whatever. They clearly try to establish their terms.

bp: I think responsible criticism has to do that. Once it's done that, it can say whatever it wants, because the terms are understood. Not just "responsible," which has that moralistic tinge to it, but, I think, intelligent criticism has to foreground its terms and approaches.

Were you doing a weekly column of art criticism, you shouldn't have to reiterate this constantly. Presumably your readers have read enough or are following along to some degree. One thing I have always liked about John Bentley Mays' criticism is that you know exactly what John thinks and believes, where his taste resides, what rings his bell and what doesn't. He's always been very up front about that and he will in fact seize the occasion to talk about the subjectivity of his response. This is particularly rare in newspaper critics. It's a bit more common in the writing of magazine critics or feature article critics. That's where I think John's been very responsible, personally speaking, in putting that forward. Partly because, when you are in that kind of an immediate feedback situation of the newspaper review you have, unfortunately, the power to make or break exhibitions.

FG: There would be many in the Toronto art community who would disagree with you about his writing. Many find him irresponsible, and many suggest that there should be a greater diversity of art critics/reviewers in what is called our national newspaper.

bp: Well, that's not so much John's problem. That's a problem, I think, of having one set of tastes being the sole or major reviewer. On the other hand, that's the history of newspaper reviewing. You get one very opinionated writer. Look at the Broadway stage, and we're talking way more bucks, we're talking about millions having gone down the drain on the strength of five reviewers or three reviewers.

FG: In North American society, where there has been an active literature for a number of years, there now is a situation where criticism seems to be writing's vanguard. It's no longer the writing of poetry or fiction that captures the attention of cultural producers, it's the critical writing that's exciting. It is interesting to contrast this to Latin America, where today the literature is vibrant and experimental and is a cultural vanguard, as it was in North America during, say, the late 40s, 50s and 60s. It would be reasonable to conjecture that Latin Americans are, in a sense, moving through an historical phase, one through which our late capitalist society has already moved. This notion is over-simplified, and ignores the realities of colonialism, economics, politics, oppression, cultural hybrids and so on.

With that in mind, however, it is interesting to apply this notion to Canada. In a certain way, Canada does reflect both phases of vanguard writing. This country has a colonial past, which is not that distant. Many of its artists and writers are exploring Canadian histories of all kinds, and are reclaiming these histories and representing them, not unlike the writers and artists of Latin America. From the American point of view Canada is a dim country cousin and needs guidance and policy direction and so on. Many artists and writers rebel against this. Although Canada is not an imperialist nation, as such, ...

bp: Just because it never had the chance though ...

FG: ... it's a country of regions, of great distances and so on. It's a country that has a great deal of idiomatic activity in its culture. It is also rich, economically and technologically developed. It seems that due to these conditions, as well as others, Canada has both an active and experimental literature as well as vibrant and innovative critical work. Do you have any thoughts or ideas about this phenomenon?

bp: It seems to me, I haven't really talked to any French writers about this to know how true it is in, say, France, but certainly in North America we have a situation where literary criticism has more or less left literature behind, because it doesn't need it any-more. It's become, in a certain way, self-sustaining. I don't think that it's the ascendancy of one thing over the other. I think that literary critics are no longer interested in literature per se. They've become, as is only logical, much more interested in the act of criticism and what the act of criticism means and so on. It's the translation of the act of reading into a written medium. And there's enough of it now that it's achieved a kind of critical mass, if you will pardon the pun, and taken on a life of its own. This is parallel to what has happened in writing, where writers have become interested in exploring what writing means, what happens when you write, what is your responsibility to an audience, what is an audience, what does the concept of even thinking of an audience mean, and so on. This is also why I made that earlier distinction, that I was a writer writing about writing. I am not a critic writing about writing.

There tends to be this kind of supremacy argument about which one is top dog, and I don't know how relevant that really is. I think there certainly is a criticism developing in Canada that is as vibrant and interesting as anywhere in the English speaking world. At this point we've got some pretty fantastic thinkers that are coming up. I also think that within the last 25 years we've developed an incredible diversity and range of writing.

On the other hand, one also sees big conservative streaks at the moment. That is to say, attacks on experimental writing, attacks on deconstructionism or anything that has a certain life and vitality to it and therefore tends to create enthusiasts. It's seen as somehow threatening and the old values are constantly re-invoked, and I see that in both criticism and literature, which would lead me to feel there is essentially a lot of truth in what you are saying. I am less familiar with that on the art scene. I certainly have seen the growth of a lot more established art writers, and people more or less making a living as art writers, which was almost unheard of in the 60s, so that tells us something vibrant is happening there.

FG: Clearly, institutions like Coach House Press or A Space, at certain times, were places where artists of many disciplines came together and worked together and it seemed, for an all too brief moment, that there was a line of communication developing among writers and painters and composers and so on, which today does not seem to be occurring with the kind of intensity or in the kind of numbers that it did at that time. I wonder if you have any thoughts or notions about that?

bp: Well, I think in the 60s there was a strong interest in communal activity. There was a social interest in it. Regardless of all the jokes that were made about hippie communes and so on, the fact is that if you were a young artist at that time, you were probably exploring some kind of communal activity; be it an involvement in some kind of communally run art space, or in a collaboratively based art space. Those kinds of projects seemed somehow important and vital to do.

I think they still are important and vital to do, but it doesn't surprise me that in this era of greater self-involvement, socially speaking, artists are much more single-career oriented. They don't seem to automatically seize on the option of starting collaborative projects. They don't even necessarily see the value in it. It's always been very interesting to me that if you look at the generation of writers of which I am a part — and probably the youngest member of, which would include Dennis Lee and Peggy Atwood, bill bissett, Victor Coleman and so on — that almost everyone you point to in that generation was in some way involved in the founding of a press or a little magazine of some kind. We felt a real urgency to get the work out and to create lines of communication. The only way to do that was to do it ourselves. It was precisely because that energy was there that the Canada Council responded to the initiative by writers and began to pump money into Canadian publishing. That was a case of where the impulse was there in the art community, and out of that impulse, funding was created to help. However, this did not occur overnight. The fact is that most of those presses started with no funding money at all, and usually ran for a number of years before there was even a possibility of that kind of a structure being in place in this country. I've run *grOnk* for years with no funding. I've been involved with Underwhich Editions now for ten years, and I think only three of our books ever had any funding out of 155 or so.

During those early years there was a kind of double push by writers. One was to create the means, and that was helpful to the individual writer. There was — certainly in myself, in bill, in Victor, I saw it in Dennis, I saw it in Peggy when she was involved with Anansi and she wrote *Survival* — the feeling that you should get out and argue for the writing. You should get out there and let other people see that argument.

There was more flow back and forth between, say, painters and writers. For example, visual artists at Coach House were quite interested in the quickness of the poster or the postcard as a medium. The idea that you could put up something quite fast and get very quick feedback. To have those kinds of avenues open between the arts is pretty fantastic.

FG: Is that how you became involved in intermedia or collaborative work?

bp: Writing, in essence, lies at intersections of poetry, painting and music. In a sense, to write is a visual act — to put letters on a page, to create lines with a pencil or a pen. There's a very definite visual moment. The page is a visual field and that's one of the elements of writing. It is also tied to thought. Therefore, there's a way in which it interacts with something like philosophy, with any act of thoughtfulness. It uses language, the thing we probably take the most for granted because we use it all the time. Inherent in language is a system of sounds and pitches and so on. We could say a kind of musicality is one of the elements of language. Each of these is part of what makes up what we think of as writing. On the whole, an awful lot of writers tend to exclude one or maybe two of these elements. For a tremendous number of writers, writing is that almost silent, solitary act of the pen scratching across the page. They are really not looking at what they are writing. They are thinking about the content of what they are writing. They are shaping it to get it across the best way they can. But the minute you start to look at what you write, there's a whole set of visual possibilities that opens up, and similarly the minute you start to listen to what you are saying you realize you could say it in a number of ways.

It seems to me that I was led to intermedia activity by the very fact of looking at the page and by listening to what I was doing. For me, it really grew out of trying to get more in touch with my own writing. And, of course, once you start questioning givens, and authorship is certainly one of them, there is a tendency to open up authorship to some kind of collaborative process and to see what is actually possible.

In Place: An Appreciation

1988, 1993

I think I can safely say that my name is not the first one that would spring to people's minds when asked to name writers that have been influenced by Al Purdy. Certainly by looking at my work as it is today, his influence is probably invisible. But it was so specific, and such a revelation at the time that it occurred to me, that when Russell Brown asked me, during a chance phone call about something else, whether I had any words or thots about Al Purdy and his work, his writing, that I'd want to say at a day long celebration of his work and worth, I instantly said "yes" because I instantly thot of the poem I am about to talk to you about and what it meant (said) to me when I first read it. So this is, of necessity, an autobiographical piece about how a writer's writing, in this case Al Purdy's writing, comes to influence a reader that writer doesn't even know, won't even meet for a goodly number of years. The autobiography is a necessary prelude to the act of appreciation.

The background to this, the general situation in Canada in the late 50s, early 60s, is, perhaps, familiar ground to most of you but probably worth rehearsing again. From about the age of eight on I was writing, initially in that mostly mildly unconscious way you have when you're young, writing the way you'd draw a picture, or collect stamps or read books, i.e. it pops into your mind as something to do and you do it. And tho you have influences — Dr. Seuss, Thornton W. Burgess, Kenneth Grahame, Frank L. Baum, Chester Gould and Walt Kelly in my case — you don't think of writing in those terms at all. Writing is just an activity among other activities, a choice you make, and it's the pleasure you take out of the activity, and the recurrence of it as a choice, that probably determines whether you go on with it as the years progress. Certainly by the time I was 16 or so I was making up single copies of books to give to friends, books full of quite terrible poems that I was very very proud of and, of course, very protective about. And it was around that same time that sources/models/influences began to enter my consciousness as an issue. Who did I *like*? Whose writing was my writing *like*? It's about 1960. I'm living in Vancouver. There is no such thing as Canadian poetry that I am aware of. Poetry seems to be something that's done by dead Englishmen or dead American men or, very occasionally indeed, dead English and American women. So that even tho I'm writing I'm not really connecting the activity to a living present, to a public act, because I have no instance, no model, on which to base that notion.

Strange times. Fortunately I meet David Phillips and Jim Alexander and among the three of us, and a few other friends, we begin to discover other cultures, other writings, and, thank heaven, some little magazines. Jim in fact is publishing a little magazine and, tho he never publishes me (my writing at that time is, after all, dreadful), I realize that living people, and yes living Canadians, can write and can publish. Wow!

Fast forward to 1962. I'm now reading all sorts of things: Chinese poetry in translation, Kenneth Patchen, Edith Sitwell, the earlier version of Emily Dickinson and, of course, because it was very big in Vancouver at the time, *The New American Poetry* anthology from Grove Press. *Tish* is on the scene. Ross Clark lends me his copies as he gets them. The first *Blew Ointment* will soon appear. Influences are pressing in from all sides and I'm doing that thing you do at that point in your writing life which is to carry on an argument in your head with all of them. "This is great!" "This sucks!" "Where does he/she come off saying that?" etc. And tho I'm doing all this in Vancouver, Canada, I have no real imagination of myself as a Canadian writer.

So that sets the scene. One day I'm browsing thru the poetry section in Duthie's Books when I come across *The Blur in Between* by one Alfred Purdy. It is a very beautiful book to my eyes, obviously hand set, with what look like silk screen prints, and, when I give the pages a fast scan, the poems look good too. It's only $1.50. This fits within my book budget, so I buy it. At home, seated in my room at 777 West 70th (phone Fairfax 77208), reading through the first poems of Alfred Purdy's I've ever read, I come across the following, the first section of a three part poem called "Towns" and it goes like this:

> If I were a panhandler I'd live in Vancouver,
> On skid row when the seiners come in,
> Where the stink of fish would stun a strong man
> (But they passed a by-law forbidding that,
> And another forbidding sin) …
> And the city would take me to its bosom:
> The old derelict street cars over Cambie
> Bridge and Oak Street resurrect for me to ride on.
> Yea, I'd be a bum at Hastings and Main,
> Among the loggers, Chinese, and bleary Indians,
> The fat klootch girls stumbling out in morning,
> The Salish girls with black eyes and bruised lips
> Their lovers inflicted when the wine was red.
> At Prospect Point (the city's high front porch)
> In fog, the cry of mating tugboats
> In the suburban sea becomes in the tuned mind
> A stealthy, horned, prehistoric head
> Scouting our ramparts from scummed black water …
> The soul of the city is its poignant dinginess,
> The dumb voices of grime, the story of dirt —
> A bright orange bobbing where ferry boats cross
> To the North Shore, and ending in Coal Harbour.
> O Vancouver, I was the swimmer out of sight
> Of land in your backyard ocean, fighting the grey ways,
> The driftwood turnings and foam roads going nowhere,
> I was that man.

Now there's a romanticized beat sensibility about this poem: "If I were a panhandler"; "The old derelict street cars over Cambie Bridge and Oak Street resurrect for me to ride on"; etc. And, at the time, given my dedicated reading and rereading of *The New American Poetry*, Jack Kerouac's *On the Road*, etc., that definitely appealed to me. The image of the tugboats making love tho, on the one hand, slightly funny — i.e. when I start imaging it the images that come get pretty bizarre — is accurate on a sound level. I'd heard that noise. I knew *what* he was talking about. (The line later influenced a bad poem of mine in which two lovers in a forest hear "the distant sounds / of deer / making love," i.e. presumably the crashing and thrashing of falling trees and some passionate snorting and/or whinnying; I'm not sure; I'd never heard deer make love when I wrote the line and I still haven't availed myself of the opportunity.) But what stopped me cold in my tracks and literally sent a shock of recognition thru me were the last four lines of the poem:

O Vancouver, I was the swimmer out of sight
Of land in your backyard ocean, fighting the grey ways,
The driftwood turnings and foam roads going nowhere,
I was that man.

Lost as I was in those days, an 18 year old would-be-writer trying to sort out for himself that hoary question about the meaning of existence, his existence, any existence, I absolutely identified with those lines. And particularly I absolutely identified with their occurrence in place, the place I lived in — Vancouver. This wasn't someone who was experiencing all this anguish in Paris or New York or London, this was an I that was lost in the town I lived in. This was my I. Alfred Purdy was talking about my I.

Looking back on it now I think the other thing that was most striking for me in these lines was the use of the invocatory voice: "O Vancouver." This *sounded* like *real* poetry, i.e. the kind of stuff they taught you in schools. And because of that, because of the way it sounded, the tradition of English language poetry suddenly intersected for me with my experience, with the possibility that I could be a Canadian, live in Canada, and still be part of the continuum. I could be in place and still have a place. I read those four lines over and over again. I read them over so many times that I ended up memorizing them and for years afterwards could drop them at will into conversations about Canadian poetry and/or Vancouver and/or Al Purdy (the "-fred" having disappeared as the years went by).

I've never told Al this, tho we've talked many times. And now certainly seems the right place and time to acknowledge the influence that that poem had on me. Because the shocks of recognition that went thru me when I read those lines also opened the door for me to the particularness of my own writing. To be in place, write about my place, and have a place, was to begin to allow my own vocabulary, my own language, to develop. Those four lines created a sense of possibility that launched me on the course I've followed to this day. And tho that course has shaped my poetry in a different way than it did Al's, it was Al working to be himself, to have his own vocabulary, his own language of place and occasion, within, nonetheless, a tradition, that first opened my eyes to what was possible. It changed how I read and what I read.

I continued and continue to read Al's poetry, and tho there are many poems in Al's considerable, sensitive and finely crafted body of writing that I like more than the section of "Towns" I've just been talking about, there is no poem of Al's that has affected me more. Writing is such a strange activity. You sit by yourself sweating over words you hope will communicate to some imagined other, will somehow reach and maybe even affect, change them in some way. Well this is an appreciation from one such imagined reader. And it seems worth saying after all these years, as I would have had it been a conversation, "Hey! I know what you're talking about Al, boy can I feel that, that's exactly what I wanted to say!"

> O Vancouver, I was the swimmer out of sight
> Of land in your backyard ocean, fighting the grey ways,
> The driftwood turnings and foam roads going nowhere,
> I was that man.

In/Ov Native Writing: Taking on the Book in Canadian Literature

REVIEW
The Abbotsford Guide to India, by Frank Davey
Diary of Desire, by Judith Fitzgerald
Skrag, by David Arnason

1988

The continuing argument about the appropriateness of political content in poetry is, of course, made foolish by the politics of reputation in poetry. In English-language literature the war for significance and greatness is between British and American poetry. And anyone who thinks that "war" is an inappropriate metaphor here need only look at how Irish literature has been subsumed by the British (the subsuming being helped along by the amorphousness of the term "English"), not in Ireland certainly, but elsewhere through the agency of those "official" arbiters of taste, the anthologies and their editors. North of the 49th parallel one confronts this reality all the time. It is part of what Canadian writers take issue with in their writing, directly or indirectly, and tends to inform any discussion of writing in this country.

It seems to me, as an admittedly subjective observer, that the awareness of the politics of literature, of the workings of cultural chauvinism, what we might term "culturist" thought forms (a not very well concealed xenophobia), has led many Canadian writers to appreciate and confront the political/cultural/emotional content of book forms — i.e. what the larger structure of the book, the frame within which the poetry is operating, says. Each of the writers I'm going to consider in this brief review has chosen to take on a specific form of the book (or books), and none of these books can be fully appreciated without a reading of its structure.

Frank Davey's *The Abbotsford Guide to India* is a case in point. Davey has chosen to take on that hoary Canadian tradition, the travel poem, while operating within the glibbest of book structures — the travel book. The confrontation is a delight. The lists of what to take, what to wear, what to say, what not to say, what to visit, etc. are all there. But can we trust them? In the midst of each list there are items that don't make sense, that seem skewed, that point, with irony, to the position the traveller occupies in any culture, how that position undermines the validity of his/her insights and makes suspect the poems and novels she/he writes out of such experiences. The title itself points to this, a play on such institutions as *The Michelin Guide*. By naming his guidebook after the small British Columbia town he was born in, Davey indexes how all viewpoints are finally local events, cannot possibly encompass the totality of that which is vaster. Precisely because of that, we should suspect the "advice" we will be given, the authoritativeness of the traveller's voice. And Frank Davey's "advice" is, in fact, laced with irony, a politically sensitive mirror held up to the politically insensitive (for any number of reasons) tradition of the travel text. To make this work, Davey eschews the look of poetry, opting instead for the prose poem, using the sentence as his basic unit of composition. Precisely because of the Canadian tradition of the travel poem, he deliberately rejects the potentially romanticizing effect of putting his texts on India into a "poetic" form. He is arguing for what one has to say being taken on its own terms and not for the exoticness (in either the reader or the writer's mind) of its content or, indeed, author. *The Abbotsford Guide to India* is Frank Davey's most radical work to date. Not too coincidentally, it is also one of his best.

Judith Fitzgerald has chosen an "unofficial" book form as the structure of her latest publication, *Diary of Desire*. The diary is an essentially private book-structure in which the "I" is allowed free rein. The true free rein of the "I" is in itself an attack on the almost snobbish notion of objectivity that so many poets and poetry editors harbour; "no confessional poems" say the notices soliciting material for many little magazines. A title like *Diary of Desire* carries, therefore, expectations of "private" information, revelations of personal feeling, of, as the title says, desire. The book is *big*, physically: 8 1/2" x 11". We associate "diary" with small, with tiny locked volumes capable of being concealed, and the very size of *Diary of Desire* (book structure on another level) is part of Fitzgerald's strategy: the outering of that which tends to be interiorized; the *publi*cation of emotions we suffer in private. This is made explicit throughout the book. And the fact that "diary" tends to be seen as a woman's medium (as opposed to the more neutral if not slightly masculine connotation of "journal") is also part of her concern. And the emotions contained in it as potentially "hysterical" (and we are familiar now with the history and problematics of that term) or, as Fitzgerald chooses to focus on in her poem "Letters," "maudlin." Beginning with the etymology of that word in the name of Mary Magdalen, Fitzgerald rhymes the ambiguity of its origin (the woman who is revered but whose feelings are viewed as mawkish and sentimental) with the plight of the "I" in the text: "Hard times, hard music, each of us hardened against / the beautiful psychic vulnerability, the open note, the pure pitch of pain." And the "diary" can be seen as the preserver of that "I," the preserver of the true voice of women through the years of repression, the place in which women's language has survived. Fitzgerald writes in "Typography of Tears": "Inexpressible. To speech to speak not profoundly but with intervals / of faith a flag, an emblem, a motif of celebration. Language binds us / together, marks the atomic density of desire, ultimately breaks us / down." And this is precisely one of the functions of a diary: to record that which is otherwise inexpressible, the full weight of desire. Fitzgerald's book is a powerful voicing of these "forbidden," in that sense, feelings, those very emotions that mark us as human.

In David Arnason's new book, *Skrag*, the Winnipeg writer takes on not simply one book form, but four. *Skrag* is not divided into sections (no section numbers appear above its four parts and each part has its own title page); rather, playing off the useful multifacetedness of the term "book," Arnason sets out to examine the options open to a writer.

The opening (and title) text is Arnason's take on that most revered of Canadian book-length forms, the biographical poem. But in Arnason's case the subject of the biography is a dog named Skrag and in that choice of a figure, Arnason takes on not only the problematics of the biographical poem, its gossipiness, its tendency to accept the given details of a life as sufficient frame, but also the Disney anthropomorphization of, say, *Old Yeller* (this is echoed in the choice of yellow as the background colour for the repeated image of a dog on the book's cover, a wallpaper-style repetition that in itself works as a sub-text), as well as the enduring (and often sickeningly endearing) prairie (and therefore in dialogue with some of the issues inherent in Canadian prairie writing that also impinge on trans-border issues) myth of a boy and his dog. It's certainly possible to read the poem simply as an affectionate tribute to a dog, but the darkness of the imagery, the unspoken suicide that is central to the story and never explained, the implicit strategy in focusing on a figure that sits outside human language, all point to the poem's larger purpose, to question the meaning of any life and the glibness of using the notion of "biography" without questioning its assumptions. The final image in the poem, the killing of an aged, sickly Skrag as the true meaning of love, segues into the second book of this book — "The Cottage Poems."

"The Cottage Poems" is an image-rhymed collection of lyrics. Formally this is what you might describe as a typical second-book structure; having gotten their first book of poems out of the way (usually a selection of the best of what they've written in the years leading up to its publication), poets generally go on in their second book to write towards a book, typically utilizing this kind of image-rhymed structure. But Arnason is once again working against the structure he has chosen; his voice is deliberately laconic or muted, and even when he reaches for the exquisite summary phrase (as he does) he simultaneously rejects the romanticization inherent in such a structural choice. The cottage remains a cottage; the animals are simply animals; love is love and is celebrated for that fact rather than for what it can be compared to.

If "The Cottage Poems" is Arnason's take on a second-book structure, and the title poem, "Skrag," could be described as a third-book structure (which it can and should be), "Selected Lyrics," the third book in Arnason's collection, is the quintessential first-book structure. The title says it all: a selection of lyrics, poems written with no book structure in mind but with a book structure now imposed upon them. The lyrics touch on all the topics you would expect a first book to touch upon: mother, father, family, lovers, work, and the political scene. But they are also about the failure of communication, the failure of the I's attempt to be more than what it is — human and therefore imperfect and transitory. Implicit in this book, and in the one preceding it, is a rejection of the romanticization and aggrandizement inherent in the use of the lyric voice, a rejection of the social clichés surrounding the role of poet in our society. And having reached this point where does the writer go?

As should be obvious by now, Arnason is moving us backwards through a history of forms. There is a tone of both structural analysis (in terms of the emotional content these

```
it's  a  good  idea,  at  least  from  time  to  time,
to  let  the  language  speak.
```

structures can carry) and self-analysis in the first three books of *Skrag*. The two, in fact, are married. He's taken us from a third-book structure, through a second-book structure, through a first-book structure and now, in the final part, he leaps straight into the deep past in order to take us straight into the present which, to all intents and purposes, is also our future. "René Descartes and Deadwood Dick" departs from the more usual notion of book-structure the previous parts of *Skrag* have presented. In fact, it rejects them. Cutting back and forth between the florid prose of the Victorian penny dreadfuls and a dialogue with René Descartes, Arnason charts the search for an absent poet/poetry using cheap jokes, sound poetry, and any other technique he can muster that seems appropriate to the quest. He goes premodern in order to take us postmodern and the entire history of writing becomes available to him and us. He is outside eras and outside genres. As the quest nears its end he addresses a final desperate plea to Descartes:

> René, I said, give me a sign.
> Give up poetry, he said. It's a mug's game.

And in the final stanza of the poem, even as we go to close the book (within which books exist), everything is swept away in a flood — the house, the horse and René Descartes. And we are swept out of the book knowing the writer is free to do whatever she/he chooses from this point on. *Skrag* is a brilliant example of where the macrotext absolutely informs our reading of the text. The reader who enters this book, or any of the others, like some crazed anthologizer looking for the "best" poems, will leave the book not having read it, even though her or his eyes took in every word on every page.

There is a way in which this ending rhymes nicely with a comment Richard Elliott Friedman makes in his recent book *Who Wrote the Bible?* (Summit Books, 1987):

> It is currently in vogue to debate whether the Bible is more a work of literature or a work of history. I think that the ancient Israelites ... would have found this a pointless question. There are no words for "history" or "literature" in Biblical Hebrew. To them it was: a book. (215)

And this is where Arnason leaves us at the end of *Skrag*. Read the book reader. Read what the book says.

Who's in Control: The Poet or the Language?

1988

In response to any question on the nature of control one would like to imagine the best, i.e. in this case, ideally, it's neither the poet nor the language but rather the two of them, together. Having said that tho, there is something interesting in the question that remains unanswered. I've often used the language of surrender when talking on this point: "Let the language lead you ; Listen to what the poem wants to say", etc. And tho I prefer the language of surrender (& hence desire) over the language of control (tho control does come into play on the level of technical facility), I don't feel I've answered the particular question when I talk that way either.

It seems to me that what the question raises is the fundamental issue of consciousness, the nature of consciousness. Are we, indeed, always in control? Historically, the poet, as opposed to the prose writer or playwright, associated with *ekstasis*, with the poetic trance induced by divine inspiration. Those who wish to account for Shakespeare's genius attribute the telling difference to his being "a poet"; or, to really drive the point home, "a real poet." And I think most poets at one time or another must have that experience of dictation, where the poem seems to write itself and you literally don't know where it's coming from. At such moments precisely because one does not feel "in control" one is tempted to answer today's question with the answer "the language is in control."

But it's precisely the answering of that question that makes you realize you are talking about consciousness — states of consciousness. I think there is a state of mind you achieve out of which you write. It is a meditative state, one in which you focus your energy and your thot. Given that it is such, it is totally unlike other states of consciousness, i.e. love-making, eating, going to the bathroom — each of these involves a unique, focused mind-set (whatever the other physical urgings that might have led one there) and so too with writing. Which at least partially accounts for the feeling one has of "coming to," i.e. coming back to consciousness, after a period of dictation — one is passing from one mind-set to another.

There are often issues indexed by the question, i.e. spirituality, the nature of language, the relationship between the spiritual, consciousness & language. But these are just supposed to be some opening remarks so I'll draw it to a close here. I should add that I don't believe poets to be any more, or differently, inspired than prose writers or playwrights. The very word "inspiration" suggests the obvious connection that it's as natural as breathing.

Fred Wah says the etymology of "control" is "counter the role," i.e. "stop the revolution" literally.

Editorial Notes

INTERVIEWS

The visual text with "Meanwhile!" at the top, which is placed at the beginning of each interview, has been taken from "TRG Report 2 (Narrative, Part 5) — The Search for Non-Narrative Prose, Part 2," with Steve McCaffery, in *Open Letter* 3rd Series.2 (Fall 1975): 39. It is also reproduced in *Rational Geomancy: The Kids of the Book-Machine, The Collected Research Reports of the Toronto Research Group 1973-1982*, edited by Steve McCaffery (Talonbooks, 1992), 116. A few cloud images, taken from Book 3 of bpNichol's *The Martyrology*, are used to signify sections of interviews not included.

With George Bowering. "Cutting Them All Up: An Interview with bpNichol," was taped on August 30, 1968, and published in *Alphabet* 18-19 (1971): 18-21. It is included here in total.

With Raoul Duguay (excerpt). This interview, dated Ottawa, July 24, 1973, is what Nichol, in a note for its publication, calls the "companion piece" to his own interview with Raoul Duguay that appeared in *Open Letter* 6th Series.6 (Fall 1973): 65-73. It was finally published in *Brick* 23 (Winter 1985): 25-31, alongside two other pieces written many years before, "Passwords: The bissett Papers" and "A Letter to Mary Ellen Solt."

With Nicette Jukelevics (excerpt). Nichol was interviewed for Jukelevics' MA thesis, "A Bibliography of Canadian Concrete, Visual and Sound Poetry 1965 1972, with an Introduction" (Concordia University, 1975). Her "Interview with b. p. Nichol," dated June 26, 1974, appeared as an Appendix.

With Pierre Coupey, Dwight Gardiner, Gladys Hindmarch, and Daphne Marlatt (excerpt). This interview — more a discussion session — was edited by Nichol and Marlatt for publication in *The Capilano Review* 8-9 (Fall 1975-Spring 1976): 313-346. A note informs readers that it "was held with great hilarity in the kitchen of Gladys Hindmarch's house on the afternoon of September 19, 1974, the day after bp's reading at Capilano College ... The original transcript is unfortunately much too long to reprint in full, so what follows are essentially excerpts from the mainstream of conversation ..." Brian Fisher was also present but he does not speak in this excerpt.

With Nick Power and Anne Sherman (excerpt). This interview was conducted for the University of Toronto student newspaper, *The Varsity*, February 28, 1975: 10-11. Anne Sherman later changed her name to Caroline Bayard.

With Caroline Bayard and Jack David (excerpt). The introductory note to this interview sets its time and place: "We talked with Nichol at Caroline's Toronto flat on February 10, 1976, interrupting the conversation at one point to drink some wine and eat a salad." It was published in *Out-Posts* (Erin, Ontario: Press Porcépic, 1978), 15-49.

With Ken Norris (excerpt). The first interview by Norris, "Interview with bp Nichol, Feb. 13, 1978," appeared in *Essays on Canadian Writing* 12 (Fall 1978): 203-250. The second interview, previously unpublished and dated December 1979, is taken from the Nichol Papers at SFU. Thanks to Ken Norris for suggesting its inclusion.

With Stuart Ross (excerpt). "bpNichol Talks about Consumer Resistance" was published in Ross' journal, *Mondo Hunkamooga: A Journal of Small Press Reviews* 2 (October 1983): unpaginated. Ross begins his interview with a question on Nichol's novel *Still*, the winner of the International 3-Day Novel Writing Contest sponsored by Pulp Press (1982).

With Geoff Hancock (excerpt). This interview has taken 15 years to reach publication. Initially conducted in July 1986, it has appeared in *Rampike* 12.1 (Winter 2000-2001): 16-22.

With Steve McCaffery (excerpt). This interview takes the form of a constructed dialogue undertaken between May and September 1987 for submission to *Tracing the Paths: Reading ≠ Writing* The Martyrology (Vancouver: Line/Talonbooks, 1988), 72-91.

With Clint Burnham. A slightly shorter version of this interview appeared in *Tracing the Paths: Writing ≠ Reading* The Martyrology (Vancouver: Line/Talonbooks, 1988), 292-95. The version included here in total is based on the typescript of the interview in the bpNichol Papers, dated in Nichol's hand, June 1987. Burnham's note describes its circumstances: "This talk was originally conducted over a very bad telephone line between Victoria and Toronto. It was first edited for sound, then, not used as a radio interview, transcribed in this form. bpNichol has been very kind in helping to make a few changes."

With Fred Gaysek. This *Artviews* interview, conducted by its editor, was dated December 15, 1988 (should be 1987) in *Artviews* 14.1 (Winter 1987-88): 21-23.

CRITICAL WRITING

Waiting (1973). First published in *Open Letter* 2nd Series.5 (Summer 1973): 17-21, as part of "TRG Report 2: Narrative (part 1)." It was republished as the opening piece, untitled, in *Craft Dinner: Stories & Texts 1966-1976*

(Toronto: Aya Press, 1978), unpaginated.

Letter to the Editor, *Open Letter* (1966). Published in *Open Letter* 1st Series.4 (June 1966): 6–7.

statement, november 1966. Published in February 1967 as part of Nichol's first Coach House Press publication, *bp*, a boxed collection of diverse works, including a book of poems, *JOURNEYINGS & the returns*; an envelope of visual poem/objects, *Letters Home*; a recording of sound poems, *Borders*; and a flip poem, *Wild Thing*.

Scattered Notes 1966 - 1971. A compilation made by Nichol and which appears to have been ear-marked for a collection of essays. One section, "A Contributed Editorial," is considered in this collection of such importance to warrant its own space.

aaaa a a a a a a: d.a. levy and the Great Society (1967). Published in *grOnk* and also in *D.A. Levy: A Tribute to the Man: An Anthology of His Poetry* (Cleveland, Ohio: Ghost Press, 1967), edited by RJS (Robert J. Sigmund). It is dated February 26, 1967, with Nichol's note: "...the following Rticle was taken from isshue #3 of *grOnk* (march 67), flcyc press, toronto."

Review of *Notations,* by John Cage (1969). Published in *The Canadian Forum* 48 (March 1969): 285–86.

"an introduction" to *Pnomes, Jukollages & Other Stunzas,* by Earle Birney (1967). First published in *grOnk*, Series 4.3 (1969), then reprinted in *Earle Birney*, edited by Bruce Nesbitt (Toronto: McGraw-Hill Ryerson, 1974), 171–72. It is excerpted in *Contemporary Literary Criticism* Volume 6 (Detroit: Gale Research Company, 1975), 75.

Passwords: The bissett Papers (1971, 1985). Published in *Brick* 23 (Winter 1985): 5–18, but as Nichol says in his introductory note, earlier versions of parts of this essay were previously published: as "The Typogeography of bill bissett," an afterword to bissett's *We Sleep Inside Each Other All* (Ganglia 1966), and as "Zounds!! — the sounds of bill bissett," a review of bissett's *The Jinx Ship and Othr Trips*, in *Quarry* 16.4 (Summer 1967): 43–46. A typescript of this essay in the Nichol Papers is dated August 1971. When printed in *Brick*, it became one part of "Not in Time: Three Uncompleted Projects from the Early 70's." The other two pieces are "A Letter to Mary Ellen Solt" and "Raoul Duguay Interviews bpNichol."

some beginning writings on Gertrude Stein's Theories of Personality (1972). Published in *Open Letter* 2nd Series.2 (Summer 1972): 41–48. Part two of this essay was published in *White Pelican*. Nichol worked on a series of essays on Stein over a period of many years. There is a manuscript of this work in process in his papers called "Notes Towards an Essay on Gertrude Stein's Theories of Personality as Revealed in *The Making of Americans*," which ends with "a review of bpNichol's 'some beginning writings on Gertrude Stein's Theories of Personality' as published in *Open Letter* 2/2," by pbLichon. A more complete editing of Nichol's writing on Stein remains beyond the limits of this collection and calls for a separate critical edition.

from some beginning writings on Gertrude Stein's Theories of Personality as revealed in *The Making of Americans* (1972, 1983). Published in *White Pelican* 3.4 (Autumn 1983): 15-23.

a review of bpNichol's "some beginning writings on Gertrude Stein's Theories of Personality" as published in *Open Letter* 2/2 (1972). Taken from the Nichol Papers where it follows the manuscript of the *White Pelican* publication.

Review of *Typewriter Poems*, edited by Peter Finch (1972). Published in *Open Letter* 2nd Series.3 (Fall 1972): 78-81. A typescript in the Nichol Papers is dated June 21, 1972.

Sound and the Lung Wage (1973). Taken from the Nichol Papers where it is dated March 1973.

A Letter to Mary Ellen Solt (1973, 1985). Published in *Brick* 23 (Winter 1985): 18-19. Nichol prefaces its publication by explaining what initially prompted this letter: "This was a statement on poetics for an international anthology of visual poetries that Mary Ellen Solt was editing for a European publisher and then abandoned as the sheer scope of it became too much. The letter remains an accurate summary of what I knew of my poetic practice circa spring 1973. I've included some of the texts mentioned (as illustration)." The letter is dated Spring 1973.

What Is Can Lit? (1973). Published in *Open Letter* 2nd Series.4 (Summer 1973): 69-70.

Letter re James Reaney (1973). Published in *Open Letter* 2nd Series.6 (Fall 1973): 5-7. A typescript in the Nichol Papers has the title, "A Few Words on Why James Reaney Is Important to Anyone Writing Now (for Frank Davey)."

Two Pages on the Nature of the Reality of Writing (1973). Published in *Open Letter* 2nd Series.6 (Fall 1973): 104-105, as part of "TRG Report 2: Narrative (part 2)." It is reproduced in *Truth: A Book of Fiction,* edited by Irene Niechoda (Mercury Press, 1993), 139-140.

Overwhelming Colour: Review of *White*, by Douglas Barbour (1974). Published in *Open Letter* 2nd Series.8 (Summer 1974): 110-112.

Review of *Lists*, by Jean-Jacques (1974). Published in *Open Letter* 2nd Series.9 (Fall 1974): 107.

A Letter to Michael Gibbs (1975). Published in *Kontexts* (Holland) 6-7 (1975): unpaginated.

Some Notes for Jack David on Earle Birney's "Solemn Doodles" (1977). Published in *Essays on Canadian Writing* 9 (Winter 1977-78): 109-111. It was published without the graphics attached to the typescript in the Nichol Papers, dated December 1, 1977.

A Contributed Editorial (1978). Published as the Preface to *Open Letter* 3rd Series.9 (Fall 1978): 5-6, and dated December 11, 1978.

Tabling Content: writing a reading of Shant Basmajian's *Quote Unquote* (1978). Published in *Open Letter* 3rd Series.9 (Fall 1978): 135-149, and dated by Nichol, "New Port Richey — Montreal — Clearwater 1977-1978."

A Conversation with Fred Wah and Pauline Butling (1978). Published in *Open Letter* 3rd Series.9 (Fall 1978): 34-63. A subtitle presents the interview as a TRG (Toronto Research Report) project, "Report One: Translation (Part 3)," the connections to which are clarified in Nichol's introductory note on the date and focus of the conversation: "The following conversation was recorded in Castlegar, British Columbia in the home of Fred Wah and Pauline Butling on January 26, 1977. I have edited it and reworked sections of it on the basis of subsequent conversations with Fred, most notably in Toronto in late January 1978. The conversation centres on Fred's *Pictograms from the Interior of BC*, his compositional process and the relationship of it to the issues of Translation that the Toronto Research Group has been exploring."

some words on *the martyrology* march 12, 1979. Published in *The Long Poem Anthology*, edited by Michael Ondaatje (Toronto: Coach House Press, 1979), 335-7, as part of the section, "Statements by the Poets."

Introduction to *The Arches: Selected Poems of Frank Davey* (1980). Published as the editorial introduction to *The Arches: Selected Poems of Frank Davey*, edited by bpNichol (Vancouver: Talonbooks, 1980), 7-21. Dated at the end, "Toronto/Milwaukee/Toronto / February 8 to April 5 1980."

Some Sentences, Paragraphs & Punctuations on Sentences, Paragraphs & Punctuation (1982). Published in *Open Letter* 5th Series.3 (Summer 1982): 17-23. A typescript of what is called the "1st draft" in the Nichol Papers is dated November 10, 1981.

"Syntax Equals the Body Structure": bpNichol, in Conversation, with Daphne Marlatt and George Bowering (1982, 1985). Published in *Line* 6 (Fall 1985): 22-44. I edited this discussion that took place on July 21, 1982, and provided a background note: "During the summer of 1982, bpNichol was a special guest in a graduate course on Contemporary Canadian poetry. *The*

Martyrology was on the course, and among other long poems, George Bowering's *Autobiology* and Daphne Marlatt's *Steveston*. Since both Bowering and Marlatt lived in Vancouver, they were invited to join bp to form a panel … The edited portion of the discussion attempts to retrieve the threads of continuity without losing the texture of the conversation, though much, some two-thirds or more, was left behind on the tape — and given the disproportionate amount of speech recorded to text printed, I resorted to some splicing for the sake of form. Readers who would like to listen to the talk in all its raw entirety can do so in Special Collections, The Contemporary Literature Collection, in the Simon Fraser University Library, where the tapes are housed. The event was recorded by Kurtis Vanel, and I am very grateful to Susan Lord and Lisa Goldberg for doing the initial transcription for editing."

The Medium Was the Message (1982). Published posthumously in *Journal of Canadian Poetry* 4 (1989): 1-3. This issue of *Journal of Canadian Poetry* was dedicated to Nichol. A handwritten note on the typescript, dated October 4, 1982, in the Nichol Papers says it was written for a book on Marshall McLuhan to be edited by "Flahiff & Watson," presumably Fred Flahiff and Wilfred Watson.

The Prosody of Open Verse, with Frank Davey (1982). Published in *Open Letter* 5th Series.2 (Spring 1982): 5-13. It was the first in a series of articles they wrote for the special "Notation" issues of *Open Letter* which were edited by Nichol.

Notating Sound Poetry — An Introduction to *The Prose Tattoo* (1983). Published as the introduction to *The Prose Tattoo: Selected Performance Scores, by The Four Horsemen* (Milwaukee: Membrane Press, 1983), unpaginated. It is dated at the end: "January 1982, January 1983."

When the Time Came (1983). Published in *Line* 1 (Spring 1983): 46-61. Dated by Nichol, "October 1982 thru February 1983," it was first presented as a talk at Simon Fraser University. It has been reprinted, but with the handwritten comments replaced by typeset copy, in *Gertrude Stein and the Making of Literature*, edited by Shirley Neuman and Ira B. Nadel (Boston: Northwestern University Press, 1988), 194-209.

Talking About the Sacred in Writing (1983). Published in *Tracing the Paths: Writing ≠ Reading The Martyrology*, 233-36. Nichol presented this talk, initially transcribed by Lisa Goldberg, for a panel discussion, "Poetry and the Sacred," with Robin Blaser and Sharon Thesen, at Simon Fraser University, July 6, 1983.
Multiplex letraset a language event: Review of (Untitled), by Peggy Lefler (1983). Published in *Mondo Hunkamooga* 2 (October 1983): unpaginated.

Notes for "Journal" Conference Paper (1984). Unpublished draft notes, dated

May 12, 1984, in the Nichol Papers, which may have been initially directed towards Nichol's presentation at the Long-Liners Conference, York University, May 29-June 1, 1984. A handwritten question at the bottom of the first page, "Journal? or Notebook?," suggests that Nichol had second thoughts on terminology for his process-based writing.

Note Book a composition on composition (1984). Published in *Open Letter* 6th Series.2-3 (Summer-Fall 1985), a special issue devoted to the Long-Liners Conference, edited by Frank Davey and Ann Munton. Written as what Nichol called a "shuffle text," this essay was distributed in sections throughout the publication. A similar form has been enacted here but less randomly: the opening section begins in the chronological order of this collection with the remaining sections distributed throughout in the order they appear on the typescript in the Nichol Papers.

The "Pata of Letter Feet, or, the English Written Character as a Medium for Poetry (1984, 1985). Published in *Open Letter* 6th Series.1 (Spring 1985): 79-95. A footnote explains the circumstance of this essay: "A draft of a talk delivered to the York Fine Arts Department and the Lethbridge University English Dept." Nichol was writer-in-residence at the University of Lethbridge in October 1984.

Sketching (1984). Apparently unpublished. The typescript in the Nichol Papers is dated "Toronto and Lethbridge / August 6th thru December 3rd 1984."

The Book as a Unit of Composition, with Frank Davey (1985). Published in *Open Letter* 6th Series.1 (Spring 1985): 39-46.

Poet Tics (1985). Published in *Line* 8-9 (Spring-Fall 1986): 90-2.

Narrative in Language: The Long Poem (1986, 1988). Initially delivered as a talk at the University of Alberta, March 1986, and later published in *Tracing the Paths: Writing ≠ Reading* The Martyrology, 35-7.

The Dart, Its Arkness: David McFadden's *The Art of Darkness* (1986). Published in *Brick* 28 (Fall 1986): 35-37.

Introduction to *The Last Blew Ointment Anthology Volume 2* (1986). Published in *The Last Blewointment Anthology: 1963-1983, Volume 2*, edited by bill bissett (Toronto: Nightwood Editions, 1985-86), 9-10. It is dated December 7, 1986.

Primary Days: Housed with the Coach at the Press, 1965 to 1987 (1987). Published in *Provincial Essays* 4 (1987): 19-25. A typescript in the Nichol Papers is dated "January/February 1987."

R-Toys-Us? (1987). Published in *The Journal of Wild Culture* 1.1 (1987): 13.

In Place: An Appreciation (1988). This essay was presented at "A Celebration of Al Purdy," University of Toronto, March 25, 1988. The typescript in the Nichol Papers is dated March 25, 1988. It was published posthumously in a special Al Purdy issue of *Essays on Canadian Writing* 49 (Summer 1993): 27-31.

In/Ov Native Writing: Taking on the Book in Canadian Literature (1988). Published in *American Book Review*, May-June 1988: 5-7. It appeared without the subtitle used in the undated typescript in the Nichol Papers.

Who's in Control: The Poet or the Language? (1988). Unpublished talk in the Nichol Papers, dated "Weyburn, April 16th 1988."

LIST OF VISUAL TEXTS

Page 41: "Frame 9 & 12," in *Love: A Book of Remembrances* (Vancouver: Talonbooks, 1974), no pagination.

Page 50: from "Emblems," in *Zygal: A Book of Mysteries and Translations* (Toronto: Coach House Press, 1985), 17.

Page 63: from "Emblems," in *Zygal*, 22.

Page 89: "Toth 4," in *Zygal*, 110.

Page 97: "Mind Trap," in *bp* (Coach House Press, 1967), unpaginated.

Page 103, Untitled, in *Art Facts: A Book of Contexts* (Tuscon: Chax Press, 1990), 79.

Page 115: "Doors 1," in *Art Facts*, 37.

Page 117: "Frame 16," in *Love*, unpaginated.

Page 136: "Sine (Horizon 17)," in *Truth: A Book of Fictions*, edited by Irene Niechoda (Toronto: Mercury Press, 1992), 95.

Pages 147, 149, 151, 153, 155, 157, 159, 161: *Aleph Unit* (Toronto: Seripress, 1973).
Page 185: from "Scraptures: Lost Sequence," in *Gifts: The Martyrology Book(s)* 7 & (Toronto: Coach House Press, 1990), unpaginated.

Page 242: "Allegory #23," in *Love*, unpaginated.

Page 264: "Ocean Song," in *Art Facts*, 9.

Page 272: "Water Poem 5," in *Art Facts*, 142.

Page 293: "Allegory #6," in *Love*, unpaginated.

Page 300: "Allegory #25," in *Love*, unpaginated.

Page 337: "Allegorical Return: H is I," in *Zygal*, 123.

Page 349: from "'He Was Born in the Happy Ever After'," in *Zygal*, 69.

Page 377: "Sixteen Lilypads," in *Art Facts*, 57.

Page 393: Untitled, in *Art Facts*, 109.

Page 403: "Love," in *Concrete Poetry: A World View*, edited by Mary Ellen Solt (Bloomington: Indiana University Press, 1971), 216; typography by Hansjörg Mayer. This poem, titled "Blues," was published in *KonfessIonS of an ElizAbeThan Fan Dancer* (London: Writer's Forum, 1967; revised edition Toronto: Weed/Flower Press, 1973), unpaginated. The Mayer version was used for the cover for *Love: A Book of Remembrances* and is included in *As Elected: Selected Writing 1962-1979*, edited by bpNichol and Jack David (Vancouver: Talonbooks, 1980), 36.

Page 431: "From 'S,A's' by A. Gold & N. Guppy," in *Truth*, 124.

Pages 433-38: "Eyes," in *An Anthology of Concrete Poetry*, edited by Emmett Williams (New York: Something Else Press, 1967), 224-25.

"Remains in Process": An Editor's Afterword

> this business of process
> nothing more than
> the moment's grace

> — "The Grace of the Moment," *The Martyrology: Book 6 Books* (1987)

THE ENTRANCE

In "Talking about the Sacred in Writing," bpNichol acknowledges the centrality of "process" in his work. "You know how you set yourself these goals," he says, " — like I decided when I was 18 that I believed in process in writing, and then about a year and a half ago I woke up one night in the middle of the night, and I woke up Ellie and said 'Why process?' You know, after something like 20 years" (336). This preoccupation with "process," which for Nichol encompasses both belief and practice, occupies so many of the seams making up the multiple forms of his oeuvre that it sounds their "bass note / plunk it" (see the title page of *Gifts* (1990) where the reference is to Plunkett, Saskatchewan, a familial site of beginnings in his biogeography). The implications of its resonance in his work have suggested for me, as editor, a point of entrance to the subjects and procedures — and the personal refractions — of the critical material collected in this book, *Meanwhile*.

"So you get these little underpinnings you're working from ..." (336), Nichol continues, as he goes on to explain that the writing act has been for him the performance of process in the material conditions of language. But then again, the fascination with "process" had also become apparent in the more mundane setting of train travel through geographical spaces, another of the "little underpinnings" that Nichol would draw out of the drama of his family life. That movement would remain the imagined site par excellence for thinking through the material production of writing. In one poem, for instance, "it" all begins — i.e. the connections that link writing to process to trains — in the appearance of letters, that is, in the letteral language on the page/field which functions as the constitutive site of production. Here, in an inaugural poem of "Trans-Continental" in *Love: A Book of Remembrances* (1974), we hear the voice of the poet "bpNichol" assume speech, movement and graphic visibility:

> o dreaming
> l sets
>
> r rises black
> blue blue blue
>
> even the white turns green
> purple
>   black
>
> black black black
> back to blue
>
> e rises
>
> no
>
> e does not rise
> it is a dream
>
> somewhere on this train
> ryme schemes

Later, the poet comes to recognize "a trance state" — and the writing proceeds to undergo its states of consciousness as a performance of textual space. If we knew nothing else about this poet, "bpNichol," we would know that he has an extraordinary capacity to bear witness to the appearance of letters and to write himself into the indeterminate but always unfolding drift of their movements. Readers need only check out pretty well everything he would write in all genres to appreciate the playful-serious ways this negotiation — this love affair — with the elements of language is sustained in his work.

Nichol himself recalled in one interview that he committed himself to "play with the language" around 1963 (with Nick Power and Anne Sherman 158). He was then 19 years old, only one year after he dedicated himself to "process" in writing. A necessary fiction? Perhaps, but the trajectories of his writing life keep returning to the discourse of a journey — Nichol's first book of lyric poems was called *JOURNEYING & the returns* (1967) — a journey that has all the elements of a quest to discover in writing a means of liberation and social transformation. The critical work that emerged — in essays, reviews, letters, notes, dialogues, and interviews — holds together precisely because Nichol consistently approaches critical thought as a responsibility to the specific projects, events, magazines, small press publishers, and writers that shaped "that life," "outside these books," as he writes in dedicating *Gifts*, Books 7 and 8 of his acclaimed long poem, *The Martyrology*, to his wife Ellie.

A brief sketch of "that life" may help readers understand the intersection of the personal with the cumulative history of the critical work in *Meanwhile*.

THE BRIEF BIO

> 'because i criss-crossed the west with
> my mother & father'

> 'because i was raised on trains'
> ("Continental Trance," *The Martyrology: Book 6 Books*)

Barrie Phillip Nichol was born on September 30, 1944, in Vancouver, the youngest child of Glen and Avis (Workman) Nichol. A sister Deanna was born in 1940, brother DJ (Donald) in 1937, and brother Robert in 1935. Donna, the first-born sister, had died in 1934 at three months old (and her absence would haunt Nichol, carrying "on" as he did the D-N-A in her body). Nichol's father was born in North Dakota, moving up to Alberta in 1908 where he was raised; his mother was born and raised in Saskatchewan, near Plunkett. With his father working for the

Canadian National Railway (CNR), Nichol found himself in many different locations as he grew up. From an early childhood in Burnaby and Vancouver, he lived in Winnipeg (1948-52), Port Arthur (1952-56), and Winnipeg again (1956-60). He returned to Vancouver in 1960 where he competed his high school education.

Nichol recalled getting train passes to travel back and forth, between Vancouver and Toronto. "It is a trip that I took a lot as a kid, but I think it is kind of the quintessential Canadian experience in a way," he explained in one interview. His poem, "Continental Trance," thus becomes for him "an imagination of how life is lived and how a story gets told, in the sense that one foot follows another, one mile comes after another. To a degree, just moving on in time creates a narrative, a narrative moment, a sequence of events. Along the way I'm allowed the chance to talk about issues that have been on my mind" (with Clint Burnham 451).

As early as in his high school years Nichol already found himself attracted to typographically innovative texts and to sound and performance poetry — to Dadaism, the visual poems of Kenneth Patchen and Apollinaire, and the *Ghost Tantras* of Michael McClure (who came to Vancouver from San Francisco in 1962). The more inspirational examples in his local world came from the radical work of bill bissett and the textual dexterity of Sheila Watson's *The Double Hook*, a book he found in a Salvation Army junk shop in Winnipeg while visiting the city in December 1962. In short, writing as a life activity was an "in / vocation" (CODA: Mid-Initial Sequence," *The Martyrology*, Book 3 (1976)) right from the outset of his creative journey.

After completing his first-year university at King Edward Collegiate, in 1963, Nichol thought of becoming an elementary school teacher. He enrolled in the College of Education at the University of British Columbia and received an Elementary Teaching Certificate. He visited Toronto for the summer of 1963 — and so was away during the Vancouver Poetry Conference at UBC organized by Warren Tallman — and returned to take a teaching position (grade 4) in Port Coquitlam. Unable to complete the year, he resigned in April 1964 and decided to relocate to Toronto. There he entered into therapy with Lea Hindley-

Smith (Books 1 to 5 of *The Martyrology* are dedicated to her) and got heavily involved in Therafields, a collective of lay therapists trained by Lea Hindley-Smith. In their practice they sought various methods, including theradrama, to liberate subjects from what they understood to be the repressive structures of social and cultural norms and regulations. During the 1960s and 1970s, Nichol become a lay therapist and worked in the Therafields Foundation as one of the key movers in its institutional development. He provides an encapsulated account of his Therafields work, from 1966 to 1982, in a CV now in his papers at Simon Fraser University:

> Vice-President, Therafields Environmental Centre (York Ltd., Toronto). Input into budgets, involvement in all levels of decision-making, ideation & supervision of various building programs, liaison & arbitrator between creative professional & business management divisions, publisher & originator of various internal & community-oriented newsletters, public relations.
>
> Co-chairperson, Therapists' seminar, 1969-1981.
>
> Archivist (from 1973). Helped establish & supervise maintenance of collection.
>
> Therapist, Toronto. Established & sustained an individual practice (averaging 15 people per year) & group practice (groups ranged in size from 16 to 40 people) both independently & in connection with the ability to articulate both their life experiences & goals, & in the resolution of difficulties arising in inter-personal relationships. Worked in relationship counselling. Specialized in group work with artists in the practical resolution of creative blocks.

Soon after settling in Toronto, and prior to his commitment to Therafields, Nichol worked in the library of the University of Toronto where he established close friendships with poets David Aylward and Margaret Avison. Hesitant to jump into the contemporary poetry circles as yet another conventional lyric poet, he focused instead on language, and composed what he would call "ideopomes." These are typewriter poems exploring the materiality of language through letteral transformations and patterns that interact with the productive space of the page. They were collected in a book published in England with the marvellous title, *KonfessIonS of an ElizAbeThan Fan Dancer* (1969). An exception at the time were the lyric poems he submitted and had accepted for the Contact Press anthology, *New Wave Canada: The New Explosion in Canadian Poetry* (1966), edited by Raymond Souster with crucial assistance (unacknowledged) from Victor Coleman with whom Nichol would form a lasting friendship. During this time Nichol also wrote and recorded his first sound poem, "Beach at Port Dover" recorded on *Borders* (1967), included in *bp* (1967), while on vacation at Port Dover, Lake Erie. His first published poem, "Translating Apollinaire," appeared in 1964 in bissett's journal, *blew ointment*, a moment Nichol recalls in his "Introduction to *The Last Blew Ointment Anthology Volume 2*" (418). bissett had introduced him to the work of Gertrude Stein, and her work would quickly become a singular model for writing modes he believed would enable him to articulate the "new humanism" he envisioned in his prescient "statement, november 1966," a writing whose forms would be open to his own process-oriented poetics. It was a struggle to find new ways of relating to one another, as he wrote: "the other is emerging as the necessary prerequisite for dialogues with the self that clarify the soul & heart and deepen the ability to love" (18).

From the mid-1960s on, Nichol's creative work would take root and begin to flourish in the Toronto milieu, notably through the liaison with a new radical press, The Coach House Press, which in turn led to collaborative publishing ventures with Stan Bevington, Wayne Clifford, Victor Coleman, and others. With David Aylward, he would launch his own non-commercial publishing projects, editing Ganglia and grOnk, all the while immersing himself in his own writing, producing an array of texts, such as *The Captain Poetry Poems*, *Scraptures*, and his first major — identity making — collection, *bp*, a boxed text that assembled various works: a book of poems, *JOURNEYING & the returns*; a flipbook, *Wild Thing*; a record, *Borders*; and an envelope of visual poems and pamphlets, *Letters Home*.

By the late 1960s, while his international reputation as a concrete poet spread, he would meet up with Steve McCaffery, who had recently moved to Toronto from England. Instantly attracted to mutually shared interests in concrete and sound poetry and in process writing, they soon began a long-term collaboration on what they identified as "research." Under the auspicious mantle of The Toronto Research Group, they became, in McCaffery's phrasing, the "kids of the book machine," producing a series of collaborative essays, or "reports," that still remain the most stimulating thinking in Canada on textuality, language, and form. Their essays appeared in installments through Frank Davey's *Open Letter*, a journal with which Nichol began associating in 1972, largely because, as he later explains, Davey "offered me carte blanche — a section in each issue of *OL* in which i could do whatever i wanted" (189). The reports published in *Open Letter*, which are not included in *Meanwhile*, are available in the collection edited by Steve McCaffery, *Rational Geomancy. The Kids of the Book Machine* (1992). The friendship with McCaffery would also lead to the opportunity for Nichol to develop his interest in sound and performance texts. With Paul Dutton and Rafael Barreto-Rivera, he and McCaffery would form The Four Horsemen, a performance group that would garner a national and international audience throughout the 1970s.

During the 1980s, as his involvement in The Four Horsemen waned and as he severed his ties with Therafields, Nichol turned to other means of supporting himself. He taught creative writing courses at York University and began to make a name for himself as a script writer for children's TV programs, *The Muppets* and *The Raccoons*. When he died suddenly on September 25, 1988 while undergoing a complicated operation to remove a tumour in his spine, Nichol had become one of the most influential and well loved writers of his generation.

THE EDITORIAL

In compiling this collection I have been attentive to Nichol's explorations of the multiple dimensions of writing as process and the intellectual and social implications of this concern. Nichol came of age in the 1960s, a period marked by the belief that radical transformations of consciousness, and consequently social change, were possible through the power of creative forms. The performance of creative thought was assumed to release a psychic and libidinal reserve of energy that could provide the impetus to produce more inclusive and collective forms of social interaction and communication. The young Nichol, who first sensed a "future music" in the first book of *The Martyrology* (1972) while still in his late teens in Vancouver and who moved to Toronto at 22, was receptive to the undercurrents of new writing coming from his own generation. The writers who figure in Nichol's critical writing — bill bissett, d.a. levy, David Aylward, Margaret Avison, Frank Davey, Steve McCaffery, Daphne Marlatt, George Bowering, Michael Ondaatje, Victor Coleman, Peggy Lafleur, and so on — became the locus of his own interactions, generating a network of relationships out of which he fashioned himself as a writer and critical thinker.

It was out of a continuous engagement with "the actual life of language" (156) that Nichol worked out — and through — the complex of subjects that define the intellectual range of *Meanwhile*. Now is not the occasion to undertake a detailed critical inventory of these subjects, but readers will become familiar with Nichol's participation in the Canadian version of "pataphysics, his investigations of notation and the notational practices of process-oriented writers, his work in sound and concrete poetry, his own publishing initiatives through Ganglia and grOnk, the history of his affiliation with Coach House Press, his personal involvement in Therafields as a corollary to his work in open form poetics, and his study of other writers — Gertrude Stein, for instance — and many of his contemporaries who shared his preoccupations.

In "A Contributed Editorial," Nichol talks about his critical writing as a "desire to articulate for myself a way of replying to other writing that honours my awareness of it," and adds: "By this i mean then not a criticism which presumes to know more than the writer of the text ... but rather an articulation of a particular (to this writer) understanding (and i'll take that literally as standing under or subservient to the text) which may offer a way in for others if they choose to take it" (188-90). He says as much in the last interview included in *Meanwhile* where he explains his relationship, as writer, to critical thought: "I think of myself as a writer who writes about the act of writing. Though I have written what you would call criticism, on the whole in that work I've always tried to foreground the fact that I am a writer writing about other writers" (with Fred Gaysek 454).

The idea of collecting his critical writing was on Nichol's mind at the time of his death, as a file of essays, named "Overdues," in his papers at Simon Fraser University makes clear. In editing *Meanwhile*, I began with Nichol's file and, following a search for additional pieces, added a few titles, including a sampling from the rich body of unpublished material housed in the Nichol Papers. In the archives is a companion file, named "Intervues," where Nichol had been collecting the interviews he had either conducted or given over the years.

My first plan was to concentrate primarily on Nichol's critical work, a substantial manuscript in itself, setting aside the interviews for perhaps a future project. As the collection took shape, though, I found myself making mental references to comments Nichol made in interviews, comments which often complemented or otherwise enhanced through nuance and personal voice the intellectual substance of the essays. The continuities in Nichol's work are such that the interviews are themselves versions of a critical statement or argument — but how to make use of them without having the manuscript sprawl too much? The interviews of a writer, moreover — and Nichol's are no exception — often contain statements that tend to be repetitious, not surprising because interviewers often ask a similar range of questions. There was also the difficulty of tracking down some interviewers to get their permissions. After several months of mulling over what to do I decided to splice the interviews into the critical writing, a few in total and several more through excerpts. What has been included is far from complete but I hope representative enough to foreground the interview form as itself a mode of critical thought for Nichol. They offer moments of intervention in which readers can hear the voice of Nichol as he converses with his interviewers and speaks about his writing in more direct and personal terms. The combination of the critical writing and the interviews offers readers a major collection that tracks Nichol's critical thinking over a period of some 22 years, from 1966 when he was 22, until the year of his death, 1988, at the age of 44.

In working out a structure for *Meanwhile*, I decided early on not to resort to an arrangement based on generic categories (e.g. essays, reviews, statements and so on), or even on sections as suggested in Nichol's own files (e.g. essays on poetics, on other writers, and reviews). What presented itself as the most obvious structural principle — the chronological — also seemed the most appropriate for this collection. The reader can then read each of the pieces without the critical fiction of artificial divisions. Of course, the determination of simple chronology, especially because of the "illusion of publication versus the reality of composition" (247), can itself be deceptive and uncertain. While acknowledging the publication dates, wherever possible, I have attempted to follow evidence, usually Nichol's own note, that records dates of composition. (Even in deferring to such documentation, however, I realize that further research in the Nichol Papers will likely expose some inaccuracies of dating.) In the absence of such information, I have gone with publications dates, as indecisive as they can be for periodicals. On the whole, the arrangement I settled on attempts to follow Nichol's writing life from the mid-1960s to 1988 — with the exception of the opening and closing pieces, both of which appealed to my own editorial sense of an entrance and exit, and the three Gertrude Stein essays, which seemed more comfortably grouped together.

THE EXIT

Editing Nichol brought its own pleasures, especially in the face of the recent return to more normative forms in creative and critical texts. Nichol's language and style were charged in the crucible of the 1960s when linguistic play and the abandoning of conventional forms of typography and punctuation were read as vital intellectual acts. In working to bring this collection to published form I have tried to find that critical tension between decisions that would produce the unity and cohesion of a "book" and those that respect the specificity of Nichol's modes of thought as performed in his writing practices. I have, for instance, retained those instances in which Nichol uses a characteristic step-down pattern for paragraph indents — i.e. starting the next paragraph on the next line a space after the last word — a pattern that enacts the way thinking occurs in the passage from one paragraph to the next. These indents are routine for the typewriter, but quite demanding for the computer, and indeed could not be accurately inserted until the whole text was set. During Nichol's lifetime I had the good fortune to work with him on some of his texts and recall that he was always open to editorial suggestions. In editing this collection, I have tried to match the spirit of those interchanges, often pausing to reflect on what I imagined would be his responses to the decisions I was making.

As "a writer who reads," the Nichol we encounter in *Meanwhile* always keeps returning to the act of writing, circling its complexities to probe and articulate what attracts him to its sites of production. Written for the most part for specific occasions — specific calls for a critical response — Nichol's writing itself always "remains in process." This RIP is a characteristic pun in a drawing that goes further, as most of his drawings do, and suggests that the "death" of signification prepares the ground for its emergence in new forms of reception, in other words, in new forms of translation. Just as Nichol's own critical thought remains open to readers so readers coming to *Meanwhile* are encouraged to dialogue his language into the conditions of their own present. "words, finally, to anyone who wants them" ("in place of Hour 28," *The Martyrology: Book 6 Books*).

ACKNOWLEDGEMENTS

An editorial project with the scope of *Meanwhile* has benefitted from the knowledge and assistance of many fellow readers and writers, much of this spanning the (now) considerable passage of time since the 1970s when I first started reading bpNichol's work and formed a friendship with him. So much of the conversation that swirled around his "work in process" during the years prior to 1988 were exchanged at literary events, chance meetings, and conferences, and these involved a network of readers and writers connected by friendship and a sense of collective interests. I personally have been fortunate in being able to consult with many who shared my enthusiasm for bp's writing. My appreciation is especially extended to Nelson Ball, George Bowering, Pauline Butling, Frank Davey, Jeff Derksen, Paul Dutton, Smaro

Kamboureli, Robert Kroetsch, Jacqueline Larson, Daphne Marlatt, Steve McCaffery, Irene Niechoda, Lola Lemire Tostevin, and Fred Wah. Carl Peters, who completed his PhD dissertation on bpNichol at Simon Fraser University while this book came together, assisted in locating some material in the Nichol Papers. Our conversations and his scholarship on Nichol helped clarify some editorial conundrums, and I am grateful to him for bringing to my attention the RIP drawing which immediately took on resonance for my Afterword. Thanks to librarian Gene Bridwell, who worked in Special Collections during the time of my research, for always accommodating my search for material in the Nichol Papers. Thanks also to Linda Charyk Rosenfeld for allowing us to use her photo of bpNichol; to Barbara Caruso from Seripress for permission to reproduce *Aleph Unit*; and to Isabelle Basmajian for permission to reproduce *Quote Unquote* by Shant Basmajian; and to all the interviewers for permission to reprint their interviews. Special thanks to Lori Emerson for assistance in proofing the manuscript in the initial phase of editing. I am grateful to the bpNichol Memorial Fund (Phoenix Community Works Foundation) for a grant in the early stages of editorial work to assist in the preparation of the manuscript. In taking *Meanwhile* through the production process, I have had the good fortune of working with Shyla Seller at Talonbooks. She took on the challenging work of design and layout with a sensitivity and efficiency that made pleasurable what would otherwise have been an onerous chore. I am also thankful to publisher Karl Siegler for ensuring that the work of bpNichol is available to a new generation of readers and for refusing to sacrifice substance to the exigencies of the market. Finally, I would like to acknowledge my deep appreciation to Ellie Nichol for her care and friendship — and for responding with good humour to all my questions and requests.